*Also by Peter Schrag:*

VOICES IN THE CLASSROOM
VILLAGE SCHOOL DOWNTOWN
OUT OF PLACE IN AMERICA
THE DECLINE OF THE WASP
THE END OF THE AMERICAN FUTURE

"Those of us who went to Los Angeles," writes Peter Schrag, "to cover the trial of Daniel Ellsberg and Anthony J. Russo, Jr., the so-called Pentagon Papers trial, came looking for one thing and found something else. The facts of the case...were supposed to be relatively simple. Ellsberg and Russo were on trial in connection with the copying of the Pentagon Papers in 1969; Ellsberg had admitted giving the Papers to **The New York Times** in 1971, but that act was not part of this indictment.... The charges were conspiracy, conversion (i.e. misappropriation) of government property, and violations of the Espionage Act. . . . But beyond those facts lay an immensely complicated story that went back at least to World War II and that involved the experience of a generation which had been shaken to its soul by the failures of the intellectual and political assumptions on which it had been raised."

In this timely and brilliant book, Peter Schrag describes the most important legal, constitutional confrontation of the decade—the Pentagon Papers trial.

Ellsberg had been privy to enough Top Secret discussions to have reached the conclusion that "there existed [in the Pentagon] people capable of writing, on demand, plans for the Nazi general staff...." The trial that ensued graduated from a simple challenge con-

dment rights to ut blind allegi-conscience, and pt by the Nixon p out any chal-y the end, the rcle. Watergate inistration had berg's medical nce and bribe [atthew Byrne, urt.

g writes, "there that what we oisoned politi-ome difference who had been never trust the l—any word—rhaps the trial e the country tion that had eginning."

**peter Schrag**

# TEST OF LOYALTY

Daniel Ellsberg
and the Rituals of
Secret Government

## PETER SCHRAG

SIMON AND SCHUSTER    NEW YORK

SBN 671-21787-9
Library of Congress Catalog Card Number: 74-111
Designed by Jack Jaget
Manufactured in the United States of America
By American Book - Stratford Press, Inc.

1   2   3   4   5   6   7   8   9   10

FOR BILL FARR

# Contents

the cause must be found in some flaw of character and spirit. All California sometimes has the look of a Hollywood set, a beautiful front with little behind it except rotting timbers and rusty nails. The test is performance: how do I look? Very American in a way, but exaggerated, and especially in Southern California. There is a temptation to seize on manifestations and symbols and mysteries: the familiar cults, the sects, the Great I Am. These things seem more understandable in terms of Hollywood than as the reductions of historical American fundamentalism and innocence which they are often said to be. It is the intensity that counts, whether the substance is transplanted Oklahoma Baptism, Jesus freakery, encounter therapy, perpetual care at Forest Lawn, or the games of war and intelligence at the Rand Corporation. All share a belief in ultimates and seek or indulge in similar rituals of affirmation. Deep inside, very deep, there must be an ultimate secret.

II

Those of us who went to Los Angeles to cover the trial of Daniel Ellsberg and Anthony J. Russo, Jr., the so-called Pentagon Papers trial, came looking for one thing and found something else. The facts of the case—the facts that the reporters put into the third or fourth paragraph of each of their daily stories—were supposed to be relatively simple. Ellsberg and Russo were on trial in connection with the copying of the Pentagon Papers in 1969; Ellsberg had admitted giving the Papers to the *New York Times* in 1971, but that act was not part of this indictment (although it was the subject of an extensive grand-jury investigation in Boston and could have led to another indictment). The charges were conspiracy, conversion (i.e., misappropriation) of government property, and violations of the Espionage Act. Two other persons were named as unindicted co-conspirators: Lynda Sinay, now Lynda Resnik, who ran an advertising agency in Los Angeles and was a friend of Russo's at the time the Papers were copied —she owned the Xerox machine—and Vu Van Thai, at one time South Vietnamese ambassador to the United States,

# ONE

# Prologue

I

LOS ANGELES is a good place for trials and purges. Perhaps it is the *auto-da-fé* of the sun, or the Santa Ana wind, which is said to cause some ionic madness among the inhabitants when it blows down from the mountains, or simply the warmth of the climate, which causes the withered dreams of other regions to bloom with renewed and often rank vitality. There are still believers here, believers in redemption and ultimate truth, believers in witchcraft and magic, believers in The Word, and believers in those tests which will show The Word to be Revelation. This is the place where, as Joan Didion once said, we run out of continent, and, because that is so—and because this is also where, in a manner of speaking, we run out of time—all the messianic impulses, the hopes for happiness, the national instincts, turn upon themselves, producing confrontations which the frontier delayed.

But there is also the element of performance. The atmosphere induces its inhabitants to play at the role of fulfillment and perfection, and so façades are easily confused with substance. If one cannot be perfect and happy in this region, then

a former consultant to Rand, a friend of Ellsberg's and subsequently a United Nations official in Europe. But beyond
those facts lay an immensely complicated story that went back
at least to World War II and that involved the experience of
a generation which had been shaken to its soul by the failures
of the intellectual and political assumptions on which it had
been raised.

At the beginning, as at the end, the trial seemed an appropriate symbol for an age. The defendants themselves were
symbolic figures, even allegorical characters, for a generation
which had changed its mind. But between the spring of 1971,
when the Pentagon Papers were first published, and the end
of the trial two years later, both the symbols and the age had
changed. What I write now is not what I intended to write
two years ago, nor even what I would have written immediately after the election of 1972. What had seemed like a land-
mark in 1971, a major confrontation between the government
and the press, had, by early 1973, become more like a representative skirmish, a rearguard engagement behind a front
that had already moved. The sense of futility which attended
the last years of the peace movement had survived the cease-
fire in Vietnam, and the arrogance of power in government
was just as evident in negotiating peace as it was in escalating
the war. But, while the original issues about the case were still
very much the officially discussed issues at the end, they no
longer seemed to matter nearly as much; whatever the outcome of this test, the repressive administration mood and the
corresponding public apathy would be likely to grow. The
trial went on in counterpoint to the war in Vietnam, to the
Nixon Supreme Court, and to political developments in
Washington: reporters were being sent to prison, Nixon had
been overwhelmingly reelected, and the country had officially
abandoned the promises of racial equality and economic opportunity of the sixties. As a consequence, the context of the
prosecution began to shift, became increasingly a celebration
of the mystique of information, and seemed to reflect an
atmosphere of power and privilege already beyond judicial

remedy. The case, which we had once seen as perhaps the most important test of First Amendment rights since World War II, seemed in addition, if not instead, a demonstration of executive power unaffected by criticism, an example of arrogance untouched by free expression. After Mylai, and the Christmas bombing of North Vietnam in 1972, and Nixon's assaults on the press, did anyone still really care? Who wanted to know? Perhaps it didn't matter anymore what anyone said about the bastards in Washington, nothing could change their politics, their behavior or their power. Just before the end, it was still possible to see the case as a situation where the totem was information and even its possession might not make any difference.

It was the link with Watergate that put the case back on the front lines. It was now clear that Ellsberg had been something more than a footnote to the history of the Administration's intrigue, had indeed been a central object in the campaign of wiretapping, espionage, burglary and intimidation. The revelations about E. Howard Hunt and G. Gordon Liddy, about John D. Ehrlichman and Robert C. Mardian and Henry Kissinger, and about the President himself, brought the case full circle and overshadowed what had seemed to be the paramount issues, free speech, secrecy, the war, yet at the same time reinforced them. If the climax matched the wilder dreams of a demonic Hollywood producer, it also rejoined the threads of two eras, and made clear that what had seemed different practices abroad and at home—the CIA, the FBI, the White House, the Department of Justice and the Department of Defense—were parts of a single and consistent story. The case of the Pentagon Papers, the trial of Russo and Ellsberg, was perhaps the most important case of its time, but between its beginning and end both its time and its meaning had changed.

The case itself had always been about words; it was gorged with words, words as secrets, words as lies, words as obfuscation and deceit, words as revelation, words about words, and words about words about words. In the beginning they had seemed to mean something; they applied to Vietnam or to the government's use of information or to the arrogance of two defendants (depending on your point of view) who had taken upon themselves the responsibility for disclosing what the executive branch of the government officially regarded as militarily and diplomatically sensitive material. This had seemed to be, when you came down to it, a literary prosecution—part obscenity case, part heresy trial—an inquisition into the meaning, use and control of The Word. Yet it was never clear whether The Word itself was merely the stuff of prurient interest, the pornography of Vietnam (or, by another interpretation, the material of a theological dispute between schismatic sects of data worshipers), or whether it really symbolized, as the defendants seemed to believe, the principles of the First Amendment as opposed to the government's deceits. The symbolism changed; as the case became more complex it slowly began to suggest the possibility that one was witnessing not a classic battle about free speech but rather the revelations of a cult which had, in some strange way, come to possess us all, and from which there was little chance of escape. Perhaps what one knew no longer mattered, and all that did matter were the incantations which were pronounced over the knowledge and the degrees of restriction on its possession. Perhaps knowledge was not power, only its symbol. Yet, at the end, there was also the possibility that what we had learned about the poisoned political system might make some difference after all, that even those who had been cynical all along would never trust the government or the word—any word—in the same way again. Perhaps the trial and Watergate would free the country from the faith-in-information that had obsessed all of us at the beginning.

III

It was impossible for any reasonable journalist not to regard himself as part of the case. Russo once described himself as a surrogate for the *New York Times,* which had first published the Pentagon Papers, and which was the most important recipient of the allegedly stolen goods. We were all potential receivers, were all affected by the climate of press repression, espionage and sabotage of which this case was a part, and were all regarded by the Administration as potential enemies. Published comments in national periodicals, the government argued in one of its pretrial briefs, portrayed the defendants as "champions of a free press and of a public and congressional 'right to know'; supporters of the Constitution; moral giants who performed acts of conscience at great personal risk and sacrifice; victims of racist attacks, government mistreatment and harassment; and courageous patriots whose only motive was to achieve peace." So much adulation had been heaped upon Ellsberg and Russo, the government argued, that readers of the *New York Times,* the *Washington Post, Harper's, Atlantic, Esquire,* and *Saturday Review* should be excluded from the jury. The defense, which always regarded the trial as an opportunity to "educate the public" about the origins of the war, the contents of the Papers and the practices of information management in Washington, maintained an active, well-run and often extremely helpful press and public-relations operation, and, in a more general sense, it held out a standing invitation to journalists to regard themselves as unnamed co-defendants in the case; if Ellsberg and Russo were convicted, the defense kept telling us, then any government official who leaked anything could be prosecuted and any journalist who published such a leak could be indicted as a conspirator or a receiver of stolen goods. The prosecution was distant and unresponsive; queries were referred to the Justice Department in Washington, where they remained unanswered. As a consequence, the reporters, who usually sat on the government's side of the courtroom, would often talk behind the back of the chief government prosecutor, David R. Nissen, like schoolchildren discussing an unpopular and somewhat frightening teacher. There were remarks about Nissen's compulsiveness, the perfect part in his straight black hair, the way he flicked specks from the sleeves of his jacket, the rigid line of paper clips on the table in front of him, the angularity of his gestures. Nissen's two colleagues, Warren P. Reese and Richard J. Barry, were regarded as more friendly, but neither of them was permitted to say anything of substance to the press. Besides, they were part of the government, and the government was the enemy.

Not that the defendants were universally loved. Ellsberg, the supposed hero of the affair, was often ignored and occasionally avoided, and he sometimes asked me why some journalists never interviewed him, why they didn't even ask a question. His ego, of course, had become a cliché, but reporters often pursue far larger egos than his and manage to enjoy it. What was more likely was that Ellsberg himself had simply ceased to be news; he could be counted on for comments about the various turns in the Vietnam War, the negotiations, the escalation, the bombing—something would always be quotable—but as a personality he was too one-sided, too linear and too familiar to remain journalistically interesting. For a year he had been mined by the press, and now he was exhausted. Who could be fully sympathetic with a man who could say, without embarrassment, that he never tired of reading the Pentagon Papers, or who could declare that he did not recall one waking hour in the past eight years when he hadn't thought about Vietnam? What was fascinating about him fell outside the bounds of the reporter; it belonged to psychoanalysis, to literature, and to theology. I often wondered, as I got to know him, whether he was the Young Man Luther of our generation—the representative convert of the age of information, a subject more appropriate for an analyst like Erik Erikson than for a reporter. His very act of disclosing the Papers had a finality about it: it had made him a national figure, but there was obviously no chance that he could ever do such a thing again. He and the Papers were chained together. The Berrigans were something more than Catonsville or Harrisburg; Jerry Rubin and Abbie Hoffman had not been created by the conspiracy trial of the Chicago Seven; and Benjamin Spock had been Dr. Spock long before he was indicted for counseling draft resistance. But Ellsberg was only the Papers. Perhaps he knew other secrets, about the Pentagon and about himself, but he wasn't saying. Again, it was Watergate which would temporarily rescue him from oblivion and give him new relevance.

Russo remained in the shadows, partly because of Ellsberg's ego, partly for legal reasons—if he had more to do with the disclosure than merely providing help with the copying, as charged by the government, no one could, or would, say—and partly because he was just an ordinary human being with something more than ordinary courage. We were all certain that Russo really didn't belong in the case at all; he had been indicted for punitive reasons and to add the portentous element of conspiracy. Having refused to cooperate with the government in its investigation—a refusal for which he spent forty-seven days in jail—Russo became part of the conspiracy, became a symbol for the press, and became an object of David Nissen's vengeance. His addiction to movement language—the language of "war crimes," "mass murder," "genocide" and "imperialism"—made him politically difficult for the press; no one was willing to quote that stuff seriously. It was apparent, moreover, that even Ellsberg tried to detach himself from Russo's more extreme statements and associations—the scruffy people who sometimes surrounded him in the halls outside the courtroom, the declaration that Lieutenant General William De Puy, an expert witness for the government, was a war criminal, the suggestion that the trial be carried to the streets and that demonstrations be organized. Yet it was Russo who, in this peculiar and often ill-fitting association, usually seemed the more reasonable man and the more complete human being. Russo was Sancho Panza to the Great Don: it was he who intuitively understood the irony of his position—if he was just an innocent victim, then he really had no claim to anything but symbolic attention—and he seemed to understand the corresponding irony of the case, but he never fully managed to articulate those things in anything but the most inadequate movement rhetoric. Perhaps there was no way to say those things well;

perhaps, moreover, as he himself seemed to understand, being a victim of the Vietnam War was itself a role that had become banal and was therefore no longer worthy of attention.

Any extended trial begins to generate an incestuous atmosphere, becomes, in many ways, a ship of fools. But in a case where the facts are not really in question, where no great revelations are expected, and where words themselves are at issue, the incest is intensified. We had moments of relief—most of them provided by the government's own demonstrations of contempt for the judicial process—but that relief only seemed to highlight the tedium of endless days in court. Martin Arnold, who covered the proceedings for the *Times,* once remarked that we would wake up one day and discover that we had all been killed in some freeway accident and had been assigned to this courtroom for purgation. The tedium was part of the material of the case, and after a time it became one of its central elements, the tedium of ritual and the tedium of detail. Out of necessity we became engrossed in those details, became addicted to our motions and countermotions, to minor issues of fact and personality, and to the technical points of law and evidence which related to the case. For the press, the defense and the small band of regular spectators, these things became familiar parts of language and daily concern, and gradually, almost without knowing it, we began to isolate ourselves from the world. Because the stuff was too trivial and too complex, we found it impossible to discuss it with others; it had become the sickest kind of shop-talk. The job became an affliction and the affliction a way of life. Having come ostensibly to resist the processes of secrecy and to expose synthetic mysteries, we had ourselves become citizens of a separate country with its own language and concerns, and we began to develop institutional habits of dependency not unlike those of inmates in mental institutions. The better that one adjusted to this life, the crazier one became. Complexity created its own madness, and tedium induced forms of childish behavior—passing silly notes in the courtroom, giggling, making eighth-grade jokes about the legal issues involved in the so-called "Heine defense"—which I doubt any of us will want to remember.

Until just before the end, the essence of the case lay in abstractions, and so the proceedings were necessarily filled with totems, spooks and allegorical figures. The larger issues —restrictions on the First Amendment, the use of the classification system, and government control of information—made only symbolic appearances: the jury was exposed to a hypothetical "foreign analyst" enjoying an "intelligence windfall" in the event the Papers had fallen into his hands, a hypothetical foreign government sabotaging secret negotiations between Washington and Hanoi, and a hypothetical North Vietnamese general assessing hypothetical plans for the phased withdrawal of 500,000 troops in 1969 by studying a discarded proposal for the removal of 16,000 troops in 1964. Great cases, it is often said, make bad law, but they also make for bad journalism because they hinge so much on judicial interpretations of constitutional language, on the uncertainties of Supreme Court decisions and, in this instance, on the subtleties of expert testimony about what did or did not relate to the "national defense," one of the elements of proof required by the language of the Espionage Act. There was, moreover, the immense volume and complexity of the various elements of the case. The government's unprecedented attempt to enjoin the *Times* and the *Washington Post* from publishing the Papers, the subsequent grand-jury investigations in Boston and Los Angeles, the pretrial litigation in the Ellsberg-Russo case, the trial itself, and the various appeals to higher courts which those proceedings generated involved at least ten federal district court judges, five appellate courts, including the Supreme Court, and hundreds of lawyers and witnesses. Two of them, Russo and Professor Samuel L. Popkin of Harvard, spent time in prison for their refusal to testify before grand juries, one trial jury in Los Angeles was impaneled and dismissed without hearing a word of testimony, and nearly a year of pretrial arguments produced some six thousand pages of transcript and an additional five thousand pages of motions.

By the time the case was dismissed in Los Angeles, the trial transcript had run to another sixteen thousand pages, a total of 22,691 pages, and the proceedings had cost the defendants alone (there is no estimate on what it cost the government) somewhere in the vicinity of one million dollars. The pieces of the story ran to almost every segment of our national life —the press, the universities, the government—and substantially altered the lives of countless people.

TWO

---

# The Convert

FOR a few months in the summer and fall of 1971, Daniel Ellsberg enjoyed an heroic age. In certain circles, publication of the Pentagon Papers had made his name a household word, as perhaps the best example of what then seemed like meaningful civil disobedience. Stewardesses recognized him on airplanes and asked for his autograph, strangers stopped him on the street, and countless organizations wrote to ask if he would lead a new movement, some final effort to end the war. He was a traitor, a hero, an ego-tripping maniac, a true believer, a saint, a jet-set playboy, a symbol of whatever might ail or save the nation. By early fall, he had reached a sort of apotheosis: he had been the subject of an interview in *Look,* had been given the full ninety minutes on *The Dick Cavett Show,* was being pursued by half a dozen writers for national magazines, and had appeared at virtually every major gathering of peace movement people in America. In November he would be the featured speaker at a mass rally that drew twenty thousand people to the Los Angeles Sports Arena.

The apogee came on October 1. Ellsberg and Tony Russo, self-acknowledged collaborators on the Xerox machine, had flown to Chicago to attend the "American Peace Awards" ceremony of BEM, Business Executives Move for Peace in Vietnam. As usual, Ellsberg was late; he was habitually missing planes, canceling appointments, observing schedules and priorities that seemed to exist only in some secret, distant place accessible to his eyes alone. He and Russo missed a scheduled press conference and a party for the celebrities, and while they were missing them the young men who were helping to run the affair reported his movements from O'Hare Field into the city as if it were the progress of a mysterious higher presence, the arrival of a personage in touch with forces and motives not fully comprehensible to ordinary men.

It was three months after the Pentagon Papers had first begun to appear in the *New York Times* and, as Ellsberg later told his audience, precisely two years from the day when he had called Russo to ask him where they could get a Xerox machine. By now, the Papers—officially known as *United States–Vietnam Relations, 1945–1967*—were available in three separate editions, one of them published by the government itself. Yet hardly anyone had read them. The shortest version, published by Bantam, constituted nearly seven hundred closely printed pages of bureaucratese—memos and cables, intelligence estimates and security analyses—covering more than twenty years of American interest in Vietnam. The congressional hearings into the origins of the war that Ellsberg had expected were never held, the war itself was represented in the press and the polls as a waning issue—the troops were being withdrawn—and Nixon had somewhat defused its last explosive potentialities with the announcement of his forthcoming trip to China. It was more than likely that the Papers would have gone almost unnoticed had the Justice Department not decided to try to stop the *Times* and the *Washington Post* from publishing the documents and the articles derived from them. The radicals in the peace movement having decided long ago that American Presidents and Secretaries of State were perfidious manipulators, the detailed record of American Vietnam decisions in the administrations of Truman, Eisenhower and Kennedy was, at best, of academic interest. From all indications, the majority of Americans were eager to forget the war and were more impressed with the removal of American ground troops than with the fact that we were still killing Vietnamese. What Ellsberg did not seem to realize was that the act of releasing the Papers was far more significant to his audiences than the Papers themselves. He wanted them to study the war, but instead they came to study him.

Yet the respectable wing of the movement, for all its divisions and uncertainty, was still alive, and Ellsberg had become its hero. This was not some scruffy radical, a burner of draft cards, a long-haired freak, but a person who had the proper academic credentials, spoke the right language and could more than hold his own in any gathering of proper people. If he challenged the converted middle class to ask themselves why they hadn't done more—if he had himself become a symbol of risk—he also reassured those who had arrived late in the camp of peace that it was nothing to be ashamed about.

At Orchestra Hall that night, a few blocks from the center of the demonstrations against the 1968 Democratic convention, the respectable wing of the movement had gathered again. Many of these people had been together before, in New York and Washington, in Cambridge and right here on the streets of Chicago, at rallies and marches, teach-ins and trials, but rarely had there been such an assembly of movement stars. The BEM ceremony was supposed to be a celebration, but there wasn't much to celebrate, and a threat of banality hung over the proceedings. Most of the evening was polite, too polite, as if the well-dressed, well-heeled crowd in Orchestra Hall had come to see another performance. Someone said later that it was encouraging to see business executives doing this sort of thing at all, to see them associating with such people. Ramsey Clark, who, as Attorney General, had prosecuted Benjamin Spock for counseling draft resistance, would now give him an award for peace; Irv Kupcinet, a Chicago television talk-show host, who had been a hawk through most of the sixties, accepted an award on behalf of Bill Mauldin, the cartoonist; a group of actors read from *The Trial of the Catonsville Nine,* although Philip Berrigan, awaiting another trial, remained otherwise unmentioned. There were awards for Harvard biologist George Wald, John Kerry, the head of the Vietnam Veterans Against the War, Wayne Morse, Joan Baez, David Schoenbrun, and for others in absentia—Pablo Casals, J. William Fulbright, Ralph David Abernathy, and the late Martin Luther King, Jr.—who were represented by stand-ins. The funkier peaceniks, the conscientious objectors, the jailbirds and the freaks were hardly represented at all; no new action was contemplated, and nothing, other than patience, was expected of the audience. One just had to sit through it. Like the war itself, the ceremony threatened to become chronic, an interminable event gorged with words. It demonstrated, for anyone with lingering doubts, that opposing the war had gone midcult; it also demonstrated how badly they needed an Ellsberg.

The decorum of the evening suffered only two notable interruptions. The first occurred when Joan Baez, saying something about obscenity, took the American flags which had been standing on the platform and laid them on their sides. (Later, Congressman Paul "Pete" McCloskey of California, who was then preparing to run against Nixon in the Republican primaries, and who would give Ellsberg his award, put them up again.) The second came when Ellsberg introduced Russo. Russo had gotten out of jail that morning after having served forty-seven days—twenty of them in what he called the "hole"—for refusing to testify in secret before the Los Angeles grand jury. A federal judge had ruled that Russo could quote in public from the transcript of his grand-jury testimony, and on that basis Russo had agreed to testify and he had been released. (As it turned out, he was not called and was later indicted with Ellsberg as a fellow conspirator.)

He was still wearing the clothes he had worn that morning in prison, a T-shirt and heavy corduroy trousers, and his long hair was held together at the back of his head with a rubber band. Now, at the microphone, he became not only an advocate of action—against the war, and against the horrors of the society that had brutalized him in prison (they had chained him, he said, and beaten him)—but also an exhibit, a representative victim who could explain everything, could tell them what had happened to him, only by speaking forever.

He tried to talk of his fellow prisoners, about the guards, about the Attica Prison uprising and the subsequent murder of the prisoners, about the war and resistance, about a hunger strike he planned to continue in sympathy with "my fellow members of the convict class," and about a whole society which regarded men as expendable—wandering from his subject, sometimes incoherent, searching for words, for order, for anything that might make the agony real. In the disjointed half hour—now long past midnight—before he was nudged from the microphone, he had begun to suggest to his audience how easy (and fashionable) it had become to be against the war but how difficult it was to act, and for an instant the ugliness of the age broke through the decorous caution of the moment. It was an embarrassment, an unwelcome reminder of all the things the Good People had tried to forget, ignore or deny. They had come to celebrate themselves, and Russo spoiled it. As they took him from the microphone, Ellsberg put his arm around Russo's shoulder. "When you decide to change the world around," Ellsberg told the impatient and the uncomfortable, "I hope you have a friend like this hungry and very brave man." Russo and Ellsberg temporarily rescued the movement from its own banality.


Ellsberg had always been the unimpeachable man. Now an attractive forty-year-old, he was a former rising star of the military-intellectual complex, a man once photographed

by *Life* holding a submachine gun in Vietnam, and an intellectual with Harvard and Cambridge credentials. In the period
that began with Camelot and closed at Mylai and Attica, he
was a consistent shining example: McGeorge Bundy's kind
of man, an assistant to Robert McNamara, the military intellectual in the Defense Department, the researcher at Rand,
the Marine lieutenant, but now a symbol of a time whose
most representative form of national service might begin in
the military and end in prison. His major academic interest
had been the theory of bargaining, perhaps the most fashionable subject of the Cold War intellectuals, and in 1959, barely
out of graduate school, he had delivered the Lowell Lectures
in Boston on "The Art of Coercion." (In the audience there
had been a young woman named Gloria Steinem who was
so impressed by him that she thought of asking him to participate in a meeting that she was then helping to organize as a
counter to the Communist Vienna Youth Festival—and that
later turned out to have been CIA-sponsored. As it happened, she never asked him—it was only later that Ellsberg
learned she had been there—and that summer he went off
to Rand.) Among his government assignments were consulting jobs for the State and Defense Departments in Washington during the Cuban missile crisis, a project calculating
Soviet nuclear capability, and another estimating the scope
of the so-called missile gap in the early months of the Kennedy Administration. In 1964 he became a special assistant
to Robert McNamara in the Office of the Secretary of Defense; in 1965, as a member of a State Department task force
under General Edward T. Lansdale, the man who in 1954
had conducted sabotage operations in Hanoi (among other
things, by putting sugar in the gas tanks of the city's buses),
he went to Vietnam to study the pacification program; and in
the summer of 1967, suffering from a severe case of hepatitis,
he returned to the United States to participate in the study of
American decision-making that McNamara had commissioned and that he would eventually leak to the press. It was
because he had done all these things—because he had the

credentials, had lived among the gods—that he now became the Prometheus of the movement.

But making peace was even more difficult than pacifying villages or Vietnamizing the war or planning protective-reaction strikes. It was certainly harder than writing memos for McNamara or interviewing village chiefs in South Vietnam. There were no beaches to capture, no limited operations to conduct, and therefore no priorities for a man in Ellsberg's position; no absolutes, except, of course, for the cause itself, no style that was fully comfortable. When Ellsberg first arrived in Chicago that evening, he told a waiting television interviewer that in giving the Pentagon Papers to the press he had not gone outside the system. "I've joined a larger system," he said. "The Constitution is larger than the executive branch." And yet that larger system, as he well knew, had no command structure, no precise objectives, and no certain method for calculating success. Its breadth leveled all the specifics—the marches, the speeches, the rallies—to an irrelevant equality.

It had not always been that way. In the Marine Corps, fifteen years before, he had been well-disciplined, organized and systematic. He had commanded one of the best companies in the First Marine Division, the company with the highest rifle scores and the lowest AWOL rate, had been so successful that even though he was only a lieutenant he kept his command; normally, the command of rifle companies went only to captains. In the Defense Department and the Department of State there was always a boss, a person who kept the thing functioning and who decided what was important. But now Ellsberg wanted to belong to a generation that would never feel the same way about the boss again, a generation whose larger system, if it was a system at all, was so loose and unfocused that nothing was more important than anything else. The Congress, he believed, had refused to exercise its responsibilities about the war, and the movement itself was so divided and often demoralized that he had spent four years looking for some means to be effective, talking to any United States Senator who would listen, making speeches, writing articles, and suggesting that he himself might be a war criminal, a man whose moral complicity in American war crimes might be no lighter—though perhaps more limited—than the parallel guilt of the Nazis who were tried at Nuremberg.

In the eighteen months between the fall of 1969, when he first copied the Papers in Los Angeles, and March of 1971, when he delivered them to Neil Sheehan of the *New York Times,* Ellsberg had participated in countless teach-ins on the war and visited scores of college campuses. The talks often contained references to the Nuremberg documents and to the memoirs of Albert Speer, who had been sentenced to prison as a Nazi war criminal, and to the matter of war crimes in general. In the last speech he made before the Papers were published (but after the *Times* already had them) he told an audience in Boston, "It is my own long *persistence in ignorance*—of the history of the conflict and of our involvement and of the full impact of the American way of war upon the people—that I find most to blame . . . It is a heavy load of blame. But if that is true for me, how should we weigh the responsibility of those ultimately responsible for informing themselves and the public and to whom recommendations for investigation were made repeatedly, each time to be rejected?" In the Pentagon, he said, he had discovered that "there existed people capable of writing, on demand, plans for the Nazi general staff. . . . These were people capable of imagining, in fact writing, plans for the genocide of entire nations. . . . I had the feeling that I was reading the Nuremberg documents for the second time in my life—and not the last." In making the Pentagon Papers public, he said later, he hoped to set an example for other defectors and that "a few other ex-officials would come clean." But the act was also an effort to establish credibility with the people he was trying to reach. The students were always polite during those campus visits; there were no hecklers, yet there remained Ellsberg's own unresolved feeling of personal complicity. "When I first started facing such audiences and the person introducing me felt compelled to go down the whole list of my past associations, my heart would sink with each sentence." If a man was willing to risk death for a nation in war, he often said, should he not also be willing to risk prison to stop a war he regarded as brutal and unjust?

## II

Standing on a platform or sitting with an interviewer, Ellsberg seemed somehow smaller than he should be, smaller than the act or the symbol, smaller than the man on television, and infinitely younger, more boyish, more vulnerable. It was only the eyes that marked him: deep blue, intense, at times piercing, looking for something inside himself. The snippy people on the right would find it easy to call him an egocentric fanatic, a man "with a strange secret smile, those funny anticipatory noddings . . . and above all, those eyes— extremely bright, the stare intense—and just behind them a wary look, the look of a frightened deer." It would be easy, moreover, to surmise that he was a nut or perhaps even a tool of the Nixon Administration in its efforts to blame the war on a covey of Democrats; no reasonable man, after all, does such things on his own. The charge was comprehensible because Ellsberg himself was an embarrassing man, because his very presence suggested the question "Why haven't I done the same?"

People were now encountering him, he once said, "several years into my alienation. I've had almost four years living with those documents. Some of them think that the only person who can make a real commitment is one who thinks he knows all the answers, so they say to themselves, 'I don't have all the answers, so I'm not expected to make commitments.' I don't think the test is a willingness to go to prison, although when I did this I expected to go to prison for a long time. The test is 'What would I do to end the war if I were willing to risk my job, the adverse criticism of my friends, and social ostracism?' " What had the Congress done, he often asked, what risks had it taken "against mur-der"? Every institution of the society had some complicity in this war. How much did a vote for the Hatfield-McGovern amendment (requiring withdrawal of American troops) mean by itself? Who had been willing to filibuster against the war or against the military? Who had taken what risks? "I've been searching through this society for people who will exercise authority and assume responsibility. The Congress tries to pass responsibility for the war to the President, but the President has the effective consent of the Senate and the House. They have not acted." He was forever searching, it seemed, and the material of his judgment came from sources so deep and complex that it was often difficult to determine what demons possessed him or what deities were still to be honored. He was completely at home with the style of the middle-class liberals but increasingly distant from their mod-erate politics; he was comfortable with the politics of the radicals but out of place with their manners. And so he was searching for a new home, a place to belong. "He's always looking for gurus," said an acquaintance who knew him in California.

There were new friends now, people like Noam Chomsky of MIT, a man who had himself taken risks for the cause, and with whom Ellsberg had discussed the possibility of leaking the Papers to the press, and Howard Zinn, the radical historian at Boston University, yet most of them were more like comrades-in-arms than friends, intellectual companions with whom one could apply the old techniques to new assump-tions, and even some of them were saying that Dan still didn't get it, hadn't really changed, was just the same old Ellsberg playing for the other team. And yet, other than speaking or writing, what could a man do? What were the priorities of the larger system, and what, indeed, was the system? What was left after the Papers had been published? What was Daniel Ellsberg other than the man who had given the Papers to the press?

Most of all, he was regarded as a convert, a representative

member of a generation whose adolescence coincided with
the end of World War II and which had grown up to identify
strongly with the actions of its nation, its government, and
particularly its President. Ellsberg was fourteen at the time
of the bombing of Hiroshima, a kid growing up in Detroit.
"Even then," he once said, "I had a feeling that that was a
decision that would better have been made in more anguish
than President Truman has ever admitted or indicated." But
that clearly was the statement of hindsight; most kids had no
such sensation; as another fourteen-year-old growing up in
New York, I was delighted that we had leveled an entire
Jap city, and I don't think I knew anyone my age who felt
otherwise. Even at the time of Korea, which seemed in its
own time a doubtful and perhaps unjustified war, few people
would even have considered the possibility of refusing to
serve in the armed forces—conscientious objectors were
rather special people, a little like religious fanatics—nor
could anyone imagine a time when America would wage a
war that was regarded as so immoral that draft resistance
would represent a serious and respectable alternative. American leadership since World War II, Ellsberg once said, has
tried to portray every enemy as Hitler: "Castro as Hitler,
Ho Chi Minh as Hitler, Mao as Hitler." I doubt that most
Americans of our generation really believed that pretense—
I think most people knew better—but I'm also certain that
we had a nearly unshakable faith in the executive branch. It
was the Congress that had been made up of isolationists and
America Firsters; it was the Congress that had always resisted foreign aid; it was always a recalcitrant legislature that
stood in the way of a progressive President. Ellsberg once
said quite correctly that political science in America was
oriented toward the views of the executive branch—something that he hoped the Pentagon Papers might help to
change. Because of Roosevelt, the President had become the
heroic figure—at least for liberals—in a nation that our
generation was raised to believe could do no wrong. Despite
Eisenhower, whose major flaw, in the liberal view, was not

misuse but nonuse of executive powers, it was in the presidency that progress resided.

The entire government style that produced Vietnam—the style of Kennedy and the counterforce intellectuals, the style of the think tank and the game-theory planners—represented the liberal answer, the modern answer, to John Foster Dulles and the doctrine of massive retaliation. The objective was to achieve the capability to fight brush-fire wars without blowing up the world, without confronting the choice of doing nothing or doing too much. Kennedy had created the Green Berets for precisely that purpose at a time when it was the hydrogen bomb and not Laos or Vietnam that was considered the ultimate obscenity. In his Boston speech, Ellsberg had spoken of "an almost inevitable feeling among our 'national security managers' that we can't be doing anything very wrong if we are still refraining from the use of nuclear weapons." To some extent, most people who came out of World War II had the same feeling. Not that the entire nation supported the war in Vietnam—in the years of the Kennedy Administration few people thought about Vietnam at all—but a great many, especially among the intellectuals, were, like Ellsberg, committed to a form of reason suspicious of all absolutes: the only absolute was the intellectual system itself. We were no longer living in a world where questions necessarily had immediate solutions or moral certainty, or where one could simply choose between winning and getting out. We were beyond ideology, and every problem, finally, was a technical problem. Ellsberg frequently spoke about the practice of presidential advisers of offering three options, two of them unacceptable extremes and one, Option C, a compromise. In the intellectual and political climate of the fifties and early sixties, Option C was, by definition, nearly always right. The possibility that these approaches themselves could produce an obscene war or mass murder was simply not imaginable.

In his own chronology, Ellsberg's personal "conversion" ran roughly parallel to the conversion of his generation of liberal intellectuals. He was a believer in 1965, an apostate in 1967 and a believer in something else by 1969. At each stage he was more deeply committed or more deeply alienated than most of his contemporaries. The first time I met him in 1971, he struck me as a person who was "too perfect, perhaps, too compulsively eager to be correct, too intense, too committed, too illiberal with himself." He had, as one of his friends said, very little capacity for self-irony: "McNamara was a rationalist who couldn't conceive of another symmetry of rationality; Ellsberg is a moralist who can't conceive of another frame of morality." During the long years of commitment to the government, it appeared as if he had always been searching for the ultimate point of control, the absolute secret, the final confrontation. Later in an affidavit he would go on for a dozen pages, listing the higher than Top Secret clearances he had received, the secrets he had learned—secrets often concealed from the Secretary of Defense and the President—and the decisions on which he had been consulted. He had haunted power, at the State Department, in Defense, at the Joint Chiefs of Staff, at Rand, and in endless special committees and groups, had become an omnipresence in crisis: the Cuban missile confrontation, the Skybolt affair, the planning for nuclear war, the studies of command systems, places where Top Secret material "is regarded . . . as relatively routine, relatively nonsensitive" and where genuinely sensitive data "is carefully concealed even from the great majority of those holding Top Secret clearances." The commitment was total—commitment to the system, the war, and the elaborate security procedures that they entailed. He was a voyeur of power.

Not surprisingly, his revulsion about the war did not begin with the brutality and the killing—with moral issues—but with its futility, and with the growing realization that things were going nowhere. It was the intellectual system that was on the verge of breaking down, and people who recall meeting him during his last months in Vietnam all speak about his anger at the inefficiency, the stupidity and the inability to do things right of responsible individuals. "I had thought," he said later, "that winning the war in Vietnam was a way of ending it." In 1965, when he went over with General Lansdale to study the pacification program, the war's tactics still seemed morally justified on the assumption that the war itself was necessary—the prevalent assumption of the Cold War mentality. He recalled how he had reacted to French practices in Algeria in the late fifties—i.e., the use of napalm on civilians and the common resort to torture: "I told myself at the time that I'm glad that I, as an American, don't have to read this about my own country in the newspapers. And I sympathized with French critics like Sartre and Simone de Beauvoir who were resisting in their own country."

By 1967, after two years on the scene, he had reason to change his mind.

Two years of field work [he wrote in 1972] had discredited, in my eyes, hopes of success in almost any terms in Vietnam, given the courses we were following and the increasingly obvious unlikelihood of our changing them. The prospect was . . . one of continued conflict, at increasing levels of violence; followed some day—probably later rather than sooner, and after more and more deaths, costs, destruction and dissension at home—by U.S. withdrawal and NLF dominance.

It was not to find this—or to find out the shortcomings of American policies, practices and officials that seemed heavily at fault—that I had come to Vietnam two years earlier. The process of coming to these conclusions was, quite simply, the most frustrating, disappointing period of my life. I had come to Vietnam to learn, but also to help us succeed; and the learning was as bitter as the failure.

What he discovered, first of all, was what he regarded as systematic deception that began at the lowest echelons and ran through the entire structure from the platoon leader to the President of the United States. Every week, he said in a talk to a group of dissident federal employees, the South Vietnamese Army filed reports that there had been 1,600 patrols that week, or 2,200 or 1,800, "but everyone in Vietnam knew that there had been no patrols—not one. And I said to myself, 'If only the Czar knew.' " In 1966, after he had been in Vietnam about ten months, he wrote McNamara that

> official reporting . . . is grossly inadequate to the job of educating high-level decision-makers to the nature of the essential problems here. It did not tell them what they needed to know. Nor did official, high level visits to Vietnam (though somewhat better), in practice, fill that lack. . . . To rely entirely on official reporting to Saigon from the field . . . is to remain untutored on many critical problems of Vietnam . . .

In the succeeding months, Ellsberg's disenchantment began to mount; areas that were marked blue on the map—meaning secure against the Vietcong—were not secure at all; in one village, as Ellsberg later reported, the guides warned visitors who had come to attend a ceremony marking the elevation of the town to the "secure" classification not to stray from carefully defined paths. At the same time he became increasingly aware—as he had not been in Washington —of the human price of the war and the humanity of its victims. In a long letter to his Harvard classmates for their fifteen-year reunion report, Ellsberg wrote that he was proud to have served with Lansdale:

> I've learned fully as much as I had hoped; and learned to care deeply for this tortured country, . . . its children, its people and their future. But much of the knowledge is painful; I don't seem to have the temperament of a pathologist. It has been, most of it, an intensely frustrating year and a half, though with a good deal of excitement and moments of hope. . . . I'm more convinced than I could have been before that Lansdale's basic thoughts on political development, on nationalistic and democratic rivalry with communists for leadership of revo-

lutionary forces, and on counter-guerrilla tactics are sound, relevant to Vietnam, and desperately needed here; but *none* of them are being applied, in any degree . . .

*If only the Czar knew.*

In fact, of course, the Czar did know. Or should have known. Shortly before he left Vietnam in the spring of 1967, the increasingly disillusioned Ellsberg suggested to a friend in the Defense Department that he propose to McNamara the initiation of a study of "U.S. decision-making in Vietnam on the model of Dick Neustadt's study of the Skybolt crisis." If his hepatitis allowed, Ellsberg added, he himself would be interested in participating in the study. That request may or may not have been the stimulus for the Pentagon Papers; at any rate, Ellsberg later wrote, a few weeks after the suggestion was made "McNamara himself proposed his historical study, mentioning the Skybolt as a guideline"—by now McNamara had also become disillusioned with the war and the decisions that produced it—and, by fall, "once again employed by Rand . . . , I was at work."

III

The project had begun in the summer of 1967 under the general direction of Morton H. Halperin, then the Deputy Assistant Secretary of Defense for International Security Affairs. It was to be "encyclopedic and objective" and to concern itself with the history and background of the American involvement. McNamara did not want Halperin to work on the study full time, and so Halperin named Leslie H. Gelb, his own assistant at ISA, to head the task force. Eventually there would be some thirty-six scholars working on different aspects of the war; several of them came from the Defense Department, others from Rand and several from the universities. They would go through two decades of American involvement in Vietnam, assembling three thousand pages of analysis and history and some four thousand pages of documents—memos, intelligence estimates, and cables from a variety of executive departments (some of which had already been leaked). McNamara instructed Halperin to keep the work as confidential as possible; no one outside the task force should know except for those who would be asked to provide material; interviews with those who had made the decisions on Vietnam were not allowed—the task force would have to work entirely from written materials—and materials from the White House would not be available. Those instructions, as Halperin interpreted them, meant that the study was not only secret (i.e., classified), but also, in his words, "bureaucratically and politically sensitive." If people in other agencies knew about the study, there were likely to be recriminations within the executive branch—the documents showed, among other things, how federal agencies had bypassed one another—and demands for the release of the study to Congress. As a result, Halperin and Gelb routinely marked all the volumes (and each page of each volume) "Top Secret—Sensitive." "Top Secret" was based on the official government classification system as defined by an executive order (E. O. 10501) and derived from the fact that many of the documents used in the study were themselves classified "Top Secret." The mark "Sensitive" had no basis either in law or in the administrative classification system, but it was, as Halperin later testified, often used to designate material that was to be withheld from other government officials (and particularly from the Congress) because its contents were "bureaucratically and politically embarrassing." "Sensitive" referred to matters of bureaucratic concern rather than to military secrets. Later Gelb also confessed that in fact he knew nothing about the classification system—his only training in security had come from a film which instructed him to beware of beautiful blondes "because they might be Russian spies."

The project took eighteen months to complete (the original estimate had been three months). Ellsberg later claimed that as a *quid pro quo* for his participation in the work he was to be given personal access not only to the portion he himself was to work on, but to the entire study. Halperin, Gelb and Paul Warnke, the Assistant Secretary of Defense for International Security Affairs at the time the study was finished, denied that such an arrangement was ever made. Ellsberg, nonetheless, did get access. In December of 1968, as the Johnson Administration was about to leave office, Gelb, Warnke and Halperin, wishing to retain control of documents on which they had worked, pooled their copies of the Papers and, under a special arrangement with Henry Rowen, the president of Rand, sent them to Rand for storage (Gelb and Halperin had both been Rand employees). An incomplete set of thirty-eight volumes was sent to Rand's Washington office in January 1969; one complete set of the forty-seven-volume study was later sent to its Santa Monica office and another to its Washington office. Whether those copies were the property of the government or whether they belonged to the three ex-officials is not clear: in such cases the line between "private papers" and "government documents" has always been hazy. Every bureaucrat has always signed statements that he would not remove classified documents from government custody when he terminated his job, yet hundreds of officials from the President down have done precisely that, not only taking their "private papers" for their memoirs, but often also turning them over to libraries as a means of getting a charitable tax deduction. What was certain was that the understanding with Rowen included a proviso that the Pentagon Papers (and a number of other documents sent to Rand for storage) would not be logged into the Rand "Top Secret Control" system and would be accessible only to those who had specific permission from two of the three "owners"—Gelb, Warnke, Halperin.

Rowen himself got access for Ellsberg. He tried twice: the first time he was refused (there was, at the very least, an intimation that Warnke did not trust Ellsberg to keep the Papers confidential); then he tried again—Ellsberg, he told Halperin, was working on his Rand study on the "lessons of Vietnam" and could benefit from the Papers—and Halperin secured Gelb's consent without consulting Warnke. Ellsberg went to Washington on two separate occasions, in March and August of 1969, and brought back to Santa Monica eighteen volumes of the thirty-eight-volume set that had been stored at the Rand Washington office. (The remainder of the forty-seven-volumes would not be typed for several months.) The government later claimed that Ellsberg was only acting as a courier between the two Rand offices—it would be one of the bases of the indictment against him—and that he had failed to check them in with the proper "Top Secret Control officer" at Rand Santa Monica. The evidence indicated, however, that the "owners" had ordered that the documents not be checked into the system, and that Ellsberg had acted in accordance with those instructions. The Papers had been too sensitive for the "Top Secret" system at Rand.

Ellsberg thus became one of the few people—perhaps the only person other than Gelb and Halperin—to read the complete study. He was also unique in being the only person up to that time to have full access to the Papers who had also had extensive field experience in Vietnam. That access, he said, produced another cycle of frustration and "bitter learning":

What stood out among the internal documents was the personal responsibility of the President for the particular policy chosen. Whatever it was each President thought privately he might achieve from what he decided to do, it must have differed from the written estimates and much of the advice he was receiving in those years; it could not simply be the production of bureaucratic euphoria or deception. Indeed, in each of the crisis years—in contrast to the years in-between—there had been enough realistic reporting available to the President to make it hard to imagine that somewhat *more* truth-telling or even pessimism could have made any difference to his choice.

Could it be that none of the lying to the Presidents had mattered? If each President was told, at the moment of escalation, that what he was ordering would probably not solve the problem, what was he up to? Why did he not do more—or less? And why did each mislead the public and the Congress about what he was doing, and what he had been told?

From 1967 on, Ellsberg said, he had begun to work privately to get the Vietnam policy changed. At first, much of it was "behind the scenes—as my background dictated—as consultant to Executive officials, to presidential candidates and their advisors, and finally to the National Security Council staff of the new President."

On Christmas Day, 1968, some four weeks before the Nixon Administration took office, Ellsberg and two colleagues from Rand had gone to see Henry Kissinger at the Hotel Pierre in New York to discuss a Rand study that Kissinger had initiated for Nixon on the policy options on Vietnam. In January of 1969 a first draft of that study was available for discussion by the National Security Council. In the meantime, Ellsberg had drafted a set of questions for Kissinger "which analyzed the major uncertainties, contradictions and controversies among the agencies dealing with Vietnam." That analysis, National Security Study Memorandum No. 1 (NSSM-1), Ellsberg wrote, "Kissinger sent to each agency. I spent February in the Executive Office Building reading and helping to summarize the answers to my questions . . . for the President." Ellsberg still believed, however strong his disillusionment, that the greatest possibilities lay with the President, and that the most effective way for a defense intellectual to operate was within the old system: "I would, I told myself, have done the same for George Wallace." (Ellsberg later leaked copies of NSSM-1 to at least two members of the Senate: Mike Gravel of Alaska and Charles McC. Mathias, Jr., of Maryland. Shortly after the Pentagon Papers were published Mathias turned his copy of NSSM-1 over to the officers of the Senate and informed Attorney General John Mitchell that he had received the material from Ellsberg. Early in 1972 Gravel made his copy public, but this time there were no indictments.)

The final phase began that spring. The Kissinger studies went the way of most such projects. (One of the options that Ellsberg included in the original draft for Kissinger, withdrawal from Vietnam, was deleted from the list submitted to the National Security Council.) Kissinger went off to Europe on an errand for Nixon, and Ellsberg returned to Rand in Santa Monica with the first group of volumes from the Washington office to begin his reading and analysis of the Pentagon study. By that time, judging from Ellsberg's own recollections, the war in Vietnam had become a near-obsession, an intellectual and moral quest through political and military decisions twenty years old, through personal crises, and through a series of traumas that, in the kind of analysis that might be applied by Erik Erikson, could be labeled clinically as an identity crisis. The world was turned on its head: what characterized his own assumptions before 1967, he said later, was a "tacit, unquestioned belief that we had a right to *'win,'* in many ways defined by us (i.e., by the President); or, at least, a right to prolong a war . . . or, at the very worst, to 'lose only gracefully, covertly, slowly,': all these, even the last, at the cost of an uncounted number of Asian lives, a toll to which our policy set no real limit." By August 1969 he regarded himself intellectually and morally a different man. He had decided that Nixon had decided against "extrication"—against a definite end to American involvement:

Once more, an Administration planned to postpone failure; to buy time by maintaining indefinitely American troops (very gradually to be reduced to a sizeable residual force), and American bombing, Indochinese casualties, and the threat of worse. That was what the "option exercise" and NSSM-1 had come to. . . . One of the questions asked had been, in substance, "When would the South Vietnamese Armed Forces be made capable of handling a sizeable challenge by North Vietnamese forces without both U. S. ground forces and U. S. combat support?" (In other words, when would *"total* Vietnamization," as

the American public was later led to understand it, be feasible?)
The answer from the Pentagon in February, 1969—never revealed to the public—was clear cut: "Never." . . . Only Congress and the public, informed in time and organized in protest,
could now dissuade the President from prolonging the American war in Vietnam.

   To ask a man who had spent the last decade serving four of
these five Presidents to act on such perceptions is asking him to
jump out of his skin. Something harder than risking it, which I
had already done along with three million, mostly younger
Americans who had gone to Vietnam. We had seen that as
responding to the President. Until recently, few had supposed
that might conflict with serving our country. What was needed
now, to go beyond that, was the inspiration to find in oneself
loyalties long unconsulted, deeper and broader than loyalty to
the President: loyalties to America's founding concepts, to our
Constitutional system, to countrymen, to one's own humanity.


   *To find in oneself loyalties long unconsulted:* it was a
striking phrase, a plea to be understood, and, more than that,
perhaps, a self-conscious yet impossible wish to understand
oneself. Since when had those loyalties been neglected, and
what sins, other than the sin of intellectual error, had that
neglect produced? One would have to go back to the very
roots, to the Christian Scientist parents—both of them converted Jews—who had raised him, would have to consider
his mother, a talented and energetic woman, who had decided in his early  youth that he would become a concert
pianist, and that he must practice at least five hours a day.
There were the recollections of guilt, moments more than
thirty years ago, when playground injuries and minor ill-
nesses were treated as moral failures, as blemishes of the will.
As a reminder, there was a scar on his forehead where a gash
incurred in a schoolyard accident had been allowed to heal
without medical attention; there was the remembrance of
times "when you blamed yourself for everything," the recollection of others who knew him then that "Dan never had a

chance to be a kid at all," and the memory of days and years in the Depression when the unemployed engineer father, like so many others of his time, blamed only himself for his failure. It was not all that way, he would say; he did play sports, played tennis and soccer and boxed; yet there was also the recollection of the moment when his mother was killed in an auto accident (he was then fifteen years old) and when he thought, "Now I don't have to practice the piano anymore." He had gone to Harvard on a full scholarship; people would remember him from those days as a brilliant person, but also someone who was hard to know. By his junior year he was married to Carol Cummings, the daughter of a colonel, later a general, in the Marine Corps. There wasn't much chance to be one of the boys. He'd never been one of the boys.

In the summer of 1968, everything had fallen apart: his intellectual assurance, his political assumptions, his personal life. He had been separated from Carol since 1964 and divorced since 1965; now, after the assassination of Martin Luther King, Jr., and Robert Kennedy, and with the rejection of the Vietnam peace plank at the Democratic national convention (on which he had been a consultant), all the old systems ceased to function. Everything that had been exquisitely right in its own time came up unmanageably wrong in another.

"I spent that summer with girls," he told Studs Terkel one night, "very little work that I can remember. One girl after another. I was fighting an extreme case of powerlessness. . . . And what I was doing with one girl after another was trying in some way to remind myself, or convince myself, that I existed or that one could have purposes or satisfactions entirely apart from politics. That was sort of a lost summer for me. I never watched television for a moment, I saw no speech of either candidate. I told myself that if the bombing would stop, if they would stop the bombing altogether, then I could be interested in one side or the other. And, looking back on that summer much later, I really remembered that this succession of girls that I was interested in—I'm not clear whether I was interested in them, but this succession of girls that I was seeing that summer suddenly stopped at a very abrupt point. And I often asked myself why it stopped, and, in a way, you know, I was pursuing this obsessively . . . and it stopped the day the bombing stopped."

It was all rolled together: the war, the intellectual disillusionment, Russo's politics, the girls, the fascination with power. In the spring of 1968 he had begun psychoanalysis with Dr. Lewis Fielding in Beverly Hills, and although he was never willing to discuss what he learned in those sessions (which were to last, at the rate of four a week, for two and a half years) they seemed to reinforce the decisions he would make eighteen months later. By early 1969, after his disillusionment with NSSM-1, he began to see more of Russo, whom he had first met in Vietnam, where Russo had been interviewing Viet Cong prisoners for a Rand study. Russo had left Rand in January 1968—he had been fired six months before but was given the customary Rand grace period to complete his work and find another job—and was now working intermittently in the ghettos of Los Angeles. He had by then become a fervent critic of what he regarded as American imperialism, and he spent much of his time trying to persuade friends to drop out of the system and work for reform or revolution. By midsummer, Russo, his friend Lynda Sinay, Ellsberg, and Ellsberg's friend Kimberley Rosenberg were spending a great deal of time together, partying at the beach at Malibu, smoking pot, listening to rock music and engaging in a great deal of talk about—in the words of one of Ellsberg's friends at the time—"Vietnam and sex." He also started attending meetings on war resistance, where, among others, he met Randy Kehler, a young Harvard graduate who had joined the War Resisters' League and who was subsequently sent to prison for his refusal to cooperate with the Selective Service System. "He impressed me a great deal," Ellsberg would say later, "because he was willing to go to jail for the principle of civil disobedience." He

had also met a girl from India "who gave me a vision, as a
Gandhian, of a different way of living and resistance—truth
telling as a form of power," and what she told him would
now become part of his moral rhetoric. In the meantime Ellsberg continued reading his documents and thinking about
the "lessons of Vietnam," and concluded that the lies and
deception were systematic, not just the aberrations of particular Presidents or the result of errors in judgment. The intelligence estimates, he concluded, despite his earlier feelings
about inaccurate reporting from the field, were "remarkably
accurate." He had become privy to a new secret.

That ultimate secret seemed to have something to do with
the nature of secrecy itself. He could verge on the rhapsodic
when he spoke about what the possession of secrets could do
to the possessor, about the safes within safes, the clearances
above Top Secret, the secrets within secrets that he had discovered in the inner chambers of the Pentagon. People in
Washington derived kicks from having access to information
from those inner chambers, achieved a kind of euphoria from
knowing things that were not known by others. He would
later say that his own fascination with them might have some
relation to a parallel fascination with pornography. For years
he had collected pornography, and his apartment was full of
the stuff. Now he also possessed the hard-core information
about the war, the pornography of Vietnam. Was the language suggestive: disclosure, revelation, protection, penetra-
tion? Here was a whole literature of perversion and hidden
acts. It was the notorious addiction of Washington and the
intellectual preoccupation of the think tank, but for Ellsberg
it seems to have had a special allure. Because they were produced by the government, and because they were marked
"Top Secret," the Pentagon Papers had a relevance which
other information lacked, even if it was, in substance, the
same information. It came from the inside and was therefore
genuine. In 1968 he had warned Henry Kissinger (he would
later testify) not to be seduced by secret data, which con-
stitutes "a magic potion that turns ordinary human beings

into arrogant, contemptuous menaces to democracy," but two years later, when he saw Kissinger again, he concluded that Kissinger was "eating the secret honeydew."

III

The precipitant moment came late in September, when he read in the *Los Angeles Times* of the decision of the Secretary of the Army to drop charges in the case of the Green Berets who had been accused of murdering a Vietnamese double agent. The Secretary's explanation for his decision indicated implicitly that people at every level of command had been systematically lying about the case and, indeed about the war. "I remember very well," Ellsberg said later on the Cavett show, "thinking that this is a system that I have spent fifteen years serving, in the Marine Corps, Defense Department, State Department, Vietnam, the Rand Corporation, serving the President . . . It's a system that from top to bottom has come to act reflexively, automatically, to conceal murder for political convenience by lying. All along, I was skeptical of this policy of deception, and yet I helped write some of those lies. I was well aware of them. I did not expose them." On the day the Green Beret story appeared, Ellsberg says, he decided "to stop lying" and called up Russo.

The Xerox machine was located in Lynda Sinay's Los Angeles advertising office on Melrose Avenue. She had her own agency—had, at the age of twenty-six, become so successful that she was being called the Mary Wells of the West Coast (though she would later go bankrupt)—and she agreed to let them use the machine. Although she had listened to endless conversations and harangues about American imperialism and capitalism, she had never had much interest in politics. Russo had tried to get her to write exposés of her advertising clients and to drop out of the system, but she always refused. "We were very different people," she said much later, but she recalled Russo's warmth, his sense of fun, and her own deep emotional involvement. She participated in the project not for the cause, but for Tony and

Dan. Sinay was told that Ellsberg, expecting to leave Rand, wanted to take some documents with him; she was also told that since she had no "Top Secret" clearance, she should not read anything, but she was given to understand that Ellsberg wanted to turn the material over to Senator Fulbright.

It was relatively easy to carry the Papers out of the Rand offices in Santa Monica. "They went to ridiculous lengths on clearances," said a former Rand employee who worked there at the time the Papers were published, "but nobody checked what you took out. I took things home; everyone took things home." In his personal safe Ellsberg had copies of the eighteen volumes he had brought from Washington; those volumes, he would always insist, were his own, not Rand's, because he had received custody directly from Gelb and Halperin. Copies of some of the other volumes, however, came from one of the complete sets which had been sent directly to Rand Santa Monica and which were checked into the Rand system. In taking those volumes to be copied, Ellsberg also took part of a copy of a document which had nothing to do with the Papers, a memorandum prepared by the Chairman of the Joint Chiefs of Staff, General Earle C. Wheeler, on the Vietnam situation after the 1968 Tet offensive, and which he would also give to the *Times* in 1971. Ellsberg had brought the Wheeler Report from Washington, where he had used it in studies of the Vietnam military situation in the weeks after Tet, and deposited it at Rand. It was routine practice: Rand's collection of classified documents consisted in substantial part of bootleg materials—papers which had been brought to Santa Monica by former government officials and "contributed" to the Rand collection.

The first round of copying took several weeks—Ellsberg estimated there were some eight sessions. (There would be another copying period the following spring.) Ellsberg would bring an installment of documents in an expansion folder and would later take away both the originals and the copies. Occasionally he brought his children, who were living with his ex-wife, Carol, in Los Angeles: Robert Ellsberg was not quite fourteen and Mary was eleven; Robert, Ellsberg said later, encouraged him to do it. Together, Ellsberg, the children, Russo and Sinay ran the pages through the machine and cut the "Top Secret—Sensitive" marking from the copies, an act, Sinay later explained, which Ellsberg said was designed to enable him to get additional copies made by a commercial duplicating service. All the work was carried on at night. One night one of them tripped the burglar alarm in Sinay's office and the police appeared; on another occasion, Kimberley Rosenberg showed up with apples and "refreshments," and on still another occasion Vu Van Thai appeared to meet Ellsberg for a dinner engagement. Thai, who had been South Vietnamese ambassador to the United States and was now a Rand consultant (and a friend of Ellsberg's), had nothing to do with the copying—later Ellsberg insisted to his lawyers that he couldn't even remember that Thai had ever been there. Still later Ellsberg recalled that he had seen something in one of the volumes that he wanted to show Thai; he took the document, which dealt with diplomatic contacts through neutral countries with North Vietnam, handed it to Thai, and Thai leafed through it; as a consequence, the FBI would find Thai's fingerprints on the document, and Thai would find himself an unindicted co-conspirator in the case. The kids, of course, told their mother, and she would later tell the FBI.

I spoke to my former husband about this [Carol Ellsberg said in an affidavit filed later in a Los Angeles federal court] and told him that I was extremely concerned since, in my opinion, this was a criminal act. and he could go to jail for it. Daniel Ellsberg told me that he had done nothing illegal because there was no official secrets act in this country. I asked him what he thought would happen if he were to go to prison and he replied that he did not think there was much stigma to that anymore. He further said that people did this sort of thing all the time in their memoirs and that they mentioned things in print that had been top secret. My former husband told me that he was very concerned about the war in Vietnam and that he was going to be actively working against it and that there were things that had not been disclosed which should be known. He then said that he would give it to authorized people like Senators Fulbright and Goodell.

Ellsberg delivered a copy of the Pentagon Papers to Fulbright—a sampling at first, then most of the rest. There was still some hope of working within the government if the Senate Foreign Relations Committee, of which Fulbright was chairman, would, as Ellsberg then expected, hold hearings into the origins of the war. He clearly believed that the Papers alone, made public, would have a major impact in ending it. But Fulbright, partly to protect Ellsberg and partly because "it wasn't clear then of what use they actually were in stopping the war," decided to proceed more cautiously. He wrote to Defense Secretary Melvin Laird, requesting a copy of the study. Laird refused: "Access to and use of this document has been extremely limited. It would clearly be contrary to the national interest to disseminate it more widely." In succeeding months, Fulbright tried once more, without success, and Ellsberg then began to seek other possibilities. (Ellsberg later claimed that Fulbright told him that the best way to get the documents out was not through Congress but through the *New York Times*.) In the winter of 1969–70, he worked as a consultant to Senator Charles Goodell of New York (who would later become one of his defense lawyers) in drafting a statement on Vietnam policy that Goodell could use in testimony before the Foreign Relations Committee to support his call for immediate withdrawal. He did not tell Goodell about the Papers, but, as Goodell later recalled, "it was obvious that the guy knew something. We had to round off the figures and fuzz the details so people wouldn't think we had access to some sort of classified data." In the succeeding months, Ellsberg also tried to pass samples of the Papers to Senator George McGovern, who had by then become the best known of the Senate doves, but McGovern refused. "We didn't know," said Gordon Weil, one of Mc-Govern's aides, "whether we were dealing with some kook; we didn't know who the guy was." There would never be much love lost between McGovern and Ellsberg; to Mc-Govern, Ellsberg was an unreliable true believer who had helped create the problem in the first place; to Ellsberg, McGovern was a man unwilling to take chances for the cause that he was supposed to represent.

Ellsberg had by now decided to become a Witness. "The guy was all over Washington," said an assistant to another member of the Senate. "He was seeing anybody who might help." At the same time, he also began carrying his case to the public, helping to draft a letter to the editor of the *New York Times;* it was signed by Ellsberg and five of his Rand colleagues, and reflected weeks of discussion among a handful of Rand employees. "We believe," it said, "that the United States should decide now to end its participation in the Vietnam War, completing the total withdrawal of our forces within one year at most. . . . The human and material costs of continuing our part in the war far outweigh any prospective benefits and are greater than the foreseeable costs and risks of disengagement." (The *Times* did not publish that statement in its "Letters" column, choosing instead to print it as a news article. The *Washington Post* published the full text a few days later.) Thereafter, Ellsberg's efforts to tell the story—even to castigate himself as a war criminal—began to escalate. He explored the possibility of starting legal action to end the war—"not necessarily criminal, but civil suits or injunctions claiming the unconstitutionality of the war," he told an interviewer from *Look,* "[which] would provide a channel whereby the Pentagon documents would enter public consciousness." The lawyers to whom he spoke were skeptical—there wasn't sufficient documentation—and Ellsberg replied that they "shouldn't think it impossible that documents as comprehensive as those available at the Nuremberg War Crimes Tribunal would be available." To some, he mentioned the study—"In fact, I proposed myself as a possible defendant or witness if somebody could get a case going. . . . Nobody rose to that at all."

He took increasingly to the stump; he started making the college circuit (once, in the early days of the campus teach-ins, he had defended the war—now he talked about deception and lies and murder), he began writing the journal articles, among them the brilliant "The Stalemate Machine and the Quagmire Myth" (first given as a paper to the American Political Science Association in September 1970), which, with later hindsight, were obviously based on something more than casual information; he testified before congressional committees; and he wrote letters to the *Times*. At the same time, he began to see Patricia Marx again. They had first met in 1964, Ellsberg the hawk of the think tank and Patricia the liberal dovish daughter of the hawkish president of Marx Toys (admirer of J. Edgar Hoover, companion of U. S. Army generals, supporter of Nixon). They had started going together in 1965, and that fall, as a part-time radio reporter for WNYC in New York, she had come to see him in Saigon. But that had gone wrong, partly over political differences and partly, as she said later, "because our values were very different." Ellsberg, who often recalled dates in his life as if they were the landmarks of an odyssey, remembers the date of the reunion as November 2, 1969, about a month after the Xeroxing began. By now, Patricia told Terkel, he was a different man from the person she had last seen in Saigon: "He had the same dedication, but it was infused with a compassion and a humanity. And we were able to love each other then . . . As a human being, he changed, not only intellectually, but as a man." In the spring of 1970, he decided to leave Rand—was forced out, some said, because he couldn't complete his projects—and in September, as a research associate in international affairs, he went to MIT, finally free, Patricia said later, "to speak out against the war." That summer they were married.

Yet there was still that great weight, "this weight of truth," Patricia said, "that he was carrying around." In physical terms it must have been about sixty pounds and, as he said at the Chicago BEM celebration a year later, he wished every Congressman had to carry it around for a while even if all of them didn't read it, "to feel how heavy the extracts of twenty-five years of classified lies and brutality feel." Yet through the fall and winter of 1970–71, despite months of debate, the Congress took no substantive action; earlier that year the invasion of Cambodia had produced some of the most massive and serious protests of the entire war—it produced Jackson State and Kent State, and it brought thousands of middle-class, middle-aged recruits into peace activism for the first time—but by late fall both the invasion and the protests were nearly forgotten. The withdrawal of American troops had begun, and the politicians were beginning to predict—correctly, judging by the election returns that fall— that the war was becoming a secondary issue. At the same time, the air war continued, and Laos became an increasingly important theater of operations, the site of a clandestine war whose existence was largely denied in Washington. Nixon, despite the talk of Vietnamization, represented no major change in policy or in the way that policy decisions were made. Opposition to the war had by now become respectable, but that made no difference; it may, indeed, have represented a coming to terms with the issue because it had been deradicalized. While the boys were starting to come home, the war turned chronic and electronic; the ultimate aim of the Administration, Ellsberg decided, was an "invisible war."

Nixon's plan was to reduce those dimensions of the war that were most salient to U.S. media and the public—U.S. casualties, U.S. ground presence, draft calls, and costs—and transfer the greater part of the combat to the Indochinese and to areas where reporters could less easily follow—to the air, and to Laos, Cambodia, and North Vietnam. He was gambling that the indefinite prolongation of the war would then cease to be a matter of concern or even of awareness to most Americans. The war would become invisible to them. With the human burden of the war falling almost exclusively upon the Indochinese, statements that "we are getting out of the war" or "the war is ending" would meet no challenge, even while U.S. bombing continued and expanded in area coverage, and Indochinese died in combat or became homeless at increasing rates. If the strategy were successful in these terms, . . . Orwell's slogan, "War is peace" would be political currency in the U.S. a dozen years ahead of 1984.

The war, of course, had largely been brought home in terms of American casualties and domestic costs. There were people at BEM who defended their anti-Vietnam position by saying that Vietnam was bad for business (just as there were others who would say that it was draining resources from domestic programs). To assume that the Pentagon Papers would create a reaction sizable enough to stop the war—at a time when, moreover, American casualties were going down—was therefore to demand a unique level of national morality. It also demanded the sort of moral intransigence that no real political world—a world of compromises and adjustments—can tolerate. As a personal attitude, as *faith,* it had meaning, but as politics it was asking too much.

In March, Ellsberg decided to escalate. It was a matter of responsibility, and responsibility, one of Ellsberg's favorite words, involved a tangle of ideas and feelings more closely related to religious than to political meanings. It was there in the idea of the Christian witness, in the tradition of the Prophets, in all those loyalties long unconsulted, and it represented the translation of newly discovered virtues into necessities for national politics. No one had taken the responsibility, but hadn't he learned long ago (and now, belatedly, remembered) that, finally, all responsibility was personal, that if the personal anguish was in any sense derived from the Puritan's reading of the Old Testament, the particularized sense of culpability was remediable only through one's own faith and deeds? *Speak truth to power.*

What had been wrong before was that as a bureaucrat you spoke truth *for* power.

> You don't influence power that way. You share in the crimes of power that way. You become an accomplice . . . You live the life not of an intellectual but of an informer. This war is not going to be ended ever by people who see themselves in their official capacity as powerless except as they do the bidding of their powerful superiors . . . , who see themselves as nothing unless they have a direct dependence and relation upon these powerful people . . .

And so, in March, he called Neil Sheehan of the *Times,* whom he had met in Vietnam when Sheehan was a reporter for UPI and who was now in the Washington bureau of the nation's most prestigious, if not its most enterprising, newspaper. In a sense, contacting the *Times* did not represent much of a radical departure from Ellsberg's earlier tactics; the newspaper was, after all, an establishment in itself—not quite the fourth branch of the government (although there are *Times* people who entertain such fantasies), and yet a Presence, an institution that would rather be mute than be considered Irresponsible. By rights, the story belonged much more nearly to a publication like *Ramparts,* which, with far more limited resources, had been muckraking the military and the war for years, or to one of the more intelligent undergrounds, which, as Ellsberg later acknowledged, had been far closer to reporting the brutality and the associated deceit of the war than the commercial press. But the *Times* was, of course, the paper that Everybody Read—which suggested something about the nature of Ellsberg's own conversion and the kind of people he wanted to reach. The *Times,* as he knew, was the Paper of Record; if the *Times* published something, it was a Fact; if the *Times* ignored it, it could properly be considered not to exist at all.

Very likely, no one will ever know the details of Ellsberg's arrangement with the *Times.* According to Sanford Ungar's well-researched book *The Papers and the Papers,* which covers the details of the internal debates at the *Times* and the *Washington Post* and the subsequent legal battle over the government's attempt to suppress publication, Sheehan and his wife, Susan, a writer for *The New Yorker,* went to Cambridge late in March and picked up the goods. Ellsberg did not give them the last four volumes of the documents, dealing with attempts to negotiate a settlement through neutral countries—the so-called "diplomatic volumes." ("I didn't want to get in the way of diplomacy," he told Ungar. "I wanted to get in the way of the bombing and killing.") And so the Great Weight was on its way to Washington and, a few weeks later, to New York.

## IV

Aeschylus does not tell us whether men knew of the existence of fire before Prometheus, taking pity on their miserable lot, purloined the secret from the gods, but Aeschylus operated in the realm of myth and art, and not in the realm of politics. What seems reasonably certain is that men would have wanted to know the secret had they suspected that it existed. In the case of the Pentagon Papers, the corollary proposition is far more doubtful: Who really wanted to know? A month after the *Times* began publication, Ellsberg appeared on *The Dick Cavett Show* and spoke about "a need not to know, both on the public's part and on the part of the press. They did not hear what they did not want to hear. They still don't do that, and the press cooperates with that. . . ." But, in the euphoria of those early postpublication weeks, Ellsberg seemed to miss the full meaning and irony of what he was saying. In the context of that evening, the "need not to know" referred specifically to the public statements of people like Lyndon Johnson, which had always been reported in their most reassuring light, when, on a closer reading—and with hindsight—they turned out to be highly ambiguous, leaving open precisely those steps of escalation which were subsequently taken. What Ellsberg did not appear to understand was that the need not to know was much broader, that, in some sense, the reporting of American atrocities and the more serious criticisms of the war were treated by many people as more of a public nuisance and generated more resentment than the war itself; the national response to the Mylai massacre should have made that clear. Ellsberg spoke a great deal in those days about the relationship that secrecy and brutality in Vietnam bore to secrecy and brutality in America. A few years before the Papers were published, he had heard Tom Hayden, one of the Chicago Seven and long a militant member of the peace movement, talk about Vietnam as a mirror of American society. "At that time," Ellsberg said later, "I thought of Vietnam as an excrescence of our policy, as an aberration, and I wanted to say that this isn't what America was like." But by the fall of 1971, with what he had seen in his visits to American prisons and what he had heard from friends, he wasn't sure. The prison bureaucracy, he said in a speech in Washington, is the perfect bureaucracy; there are no restraints, no accountability, and so Attica became the analogue of Mylai, and the Pentagon bureaucracy the corollary of the prison administration at San Quentin. But he apparently had not asked himself whether perhaps those perfect bureaucracies, which had often succeeded in representing murder as self-defense (the prisoners slit the throats of the hostages, the student demonstrators were sniping at the police, the Vietnamese children were armed, the Panthers began the shoot-out), had been *created* by the general need not to know. Did the perfect bureaucracy function as a mechanism to do what most people wanted done, but which they refused to acknowledge—a device whose very purpose is secrecy—or was it a self-serving organism whose social product, if any, was incidental? Were there, in fact, two larger "systems" uncomfortably coexisting side by side, a constitutional system of due process, civic responsibility and all the rest *and* a large and equally pervasive social understanding that a lot of dirty work was necessary (or, at the very least, in demand) and that the very essence of such dirty work was its success in protecting the citizenry from its uglier moral implications?

What, in fact, had Ellsberg done—not for himself, but for the nation? The substantive content of the Papers, let alone the implications, was itself subject to question, and the academic controversy began almost immediately after the Papers were published. (In some respects, and with hindsight, it may even be said to have begun before; a huge number of articles and books published before June 1971 included material from the study or the original government documents on which the study was based, usually without specific acknowledgment.) Within months, the Bantam edition with Neil Sheehan's introduction became a staple in college bookstores; the American Historical Association scheduled a special session on the Papers at its annual meeting in December, and the salvos that started reverberating through the journals were sufficiently fierce to promise a debate that would last for years. Ellsberg himself believed that the Papers destroyed the old quagmire theory, the belief that the war was essentially the consequence of a series of tragic mistakes—generally well-intentioned—by a succession of administrations trying to "stabilize" a situation (or to beat the Viet Cong) without resort to all-out war. But even if one did not accept that interpretation, the Papers threatened to turn a number of other and equally fundamental assumptions on their head: the general intellectual presumption in favor of the executive branch as against the Congress, the larger faith in the candor of the federal government, and the common theory that Vietnam was an aberration in American history, a momentary departure from a tradition (with perhaps a couple of minor exceptions) of just wars waged in a just cause by a just government. Instead, the Papers suggested chronic manipulation, secrecy and deceit:

> The segments of the public world—Congress, the news media, the citizenry, even international opinion as a whole [wrote Sheehan in this introduction]—are regarded from within the

world of the government insider as elements to be influenced. The policy memorandums repeatedly discuss ways to move those outside "audiences" in the desired direction, through such techniques as the controlled release of information and appeals to patriotic stereotypes. The Pentagon Papers are replete with examples of the power the Executive Branch has acquired to make its influence felt in the public domain.

The revelations touched the very center of the governmental process: the relationship between foreign policy and domestic politics, the connection between secrecy and violence, the issue of executive power and responsibility, and the constitutional matter of the separation of powers within the government. The Papers demonstrated that Lyndon Johnson was the heir and not the originator of Vietnam policy, that as far back as the administration of Harry Truman the government had portrayed Ho Chi Minh as a man with "Communist connections" and therefore an enemy, and that it had therefore ignored Ho's appeals for American support in ending French colonial rule, something that the rhetoric of World War II had committed us to do. They also indicated that the CIA had been making pessimistic intelligence reports about the Vietnamese situation for years—pessimistic, that is, in terms of American Cold War objectives—and that those reports were frequently ignored in favor of a policy of gradual escalation by Presidents unwilling to make all-out war but each afraid of becoming the President who had "lost" Indochina as Harry Truman had "lost" China; that available intelligence reports frequently belied public announcements that "we can see the light at the end of the tunnel"; and that at no time over a period of twenty years did the policy-makers take into account the human and material costs to the Vietnamese themselves.

Four . . . administrations [Sheehan concluded] built up the American political, military and psychological stakes in Indochina, often more deeply than they realized at the time, with large-scale shipments of military equipment to the French in

1950; with acts of sabotage and terror warfare against North Vietnam beginning in 1954; with moves that abetted and encouraged the overthrow of President Ngo Dinh Diem of South Vietnam in 1963; with plans, pledges and threats of further action that sprang to life in the Tonkin Gulf clashes in August, 1964; with the careful preparation of public opinion for the years of open warfare that were to follow; and with the calculation in 1965, as the planes and troops were openly committed to sustained combat, that neither accommodation inside South Vietnam nor early negotiations with North Vietnam would achieve the desired result.

The war itself was based on manipulation. Its only constitutional base was the Tonkin Gulf Resolution of 1964, which, as the documents demonstrated, was prompted by a trumped-up "incident"—an alleged attack by North Vietnamese patrol boats on American destroyers—whose facts were deliberately distorted by the Johnson Administration in order to secure Senate approval.* Part of the problem lay in the ambiguities of Option C, which, as Leslie Gelb suggested, was full of contradictions—"We tried to both bomb more and to negotiate seriously, even though bombing prevented negotiations." Another lay in the inability of the policy-makers to question their assumptions, both through blindness and through the fear of being considered weak by their superiors, and in a bravado of certainty about decisions where no certainty was possible. Long before Vietnam became anything resembling a public issue, successive American administrations, wedded to Cold War assumptions, the ideology of containment, and the domino theory, had been waging a clandestine war in Southeast Asia, carrying on covert attacks against North Vietnam, violating the Geneva Accords of 1954, and basing the justification for American involvement on a diplomatically illegitimate "two Vietnams" policy in no way supported by international accords. The Geneva agreements, which ended French rule in Indochina,

---

* The lone dissenters were Senators Wayne Morse and Ernest Gruening.

never contemplated two separate Vietnams; they called for a supervised election within two years that would establish a single government for the entire nation. American policy helped to sabotage that stipulation. The United States, said Secretary of State Dulles in a cable to Saigon, should do nothing "to speed the present process of decay of the Geneva accords," but neither should it make the "slightest effort to infuse life into them."

What was perhaps most significant about the Papers lay in their revelations about the connection between the processes of bureaucracy, the necessity for being tough, and the existential brutality of the war. The Orwellian language, familiar enough already (and later to become more familiar through the revelations of American plans for weather modification, the creation of fire storms, and defoliation) were supposed to render the brutal facts palatable by describing them in abstract terms. (However, when she read the Papers, Patricia Ellsberg noted that references to "turning up the screws" and "the rachet effect" reminded her of the language of torturers.) It was one of the blessings that intellectuals had brought to the making of war. But beyond that there was the bureaucratic imperative about "reality"—the need to be tough-minded and therefore to behave in such a way as to leave human considerations behind, making "efficiency" and "reality" into euphemisms for *machismo*. The bureaucracy taught its functionaries that power existed only in relation to the organization, that a person alone was powerless; at the same time it also treated any sign of softness with suspicion and demanded expressions of toughness as conditions for organizational acceptability. You were powerless outside the organization, and unless you played it tough your acceptability inside was open to question. The civilians dealing with the Pentagon, one might assume, were always trying to prove that they were as hard, mean and ugly as the generals; the fear of political error—"losing" Vietnam, for example—was therefore compounded by what one might imagine was the even greater fear of not being thought a man.

By the time the Papers were published, Americans had already learned a great deal about the futility, deceptions and frustration of Vietnam. What the Pentagon Papers provided was documentation, and documentation was important for those who were reluctant to reach "hasty" conclusions, those liberals and intellectuals who were suspicious of people who were too ready to ascribe all error to evil purpose. It was these same liberals who had once defended a President (Roosevelt) against charges that he had concluded secret treaties and who had castigated the Congress as a usurper of the powers and prerogatives of the executive branch. The very bulk of the Papers was therefore persuasive, even if the documents themselves went largely unread. Moreover, the secrecy of the documentation, combined with the government's attempts to suppress publication in the days after the Papers began to appear, seemed to verify those suspicions about Vietnam policy which still remained unconfirmed. The Papers became a totem, a symbol for the war, just as Vietnam had become a symbol for a series of other controversies in American belief and society. Publication in the *Times* confirmed the legitimacy of the revelations, and the government's attempt to block publication underlined it. Later there would be stories that the Administration feared that its negotiations with other countries (and particularly the discussions, then in progress, about Nixon's trip to China) would be jeopardized if the United States came to be regarded as a nation that could not keep sensitive material out of the press. But publication of the Papers legitimized both the conversion and the inordinately long time that it took so many people to make it.

The conclusions to be drawn from the study were only pieces of evidence and not a complete history of the war—whatever that might be. What the various Presidents were thinking as each decision was made remained a mystery. Arthur Schlesinger, Jr., on the basis of his own experience in the White House *and* on the basis of the documents, quickly questioned the challenge-to-the-quagmire thesis by asserting that often the judgment of the experts about a particular step was optimistic, that the intelligence reports were not full of unrelieved gloom, and that ignorance rather than cynicism underlay most of the decisions.

> By the spring of 1962, [he wrote in the *New York Review*] Kennedy was assured and probably believed, at least till the next December or January, that South Vietnamese forces, stiffened by American advisors, could defeat the few thousand Viet Cong guerrillas.
>
> Nor do I think that President Johnson was kidding when he talked about nailing the coonskin to the wall; or that Ambassador Lodge was dissembling when he looked forward to the withering away of the Viet Cong; or that General Westmoreland was lying when he ran through his litany of famous forecasts about the military progress of the war. I fear something almost worse: that these men really believed these things . . .
>
> The Pentagon Papers reinforce the view that the system did *not* work, that it failed wretchedly, and that the Vietnam adventure was marked much more by ignorance, misjudgment and muddle than by foresight, awareness and calculation.

Schlesinger's argument was compounded by the question of options: What was the alternative to Option C, even if one assumed that the President had reason to believe that the measures he was taking would do no more than postpone failure and prolong the war? It is far from certain, despite the assumptions of most liberals, that absolute candor—inside the White House and outside, with the press and the public—would in all instances have produced more pressure for withdrawal than for all-out war. Barry Goldwater's position in regard to a major escalation of the air war in 1964 was as well served by the failures of Option C as the argument for a quick withdrawal. Historically, Americans always regarded war as something simultaneously temporary and total; when the Birchers said, "Win, then get out," they were talking American. The analogue to the Vietnamese blood bath that Nixon always predicted as an aftermath to unilateral withdrawal was the right-wing political blood bath that Henry Kissinger imagined might take place at home. Ellsberg once argued that fear of a new round of post-Vietnam McCarthyism was unjustified—data from the original McCarthy period, he said, indicated that while sympathy for the Wisconsin Senator was strong, it did not translate into widespread impact at the polls—but the fear did exist and therefore constituted a limitation on presidential choice.

Most significant among the open questions, however, was the impact of the changed attitudes. In the context of 1971, the decisions of the fifties and sixties appeared patently duplicitous, arrogant and unwise. Yet, in the context of their own time, they were obviously defensible.

> With the best of motives [Gelb said in an article in *Life*], I believe our leaders were convinced that they knew best. Issues of diplomacy, war and peace, so the foreign policy community has reasoned, are too subtle and sophisticated for the common man. Besides, it was further reasoned, telling the full story to their own people makes for "complications" with other nations. In their desire to do the best for the nation, our leaders felt they had to protect themselves against public pressures, and, in the process, they shielded us from the information we needed to make up our own minds.

All that, however, came from a belief among intellectuals (and within the "foreign policy community") that too many other opportunities had been destroyed by a public or a Congress too ignorant of national interest to support wise policy: wasn't that what had been taught for a generation about the Senate's rejection of American membership in the League of Nations, about American isolationism in the thirties, about foreign aid, and about a series of other errors (in the liberal, internationalist view) which had created serious problems for America later on? What was the proper function of "candor" after the Russians shot down Francis Gary Powers in the U-2 spy plane, just before Eisenhower was to meet the Russians at the summit? The vast and brutal escalation of the air war in response to the North Vietnamese offensive in the spring of 1972 made it quite apparent that as Option C became politically more difficult, the attractions of A and B increased. The mining of the Haiphong and other North Vietnamese harbors was far more dangerous (or cynical, assuming a deal was made with the Russians) than any other act of the war; the indiscriminate bombing of the North was more brutal and ugly since, as Pete McCloskey later said, it was done not to protect our troops but to save our pride. Yet neither of these measures produced more than a routine wave of protest; the same polls which for two years had shown popular opposition to the war seemed to indicate support for the government's escalation of the air war and its blockade of the harbors. It was Option C, not the killing, that had produced the revulsion.

The Papers documented failure and misjudgment; they shattered the faith of the old liberals and intellectuals in the paternal style to which they had clung since before World War II. Leslie Gelb called it "the courtly conviction that the American people cannot appreciate the problems and have to be 'brought along.' " All that was now gone, a whole set of attitudes and convictions invented not by militarists and dictators but by intellectuals and "progressives" who imagined that they understood the national interest and could protect it from the contamination of daily politics. Now the villains were not the Burton K. Wheelers, the Martins, Bartons and Fishes, the Robert Tafts, the America Firsters, but the Dean Rusks, the Mac Bundys, the members of the Council on Foreign Relations, the Kennedys, the Schlesingers and the Rostows. Well before the Papers were published, their prestige had begun to decline: the whiz kids had lost their halos, and the national faith in the wonders of systems analysis, computers, programmed budgeting systems and conflict resolution—the overblown faith that had made the think-tank the shrine of a new religion—had succumbed to the disaster of Vietnam, had indeed become so discredited that the university itself had become a battleground. The documents merely provided further evidence—in the light of the new disbelief—for their failures. Ellsberg's conclusion that the Pentagon Papers indicated that "remarkably accurate" intelligence reports were ignored by a series of Presidents fearful of the consequences of "losing" Vietnam therefore constituted an ironic defense of the intellectual system, a last expression of the old Eisenhower-era faith that, in the long run, intelligence and morality were mutually reinforcing, that "enlightened self-interest" was the greatest of social virtues. The intellectual system, Ellsberg seemed to suggest, was effective; it was the politicians who had misused it or failed to use it at all. In the end, he would be willing to castigate himself as a war criminal, to accept guilt for his complicity in the war, if only he could cling to his faith as an intellectual. The same intellectual techniques that had been used to serve the boss could be used to serve a larger cause. The question that remained, therefore, was whether those Presidents deceived only the public or whether they also deceived themselves.

The radical kids would never understand—they were constantly asking Ellsberg what took him so long—because there was no way for them to know how deep that faith had run and therefore no way to assess how fundamentally the liberal and intellectual convictions of the previous generation had been shattered. Although conflicting readings of the Papers were possible—Gelb and Ellsberg would argue that the system worked, that the Presidents knew what they were doing, Schlesinger would argue that it failed—the interpretations overlapped in the common conclusion that since lying and deceit of the public had been part of the policy, the government must never be trusted as deeply again. They also suggested that intellectuals operating in secret cease to be intellectuals at all, that in "speaking truth for power" they come to recommend or to support only those things which they believe will be acceptable rather than those which they believe to be true or effective. "What I was proposing was something which I thought had a fair chance of being persuasive," George Ball had said in a television interview after the Papers were published. "If I had said let's pull out overnight or do something of this kind, I obviously wouldn't have been persuasive at all. They'd have said the man's mad." Most important, the Papers punctuated the end of an era when the nation, all evidence to the contrary nowithstanding, had believed that the forces of Providence, if nothing else, were on the American side.

The country, despite everything, had learned a lot from the kids: it was we, the people over forty, who were the alienated generation. The kids couldn't believe that we could ever have been so naïve as to believe so deeply in the system. But by the time the Papers were published, many of us, like Ellsberg, had started to look for "stimulation from the people who had been right all along." When, he often asked, do you stop obeying the boss? It was a question that meant much more to a person of forty than to a kid of twenty or twenty-five. "In the end," Gelb had written, "we must act like a democracy if we are to remain a democracy . . . This must entail a move by our leaders toward openness with the American people. It does not mean no more secrets on a daily or weekly inspection of the decision-making process. It does mean that our leaders need to err on the side of telling, for if they do not, Americans will come to believe that everything the government says is a lie and that all governmental actions must be opposed." Leslie Gelb was the man who stamped the Pentagon Papers "Top Secret—Sensitive."

V

The BEM ceremony finally came to an end at 12:30 A.M., an orgy of speechifying without a climax. But a number of the peacemakers had another engagement, an invitation from Hugh Hefner for late supper at the Playboy Mansion. Benjamin Spock and Joan Baez declined, but the Ellsbergs and Russo joined Ramsey Clark, Pete McCloskey, John Kerry, George Wald and Wayne Morse for the festivities. Also present was J. Anthony Lukas, a writer for the *New*

*York Times Magazine* who had been following Ellsberg around that fall; later, Ellsberg would regret his presence.

> Hefner, in black slacks and embroidered shirt [Lukas wrote], greets his guests at the door. There are no bunnies in attendance, just one striking blonde who is introduced as January's Playmate, and several other women guests.
>
> After an hour of drinking, some people began drifting downstairs to the heated pool and cozy bar which looks into the pool's blue waters through a large window. I'm sitting at the bar, talking with Patricia [Ellsberg] and John Kerry when suddenly, Dan appears at the window, in one of the Mansion's brown bathing suits, making fish eyes at Patricia. A few minutes later, he is followed by Tony Russo and George Wald. I turn back to the bar, when I hear a little giggle from Patricia. Turning around, I see two naked women at the window. A tableau of the American peace movement in 1971—Ellsberg, Russo, Wald and four breasts bobbing in their wake.
>
> As usual at the Mansion, it's all antiseptic. No real sex, not even any touching. Soon, everybody is clothed and upstairs for the buffet supper; gradually most of the guests drift off. At 3:30, only Hefner, Tony, Dan, Patricia and I are left at the long table. "Like to see my private quarters?" Hefner asks. Dan and Patricia nod enthusiastically and Hefner leads on through his bedroom with its famous revolving bed, down a spiral staircase to the "Roman Baths" and their control panel which can set off a spectacular panorama of showers, sprays and neon lights.
>
> At 3:45 A.M., Hefner sends us home to the Executive House in his chauffeured limousine.

It had been a long day—for Ellsberg it had started in the federal courthouse in Los Angeles, for Russo it had started in jail—and the visit to Hefner's pad appealed to Ellsberg's sense of humor; it was a way of keeping the surrealism intact, he later explained. Yet he was also hurt by Lukas' piece —he felt that his trust and openness had been violated—just as he would be hurt by other intimations of frivolity and idiosyncrasy, reports that suggested a penchant for a jet-set existence: the two apartments, one in Cambridge and one on Sutton Place in New York; the small boy's pride in associating with the powerful and the famous; the circuit-riding search for places where he could feel at home; and the apparently unbounded and often enviable adulation which Patricia invariably expressed toward him, at least in public.

What Ellsberg failed to understand was the sheer impossibility of escaping the surrealism, no matter what one did. The Playboy Mansion was, after all, just another Pentagon, a high shrine for the plastic society. What the Pentagon or the Rand Corporation were to war and killing, *Playboy* and Hefner were to love and sex; through technology you rendered these things antiseptic, stripped them of real feeling and thus made them manageable for people incapable of dealing with moral or psychological complexity or of confronting the human experience of whatever act they contemplated.

In a sense, the whole world had been living with the illusion of fail-safe, a universe in which one could have his cake and eat it too. The war was part of that illusion, the peace movement all of it. You could kill without pain or suffering or moral consequence, make love without feeling, disarm without danger, calculate without error, destroy without thought. Every day the pilots would return from their high-altitude missions over unknown targets and sit by the pool with their drinks; every day the people of fashion, drinking the same drinks, would sign petitions, curse Nixon, and collect their dividends from General Electric and Dow and Boeing. It was not simply that organizations and bureaucracies created the illusion of power, the feeling that a person is powerless without them, but that they sustained fictions of meaning, which is to say that they preserved identity itself. It would be easy to run Ellsberg down, to call him a public penitent, and to suggest that either his courage was contaminated by madness or his act was the same old Cold War zealotry in reverse. It would be even easier and more persuasive to charge the opposite: to say that it had never been Ellsberg's style to do anything graceless or unfashionable.

After one of his speeches in New York, a member of the audience asked him, "If the war had been popular, would people care about what you did? Can you divorce any possible consequences of your actions from the intensely unpopular sentiments that have surrounded the war?" She might even have asked whether, had the war been popular, he would have done what he did at all. "I'm not a masochist," Ellsberg would say in response; clearly he expected that the gamble would have a chance of paying off.

I have often been struck, without quite knowing why, by the similarities between Ellsberg's "conversion" and Erikson's analysis of Martin Luther's. In both, a pervasive institution served as a moratorium, offering a possible way, as Erikson said, "of postponing the decision as to what one is and is going to be": for both there came a point in life "when he half realizes that he is fatally overcommitted to what he is not," in both there was rebellion and subsequent commitment —some would say an overcommitment—to an alternative True Church. Ideologies, Erikson wrote, "serve to channel youth's forceful earnestness and sincere asceticism, as well as its search for excitement and its eager indignation, toward that social frontier where the struggle between conservatism and radicalism is most alive. On that frontier, fanatic ideologists do their busy work and psychopathic leaders their dirty work; but there, also, true leaders create significant solidarities." There was something about Ellsberg, for better or worse, in Erikson's description of *homo religious:* "He is always older, or in early years suddenly becomes older, than his playmates or even his parents and teachers, and focuses in a precocious way on what it takes others a lifetime to gain a mere inkling of: the question of how to escape corruption in living and how in death to give meaning to life. Because he experiences a breakthrough to the last problems so early in his life, maybe such a man had better become a martyr . . ."

Quite clearly, most of those who work in the Pentagon never shared Ellsberg's commitment, at least not as he and those who remember him now recall it. I suspect that there are thousands of people who approach their work with considerably more detachment, even humor, than he did, and many who leave (perhaps out of revulsion, perhaps merely to get a better job) without the pervasive sense of guilt that turns the commitment on its head. Yet, just as clearly, there was and is an endemic, pervasive quality about the symbolism of the Pentagon, an inescapability that makes detachment and humor the very essence of the higher madness. One has to be crazy to care so much, to believe so deeply, but doesn't one have to be equally mad to care too little? At what point could one stop looking at the picture of the children aflame with napalm, at the pockmarked landscape, at the faces of those people, and become indifferent? And if one did not become indifferent, where did one go to talk, to resist, to act? And so Daniel Ellsberg is sitting in the Playboy Mansion comprehending too little of the irony, and there are Patricia and Hef, and there the girls with the bare boobs swimming behind the fish-eye window. It was possible to go from anywhere to anywhere else within a day, from jail in Los Angeles to the Playboy Mansion, from the officers' club to the peasant village, from the air-conditioned penthouse to the ghetto. One told the story of brutality and systematic killing on television talk shows surrounded by the hoopla of show biz, cosmetic commercials and an applauding audience, and one carried one's case for peace or civil rights or the migrant farmworkers through cocktail parties and receptions where the latest novel, the infighting of New York publishing and the shortage of babysitters in East Hampton were topics of equal interest.

The only meaning lay in the act and its consequences. It suggested a form of disobedience that struck the system where it might be most vulnerable, for if one could assume that information was power (and that, of course was an assumption that Ellsberg and the government shared, both before and after the act), then publishing information was a way of giving power to the people. It was a symbolic act and

Ellsberg was a symbolic man, but it was or might be also an act of genuine substance. The government's attempts to suppress publication and prosecute Ellsberg confirmed its intention not to change its style and attitude. In the surrealistic universe that Ellsberg failed fully to understand on that October night, the only order possible was the order which lay in the consequences—legal, political and moral—of what he and Russo had done. It had not been a fail-safe act; Ellsberg quite sincerely believed that in copying the Papers and making them public he risked "going to jail for a long time." He therefore violated not only the systems of the Pentagon, broke the rules of the club, but also violated the no-consequence morality of the world of *Playboy*. He could be charged with moral absolutism because he acted as if universal surrealism were not inevitable. But it was also for him an act of immense magnitude, unprecedented and nearly inconceivable in a tradition of caution and obedience. The risks a man took for the boss were limited—even if they involved the possibility of death—because they were condoned by the system; the risks one took against the system were boundless because one carried them out alone.

# THREE

# Disloyalty and Disorder

MIDWAY into 1971, the Nixon Administration had taken over the remains of World War II liberalism, introduced its version of law and order, and unveiled the results as a new strategy for peace and domestic security. Although the roots of the Administration's policy extended deep into American history—to the Alien and Sedition Acts, the Red Scare and the Palmer Raids of the 1920s, the McCarthyism of the 1950s, and a dour puritanism that the country never quite outgrew—two years of Nixon had produced strategies which, even in their overt manifestations, had already run far beyond the fears of all but the most paranoid civil libertarians: the use of conspiracy charges against political activists of the Left; the employment of grand-jury investigations to gather political information and personal data on individuals suspected of no crime other than dissent; the growing use of wiretapping and other forms of electronic surveillance both to amass information and to intimidate those prone to political resistance; the flagrant attempt, often successful, to coerce the media through the attacks of the Vice-President and through the use of subpoenas to gather unpublished notes, photographs and film; the growing use of infiltrators, informers and provocateurs; and the employment of mass arrests on unspecified or nonexistent charges to control demonstrations. All these things were known long before Watergate and should have given an indication of what lay beneath the surface.

Some of it wasn't new. Many of the techniques were developed by the Justice Department under Robert F. Kennedy long before Nixon and John N. Mitchell came to public office in 1969, and some—including the burglary of selected "targets" in "national security" investigations—had been employed under prior administrations and later dropped. Despite the claim that Robert Kennedy was unaware of wiretapping by his own subordinates and that he was unable to control J. Edgar Hoover and the FBI, the New Frontier and the Great Society had been waging electronic war since the early sixties. Nor was it merely the FBI which had been tapping telephones or photographing selected political or "criminal" targets or collecting dossiers: electronic surveillance had also been conducted by Kennedy's organized-crime investigators, by local and state police departments in "cooperation" with federal investigations, and by the National Security Agency, which, under its mandate for intercepting and decoding foreign communications, had tapped transatlantic phone calls by U.S. citizens; the Army had used undercover agents to collect information on demonstrators, members of Congress and other domestic political figures; and the FBI had engaged in second-story work against foreign embassies and other suspect institutions at least since World War II (the practice was stopped in 1966). It was the Justice Department under Robert Kennedy that had refined the technique of using grand juries (in organized-crime investigations) to coerce recalcitrant witnesses, gather information unrelated to any specific criminal act, and assemble dossiers; it was Kennedy's Justice Department that had stretched the concept of interstate crime—which would permit federal investigations and prosecution—to include anything that involved telephone calls across state lines (to make a bet, for example), checks on out-of-state banks, and interstate travel. (Appropriately enough, in the middle of the Ellsberg trial Jimmy Hoffa would come to Los Angeles in an attempt to hire Leonard B. Boudin, Ellsberg's chief counsel, in his fight to regain standing in the Teamsters' Union.) "The new federal grand jury, with its devastating attacks on the Left," wrote Michael E. Tigar and Madeleine R. Levy, "was pioneered by Bobby and only put into statute when some federal courts found that there was no authority for Bobby's agents to conduct themselves in the free-wheeling way that was their wont. There is no question that the 'hit list' technique, seeking to drag up any charge at all against preselected target figures, was developed by Bobby . . ."

The Department of Justice under Nixon and Mitchell had adapted the techniques, added others, and revised the hit list. It also brought to its activities measures of corporate efficiency, obsessive fear and ideological zeal unknown in prior administrations. From the first days of his administration, Nixon used the department as a Politburo where considerations of political strategy, internal security and federal law enforcement were intertwined, and where the principal officers represented the Administration's most important link with its constituents of the radical right: John Mitchell, Nixon's former law partner, had been the President's campaign manager in 1968, and unfil after the Watergate burglary he managed the campaign in 1972; Deputy Attorney General Richard Kleindienst, who would himself succeed Mitchell at Justice, had been Barry Goldwater's campaign manager in 1964; and Robert C. Mardian, the head of the Internal Security Division at Justice, was a major contact with the Administration's base of right-wing support in California and the Southwest. Mardian, an ideologue who seemed unable to express even perfunctory concern with civil liberties, followed Mitchell from the Justice Department to the Committee for the Re-election of the President in the spring of 1972; in both places he was disappointed that he was not promoted to more responsible jobs—he wanted to become Deputy Attorney General—and complained that he was always the one to be given the dirty assignments. He would be the person who would "de-brief" Gordon Liddy after the Watergate burglary in 1972.

Yet through a series of political decisions in the period between 1969 and 1971—the Chicago conspiracy trial, the Harrisburg indictment of the Catholic activists, the nominations of G. Harrold Carswell and Clement Haynesworth to the Supreme Court—it was not certain whether it was the pragmatic or the punitive that prevailed. Had the Department of Justice, either to please itself or to please its right-wing constituents, taken those steps merely to spank the unwashed, the unpopular and the obstreperous, did the Administration really believe that its targets constituted serious threats to national security, or were there more pragmatic long-term reasons? Until the Watergate disclosures it was at least possible for cautious men to assume that the investigations and prosecutions inaugurated by Mitchell and Mardian reflected nothing more than excessive concern with demonstrations and national security, and that they could not be considered as parts of a broader strategy to condition Americans to acquiescence, soften the Left and foster silence. In the first years of the Administration there were indications that the pragmatism was largely self-delusion; the voters did not respond to Agnew's attacks, the juries in Chicago and Harrisburg did not convict (except on minor charges)—the notorious trials, in both state and federal courts, succeeded more often in converting the jurors than in convicting the defendants—nor did the attempts to coerce the voters with fears of riot and insurrection in the 1970 elections generate conclusive results. Quite possibly, the punitive mind had misjudged the independence and decency of the people it sought to influence, and had therefore deceived itself. Thinking itself shrewd and calculating (and often the "realists" in the White House confused shrewdness with hardness), it had allowed its punitive instincts and its paranoia about demonstrations and dissent to get the better of its pragmatic illusions. There was a great deal of rhetoric in 1969, 1970 and 1971 about the government's fascist inclinations, but even the people who used it seemed unable fully to believe it.

What no one understood at the time was the depth of the Administration's obsessive need to control every aspect of the political environment, or the degree to which the Administration was prepared to use all agencies of government for political purposes seen as "national security." Nixon and his people, it turned out, simply could not distinguish, or conceive that there might be a distinction, between the nation's interests and their own. Nixon's urge to imagine enemies, his need to regard himself as besieged by Communists or rioters or "bums," and his inability to shed what Gary Wills called "his outsider's resentment" produced an Administration which, almost from the day of the inauguration in 1969, began to dabble in "covert activities," secret intelligence plans, and special investigative units. John Caulfield and Anthony T. Ulasewicz, the former New York cops, were brought to Washington in March 1969 to establish "a private security agency . . . for purposes of providing investigative support for the White House," and particularly for the purpose of assembling dossiers on the private lives of potential political opponents. By the spring of 1970, White House Counsel Charles Colson had started compiling his "enemies" list and thinking of ways to use federal agencies, particularly the Internal Revenue Service, to "screw" opponents. By summer of that year Nixon himself had approved the National Intelligence Plan, which included the tactics that would become familiar in the Watergate investigations three years later. Despite CIA reports to the contrary, the White House had persuaded itself that domestic radicals, Black Panthers and other dissidents were supported by foreign governments, in particular Cuba and Algeria, and that attacks on the Administration were foreign-inspired. In an attempt to explain the White House tactics, former presidential assistant John D.

Ehrlichman was to testify that the White House was not paranoid: the protests and demonstrations in 1969–71 could not
be regarded as "just a garden-variety exercise of the First
Amendment." They represented a coordinated attempt to
influence American policy in support of the objectives of
North Vietnam. The White House was not the last domino;
it was the first.

The intelligence plan drafted in the summer of 1970 and
approved by Nixon on July 15 called for coordinated "national security" operations involving the CIA, the FBI, the
Defense Intelligence Agency (DIA) and the National Security Agency and included, among other things, authority (in
the words of Nixon's own subsequent explanation) "for surreptitious entry—breaking and entering, in effect, on specified categories of targets in specified situations related to
national security"; authority for the National Security
Agency, perhaps the most secret of all U. S. intelligence
organizations, to wiretap international telephone calls by
American citizens (something it was probably doing anyway
in certain "national security" cases); instructions for "the
intelligence community . . . to intensify coverage of individuals and groups in the United States who pose a major
threat to internal security"; "coverage" of foreign nationals
and diplomatic establishments in the United States "of interest to the intelligence community"; removal of "restraints on
the use of surreptitious entry . . . to permit procurement of
vitally needed foreign cryptographic material and against
other urgent and high priority internal security targets"; and
the establishment of an Interagency Group on Domestic
Intelligence and Internal Security composed of representatives of the FBI, the CIA, the DIA, the three branches of the
military, and the White House to coordinate domestic intelligence activities. In effect, the Administration approved a
comprehensive domestic police operation against people and
groups that it regarded as enemies of the state. Although
Hoover, fearful that he would lose (in Ehrlichman's words)
some of his "sovereignty," opposed the plan and succeeded in

getting Mitchell to persuade Nixon to "withdraw it" (apparently it was never formally rescinded), the desire and the ideas survived. The White House, aware that it was breaking the law, was dreaming about a police-state apparatus and was prepared to implement it on its own whether or not Hoover approved.

The Administration's obsessive concern with news leaks dated back to Nixon's first months in office, when the *Times,* under William Beecher's byline, published a story about the secret bombing of Cambodia, and when the FBI, at the insistence of the White House, the Justice Department and Henry Kissinger, started tapping the telephones of journalists and of several members of Kissinger's own National Security Council staff, including Halperin's. The Cambodia story, Kissinger later explained, "was not an isolated event; it capped a whole series of leaks, including those of detailed discussions of NSC meetings on the Middle East and other internal discussions." As a liberal and a former member of the Johnson Administration, and as someone who had been suspected in connection with a leak in 1968—also about Indochina and also published by the *Times*—Halperin was a logical candidate. Kissinger confronted Halperin about the leak, Halperin denied it, and Kissinger later defended Halperin's "loyalty and discretion." But the facts of any particular leak or series of leaks were not in themselves sufficient to explain the Administration's response. Leaks, after all, had always been a way of life in Washington. The Army leaked information to embarrass the Air Force, the Defense Department leaked data to impede diplomatic negotiations which it opposed, and the Administration in general—including Kissinger—conducted "background briefings" to create impressions for which it did not want to take official responsibility: today's unofficial "high-level" declaration of optimism could always be denied tomorrow.

Part of the concern lay in the compulsive need to control and in paranoid suspicions about conspiracies against the government (demonstrations and leaks, Ehrlichman suggested later, were part of the same plot). But there was also a curious mixture—part new, part inherited—of European assumptions about the need for secrecy in diplomacy and a paternalism adopted from the Eastern establishment intellectuals and internationalists whom Agnew held in such contempt. The government's proprietary attitude about information and its corresponding assumptions about what, and how much, the public should be allowed to know for its own good would become particularly vehement when they were expressed by Mitchell's Justice Department and joined with the compulsive corporate need for efficiency in the White House. But they, along with the foreign policy to which they applied, had existed long before. Leaks were a perennial problem. By the time the Pentagon Papers were published in June 1971, Nixon had taken most of the policy for his own—the liberal hope for an accommodation with China, the putative arms agreements with Russia, and, of course, Vietnam itself—and while he thus deprived the Democrats of their foreign policy he also relieved them of the responsibility. Maybe the *Times* would have published the Pentagon Papers even if the war had been popular, if Dean Rusk had been Secretary of State, or Dean Acheson, or if Kennedy had been President. But now it would be possible for the Administration to regard these disclosures as special attacks on itself and as threats to policies and practices which had been tolerated while the Democrats held power. Now it was *Nixon*'s war, *Nixon*'s secrecy, and *Nixon*'s deception.

Three weeks before the first installment of the Pentagon Papers went to press, Richard Nixon had flown to Austin to participate in an exercise which not only symbolized the continuity in policy and Nixon's increasingly close association with Lyndon Johnson, John Connally and the Texas Democratic Party, but bore ironically on events that followed. The occasion was the dedication of the $18-million Lyndon Baines Johnson Library—"Lyndon's Pyramid"—on the campus of the University of Texas, an edifice that would house some 31 million pages of documents pertaining to Johnson's forty years in public office. None of those documents would become available for two years, and many would remain classified for at least twenty. Sharing the platform with Nixon and Johnson were Spiro Agnew, John Connally, Carl Albert, and virtually every major politician in the state of Texas, among them several who were so deeply implicated in a series of stock swindles that they would be defeated in 1972 by the normally tolerant voters of the state of Texas. Edmund Muskie, Birch Bayh and Hubert Humphrey, who had once called himself "Lyndon Johnson's Eleanor Roosevelt," sat in a special section in the audience and were hardly noticed. Members of the Kennedy family had, with their canny sense of politics, pleaded other engagements, and George McGovern, already an announced candidate for the presidency, but hardly one to be taken seriously, had not been invited. Accompanied by two aides and a reporter, McGovern watched the proceedings in the lobby of a television station in Sioux Falls, South Dakota, where he had gone to make a tape for his local constituents.

"It is all here," Lyndon Johnson said, "the story of our time—with the bark off . . . There is no record of a mistake, nothing critical, ugly or unpleasant that is not included in the files here. We have papers from my forty years of public service in one place for friend or foe to judge, to approve or disapprove."

"If that isn't overkill," said George McGovern, looking at the participants, "I don't know what is."

"This is an extraordinary treasury of insights into a critical period in our nation's history," Richard Nixon said. "It will take the scholars of future generations behind the scenes of the Johnson era."

"There's Johnson's candidate for 1972," McGovern remarked.

"Who?" The reporter asked.

"Nixon," McGovern said.

Three thousand people attended the dedication and the barbecue which followed—politicians, professors, old friends

of the Johnsons, and some of the richest people on the face
of the earth—but the busiest of them all was Connally, Johnson's old protégé, former governor of Texas, Nixon's Secretary of the Treasury, and now the political matchmaker between his new colleagues in Washington and the wheelers
and dealers of the regular Democrats of Texas. There was
the possibility that Connally would be Nixon's choice for the
vice-presidency in 1972, but that day it was enough just to
introduce the folks all around. A half mile away, three thousand demonstrators, most of them University of Texas students, were shouting "No more war!," shouts which, thanks
to a favorable wind, could be heard at the festivities. Two
thousand miles away, at the New York Hilton Hotel, Neil
Sheehan and a dozen employees of the *Times* who had been
holed up there to prevent journalistic leaks were getting seven
thousand raw pages of Vietnam documents and analysis into
shape for publication. In three weeks a little of the bark
would really be off. But in Austin that day they were celebrating something: not libraries or scholarship, but a political
marriage. The Republicans had inherited the style and the
war, and now they were trying to collect a little of estate.

The reaction to the publication of the Pentagon Papers was
surprisingly slow. The *Times* had intentionally underplayed
the story with low-keyed writing and academic headlines:
"Vietnam Archive: Pentagon Study Traces 3 Decades of
Growing U.S. Involvement." It was heavy stuff for a pleasant
Sunday in late spring. The wire services almost missed the
first story entirely, and since the *Times,* for reasons of journalistic security, had provided no advance notice to the
clients of its news service, hardly another paper in America
picked it up. Melvin Laird, scheduled to appear on the CBS
program *Face the Nation* that Sunday, called Mitchell to ask
what he should say; tell them, Mitchell replied, that the
Justice Department is looking into it. But Laird was never
asked about the Pentagon Papers, and Mitchell was not
sufficiently disturbed to do anything before Monday. Quite

conceivably, the Administration could have dismissed the whole affair: the material in the Papers did not pertain to it, was fragmentary in any case, and could have been described as just one of countless investigations, studies and reports on the war. There was no panic on Sunday.

It was Kissinger who started the panic. The concern was not merely the contents—virtually no one in the Administration had any idea what the Papers contained—but the source, the magnitude, and the principle. By the time the Papers were released, the classification system had become a monstrous joke, and the disclosure therefore dramatized the breakdown of a bad system. This was not a casual leak of a scrap of information, or a self-serving hint by a government official acting under orders from his superiors; this was the release of a huge collection of documents, two or three cartons of stuff, by a man who enjoyed no protection from any agency or department. Ellsberg was not trying to justify government policy, or even the actions of one agency as against another; he was embarrassing the government and justifying, as the White House then saw it, the position of a group of Washington exiles trying to explain or make amends for their involvement in the war. With a little imagination it might even be possible for people in the Pentagon, the Justice Department and the White House to imagine the disclosure of the Papers as the work of a conspiracy of intellectual dissidents trying to exonerate themselves at the expense of those who were trying to do the job. In an era of general confidence in the Administration, the system of secrecy-and-leaks might be regarded as tolerable, if not effective; in a time of total war, secrecy would not be challenged and could be defended as necessary. But in a time when a growing number of people suspected the good faith of the government, a period of unpopular and seemingly endless war, secrecy and news management were among the most serious elements in the general collapse of order and confidence. Even the Administration conceded that the classification system required reform, but before it could be reformed it needed to be saved. If it were

not, then every official or ex-official who disagreed with
policy, every entrepreneur with access to information, and
every egomaniac could take documents and give or sell them
to the *Times*. Lyndon Johnson called Ellsberg's act "close
to treason," Barry Goldwater said something about Benedict
Arnold, and hundreds of people would send Ellsberg angry
letters, many of them anti-Semitic, about his betrayal. But
treason was not the crime. The offense, rather, was against
order itself, and particularly against Henry Kissinger's particular sense of the order required for the proper management
of foreign affairs.

Again Halperin was involved, and again Kissinger feared
that the conduct of diplomacy would be compromised. He
argued that more disclosures could impede two sets of negotiations: the secret contacts through Pakistan with China that
led to Kissinger's trip to Peking and ultimately to Nixon's,
and the equally secret talks with the Vietnamese in Paris.
Ellsberg and Halperin had both done work for Kissinger, and
they both had access to National Security Council documents,
including the subsequently leaked NSSM-1 on the Administration's options in Vietnam. There was also reason for the
White House to believe that Ellsberg had been responsible
for other leaks, including stories about American involvement in the imprisonment of a non-Communist Vietnamese
official by the Saigon government, and that Ellsberg had
made his initial contact with Sheehan through Halperin. Part
of Kissinger's concern was based on misinformation; Halperin had nothing to do with the leak, despite his work on
the study and his friendship with Ellsberg, nor did the material given the *Times* include the sensitive documents that
Kissinger seemed to fear.

The White House, however, didn't need much prompting;
it was relatively easy for an Administration unable to draw
fine lines around "national security" to decide that it was
dealing with a major threat, possibly even a ring of spies. The
publication of the Pentagon Papers, Nixon later explained,
"created a situation in which the ability of the government to

carry on foreign relations even in the best of circumstances could have been severely compromised. Other governments no longer knew whether they could deal with the United States. Against the background of delicate negotiations the United States was then involved in on a number of fronts— with regard to Vietnam, China, the Middle East, nuclear-arms limitations, U.S.–Soviet relations, and others—in which the utmost degree of confidentiality was vital, it posed a threat so grave as to require extraordinary actions." What particularly worried the Administration was the inclusion, in the *Times*'s first installments, of the material from the Wheeler Report (not part of the formal Vietnam study) "raising serious questions about what and how much else might have been taken. There was every reason to believe that this was a security leak of unprecedented proportions." Charles Colson, then special counsel to the President, later described the discussions in the White House as "kind of panic sessions."

It all coincided: the political, the pragmatic, the punitive. On Monday, after the *Times*'s second installment appeared, the conferences began at Justice among Mitchell, Mardian and William H. Rehnquist, another Goldwater Arizonian, who was the department's legal counsel. Laird called again— he was to testify before the Senate Foreign Relations Committee and had been asked to prepare a Pentagon estimate of the national-defense aspects of the leak. And that evening, after another conference between Mitchell and Mardian at Mitchell's Watergate apartment, Mitchell sent a telegram to New York:

> I have been advised by the Secretary of Defense that the material published in The New York Times on June 13, 14, 1971, captioned "Key Texts from Pentagon's Vietnam Study," contains information relating to the national defense of the United States and bears a top-secret classification. As such, publication of this information is directly prohibited by the provisions of the Espionage Law, Title 18, United States Code, Section 793.

Moreover, further publication of information of this character will cause irreparable injury to the defense interests of the United States. Accordingly, I respectfully request that you publish no further information of this character and advise me that you have made arrangements for the return of these documents to the Department of Defense.

Mardian resolved to back up the telegram with a phone call to the *Times*. Publisher Arthur Ochs Sulzberger was out of the country, and Harding Bancroft, executive vice-president of the paper, promised to call Mardian back. At that point it was already clear what general course the government would follow; this was not the chummy relationship between an establishment government and an establishment newspaper where friendly and informal phone calls through intermediaries usually succeeded in fixing things up. Mitchell had threatened the *Times* with prosecution under the Espionage Act, and Mardian told Bancroft that if the *Times* did not desist the government would seek an injunction to stop publication of future installments. What Mitchell and Mardian probably didn't know was that the *Times* had worked diligently to make certain that it did not publish material that might be used to break diplomatic codes (there was no such material) and that the most sensitive documents, those dealing with negotiations between the United States and North Vietnam, had never been given to the *Times* at all. Had they known, the approach of the government, not only in the newspaper cases, but in the Ellsberg prosecution, might conceivably have been different.

Mardian's call to New York generated another round of debate. For two months those editors and writers who were privy to the great secret had been arguing about what to publish, in what form to publish, and whether to publish at all. The *Times*'s corporate-law firm, Lord, Day and Lord, among others, had advised against it (one of the firm's partners, Herbert Brownell, had been Attorney General under Eisenhower and had helped draft Executive Order 10501, which constituted the basis for the whole classification system), and at one time James Reston, the elder statesman among *Times* writers, had threatened to publish the whole thing in the *Gazette,* a weekly newspaper that he owned on Martha's Vineyard. Now, prompted by Mitchell's telegram, the argument, some of it involving transatlantic phone calls to Sulzberger, was revived again: should they ignore Mitchell's demand, should they wait a day, or should they take the advice of their lawyers? Later *Times* managing editor A. M. Rosenthal would declare, "I don't believe in editing or publishing out of fear of what the Government might do," but the matter that night, and indeed in the preceding ten weeks, was never that clear. In the end, the *Times* stuck to its guns—more or less: it would proceed with the next installment, but it would do so with qualifications. In an accompanying article dealing with Mitchell's request (an article that received bigger play than the story of the Papers themselves), the *Times* announced its decision:

> We have received the telegram from the Attorney General asking The Times to cease further publication of the Pentagon's Vietnam study. The Times must respectfully decline the request of the Attorney General, believing that it is in the interest of the people of this country to be informed of the material contained in this series of articles. We have also been informed of the Attorney General's intention to seek an injunction against further publication. We believe that it is properly a matter for the courts to decide. The Times will oppose any request for an injunction for the same reason that led us to publish the articles in the first place. We will of course abide by the final decision of the court.

The revealing line was the last: *We will of course abide by the final decision of the court.* It did not suggest that the *Times* might conclude that there were occasions when a powerful newspaper might itself consider forms of civil disobedience to protect what it surely must have regarded as the most essential of the nation's liberties. The paper's defense would be cautious, respectable and respectful. The *Times,* did not acknowledge its source, nor was there any indication that after delivery was made in Cambridge there was any further contact between the *Times* and Ellsberg.

What was more surprising, however, was the fact that twelve hours before the paper was hailed into court it had no lawyer. Perhaps the managers of the *Times* never fully believed that Nixon and Mitchell would really go after them. Perhaps they thought that finally Lord, Day and Lord could fix things up. Late that evening, however, after the exchange with Mardian, the law firm informed the paper that since its advice had been ignored it would not be able to take on the defense. In the middle of the night, the paper engaged Alexander M. Bickel, a professor of law and legal history at Yale who had represented the *Times* in another case and who, by sheer coincidence, had lunched with James Goodale, the head of the *Times*'s own legal staff, the day before. Bickel, of course, was totally unprepared; he was enthusiastic about the paper's decision to publish the documents—as was Goodale—but all he knew about the Papers was what Goodale could tell him, and what he had read in the *Times.* The Great Institution, which had debated for three months about whether to publish at all, would come into court almost totally unprepared.

And yet it was, in many respects, a perfect match: Bickel and the *Times,* each of them eminently respectable, untainted by association with extreme positions, and thoroughly established. Bickel, who had once been a law clerk for Supreme Court Justice Felix Frankfurter (although he himself had never argued a case before the Court) was an adherent of the doctrine of judicial self-restraint, a critic of the Warren Court for its "speed" and its "confident, single-minded imposition of solutions to problems of the first magnitude," a defender of governmental authority, and a critic of student activists as "disenchanted and embittered simplifiers and moralizers." His own detractors charged (and Bickel denied) that he had been running for the Supreme Court himself. It

was certainly clear that he identified with the judicial con-
servatives, judges like Holmes and Frankfurter who had
argued that it was not the function of the courts to keep the
President and Congress from making mistakes. In defending
the government's power to restrict travel to certain countries
and to lift the passports of those who violated the restrictions,
he had argued that "farfetched or no, the fears [of the gov-
ernment] are not irrational and national interest is identifiable, and the measures taken to protect it are tailored to fit
. . . In such circumstances it is not for the courts to intervene
and make political policy." There were no political or constitutional absolutes: "Is it possible to be certain that the
country can live, permanently and to its benefit, with . . .
large inflexible principles? Pragmatic skepticism has not been
one of the attributes of the gallant Warren Court, and even
its most widely acclaimed achievements—in legislative appor-
tionment, in certain criminal, and even in school integration
and school prayer cases—may in the end suffer from this
lack." He too was a product of the liberalism of the thirties,
when the heroics were associated with the President (and
sometimes the Congress), when constitutional limitations on
government power seemed often to stand in the way of progressive reform, and when the courts were regarded as reactionary institutions dominated by old men. "The idea of
progress," Bickel had written, "is common property."

Given the inadequacies of time and preparation, Bickel's
choices were limited. The government appeared in federal
court at ten o'clock Tuesday morning seeking an injunction
against further publication of the Papers and an immediate
return of the documents. The government's lawyers, Whitney
North Seymour, Jr., the U. S. attorney in New York, and
his assistant Michael D. Hess, (who were even more unprepared than Bickel), talked about serious injury to American
foreign relations, aiding the enemy (unspecified) and prejudice to the defense interests of the United States. The
*Times,* said Hess, had violated provisions of Section 793,
which makes it a crime for persons having unauthorized

possession of government documents to disclose their contents under circumstances that could be used to the injury of the United States or the advantage of any foreign nation. Secretary of State William P. Rogers, he declared, had said that friendly nations had "expressed concern." In response Bickel argued that the government's motion, rushed to New York overnight, represented "a classic case of censorship," that 793 specifically prohibited prior restraint, and that a newspaper exists "to publish, not to submit its publishing schedule to the United States government." He argued, in other words, that the government had no power to stop a newspaper from publishing information that it already possessed—making the comparatively limited point about prior restraint and not the broader point about the public's right to know. In the process there was generated an inference (which would later become bold and specific) that to censor a paper was one thing, but that to punish the source of its information might be quite another. The *Times* could not turn over the documents to the government since the possibility of fingerprint identification might very well betray the source, something that journalists were not at that time required to do. Bickel himself had participated on the side of Earl Caldwell, a *Times* reporter who in the Circuit Court of Appeals had successfully resisted a government subpoena to produce his notes for stories he had done on the Panthers (a decision later reversed by the Supreme Court). In that sense, therefore, the paper was protecting Ellsberg—or whoever had provided the documents in the first place. But in making the legal distinction between prior restraint and subsequent punishment, and between the press and its source of information—in failing to emphasize the broader case against illegal information control—the *Times* was not really protecting its sources.

The arguments were brief—no one, after all, had much to say. The judge, Murray I. Gurfein, who had been on the bench only a few days, first suggested that the *Times* submit voluntarily to a temporary restraining order until further arguments could be heard. When Bickel refused, Gurfein issued the temporary restraining order anyway, although he did not require the *Times* to return the documents. "Any temporary harm that may result from not publishing during the pendancy of the application for a temporary injunction," he said, "is far outweighed by the irreparable harm that could be done to the interests of the United States government if it should ultimately prevail." For four days (a period that would eventually be extended to more than two weeks) the *Times* was therefore subject to unprecedented legal prohibitions against publishing certain material; equally important, the *Times* made no attempt to appeal the order that afternoon, nor did it indicate, even for a day, that it might defy the court and publish another installment.

## II

Twelve hours after Gurfein issued his restraining order, Daniel Ellsberg went underground. That same day he had been called by reporters from the *Times* and the *Washington Post* (which would get its copy of a set of Pentagon Papers that night) to ask whether he was the source of the leak. Both newspapers had bifurcated themselves for journalistic and legal convenience and would publish speculative pieces about the identity of the person or persons who had provided them with the news. That night, moreover, Sidney Zion, a former *Times* reporter and editor of the defunct *Scanlan's* Magazine, appeared on *The Barry Gray Show,* a New York radio talk program, to announce that he had learned that Ellsberg was the man responsible. Zion, it was presumed, had learned the news from some of his former associates at the *Times,* a presumption strong enough to lead the paper to declare Zion *persona non grata* forever after. (The decision was later rescinded.) But what Zion had divulged had by then become fairly widespread knowledge. The FBI had, that same day—for reasons undisclosed—been telling members of the foreign press that Ellsberg was the man; moreover, the fact was known or suspected by many of his former asso-

ciates, by Gelb and Halperin, and by the members of the
Senate and the House to whom he had offered material or
who had heard him talk. (The FBI, it later turned out, had
known for a year about Ellsberg and the copying.) One of
them, Congressman Paul "Pete" McCloskey, the same man
who would introduce him at BEM three months later, and
who would testify for the defense at Ellsberg's trial, told the
FBI about his conversations and contacts with Ellsberg. In
April Ellsberg had given McCloskey six of the forty-seven
volumes—a sample—and McCloskey had been planning to
introduce those volumes at closed hearings of a House committee; he had also asked the Defense Department to release
the documents to the Congress, but, like Fulbright, he had
failed.

Ellsberg had already decided that if he was not identified
by the government he would not claim credit for the leak
(there was no point, after all, in daring the Department of
Justice to prosecute), but that if he was identified he would
take the responsibility in an effort to protect his friends and
the people who helped him. Yet for the moment there was
other work to do. The series in the *Times* had begun with the
Johnson years, and the press, now alert to the importance of
the case, was focusing attention on a single Administration.
"That's why I was so desperate," he said later, "when it
looked like the Justice Department might succeed in stopping
the *Times* from publishing. If it had stopped with Johnson,
people might have missed the point," which was to show that
the war and the decisions that had produced it were systemic
and not the aberrations of one man's style and policy. He
asked the *Post*'s editors to start their stories with material
from the earlier years; he also told them that they must defy
any injunction. Both requests were apparently denied—the
editors later said they accepted no condition—but in the one
story that did appear before the *Post* too was subjected to a
restraining order, the focus was on the Eisenhower Administration: "Documents Reveal U. S. Effort in '54 to Delay Viet
Election." A few hours after the story appeared, the govern-

ment was in court again; the *Post* defended its right to publish with a strong First Amendment argument, an argument that Federal Judge Gerhard A. Gesell accepted. Later that night the Circuit Court of Appeals in Washington reversed Judge Gesell's ruling, issued a staying order, and told Gesell to hear further arguments. At the last moment the type for the second installment in the *Post*'s series was literally ripped out of the front page.

Now the brush fires began. In the succeeding ten days, as the cases of the *Post* and the *Times* made their way through the appeals procedure, stories based on other parts of the study appeared in the *Boston Globe,* the *Chicago Sun-Times,* the *Los Angeles Times,* the *St. Louis Post-Dispatch,* the *Christian Science Monitor, Newsday,* and the Knight newspaper chain. Before the *New York Times* had begun publication, Dan and Patricia had taken a set of the Papers to commercial duplicating firms in the Boston area and had four additional copies made. Pat had urged Dan to make those additional sets as insurance in case the government seized the documents in his possession. A friend was sworn to try to get the copies out in the event Ellsberg was arrested; now Ellsberg himself distributed the copies to the various newspapers. He later explained that he was trying to stay a step ahead of the injunctions, leading a small guerrilla war against the government, but he never acknowledged publicly that Patricia had been as deeply involved in the second round of copying as he. All he would ever say was that he and Pat had been "partners."

The injunctions, as it turned out, were being sought selectively; there was no way—and perhaps no need—to stop all of it. Sanford J. Ungar, in *The Papers and the Papers,* quotes Mardian as saying that the Justice Department's criteria for seeking injunctions consisted of two questions: "Had the newspaper published information from a classified document, the disclosure of which could cause irreparable harm to the United States and which had not been previously in the public domain?" and "Was [the newspaper] intending to continue publication?" (In fact only newspapers which had been critical of the Administration were selected. Those which had supported Nixon in 1968 were not taken to court; perhaps they were able to reassure Mardian on one of his two points. What was more significant about Mardian's criteria was their suggestion that the Administration took for granted the proposition that it was the final arbiter of what constituted "irreparable harm to the United States"; the language of torts and damages had been turned into an argument against the First Amendment.) And yet the government was at a loss to supply the specifics to support the argument in the text of the Papers. When the courts asked the government to point to those sections which would prove the possibility of "irreparable harm" (sometimes in closed sessions) nothing was ever produced to demonstrate to the judges that further publication was likely to impair the national defense. The newspapers were able to show the judges that the most "sensitive" material in the government's injunction case had already been published elsewhere. The reporters of the *Times* and the *Post* were more familiar with the goods than was the government.

From the beginning there was an inexorability about the confrontation that was only partly relieved by the comedy and surrealism that accompanied it. Here was a great showdown between the press and the government—possibly the most portentous First Amendment case in half a century—being argued by lawyers who couldn't conceivably have had the time to prepare. In ten days the case moved from Mitchell's telegram to the Supreme Court of the United States. Like Bickel, U. S. Attorney Seymour came into district court in New York the first day knowing nothing about the Pentagon Papers except what he had read in the *Times*. Solicitor General Erwin N. Griswold, never consulted by Mitchell and Mardian until the *Post's* case was about to go to the Circuit Court of Appeals in Washington, was asked to argue the government position on three hours' notice. Bickel, the *Times's* defender, had only a dim understanding of the classification procedure (though obviously more than most of the judges whom the government tried to impress), and so, in appealing from Gurfein's decision before the U. S. Court of Appeals for the Second Circuit in New York, he failed almost entirely to attack the system as overbroad and conducted much of his argument as if, in the words of one civil-liberties lawyer, it were "a mortgage foreclosure."

The struggle that might have produced a great First Amendment decision turned into a series of skirmishes in which the newspapers, more often than not, were on the defensive and the government, despite the inadequate preparation of its attorneys, was the protagonist. Bickel conceded from the beginning "that the prohibition against prior restraint, like so much else in the Constitution, is not an absolute." Later he would proceed to get himself trapped in an irrelevant Supreme Court colloquy with Justice Potter Stewart that demonstrated how deeply the attorneys, those on the bench and those before the bench, had been influenced by World War II:

STEWART: Let us assume that when the members of the Court go back and open up this sealed record, we find something there that absolutely convinces us that its disclosure would result in the sentencing to death of a hundred young men whose only offense had been that they were nineteen years old and had low draft numbers. What should we do?

BICKEL: I am as confident as I can be of anything that your honor will not find that when you get back to your chambers . . .

STEWART: You would say that the Constitution requires that it be published, and that these men die, is that it?

BICKEL: No, I am afraid that my inclinations to humanity overcome the somewhat more abstract devotion to the First Amendment in a case of that sort.

It was not surprising that the Solicitor General, arguing for Mitchell and Mardian, would contend that where the First Amendment said "Congress shall make no law" abridging freedom of speech or of the press it did not really mean no law; every college freshman had heard about Justice Holmes's dictum that free speech does not give a man a right falsely to shout "Fire!" in a crowded theater. But it was quite another thing when the lawyers for one of the most influential newspapers on earth conceded not only that point but also the relevance of a U-boat-and-troopship analogy. There were no U-boats stalking troopships in this war; the United States was not under attack; legally it was not even at war, and there was nothing in that Pentagon study that could possibly deal with troop movements in 1971, since it was limited to a period that had ended more than three years before. Stewart's question opened up the issue of "facts"—an issue in which the Supreme Court was not supposed to be involved at all—but it also revealed the extent to which the experience of World War II and the Cold War had conditioned thoughtful Americans to lend credence to every argument, no matter how farfetched, that could in any way be supported with words like "national defense" or "security." The presumptions of the national-defense argument had themselves been detached from the context that gave them their original validity, the context of aggression against the United States, and had now become attached to virtually every government activity in the foreign or military sectors, a change which began to suggest that everything was total war.

It was also striking, as the cases moved toward the Supreme Court, how much that World War II conditioning had affected constitutional definitions. After the first restraining orders were issued, the legal debates no longer focused on the constitutionality of all prior restraint, let alone the adequacy of the government's case in supporting any restraint, prior or subsequent, but rather on the more limited question of whether prior restraint was justified in this case.

There were endless arguments about whether the Papers might contain some sort of military secret; there were phrases (as in one of Judge Gurfein's opinions) about whether newspapers could "with impunity publish . . . private information" regarding past relationships with foreign governments, and there was an ongoing assumption that any claim of the sort made by the Administration was sufficient to cloud First Amendment protections. Again and again the judges asked about troopships and atomic secrets and about the newspapers' right, as Judge Walter R. Mansfield said in an appeals court hearing in New York, to arrogate to themselves "the power to decide what is of vital national defense importance." And every time the question was asked, the lawyers agreed that there were instances when the government could stop newspapers from publishing. Bickel later said he was representing a client, not a dogma, that if one goes into such cases "with an ideological interest" one has nothing to gain or lose but one's ideology, and that that, in his view, was "the luxury of an absolutist position." "I've spent some years of scholarship, if I may say so, resisting the idea of absolutes," he told Gurfein, "and I am not now turning around and embracing it."

In its lead editorial the day after Gurfein issued his restraining order, the *Times* castigated the government's "propensity for over-classification and mis-classification of documents that by any reasonable scale of values have long since belonged in the public domain." It went on to say:

As a newspaper that takes seriously its obligation and its responsibilities to the public, we believe that, once this material fell into our hands, it was not only in the interests of the American people to publish it but, even more emphatically, it would have been an abnegation of responsibility and a renunciation of our obligations under the First Amendment not to have published it. Obviously, The Times would not have made this decision if there had been any reason to believe that publication would have endangered the life of a single American soldier or in any way threatened the security of our country or the peace of the world.

The language was revealing. On the front page the paper spoke about "investigative reporting," but on the editorial page it referred to material that "fell into our hands." It discussed its responsibility to the public, but not the public's absolute right to information; it attacked overclassification and misclassification as if they were errors of judgment, and did not argue that it might have been the government that had systematically violated the law and the Constitution. It went to great lengths to argue that the "documents . . . belong in history" and that there was nothing in what was published that would, in the paper's view, endanger "the life of a single American soldier." The paper did not say what it would have done had Neil Sheehan really been able to obtain the documents through "investigative reporting," a question that came up in the course of arguments before the Supreme Court (but which the *Times* never answered); it did not suggest that it was the Administration—the incumbent Administration as well as its predecessors—and not the newspapers, which had endangered the lives of American soldiers, nor did it point out that the documents belonged "in history" only as they concerned military tactics, not as they pertained to political decisions. It might even have argued—especially at that moment, when congressional debates about setting dates for withdrawal from Vietnam were taking place—that the very immediacy of the political issue made the First Amendment case against any sort of restraint all the more urgent.

Both Bickel and William R. Glendon, the attorney for the *Washington Post*, conceded enough of the First Amendment issue to draw questions from the old civil libertarians on the Supreme Court. "As I understand the argument of both of the lawyers," said Justice Hugo Black, "it seems to me that they have argued it on the premise that the First Amendment, freedom of speech, can be abridged by Congress if it chooses to do so." Glendon replied that he hadn't made that argument, an answer similar to one that Bickel had given a little earlier to a parallel question by Justice William O. Douglas. Yet they had both argued precisely that, not only in the Supreme Court but in the lower courts as well. It was, said Douglas, "a very strange argument for the *Times* to be making."

It was the American Civil Liberties Union, in an *amicus curiae* brief, that took the broadest position. The only information that could possibly be excepted from First Amendment protections, it argued, was that which pertained to present or future tactical military operations, blueprints or designs of advanced military equipment, and secret codes, all of which were specifically covered by statute.

> The common denominator of the above classes is that an informed citizen does not need to have access to such information to perform his role properly. In contrast, if the Government's vague and broad test of "information detrimental to the national security" is accepted, there would virtually be no limit to the Government's ability to seek injunctions in District Courts. Indeed, the concept of "national security" is a political concept, which involves in its application a matter of discretion that could be employed to stifle First Amendment rights.

The language of that argument went not only to the issue of prior restraint but to the issue of classification and secrecy in any case. The ACLU also argued that the Espionage Act never contemplated information or documents of the kind published by the *Post* and the *Times,* and that if it did it was unconstitutional. "The assertion by the Executive that it may restrain the publication of the documents at issue here combines the worst elements of the British licensing acts and the law of seditious libel. That such an assertion could have already succeeded in imposing a prior restraint of two weeks' duration is disquieting—but were it to prevail on its merits, it would be nothing short of a disaster." Those arguments anticipated part of the Ellsberg defense a year later.

On June 30, after what seemed like months rather than days of litigation, the Supreme Court ruled, six to three, to allow the papers to resume publication. But the decision, celebrated as a great victory, was ambiguous. The Court merely quoted previous Supreme Court opinions that "any system of prior restraints of expression comes to this court bearing a heavy presumption against its constitutional validity." The government, said the opinion, "had not met that burden." The Court's opinion said nothing further about the constitutionality of the temporary restraining orders, about the applicability of the Espionage Act, or about any of the other substantive issues raised by the case (though not necessarily by the lawyers). Altogether the nine justices produced ten opinions: the majority decision and a separate decision by each judge. In a number of instances the justice writing the opinion would be joined by one or more of his colleagues: Douglas joined by Black; Black joined by Douglas; White joined by Stewart; Stewart joined by White. Each of the three dissenters issued a separate opinion, but Burger and Blackmun also joined in Harlan's dissent. Only Black, Douglas and Brennan attacked as unconstitutional the temporary restraining orders issued by the lower courts. Two of the justices who voted with the majority, White and Stewart, and Chief Justice Burger, who dissented, came close to extending an open invitation to the government to prosecute the newspapers—and, presumably, their sources—on criminal charges. The Espionage Act, one could assume, might well be applied in a prosecution after the fact, even if it did not seem—at least in this case—to permit prior restraint. Blackmun, another dissenter, admonished the newspapers about their responsibilities "to the United States of America" and spoke of the possible effect that publication might have on "prolongation of the war and of further delay in the freeing of United States prisoners." If those results followed, Blackmun said, "then the nation's people will know where the responsibility for these sad consequences rests."

In the opinion written by Harlan, the dissenters seemed to argue that in matters involving foreign affairs the executive branch had prime responsibility and therefore some preemptive rights: "Even if there is some room for the judiciary to override the executive determination, it is plain that the scope of review must be exceedingly narrow. I can see no indication . . . that the conclusions of the executive were given even the deference owing to an administrative agency, much less that owing to a co-equal constitutional prerogative." What that meant, between the lines, was that the burden of proof in such cases really fell on the defendant and not on the government, and that the classification system, even if it lacked statutory justification, derived legitimacy from the "co-equal constitutional prerogative" of the executive branch. Combined with the White-Stewart opinion about criminal prosecution (and with the separate opinions written by Burger and Blackmun), it indicated the Court's general acceptance of the classification procedure's legitimacy and of the government's power to enforce it through criminal proceedings. The government, it suggested, would also have a good chance of sustaining a conviction against Ellsberg, Russo and the newspapers (the chances would become even better after Black and Harlan were replaced by two additional Nixon appointees, Lewis F. Powell and William H. Rehnquist), and it hinted that there was more than a possibility that the *Caldwell* decision permitting newsmen to refuse to divulge their sources to grand juries and prosecutors would be reversed. "I am not, of course, saying that either of these newspapers has yet committed a crime," wrote Justice White, "or that either would commit a crime if they published all the material now in their possession. That matter must await resolution in the context of a criminal proceeding if one is instituted by the United States. In that event, the issue of guilt or innocence would be determined by procedures and standards quite different from those that have purported to govern these injunctive proceedings." No one seemed terribly concerned about the idea that if the newspapers or the leakers could be prosecuted after the fact, prior restraint would soon become unnecessary. At the very moment that White was writing his opinion, such a prosecution had already been started.

### III

On Monday, June 28, two days before the Supreme Court rendered its decision in the cases of the *Post* and the *Times,* the Justice Department secured an indictment from a federal grand jury in Los Angeles charging Ellsberg with violations of the Espionage Act and with converting government documents to his own use. The indictment applied only to 1969, the period of the copying of the Papers, and not to 1971, when they were published. A warrant for Ellsberg's arrest had been issued the previous Friday—just as the Supreme Court was preparing to hear arguments in the newspaper cases. Through his lawyers, Ellsberg had promised to surrender to federal authorities in Boston, and he did so on the same day that the indictment was returned in Los Angeles. Both the warrant and the indictment were announced in Washington by John Mitchell himself.

None of these developments was surprising. By the time the warrant was issued, Ellsberg's name had become familiar enough to make it unnecessary for the writer of the Justice Department press release to identify him by anything other than name. Although he had been underground for two weeks, Ellsberg had appeared on one national television interview (with Walter Cronkite) and had been described in virtually every major newspaper and television news program as the source of the leak. Nor was there anything highly unusual about the fact that the Justice Department announcements came in Mitchell's name. Since Richard Nixon had become President (and on several occasions before) the Attorney General had helpfully called attention to a number of indictments of major political significance by announcing them himself.

What was surprising was the timing. The warrant in Los Angeles was based on affidavits from Carol Ellsberg, from the FBI agent who had questioned McCloskey, and from two Rand Corporation security officials who had responsibility for the custody of classified documents. The indictment (insofar as one can ever be certain about grand-jury proceedings) was based on very little more: testimony from Carol Ellsberg, from Jan Butler, the Rand Corporation Top Secret Control officer (who would soon be given another, less sensitive job), and from Lynda Sinay, on whose Xerox machine the papers were copied and who would later be named as a co-conspirator in the case. Robert L. Meyer, the United States attorney in Los Angeles, refused to sign the indictment; he had been bypassed by a group of lawyers from the Internal Security Division of the Justice Department who had been flown to California to conduct the investigation and to get an indictment in a hurry. Meyer's friends in Los Angeles said that he not only felt upstaged by Mardian's flying squad but also had serious reservations that Ellsberg could ever be convicted on the charges which the government had brought; a few months later Meyer resigned and returned to private practice.*

Even more surprising was the fact that the FBI had known a great deal about Ellsberg's activities ever since the spring of 1970, a few months after he began copying the Papers. Carol Ellsberg, having learned about the copying from the children, had told her stepmother, who told the FBI. As a result, agents of the Bureau conducted a number of interviews with senior officials at Rand. On April 27, according to a record kept by Richard Best, Rand's senior security

---

* The defense in the Ellsberg trial would try to get him to make a statement about his reasons for refusing to sign the indictment, but Meyer pleaded the lawyer–client privilege and declined. Less than a year later he died of a heart attack.

officer, an FBI agent named William McDermott contacted Rand to say "that they had allegations concerning Ellsberg to the effect that in December, 1969 he had entered the Rand Building and removed some classified documents and taken them elsewhere to be reproduced. Mr. Rowen [president of Rand, and, at the time, one of Ellsberg's best friends] stated that in view of the pending nature of the investigation that Rand chose not to take any action with regard to Ellsberg at that time." The FBI, according to its own reports, also knew that the documents in question were in fact the Pentagon Papers, and that Ellsberg might be planning to turn copies over to Fulbright or Goodell. Best's memo, the FBI reports and other material which emerged at Ellsberg's trial three years later indicated that Rowen and other senior Rand officials believed—or at least that they wanted the FBI to believe—that a separate investigation would be conducted by officers of the Air Force and the Department of Defense, but there is no record that one was ever started. On May 13, however, two and a half weeks after McDermott's visit to Rand, Ellsberg testified before the Senate Foreign Relations Committee and hinted that he had material that could be useful to an inquiry into the Vietnam War (all of which, of course, Fulbright already had). That set off a week of panic at Rand during which Ellsberg's safe was cleaned out (there was adequate pretext since he was preparing to leave Rand and go to MIT), inventories were made and records were checked. A few days later, on May 20, Richard Moorsteen, another Rand researcher, called Rowen to tell him that Ellsberg had given him the eighteen volumes of the Papers that he, Ellsberg, had brought from Washington and had kept in his own safe. At the trial and also to the FBI in June 1971, Rowen said he ordered them logged into the regular security system; in fact they were not formally entered until six months later. No steps were taken to revoke Ellsberg's clearance or to inform him about the FBI's visit. Rand officials subsequently told federal investigators that they took no action which would alert Ellsberg so that the FBI investigation could proceed. Ellsberg, who learned about it later from acquaintances who had been interviewed, subsequently came to believe that no overt action was taken because the Administration hoped to implicate Goodell, who was then running for reelection and who, because of his antiwar position, was regarded as an enemy of the White House. He also came to believe that Kissinger knew about the investigation; when he saw Kissinger in September of 1970, Ellsberg said, Kissinger "acted oddly."

The official spokesmen for the Justice Department denied the whole episode. Although Mardian later told people privately, "We had a file on Ellsberg as early as 1970," the Justice Department refused even to acknowledge that anyone had ever charged that the June indictment had been rushed through the grand jury in the hope that it might influence the decision of the Supreme Court in the injunction cases against the newspapers. Yet, since the indictment technically had nothing to do with publication of the documents (it was concerned only with the copying), the rush to secure that indictment now, combined with the minor embarrassment of the Meyer episode, was bound to raise questions about the government's motives. Two years later there were reports that someone, perhaps the Army or the Defense Department, had been wiretapping Ellsberg and Sheehan at least a month before the Pentagon Papers were published, and strong indications that the FBI investigation which began in 1970 had never been closed. The officials at Justice who were responsible for the Ellsberg prosecution denied that they knew anything about those tapes.

The indictment was clearly an interim measure. By the time it was returned, the panic at the White House had been mixed with a growing measure of opportunism, a mix of paranoid fears and pragmatic hopes that the leak of the Papers had been the work of an identifiable conspiracy of former Johnson Administration officials. Mitchell reported to the White House that Justice had learned from an informant in the Soviet Embassy (a wiretap?) that someone had given the Russians a set of the Papers before the *Times* began to publish, a story which later turned out to be garbled and possibly fabricated. (The Soviets denied it, and subsequent leaks from Justice Department officials indicated that the documents, if they had been delivered at all, had not arrived at the embassy until after the *Times* began publication. The person who delivered the Papers to the Russians was never identified, no evidence about the delivery was ever produced at Ellsberg's trial, and the government never explained why, if the Russians already had the material, it was necessary to pursue the injunction cases against the newspapers.) The FBI and the Defense Department had also begun to report on the involvement of Warnke, Gelb and Halperin in the case, on Ellsberg's background and associations, and on the transactions with Rand which gave him access to the study. As a consequence, the White House began to raise overlapping sets of questions about the proper way to proceed. Had Ellsberg acted alone? Was there a conspiracy among former officials of Democratic administrations, possibly including McNamara himself? Could the Papers be used to embarrass those administrations? There was also some question about the political advisability of prosecuting Ellsberg at all, and, consequently, a discussion of ways in which Ellsberg could be sufficiently discredited to destroy his candidacy for martyrdom. Mardian later explained that Nixon believed his "ability to govern" and the peace of the world to be at stake, and Ehrlichman would tell the Senate Watergate Committee that the most important issue was stopping the leaks: "This theft had evidently been perpetrated by a number of people, a conspiracy, and . . . some of the people were identified by the Department of Justice as having had ties to previous domestic Communist activities." But there was also a possibility that the disclosure could be pinned on the treachery of Democrats, be exploited as proof that prior administrations had sabotaged the effort in Vietnam, or be used to link former officials of the Johnson

Administration with the leak and with aspiring Democratic candidates. In the early months of 1971, Edmund S. Muskie led Nixon in the public-opinion polls by increasing margins; Gelb, Warnke and Halperin were all associated with Muskie, and by midsummer (if not before) they all had been placed on the White House "enemies" list. Halperin's name appeared on the select list of enemies—the twenty most wanted—with the notation "A scandal would be most helpful here." In addition to his work for Muskie (as an adviser on foreign policy), he had been temporarily associated with a challenge by Common Cause against the war in Laos. He had probably been an "enemy" since 1969 or early 1970.

Early in July, Nixon decided that the White House should conduct its own "investigation"—an inquiry parallel to the criminal investigation at the Department of Justice—and appointed John D. Ehrlichman, his assistant for domestic affairs, to organize and supervise the work of a "special unit." The unit was headed by Egil "Bud" Krogh, Jr., who was already working for Ehrlichman and who would later become (before his resignation in connection with the Watergate disclosures) an official in the Department of Transportation, and David R. Young, Jr., who had been sent over from the National Security Council by Henry Kissinger. Its members also included E. Howard Hunt, Jr., a retired twenty-year veteran of the CIA who was recommended and hired by Charles Colson—they were fellow alumni of Brown University—and G. Gordon Liddy, the flamboyant former FBI agent and lawyer who had worked for the Treasury Department until he was fired for lobbying against the Administration's weak proposals for gun-control legislation (Liddy thought there should be no controls). Nixon told Krogh (according to Nixon's statement of May 22, 1973) that the unit "should find out all about Mr. Ellsberg's associates and motives. Because of the extreme gravity of the situation, and not then knowing what additional secrets Mr. Ellsberg might disclose, I did impress upon Mr. Krogh the vital importance to the national security of his assignment." Although Nixon also said that only a handful of people in the White House were to know, and that other government agencies would not be informed, Ehrlichman immediately alerted the Pentagon, the Justice Department and the CIA and asked for their cooperation in the project.

Both the motive and the degree of Nixon's personal involvement in the creation of the special unit remain shrouded in contradictions and administrative Newspeak. A week before Colson hired Hunt they had discussed the possibility of "nailing" Ellsberg and, through him, "the real enemy," meaning the Left. Colson told Hunt, in a taped telephone conversation, "Ellsberg could be turned into a martyr of the New Left —he probably will be anyway. Or it could become another Alger Hiss case, where the guy is exposed, other people were operating with him . . . We might be able to put this bastard into a helluva situation and discredit the New Left." But Colson also appeared to be interested in using the Papers and other Vietnam documents to dissociate the Nixon Administration from responsibility for the war. "Mr. Colson indicated to me," Hunt told a grand jury in Los Angeles, "that the feeling in the Executive Branch was that it was quite necessary to dissociate the current Administration from United States involvement in the Vietnam War. And to that end, he asked me that I make a thorough study of whatever root source documents might be available in the government to make an accurate determination." In its first weeks, the unit's official mandate seemed to be confined largely to the matter of spurring other government departments and agencies to become more security-conscious and to conduct their own investigations of the leaks that had occurred. It was not until later in July, after a leak about the SALT talks, that the "Plumbers" were instructed by Nixon personally and charged with the responsibility of conducting their separate investigation. On July 24 Nixon met with Krogh and Ehrlichman and approved a plan to find the sources of the leaks—which included, among other things, the use of polygraph tests in investigating senior staff people at the State Department and the National Security Council. What is not certain is the degree to which Colson was following Nixon's orders from the very beginning—he had discussed an assignment for Hunt with White House Chief of Staff H. R. Haldeman before Hunt was hired—or the degree to which orders were subsequently given right out of the Oval Office.

Installed in Room 16 of the Executive Office Building (the unit was known as "Room 16"), the Plumbers began their work by collecting all available material on the Papers and on Ellsberg himself. Even after the government had argued in the courts that the material was highly sensitive, no one was certain what the Pentagon Papers contained, from what records they were drawn, or whether they were even genuine. Hunt was given access to State Department cables on Vietnam and, of course, to the Papers themselves, and he set out to compare them. He also studied the FBI reports (which Mardian provided for the White House), collected all available newspaper and magazine stories on the affair, and used them to assemble a dossier and chronology on Ellsberg's personal life. Hunt later testified that "there was some concern in the White House about the appropriateness of seeing the prosecution actually take place with regard to Dr. Ellsberg and his associates, and I shared that concern, my own feelings being that he would become a martyr, in looking at things politically." Hunt began to pay particular attention to information about Ellsberg's former girl friends, and especially Yvonne Svenle Ekman, a former employee of the Swedish Information Service, with whom Ellsberg had lived in the summer of 1968 and whom he saw occasionally after his marriage to Patricia. Ellsberg "consorted with females of foreign birth and extraction," Hunt later explained, and that was "a danger signal to anybody in the counter-espionage field." The FBI reports, Hunt told a grand jury,

> dealt at great length with his background—how shall I put it—his moral character, or allegations concerning his moral char-

acter, some rather bizarre sexual practices, a very unusual life style . . .

Inasmuch as the Government was contemplating at that time a major prosecution . . . it was felt, and I believe Mr. Krogh, who was the lawyer, suggested that it would be well if something could—if some way could be found whereby a judgement call could be made on Ellsberg in regard to not only his sanity, but his prosecutability.

To that end extracts were made of material dealing with Dr. Ellsberg's rather peculiar background, and we read those excerpts and concluded that the best course would be a full read-out, or a reasonably full read-out, on Dr. Ellsberg through whatever files the psychiatrist had been maintaining on him during the period that Dr. Ellsberg was under analysis.

Ellsberg was a tempting target for such an investigation. There was the psychiatrist, there were stories about Dan and Pat's involvement with encounter groups and nudist camps, and there was Dan's tendency to be more open with women than with men. Sooner or later some prosecutor (or some member of the Administration with a talent for leaking the right things to the right people) might try to tarnish his halo with a recitation of affairs, catalogues of girls, perhaps even innuendos of perversion and unmanliness: one-night stands in the summer of 1968, the stories of how he couldn't get his work completed at Rand, and those crazy funky statements of his about how if women had been in charge there might never have been a Vietnam. They might find people to say, as some of his friends had said, that he always felt more comfortable in the company of women. And so they might tag him with a double offense in the American catalogue of sin: a monumental ego among men, a suspicious softness toward women, "some rather bizarre sexual practices, a very unusual life style."

The focus on Ellsberg's personal life, Krogh explained, derived primarily from the FBI's reluctance to investigate— "a close personal relationship existed between the Director of the FBI, J. Edgar Hoover, and Mr. Louis Marx, father-in-law of Dr. Daniel Ellsberg." Ehrlichman later testified that when a senior FBI official had asked for a routine interview with Marx, Hoover ordered him transferred and demoted; Hoover, the White House believed, would simply not pursue the case with energy or give it the high-priority attention it deserved. It would turn out later, however, that the FBI in fact conducted an interview with Marx and that the only hard information Hunt possessed on Ellsberg's personal life came from FBI reports; what seemed to upset the White House was the FBI belief that Ellsberg had acted alone in disclosing the Papers, and its growing insistence that there was simply no evidence of the high-level conspiracies that Ehrlichman and the Plumbers imagined.

The material available through official government agencies soon turned out to be insufficient for the special unit. The FBI had been sent out to interview Dr. Fielding on July 20, but the analyst, through his attorney, refused even to acknowledge that Ellsberg had ever been his patient. Early in August, therefore, Young and Ehrlichman made arrangements with CIA Director Richard Helms for the creation of a secondhand psychiatric profile on Ellsberg by Dr. Bernard Malloy, head of the psychiatric unit of the CIA. The profile, said to have been the first such CIA study on a domestic figure, was based largely on the FBI reports and the newspaper clippings and was generally a flattering portrayal of Ellsberg as a sincere, patriotic and intelligent man. The study concluded:

There is nothing to suggest in the material reviewed that subject suffers from a serious mental disorder in the sense of being psychotic and out of touch with reality. There are suggestions, however, that some of his long-standing personality needs were intensified by psychological pressures of the mid-life period and that this may have contributed significantly to his recent actions.

An extremely intelligent and talented individual, subject apparently made his brilliance evident. It seems likely that there were substantial pressures to succeed and that subject early had instilled in him expectations of success, that he absorbed the impression that he was special and destined for greatness. And indeed he did attain considerable academic success and seemed slated for a brilliant career.

There has been a notable zealous intensity about the subject throughout his career. Apparently finding it difficult to tolerate ambiguity and ambivalence, he was either strongly for something or strongly against it. There were suggestions of problems in achieving full success, for although his ideas glittered, he had trouble committing himself in writing.

He had a knack for drawing attention to himself and at early ages had obtained positions of considerable distinction, usually attaching himself as a "bright young man" to an older and experienced man of considerable stature who was attracted by his brilliance and flair.

But one can only sustain the role of "bright young man" so long. Most men between the ages of 35 and 45 go through a period of re-evaluation. Realizing that youth is at an end, that many of their golden dreams cannot be achieved, many men transiently drift into despair at this time.

In an attempt to escape from these feelings of despair and to regain a sense of competence and mastery, there is an increased thrust towards new activity at this time. Thus this is a time of career changes, of extra-marital affairs and divorce.

It is a time when many men come to doubt their earlier commitments and are impelled to strike out in new directions.

For the individual who is particularly driven towards the heights of success and prominence, this mid-life period may be a particularly difficult time. The evidence reviewed suggests that this was so for Ellsberg, a man whose career had taken off like a rocket, but who found himself at mid-life not nearly having achieved the prominence and success he expected and desired. . . .

There is no suggestion that subject thought anything treasonous in his act. Rather, he seemed to be responding to what he deemed a higher order of patriotism. His exclusion of the three volumes of the papers concerned with the secret negotiations would support this.

Many of subject's own words would confirm the impression that he saw himself as having a special mission, and indeed as bearing a special responsibility. On several occasions he castigated himself for not releasing the papers earlier, observing that since he first brought them to the attention of the [Senate] Foreign Relations Committee, there had been "two invasions," more than 9,000 American lives lost, and hundreds of thousands of Vietnamese deaths.

The profile was quickly rejected as inadequate. By the time it was produced, however, someone on the team had had a better idea, reviving, in the words of Nixon's subsequent statement, the thought of "surreptitious entry . . . breaking and entering, in effect, on specified categories of targets in specified situations related to national security." Hunt told the grand jury he couldn't recall who first mentioned it, "but the possibility of a bag job on the psychiatrist's office . . . became a topic of low-key conversation around the office."

At that time I was fairly new to the White House. I said, "Well, if you want the materials, why can't we just simply get the F.B.I. to procure it?"

The answer, which I believe was provided by Mr. Liddy, was that in the last five or six years, under Mr. Hoover's aegis, the Federal Bureau of Investigation had ceased training its agents in entry operations, and that the cadre that the Bureau used to maintain for this type of operation was no longer in existence. It had dwindled away. The agents had been reassigned or lost their skills.

I recall raising the question as to whether or not the Secret Service might be an appropriate unit for such a task. The reply that was given to me, and I believe it was also by Mr. Liddy, was that the White House did not have sufficient confidence in the Secret Service in order to trust them with a task of this sort.

There came a time shortly thereafter when it was suggested that perhaps the unit . . . might be able to undertake such an operation on its own.

On August 11, Krogh and Young sent Ehrlichman a "status report" registering disappointment with the CIA profile and recommending that a "covert operation be undertaken to examine all the medical files still held by Ellsberg's psychoanalyst covering the two-year period in which he was undergoing analysis." By that time two other leaks had further increased the panic at the White House, among them a *New York Times* story (again by Beecher) on the U.S. negotiating position and fall-back strategy in the Strategic Arms Limitation Treaty talks. Since such stories were generally disclosed by hard-liners trying to sabotage negotiations, the SALT leak would hardly be the work of Ellsberg and the Left, but that did not diminish the concern or the resulting pressure on the Plumbers to get on with the investigation of Ellsberg. Nixon "personally instructed" Krogh, in Ehrlichman's presence, "that the continuing leaks of vital information were compromising the national security of the United States, and the President instructed me [Krogh] to move ahead with the greatest urgency to determine the source." Ehrlichman approved the Krogh-Young recommendation—he later insisted that "covert operation" did not mean burglary—with the proviso that it be carried out "under your assurance that it is not traceable." Someone in the White House still wanted to believe that there was one "source," and that somewhere, perhaps in Fielding's file, lay the heart of a secret.

Two weeks later, Hunt and Liddy flew to Los Angeles to conduct what Hunt called a "feasibility and vulnerability study," cased Fielding's Beverly Hills office, and returned to Washington to report that "the operation could be performed." The CIA had provided equipment and technical assistance at a series of clandestine meetings, arranged through calls to "sterile numbers," in "safe houses" in the

Washington area: a special camera fitted into a tobacco pouch ("an experimental model," Hunt said), a "voice alteration device," tape recorders, bugging equipment, and disguises. The CIA also supplied false identification papers and developed the photographs that the Plumbers took in and outside Fielding's office. (Someone at the CIA thought the pictures were photos of the Rand Building, a slip that suggested that the agency was more witting about the Hunt-Liddy operation than it ever acknowledged.) Much of the equipment was superfluous; Hunt had acquired some of it for other operations, among them an "interview" with a man in Rhode Island who promised to supply some dirt on Teddy Kennedy, but he obviously enjoyed playing with it even when it was unnecessary. Hunt, through Colson and Ehrlichman, had made contact with the CIA as early as July 7, the day after Colson hired him. Although Ehrlichman later said he didn't recall any such conversation, General Robert E. Cushman, Jr., an old protégé of Nixon's who was the CIA's deputy director (and was later to become commandant of the Marine Corps), subsequently testified that Ehrlichman asked for his cooperation and that, assuming Ehrlichman "spoke with the authority of the President," he had given it. Cushman had known Hunt in the CIA, considered him a "highly respected and honorably retired CIA employee," and arranged to meet him at CIA headquarters July 22, twenty days before the Krogh-Young request and five days before Fielding, through his lawyer, refused to talk to the FBI. Hunt, who often lived in a fantasy world—he was, among other things, the author and covert hero of some forty pseudonymous spy novels—had begun to play spook for the White House well before the Ellsberg caper was planned, and the White House, in the person of Charles Colson, had been prepared to so use him when the only concern about "national security" was Chappaquidick.

On their return from the feasibility study in Los Angeles, Hunt and Liddy secured Krogh's permission to proceed with the "bag job," provided again that no one associated with the White House would be implicated. Hunt, who had played a major part in the Bay of Pigs operation for the CIA in 1961 and who kept in touch with a group of emigré Cubans in Miami, thereupon went to Florida, as he later testified, "to look up some of my old CIA contacts." Among them was Bernard L. Barker, an American born in Havana who had also taken part in the Bay of Pigs and who regarded Hunt as the hope of Cuban liberation from Fidel Castro. It was never clear what Barker and his friends had been doing for Hunt or the CIA since the Bay of Pigs, but some relationship between Hunt and the Cubans had been maintained. Barker, who had once been recruited to work for the Havana police by an FBI agent and who was now a successful real-estate operator in Miami, believed that Hunt was enlisting him for "a national-security operation higher than the FBI or the CIA." He hoped that in return for his help Hunt and the United States government would look favorably on a renewed effort to oust Castro. He also seemed to believe that the government had been supporting a number of Cubans or their families, and that if anything should happen in the operation the government would provide lawyers and support for the families of those who were apprehended. Barker later testified that Hunt told him that Ellsberg was a "traitor" who had been furnishing information to a foreign embassy.

Barker had just the men for the job: Felipe de Diego, once a banker in Cuba, and Eugenio Martinez, a photographer and a veteran, as Barker described him, of three hundred missions inside Cuba. Both were employed by Barker in the real-estate business and both were given the impression that they would be working for the CIA and "helping the United States government." (Whether in fact they had been receiving CIA support all along never became clear, yet it did not seem strange to any of them that they would now be called on to do a job in Los Angeles that had no connection with Cuba.) In his testimony to the grand jury, Hunt said the men were "run past me" for his approval, but Barker later told a Senate committee that Hunt had in fact met Martinez—had had dinner with him—several months before. Martinez, who had been screening Cuban refugees for the CIA, was still on the agency's payroll. Hunt quickly engaged them, and arrangements were made to carry out the operation in Los Angeles over the Labor Day weekend.

The actual burglary of Fielding's office was simple, though Hunt and Liddy surrounded it with vast amounts of CIA spook talk, codes and false identity cards (including one, supplied by the CIA, that would later be used by James Mc-Cord in the break-in at the Watergate: both Hunt and Mc-Cord would be Edward Warren). The Cubans came to Fielding's office early in the evening with a suitcase containing cameras, walkie-talkies and other gadgets, told the Chicano cleaning woman (who recognized their accents as Cuban) that they were delivering something for the doctor, and left the suitcase inside. On the way out they set the latch on the office door so that it would close without locking and waited for the woman to leave and the coast to clear. Hunt, meanwhile, watched Fielding's house to make certain the doctor didn't leave, and Liddy cruised the streets outside Fielding's office building to make certain the operation wouldn't be unexpectedly interrupted. The walkie-talkies would be used to warn the burglars if something went wrong. Later that night, Barker and the Cubans returned, found the building unexpectedly locked, jimmied open a window in another office, strewed papers and furniture around to make it look like a routine burglary, and went to Fielding's office. The participants all later claimed that they found nothing pertaining to Ellsberg, that they took Polaroid pictures of the open files to prove they'd been there, and that they returned the next day (Hunt and Liddy to Washington, the others to Miami) with nothing. (Fielding was not so certain. He later testified that he did have material on Ellsberg in his files and that the burglary "left a question mark about the whole affair . . . It was not easy to set my mind at rest about it." But he never mentioned it to Ellsberg.)

Hunt reported the details of the burglary to Krogh and

Young, and Krogh informed Ehrlichman, who later told the FBI that he had not authorized any burglary and didn't know about it until after it happened. According to the FBI's report, Ehrlichman did "not agree with this method of investigation" and, on learning of it, issued instructions "not to do this again." A few days after the burglary the Plumbers briefly weighed the idea of breaking into Fielding's home—perhaps he kept the files there—but they decided that "this was not a viable type of approach." Young subsequently requested and got another CIA psychiatric profile, more extensive and less flattering than the first, but when Ellsberg examined it two years later he found nothing that could be traced to his confessions on the couch.

The Plumbers' interest in Ellsberg's psyche was matched by an interest in developing the political and legal evidence for a larger conspiracy. Ehrlichman, in subsequent attempts to explain it, spoke about "a desire in the White House to air this whole thing . . . whether the treachery was in government, whether the treachery was in the think tank apparatus, if there was . . ." In July the Administration had held meetings with members of the House Armed Services Committee, including its hawkish chairman, Representative F. Edward Hébert of Louisiana, in the expectation that the committee would conduct hearings early in the fall that could be stage-managed by the Administration for maximum political advantage. The hearings were part of a large strategy "to bring about a change in Ellsberg's image" and demonstrate that the McNamara study was intentionally distorted and subsequently leaked by a single group of conspirators who had held high posts under the Democrats. Young informed Ehrlichman that Mardian, Deputy Under-secretary of State William V. Macomber and Defense Department General Counsel J. Fred Buzhardt—all of whom were deeply involved in various phases of the Pentagon Papers investigation—had met with Hébert and Leslie C. Arends, the ranking Republican on the Armed Services Committee, and reported that the committee was ready to proceed with hearings and to conduct them along the lines suggested by the White House. (Hébert later described Young's hope for Administration-managed hearings as "sheer fantasy"; no one would tell him how to run his committee, he said. He acknowledged, however, that he had discussed the possibility of an investigation with Buzhardt.) On August 26, while Hunt and Liddy were conducting their feasibility and vulnerability study in Los Angeles, Young sent Ehrlichman a memo outlining the plans. The Congressmen, Young reported,

> would begin the investigation in a low key under a subcommittee of the House Armed Services Committee. Beginning with questions of security clearance, classification and declassification, they would move into the more specific case of the Pentagon study . . . [and they] agreed that Mardian, Macomber and Buzhardt would set the format, supply the substantive data and develop the scenario.

At the time of the meeting with Hébert and Arends, Young said, it was still believed that Ellsberg had acted alone, and the plan was

> to slowly develop a very negative picture around the whole Pentagon study affair . . . and then to identify Ellsberg's associates and supporters on the New Left with this negative image. The end result would be to show (1) how they were intent on undermining the policy of the Government they were supposedly serving, and (2) how they have sought to put themselves above the law.

That assumption was no longer valid, Young said, because

> those in Justice and Defense most familiar with this enterprise believe that substantial evidence is being developed for the criminal prosecution of individuals other than Ellsberg: namely Gelb, Halperin, Warnke and Rand executives. Buzhardt states that only the FBI is disposed to thinking that Ellsberg is the prime mover.
>
> It may well be that although Ellsberg is guilty of the crimes

with which he is charged, he did not in fact turn the papers over to the New York Times. The Defense Department's analysis of the printed material may even show that Ellsberg did not have some of the papers which the New York Times printed.

Furthermore, the whole distribution network may be the work of still another and even larger network . . .

Investigators from Defense and Justice would therefore be conducting extensive interviews with Rand officials and former employees of the government, including McNamara and Clark Clifford, both former Secretaries of Defense. (Clifford, who had served in the last months of the Johnson Administration and was an adviser to Muskie, had been marked by the White House for harassment by the Internal Revenue Service as soon as more compliant IRS officials could be appointed.) Young asked for a meeting September 9 to discuss the issues he regarded as most pressing:

(1) If there is enough to bring criminal charges against Gelb, the Rand executives, etc., do we want to prosecute or do we want to bring such material out through the Congressional investigation?

(2) If criminal prosecution is decided against for all except Ellsberg, when would it be most desirable to undertake the Congressional investigation?

(3) What strategy should be followed in the actual committee investigation if (a) only Ellsberg is to be prosecuted, or (b) if all the persons are to be prosecuted?

(4) Do we want the Congressional investigation to also get into the substance of the Pentagon study? If so, a game plan must be devised for determining what, when and how information should be fed to the committee.

(5) If the decision is made to move ahead in these substantive areas careful consideration should be given to the effect of the credibility fallout on us. For this reason it might be best to stick with specific blunders such as the 1963 coup, the miscalculation on the need of forces, etc. (Note: I am sending you a separate Hunt to Colson memorandum which attempts to select

the politically damaging material involving the Democratic hierarchy. Personally I believe a good deal more material could be developed along these lines . . .)

(6) To what extent should we try to show the lack of objectivity and the intent of the participants in the Pentagon study to distort and mislead? (Note that exploitation of this theme undercuts points 4 and 5.)

(7) Effect of South Vietnamese election on timing of investigation.

(8) Effect of Ellsberg trial which will not come up before March of 1972 on timing of investigation.

(9) How quickly do we want to try to bring about a change in Ellsberg's image? . . . If the present Hunt/Liddy Project Number 1 is successful, it will be absolutely essential to have an over all game plan developed for its use in conjunction with the Congressional investigation . . .

Young planned to coordinate the hearings with a program of leaks about Ellsberg's personal life. The situation, he told Ehrlichman, was "too big to be undermined by planted leaks among the friendly press," but he was confident that in connection with the hearings the strategy would work. The key man was Colson, the White House jack-of-dirty-trades, who had, among other things, fed damaging information on Senator Joseph Tydings of Maryland to a *Life* reporter and who had, according to subsequent testimony by John Dean, suggested to Caulfield, the former New York cop, that he fire-bomb the Brookings Institution as a cover to a planned burglary of Halperin's office. (Colson denied the story.) Young had discussed the Ellsberg matter with Colson, "and his reply was that we should just leave it to him and he would take care of getting the information out." Confusing Ellsberg with "enemy" politicians whose personal life might be an issue with the voters, they planned to "fold in the press planting with the Congressional investigation."

While Young was planning White House strategy for the congressional hearing and Hunt and Liddy were casing Field-

ing's office, another project was getting under way. In reading the Papers and related documents, Hunt discovered that
cables were missing. "A lot of stuff that should have been
there," he told Colson, "had been extracted." Colson, who
hated all the Kennedys, had already given Hunt his assignment to gather embarrassing data on Teddy; now he saw a
magnificent opportunity not only to "select the politically
damaging material involving the Democratic hierarchy" (as
Young suggested in his memo) but possibly to embellish it.
Perhaps they could get Teddy through Jack. According to
Hunt's testimony later to the Watergate grand jury, Colson
asked him how he accounted for the missing documents.

I said, "Well, obviously anybody who had been given access to
the Department of State file for the purposes of incorporating
them into material held by the JFK Library would also have
had opportunity to remove any cables that could have been
embarrassing to the Kennedy legatees."

And he said, "Well, what kind of material have you dug up
in the files that would indicate Kennedy complicity?" And I
showed him three or four cables that indicated that they had
pretty close to pulled the trigger against Premier Diem's head,
but it didn't say so in so many words. Inferentially one could
say it was a high degree of Administration complicity in the
actual assassination of Diem and his brother.

And he said, "Well, this isn't good enough. Do you think you
could improve on them?"

I said, "Yes, I probably could, but not without technical
assistance." After all I had been given some training in my
past CIA career to do just this sort of thing and had done it
successfully on numerous occasions, floating forged newspaper
accounts, telegrams, that sort of thing.*

So he said, "Well, we won't be able to give you any technical
help. This is too hot. See what you can do on your own."

So, with the very meager means at my disposal, which were

---

* Colson subsequently claimed that Hunt had "misunderstood" his instructions.

literally a Xerox machine in the White House, a razor blade and a typewriter—which was not the same one as had been used on the original cables—I set about creating two cables which bore on that particular period . . .

I was not satisfied with the results. I showed them to Colson. He seemed to like them and I said "These will never stand any kind of scrutiny." . . . I found out it would be impossible for me to get access to a similar type face [as that used in the White House and State Department at the time] . . . So there would just have to be a fast brush show on a take it or leave it basis, which I began to believe was the purpose Mr. Colson had in mind.

Not long after I completed these two cables, I got a call from them saying, "There will be a fellow over to see you. I've given him your name. His name is Bill Lambert from Time-Life and I want you to talk to him about those cables . . . Show him those cables . . . but don't let them get out of your hands."

In due course, Mr. Lambert made contact with me . . . I showed him the stack of cables, extracted three or four I had paper clipped, including the two I had fabricated . . .

Mr. Lambert was quite exultant over the find. Wanted to know if he couldn't take them immediately. I, obviously, said, "No, you may not, but you may read the text. If you care to, you may copy the text down."

So he spent some time copying them down on a yellow pad and he never saw the cables again, but he was in contact with myself and, I believe, the office of Mr. Colson, trying to obtain facsimiles of the two fabricated cables.

The efforts centered in Room 16 had little to do with plugging leaks; if they had any consistent objective, it was to reestablish control over things which, in the eyes of the Prussians in the White House, had gotten out of hand, and (if possible) to turn them to advantage. Ehrlichman later testified that the original purpose of the unit was simply to put enough pressure on the security officers in the agencies, particularly at Defense and State, so that they would be more diligent in plugging their own leaks, and that the unit had not started to do its own plumbing until those efforts failed. Yet, as the summer wore on, the unit wandered farther afield, partly to satisfy its political purposes and partly out of sheer incompetence. Young told Ehrlichman in his memo that "with the recent article on [Leonard B.] Boudin, Ellsberg's lawyer, we have started on a negative press image for Ellsberg." The article was so obscure that no one, including Boudin, could recall it when the memo was later released. The assumption, moreover, that someone could learn something from a secondhand psychiatric profile was to confuse the intelligence requirements imposed by an inaccessible and powerful foreign politician (Khrushchev, for example, or Mao) with a domestic figure who had left a trail of available witnesses to his personal life and who was being watched around the clock by federal agents. Young's confused scenario for the congressional hearings also indicated (despite his experience as a Kissinger *apparatchik*) something bordering on total ignorance of the Papers, the history of the Vietnam War, and domestic politics. To conduct hearings on the Papers, the classification system or anything else connected with the leaks, even before a friendly committee, was to play directly into Ellsberg's hands. What Ellsberg wanted was exposure, and almost anywhere one turned in the story the exposure did little to enhance the record of the participants: to nail Kennedy with a forged cable about the anti-Diem coup was also to get Republican Henry Cabot Lodge, who was the ambassador in Saigon and was involved with genuine cables; to implicate Democratic politicians was also to implicate members of the Joint Chiefs of Staff, ambassadors and, among others, Eisenhower, Dulles and Nixon himself. To get Democrats was to get Johnson.

Nixon, nonetheless, maintained an active interest in the conduct of the investigation. The President attended at least five meetings concerning the leak of the Papers: July 2, July 6, July 12, July 24 and September 18. According to documents filed by Ehrlichman's attorneys in connection with his defense on burglary charges in Los Angeles, the September 18 meeting, which took place two weeks after the Fielding break-in, was attended by Mitchell, Haldeman, Colson, the President and Ehrlichman. At that meeting "a progress report on the investigation of the disclosure of the Pentagon Papers was discussed" and "the President made further assignments regarding the investigation of the . . . disclosure." Nixon was also reported to have maintained close touch with Young at a series of personal meetings where, it was said, the former Kissinger aide kept the President in touch with the investigation. Subsequent statements by White House officials attributed Nixon's concern, at least in part, to the fear that Ellsberg had given the Russians data on U.S. nuclear targeting plans (Single Integrated Operation Plans) or that he might disclose them in the future. Ellsberg had worked on such plans, but his information was, by that time, at least three years old; nor was it likely that a man who would secretly furnish data to a foreign power would risk exposure by making what were essentially historical or political documents available to the newspapers. By 1973, when suggestions of such fears were first published, the capacity for ex post facto paranoia among White House officials (and former officials) was almost boundless. The fact that the investigation did not begin until after the Supreme Court decision in the injunction cases, a decision regarded by the Administration as a defeat, suggests that Nixon's interest was based on political and personal motives, and not on apprehension about the disclosure of military secrets.

Room 16 produced a chain of almost unmitigated failures. The editors of *Time-Life,* suspicious of the forged Hunt cables, never published them; the burglars, pursuing something they probably couldn't have used, with CIA equipment they didn't need, found nothing; the House Armed Services Committee hearings were never held (Hébert thought Ellsberg should be sent to jail, but he didn't think the case was worth an inquiry); and the attempt to conjure up a larger conspiracy of high-level Democrats to smear through Ells-

berg produced little but nourishment for the mixture of paranoia and opportunism which had inspired the effort in the
first place. If Hunt's "chronology" on Ellsberg (later found
in his White House safe) was any indication of what the
investigation produced, the White House had even less data
on the "conspiracy" than was available in the public domain
and far less than the FBI and the Justice Department turned
up before trial. Hunt and Liddy were clearly more interested
in reliving the romantic lives of spies and investigators, wearing disguises, cruising around the streets of Beverly Hills
with walkie-talkies, and congratulating themselves on a "professional operation" than in collecting evidence or conducting substantive inquiries. By late fall, their activities (in the
words of Nixon) "tapered off" and they began to attach their
fantasies to the requirements of the Committee for the Re-
election of the President, where, within a few months, they
would be working for their old employers, now playing the
role of leaders of a political campaign. As late as May 1972,
however, the Plumbers maintained an active interest in Ellsberg. Early that month, Bernard Barker, on instructions from
Hunt, recruited a team of Cubans in Miami to attack Ellsberg
at an antiwar rally on the steps of the Capitol. "Our mission,"
he told them, "is to hit him—to call him a traitor and punch
him in the nose. Hit him and run." The object was to start a
riot and discredit Ellsberg, but the attack, like most of the
other Plumber enterprises, failed. The punches landed on
people surrounding Ellsberg, and there was no riot.

IV

The attempt to establish a conspiracy was not limited to
the White House amateurs. Under Mardian and John Martin,
who headed the Evaluation and Analysis Section of the Internal Security Division, the investigation at the Justice Department proceeded on a more or less independent course
—technically separate from the White House inquiry, yet
clearly related. Mardian and Martin fed information to the
White House, and therefore to the Plumbers, and, apparently

with Mitchell's consent, authorized Hunt and Liddy to tap the telephones of at least two *New York Times* reporters. Whether any information collected by the Plumbers found its way back to Justice is unclear. Hunt and Liddy reported to Krogh and Young, Krogh and Young reported to Ehrlichman, and Ehrlichman reported to Nixon. The government insisted, literally in a stack of affidavits, that nothing from the Hunt-Liddy investigation ever found its way to Justice, and Mardian later testified that he first learned about the Fielding burglary when he "de-briefed" Liddy in June 1972. But Mardian had in fact attended at least one meeting with Young, Buzhardt and others at which the plans for the congressional hearings were discussed and where, according to Young's memo, he agreed to help "develop the scenario." The Justice Department was therefore at the very least involved in a plan to discredit publicly a person who was then under indictment, and, more likely, it was aware (through Mardian) that the burglary had taken place.

The initial work in the case, after Meyer had been end-played in Los Angeles, was done by Paul T. Vincent, an attorney in the Internal Security Division; it was Vincent who secured the first indictment, got the grand juries to work, and issued the first round of subpoenas. But within three months he too was replaced, this time (and, as it turned out, permanently) by a team of three lawyers headed by David R. Nissen, a former U. S. Army counterintelligence agent and then the head of the criminal division in the U. S. Attorney's Office in Los Angeles. The other members of the team were Warren P. Reese, a former engineer and a member of the U. S. attorney's staff in San Diego; and Richard J. Barry, a young assistant U. S. attorney from Des Moines. Clearly Nissen was in charge, set the tone and determined the style. He had already established a reputation as a tough, contentious prosecutor, a man not given to philosophical ruminations or political abstractions, and a tenacious cross-examiner who, as one of his acquaintances said, "tries every case like a bank robbery." Nissen would not be afraid to talk back to judges—on one occasion he was threatened with contempt charges himself—or to witnesses. In 1970 he had prosecuted a local *cause célèbre* in Los Angeles, the so-called Friars Club case, in which a group of card-table swindlers, using peepholes in the ceiling and secret radio signals, had fleeced a collection of well-heeled gin-rummy players from Beverly Hills out of a great deal of money. Nissen had never handled anything as political as the case of the Pentagon Papers, but that was not likely to trouble him. The politics would be handled elsewhere—"They occasionally call me from Washington," he once said; he himself was just doing his job and would go wherever the crime or the criminals led him. Although Mardian had appointed him to this assignment, he said, Mardian left him alone.

No one can be certain whether Nissen's investigation was based on some preselected hit list or whether, once started, it simply took on a life of its own. In the early months of the investigation, the FBI conducted extensive inquiries into the possible complicity of Gelb, Halperin, Warnke and the Rand officials, and by early fall several of them were fearful that they might be indicted. But the investigation, which included multiple interviews with each of them, turned up nothing that could be used in a prosecution. Nissen too was looking for a conspiracy, but the trail eventually led not to former senior officials of Democratic administrations or (with the exception of Halperin) to people on Colson's list of enemies, but into the heartland of the intellectual Left.

In the year between the publication of the Papers and the beginning of Ellsberg's trial in Los Angeles, the speculation seemed to change by the week: they were investigating the transportation of stolen goods (the Papers) in interstate commerce; they were collecting evidence on two separate conspiracies; they were preparing to indict Sheehan; they were hinting that Ellsberg had not been the one to leak the papers at all, that someone else who had gotten a copy from him became impatient and beat Ellsberg to the punch; or they were simply fishing, hoping to catch or intimidate as many antiwar intellectuals as they could. ("I have often gone fishing," Nissen said at one time, "but never in a grand-jury room.") The government remained consistent in its belief that many of the leaks from the Pentagon centered around Halperin and Ellsberg, and Nissen would later try to suggest that the disclosure of the major conclusion of the 1968 Wheeler Report, which recommended 206,000 additional troops for Vietnam, was linked to Halperin and Ellsberg. Nissen inquired extensively into the connections between Ellsberg, Halperin and Sheehan, and he would later try to suggest that they had been conspiring ever since 1967.

Nissen's prime interest, however, was in the intellectual and political figures of the New Left. The list of persons called before the grand juries and the related objects of his interest could all be charted on a map of the prosecutorial imagination—Mardian's imagination, Vincent's imagination, Nissen's imagination—where each point of investigation was, in some way, linked to every other point and where Ellsberg could be represented as one of the centers of a network of intellectual Vietnam War resistance. There was nothing novel about the technique: it had been used on bootleggers, racketeers and Mafiosi. If one assumed that the release of the Pentagon Papers was in fact a crime (and, indeed, a very high crime, a crime of state), then most of the connections on the map were logical even if the witnesses and suspects were not themselves criminals.

Copies of the Papers were handled by literally dozens, if not hundreds, of people: by Ellsberg and Russo and Ellsberg's children; by Neil Sheehan and the editors and writers of the *Times;* by Ben H. Bagdikian and his colleagues at the *Washington Post;* by Senator Mike Gravel of Alaska, who tried, on the eve of the Supreme Court decision in the newspaper cases, to read the Papers into *The Congressional Record* and who subsequently (through an aide, Leonard Rodberg) arranged for their publication by Beacon Press in Boston; by the editors of other newspapers; and by the authors of a number of books written before the *Times* published its first installment. Ellsberg himself had quoted from the study in his speech to the American Political Science Association in 1970; Ralph Stavins and Richard Falk, scholars associated with the Institute for Policy Studies in Washington, had used copies of some of the same documents in preparing two volumes of a book called *Washington Plans an Aggressive War* of which they were among the co-authors; and David Kraslow and Stuart H. Loory had used material later collected in the diplomatic volumes in their book *The Secret Search for Peace in Vietnam*. (One of them had asked Ellsberg about the Papers before they were published, but he had refused to show them.) Even Lyndon Johnson, in *The Vantage Point,* and William Bundy, in researching a book on Vietnam, had drawn on the study. Bundy, Assistant Secretary of State under Johnson, had received one of the first copies of the Papers after they were typed and assembled, and David Young's suspicions would briefly be aroused. But the investigation of the case did not concern itself with people like Johnson and Bundy; it was limited by a definition of criminality whose bounds were, on one side, the politics of the suspect, on another, the hazy lines of legitimate declassification (Bundy and Johnson, though no longer in the government, had been given "official" access to the Papers) and, on a third, by proximity to Ellsberg himself. There were clear indications, moreover, that much of the material published in books and journal articles could have come from sources other than Ellsberg (fifteen "first-generation" copies had been made of the Papers, and no one knew how many people—in accordance with general government practice—had made additional copies of portions of the study for their own files); Gravel himself, while he publicly praised Russo and Ellsberg for divulging the Papers, had never acknowledged his source, nor had the newspapers, the scholars or any of the other people who drew on the documents without official access. Yet those who were, one way or another, to be placed on the government's map could all—again in the prosecutorial imagination (and perhaps with evidence)—

be connected to Ellsberg: Ellsberg and Rodberg and Gravel; Gravel and Rodberg and the editors and officials of Beacon Press; the Beacon Press and the Unitarian Universalist Association, which owned Beacon; Ellsberg and Stavins and Falk; Ellsberg, Russo, Lynda Sinay and Vu Van Thai; Ellsberg and Chomsky and Howard Zinn; Ellsberg and Neil Sheehan; Ellsberg and Jan Butler, the Top Secret Control officer at Rand; Ellsberg and Melvin Gurtov, who had also worked on the the Pentagon study, who had been one of the six signers of the Rand letter to the *Times* criticizing the war, and who, while still a Rand consultant, had praised Ellsberg's courage in releasing the Papers; Ellsberg and Samuel Popkin of Harvard, a Vietnam scholar, though hardly a dove, who had become a good friend; Ellsberg and David Halberstam, a former *Times* correspondent in Vietnam, who was then writing his book on the origins of the war, *The Best and the Brightest,* but who had apparently never seen the Papers before they appeared in the *Times.* By implication (and by later inferences from the government prosecutors) the map also included a major segment of the American press—the *Times,* the *Washington Post,* the *Boston Globe* and, among others, columnist Jack Anderson, who would, on the eve of the Ellsberg trial, publish material from the diplomatic volumes. It was a large map.

The FBI had begun calling on Ellsberg's friends and colleagues within days after the first *Times* installment appeared, but the scope of the investigation seemed to broaden according to the distance from the event. Ellsberg himself, in the weeks after publication, said he was trying to stay clear of his old associates in the government and at Rand for fear of embarrassing or implicating them—a number of them, especially those at Rand, were livid with anger and wouldn't have spoken to him anyhow—yet he had already left behind him a trail of vulnerability so wide and obvious that no agent could miss all of it. There were the fingerprints on the documents that he had copied at Rand; there were receipts for the Papers he had signed out; and there was a string of witnesses—many of them women (plus his own children)—who had, one way or another, become aware of his activities. With the exception of his quasi-military efficiency during the underground period in Cambridge, Ellsberg represented, perhaps necessarily, a poor conspirator. People had always called him a loner, which meant that he wasn't really part of any group, wasn't one of the boys, yet that very fact seemed to create a need to confide, to be loved, even to be seduced. The whole chain of claims about his conditions concerning the release of the documents—the *Times* had agreed to get his approval on the timing of publication, the *Post* was expected to defy an injunction—suggested not so much a man deceived as a person willing to be had. There was, moreover, the impulse that had made him divulge the Papers in the first place: the intellectual's imperative to publish and to talk and, in combination with it, hardly separable from it, the partly religious, partly parental imperative to tell truth. Truth telling had come from his father, Pat would say; he was not really a political man, Harry Ellsberg, but he was proud of Dan because he told truth.

Yet, despite the obvious trail, the investigators encountered trouble almost from the start. Amateurs, believers and ideologues can be more difficult than professionals; they are not people who try to cut their losses, and they do not make deals. A few peripheral people cooperated with the investigators: Carol provided her affidavit and would later testify before the grand jury because, she told her former husband, she was trying to protect the children (although eventually she would allow Robert to testify to the grand jury without any attempt to resist, or even to get him a lawyer); Rand and the Defense Department supplied the relevant records—receipts and manuals and employment files; and the Council on Foreign Relations, the ultimate organization of the Eastern establishment, which had invited Ellsberg to give an off-the-record seminar talk, responded to a government subpoena without protest and delivered the transcript of the seminar to the FBI. Meanwhile the government also assembled copies of hundreds of interviews, articles and speeches by and about Ellsberg and Russo, and it attempted to question scores of academics, reporters and others. But the journalists wouldn't talk, nor did most of the professors, nor did Rodberg or Gravel. Martin Nolan, the Washington Bureau chief of the *Globe,* asked his interrogators (according to a story by Trudy Rubin in the *Monitor*), "Wouldn't you guys rather be chasing drug pushers at the Mexican border?" The whole investigation, he told them, "was a political game led by the same people who sought injunctions against the newspapers and who'd just as soon put a padlock on the press." And an employee of the *Monitor* confounded his questioners further: When they asked him what the basic policy of the paper was, he replied, "To injure no man, but to bless all mankind." What kind of policy was that? they wanted to know.

The burden of the government's investigation fell on what had by then become its favorite vehicle, the grand jury—in this case two grand juries. In Boston one panel was set to work on the distribution and publication aspects of the case; in Los Angeles another was hearing testimony on the activities for which Ellsberg had already been indicted. In both the government attorneys attempted to employ the familiar tactics developed by Kennedy and refined under Mitchell and Mardian. People who refused to cooperate with federal investigators (and sometimes those who did) were summoned to testify, and if they refused on grounds of possible self-incrimination (in the McCarthy days it used to be called taking the Fifth) they were offered immunity from prosecution; if they still refused they could be jailed for contempt. The choice of the grand jury in such cases "seems almost inevitable," wrote Frank J. Donner and Eugene Ceruti in a study for the American Civil Liberties Union.

Although it served in the not too distant past as a curb on unjustified prosecutions, a "people's panel," it has been turned into an oppressive tool. And the process has been accelerated during this period of political stress, whereas during similar periods in the past its protective aspects were intensified. Most people know very little about the grand jury because it is enshrouded in secrecy. This secrecy was based originally on the need to protect the independence of the grand jury by insulating it from the pressures of the crown. Although this reason for secrecy no longer obtains, the government today insists on preserving the grand jury's secrecy—in part, certainly, because it effectively cloaks abuses by prosecutors. The secrecy surrounding grand juries has thus become an instrument of the very evil it was intended to prevent.

Secrecy invites overreaching . . . There are no limits on the number of witnesses that the prosecutor . . . may choose to call . . . A desperate or irresponsible prosecutor can wildly spray members of an entire group with subpoenas, many of whom may be wholly removed from the panel's basic concerns. He may do so out of pique, to show his power, to harass the witness, and in the knowledge that it will serve no legitimate purpose.

The broad scope of the prosecutor contrasts with the limited character of the witnesses' protections. The subpoenaed witness cannot even bring his counsel into the grand jury room, although he is subject to unrestrained cross-examination. He has no right to learn the subject of the investigation, or indeed whether he himself is a target of the inquiry.

The secrecy of the proceedings and the possibility of a jail sentence for contempt so intimidate the witness that he may be led into answering questions which pry into his personal life and associations and which, in the bargain, are frequently immaterial and vague. Alone and faced by either hostile or apathetic grand juries, the witness is frequently undone by the experience . . . The very body toward which he could once look for protection had become a weapon of the prosecution. When he seeks protective guidance from his lawyer he learns that the judicial broadening of due process which has occurred in the past two decades has largely ignored grand jury matters, precisely because it was assumed that the grand jury still functioned as a guardian of the rights of potential defendants.

The witness' traditional shield is the Fifth Amendment privilege against self-incrimination, but this too is no longer secure. A witness may answer some questions, either because on the surface they appear innocuous or because he feels he has nothing to hide. He then discovers that such cooperation has been his undoing: because he answered at the beginning, his self-incrimination privilege is considered waived with respect to later questions, which may well require him to name or implicate others. More important, the very ground on which the witness stands, the privilege itself, has become unsafe. The immunity provisions of the 1970 Organized Crime Control Act . . . permit the government to offer the witness limited "use" immunity. Thus the witness is sometimes faced with the Hobson's choice of a contempt sanction or an offer of "immunity" that denied him the full benefits of the Fifth Amendment privilege against self-incrimination.

The first recalcitrant witness to be summoned before a grand jury in the Ellsberg case—and perhaps the most interesting—was Russo himself. A graduate in engineering and a political scientist by profession, Russo had, as an employee of Rand, spent two years in Vietnam studying crop destruction and interviewing Vietcong prisoners for the Rand Viet Cong Morale and Motivation Project. In time, his own conversion had run ahead of Ellsberg's, yet in many substantial respects they were totally different kinds of people. Russo, who came from a middle-class family in Virginia, was barely thirty when he helped Ellsberg copy the Papers, and he tended to identify strongly with class issues and with the general outlook of the militant young. After his own career as a military intellectual came to an end, he started to do poverty and civil-rights work in California, and ultimately became affiliated with the Los Angeles County Probation Department. In the two years before the Papers were published he had also started to work his way through the counterculture, riding motorcycles, writing poetry, traveling around the country, and trying to orient himself to a new style of life. His friends said that in 1969 he had been close to a nervous breakdown;

he would be alternately elated and depressed, tended to be emotional and often hyperbolic in his rhetoric and seemed to believe that after he started probing too deeply on his morale project in Vietnam the military authorities there tried to have him assassinated. Although his own training was analytical— he had gone to Virginia Polytechnic Institute (in physics) and then to the Woodrow Wilson School at Princeton (in political science), he was, on the whole, more interested in ending the war than in studying it, more angry than fascinated, and more comfortable with the radical elements of the peace movement than was Ellsberg. At the same time, however, he had held only junior-level jobs with Rand and had played only a minor role in the Ellsberg affair. He had obviously been encouraging Ellsberg to disclose the Papers, though he was never really in a position to disclose very much himself. Later, when his name appeared in the newspapers, hardly anyone at Rand could remember him. It was the grand-jury episode that turned him into a major figure.

Ordered to appear on June 23, Russo was asked a number of questions about Ellsberg's activities (Ellsberg was still underground), declined on grounds of possible self-incrimination, was offered full immunity, and declined again. He would not testify in secret, he said. On July 2 a federal judge held him in contempt, and on August 16, having lost an appeal to the circuit court, he was ordered to jail. On that same day Ellsberg had come to Los Angeles for arraignment, and so they appeared on the steps of the federal courthouse together—arm in arm (as they would be seen on many occasions again), stylistically an unmatched pair, the man of the street and the man of the study, proclaiming their brotherhood. He would not, Russo told the reporters, collaborate in the "attempt to prosecute Daniel Ellsberg by testifying in secret before a grand jury. I would rather tell my story openly, free of the compulsion of grand-jury subpoenas and contempt citations and not as a tool of the prosecution." Two hours later he was in jail, and within twenty-four hours he would be in solitary—maximum security—with his wrists and ankles chained behind his back, "on my belly, tied in a neat little bow." He had protested too much during the booking process, complaining to a clerk who had taken away his reading glasses, and then angered the guards again by kicking the door of his cell. Later he was beaten up when he refused to let two guards take away a journal he had been keeping. "One of my toenails was half torn off, a bone bruised, and a bump was left on the back of my head. For this I was then hauled before the 'adjustment committee,' where I was charged with 'agitating and disrupting inmates.' "

That was the first round. The normal contempt sentence for refusing to testify before a grand jury is coterminous with the life of that grand jury; in this case the grand jury was due to expire early in September. Shortly before it was to go out of existence, however, the government prosecutors had its term extended, raising the possibility that Russo might remain in jail for as long as eighteen months. His lawyer argued that he should be released, that the extension of the grand jury was in part a punitive move against Russo, but the federal judge who heard the case rejected the argument. Shortly after that rejection, however, an unexpected and unprecedented decision was rendered in Russo's favor. "On October 1," Russo later wrote in an article for *Ramparts,* "I submitted a motion to the court, requesting a transcript of any grand jury testimony I should choose to make. Earlier in the summer I had suggested this to my attorney [then Joseph Ball of Los Angeles], but he hadn't thought it would work. So I got a new attorney [Michael Balaban], who felt differently and we made the motion. If the court would grant it, I would agree to testify because a copy of the transcript could be made public. It was equivalent to letting the public into the grand jury room as far as I was concerned." Whether, in fact, that was the whole story is still an open question; in Los Angeles there were strong rumors that the judge, Warren J. Ferguson, uncomfortable about Russo's indefinite sentence, had suggested the motion himself. (He had taken over as motions judge in federal court that very day; judges in most districts rotate that responsibility, usually on a monthly basis.) Whatever the story, Ferguson did grant the motion and ordered Russo released. Again Ellsberg happened to be in town, and again they appeared together on the courthouse steps. That night they would celebrate at Hugh Hefner's in Chicago.

Russo did not testify. Ferguson's ruling ordered him to appear before the grand jury on October 18, but by October 5 Nissen had informed Balaban that the government would "respectfully decline to furnish [Russo] a copy of the transcript . . . , on the ground that the order requiring such a transcript to be furnished him is unlawful and made without and beyond the authority of the Court." In a formal opinion a few weeks later, Ferguson, while acknowledging the novelty of the order, pointed out that this was "an unusual case" and that since grand-jury witnesses were already permitted to discuss their testimony in public, the provision of a transcript would do no more than insure accuracy. Yet clearly the ruling, if it were upheld by higher courts, would represent a major dent in the secrecy of grand-jury proceedings; it would eliminate suspicion about what a person did or did not say, and would allow him to square things with those who suspected that he had said more than he actually had. It could, of course, also permit the intimidation of witnesses in organized-crime investigations who feared reprisals from the people they testified about, and it could be used by unscrupulous witnesses to destroy the reputation of any person about whom they chose to testify. Nissen could have appealed the decision, but he (or the Justice Department) decided to let it stand. If they lost the appeal, the whole grand-jury system as they were now using it would be jeopardized.

Russo appeared on October 18, but did not even enter the grand-jury room. Nissen confronted him in the hall, and a stenographer for Russo's lawyer transcribed the dialogue:

NISSEN: Mr. Russo, I was talking to Mike [Balaban] about your appearance this morning. I told him, as I had

|  | notified him in writing, we are not going to be giving a copy of the transcript to you. |
|---|---|
| RUSSO: | That is in violation of the court order. |
| NISSEN: | What I want to know is—are you willing to enter the jury room and testify under these conditions? |
| RUSSO: | Before I answer that, would you tell me why you are violating the court order? |
| NISSEN: | I don't consider it to be a violation of a lawful court order. What I want to know is, will you now enter the grand jury room? . . . |
| RUSSO: | What? You say that is not unlawful? |
| NISSEN: | Let's leave that. We are really not going to furnish you a copy of the transcript. |
| RUSSO: | But that's a violation of the court order. |
| NISSEN: | We have told you what we are going to do. You talk to your counsel. |
| RUSSO: | I am trying to understand the process—the judicial process as opposed to the executive process and the legislative process. These constitute the law of the land. You are standing there telling me that you are going to be judge, jury—you are going to decide this? . . . Mr. Nissen, I am shocked. |
| NISSEN: | You are free to express your shock. I have told your counsel that the court order requiring the government to produce a copy of your transcript is an unlawful order . . . |
| RUSSO: | (seeing the foreman of the grand jury, Patricia Jones): Mrs. Jones, are you the forewoman of the grand jury? Do you represent the people? |
| NISSEN: | Mrs. Jones is not going to answer any questions. |
| RUSSO: | Wait a minute. Mrs. Jones can speak for herself. |
| NISSEN: | Don't answer him. |
| RUSSO: | Mrs. Jones, do you oversee—do you represent the public? |
| BALABAN: | Tony, we really can't go into that. She is not the protagonist in this particular issue. |
| RUSSO: | But she represents the people. |

BALABAN:    Well, that's the grand jury process.
RUSSO:      It is a rubber stamp process, Mr. Nixon—I mean, Mr. Nissen . . .

Nissen returned to Judge Ferguson's court to inform him that the government would not furnish Russo with a copy of the transcript. It was unprecedented, he said, and would endanger the whole process. "Our respectful opinion is that if the grand jury is compelled to disclose the nature of its proceedings to the very persons it is investigating, its investigation must necessarily fail." Ferguson, however, stuck to his position and, a month later, issued a written opinion reaffirming what he had already said from the bench. Russo, purged of his contempt, was never called. On December 29 he was charged with Ellsberg in the superseding indictment on which both of them were eventually tried. Since Russo had never testified before the grand jury, the courts rejected his claim of immunity.

Covering grand-jury proceedings is only a little more certain than covering the Kremlin, and often a great deal duller. Unless the government chooses to leak its list of witnesses or the witnesses themselves talk to the press (or unless they challenge their subpoenas and thus appear in open court), there is no certain way of knowing who was called or what questions were asked. In the case of the Pentagon Papers, as in others, it was always possible that a whole string of people known only to the grand jurors and to the government willingly cooperated. In Boston, it was rumored, the government had called a number of individuals—telephone operators, motel clerks and other representatives of the marginalia of criminal proceedings. What was certain, however, is that many, if not all, of the major figures on the government's original list of witnesses—the professors, journalists, and the aide to Senator Gravel, Leonard Rodberg—resisted their subpoenas and managed to keep the grand jury tied up for months. For while the government had been refining its techniques, the tactics of resistance had also become more sophisticated. Over a period of three or four years, civil-liberties lawyers, and especially the members of the National Lawyers' Guild, the anti-establishment bar association, had learned to take advantage of constitutional provisions and a number of Warren Court decisions to retard the government's criminal proceedings against political figures. Clearly the government still had most of the muscle (and, given the new Nixon appointees to the Supreme Court, could be expected to develop more), but recent decisions concerning evidence derived from wiretapping and electronic surveillance, journalistic privileges in regard to the protection of sources (subsequently all but abolished by the Burger Court), the ethnic composition of juries, and a number of other matters provided some basis for challenge. The very breadth of the Ellsberg–Pentagon Papers investigation, combined with the government's own ineptitude, created legal situations which touched a series of constitutional issues and therefore provided a variety of openings to resist the proceedings.

The original list of witnesses for the Boston grand jury— Rodberg, Chomsky, Stavins, Falk, Popkin and Halberstam among others—had probably been prepared as early as July 1971, and certainly no later than August. Most of them were academics, and academics were supposed to be patsies under this kind of pressure. Yet they managed, despite occasional spells of minor activity, to keep the Boston grand jury from functioning for nearly a year. The hearings were delayed almost at the very beginning when one grand-jury panel was dismissed and another assembled, assertedly because there had been leaks to the press, but even the new (and, perhaps, more cooperative) panel spent a good deal of its time waiting while motions judges and appeals courts ruled on what became a nearly endless series of challenges. Stavins, Chomsky and Falk charged that they had been subject to illegal wiretapping: Stavins provided an affidavit from a wire-tapping expert who had checked his telephone and discovered unaccountable electronic signals; Chomsky and Falk submitted affidavits that they had been in telephone contact with some of the defendants in the Harrisburg trial (a situation in which the government had already acknowledged wiretapping) and asked a federal judge to quash their subpoenas. The judge, W. Arthur Garrity, Jr., ruled that they had presented enough evidence to require the government to "affirm or deny" the allegation. He gave the Justice Department a week to reply. Two months later the prosecutors filed an affidavit signed by A. William Olson, Mardian's deputy and later to become his successor as head of the Internal Security Division, declaring that inquiries had been made and that no wiretap evidence had been found; if there had been such evidence it might have jeopardized the entire investigation and would certainly have produced a demand that it be turned over to the witness-subjects of the taps. Nonetheless the language of denial in the affidavit was so indefinite that Judge Anthony Julian, then sitting as motions judge, ruled it insufficient. (An identical affidavit had been filed in connection with the Harrisburg case—it had been proven false—and when similar denials were later made in other contexts, defense lawyers began calling them "Olson Affidavits" no matter who signed them.) The government did not respond further; Chomsky, Stavins and Falk were in the clear.

Rodberg, meanwhile, raised an entirely different issue. A physicist and a fellow of the Institute for Policy Studies, an anti-establishment "radical" think tank, and therefore another link in the prosecutorial chain between Ellsberg, Stavins and IPS, he had been appointed a special assistant to Gravel on the very day that the Senator from Alaska tried to place the Papers into *The Congressional Record,* on the eve of the Supreme Court decision in the newspaper cases. Gravel, outmaneuvered by craftier parliamentarians when he attempted to read the Papers on the floor of the Senate, had hastily called a meeting of the Senate Committee on Buildings and Grounds, of which he was chairman, hoping to put them into the public domain by reading them into the committee record. He was outmaneuvered again when the Senate refused to print the transcript of the proceedings. Nonetheless the all-night session of the committee, with Gravel the only member present, gave him an opportunity to show, as he later said, that at least one member of the Senate was willing to incur some risk in the cause of informing the American public. Since Rodberg subsequently arranged for the publication of the Papers by Beacon Press—he had failed in his attempt to arrange publication by Simon and Schuster, MIT Press and Harvard University Press—and since he clearly knew a great deal about how Gravel had received the Papers in the first place, he would be an obvious witness.

Rodberg claimed congressional immunity under a constitutional provision that members of Congress "for any Speech or Debate in either House . . . shall not be questioned in any other place." That clause, like so much else in the Constitution, came from the framers' suspicion of royal or executive power: no member of the legislature should be held legally or criminally accountable to king or President for what he had said or done in connection with his legislative duties. Supported by Gravel, Rodberg argued that the constitutional protection necessarily covered not only members of Congress themselves but their staffs as well. In a separate action, Gravel also contended that since the grand jury was looking into his activities—even though he himself might not be questioned—its entire line of investigation was unconstitutional and should be stopped. The government replied that congressional immunity extended only to legitimate legislative activities and that, in any case, Gravel should "fulfill his own duty as a citizen to assist the executive branch in its own constitutional obligation to enforce the laws of the United States . . . Should questioning prove self-incriminating, the Senator would retain his own Fifth Amendment privilege in this regard."

Ultimately Rodberg and Gravel lost: in a decision rendered in June of 1972, the Supreme Court, by a five-to-four majority, upheld the government. The heart of the speech or debate clause, said Justice White for the Court, "is speech or debate, in either House, and insofar as the clause is construed to reach other matters, they must be an integral part of the deliberative and communicative process by which members participate in committee and house proceedings." Presumably the Pentagon Papers were not an "integral part" of the proceedings of the Senate Committee on Buildings and Grounds. Before that decision was rendered, however, the lower courts found sufficient ground in the Rodberg-Gravel arguments to issue orders barring grand-jury testimony on Gravel's conduct at subcommittee meetings, blocking questions about Rodberg and other members of the Gravel staff, and quashing Rodberg's subpoenas. The Supreme Court's decision restored the possibility that Rodberg might be called again and the investigation be resumed, but by the time it was handed down, Nissen, Reese and Barry were so deeply involved in other matters that the grand jury remained dormant.

The third line of attack against the grand jury in Boston arose from the decision in *United States v. Caldwell,* a case in which the U. S. Court of Appeals for the Ninth Circuit (which covers the West Coast and Hawaii) had ruled that a reporter was entitled to protect his sources by refusing to divulge them in judicial proceedings. Although *Caldwell* would be reversed by the Supreme Court on the same day that the Court ruled on Rodberg and Gravel, it was used by at least one journalist (Halberstam) to quash a Boston subpoena, was offered as an argument by a number of academics (who said that they, like journalists, had sources to protect), and probably prevented the government from calling any number of other reporters and editors—and possibly from issuing subpoenas ordering the newspapers to deliver documents related to the case, among them copies of the manuscript (Xerox) copies of the Papers themselves. Again the Supreme Court decision helped to restore the government's power to resume grand-jury activities on a wide scale; but again the witnesses had confounded the proceedings.

What had begun as a single act in a distinct arena had

turned into a cluster of sideshows where no one was able to keep track of all the proceedings or even to know what the proceedings were. While Chomsky, Stavins, Falk, Rodberg, Halberstam and Gravel were pursuing their appeals, the government issued subpoenas for the bank records of the Unitarian Universalist Association and Beacon Press, presumably to learn how much Beacon had paid Rodberg or others for the Papers; it subpoenaed Popkin to testify even though he knew nothing about the distribution of the Papers before they were published (Popkin had been subjected to FBI questions about Ellsberg's "stability"), it called Idella Marx, Patricia's stepmother, who had been in Cambridge while Ellsberg was in hiding and who was believed to know something about the distribution of the documents to the press, and threatened her with contempt charges when she refused to testify (despite which she continued to insist that J. Edgar Hoover was a wonderful man doing a good job); it issued a summons at seven-thirty one morning ordering Robert Ellsberg, then fifteen, to appear before the Los Angeles grand jury two hours later; it sent agents around Cambridge with photos of Neil and Susan Sheehan to ask people whether and where they had seen them; it took advantage of a poorly worded judicial order in Los Angeles to seize and inspect belongings Ellsberg had stored at a Bekins Company Warehouse (among them back copies of *Foreign Affairs* and Ellsberg's old marine uniform), even though it was the court's understanding —and that of Ellsberg's angry lawyers—that no such search would be carried out until further arguments were heard; and it slowly began to assemble the information to support a new indictment.

In the context of other grand-jury proceedings (at one time there were at least a dozen simultaneous Mardian-inspired investigations of left-wing activists) one could not be certain at the time whether those that related to Ellsberg were simply designed to gather information about the leak and distribution of the Papers or whether they were also part of a pattern of political intimidation—whether the government was looking for criminals or trying to find a crime. The judgment would have to come later. What was clear was that the disorder that Ellsberg had created (or which, in any case, he symbolized) had produced a contagious round of subsequent disorders. Ellsberg's act demonstrated that both the classification system and the legal structure on which it was supposedly based could survive only as long as there was general confidence in their legitimacy and in the good faith of the government. If either the legal system or the administrative practices relating to classification were to depend entirely on literal interpretations of the law, or if classification became malignant, neither would be able to function. Classification, like law-and-order, required self-restraint and a concommitant belief that both were being applied to achieve legitimate ends. Now both had started breaking down. Clearly Ellsberg had violated some sort of trust: he had revealed documents to which he had obtained access with promises not to reveal. Just as clearly the government had violated an implicit trust not to abuse its power—however justified—to maintain secrets. Yet neither Ellsberg's act nor the government's practice was specifically covered by law. The Congress, dependent as it was on leaks, had steadfastly refused to pass an official-secrets act on the British model. There existed statutory prohibitions against divulging atomic secrets, certain kinds of military information, and cryptographic material, and there were specific sanctions against divulging information with the intent of injuring the United States or aiding a foreign power, but the entire process of classification —a process that had, by the government's own admission, grown malignant—was based largely on Executive Order 10501, and not on statutory provisions. It operated outside the law, and its enforcement depended primarily on administrative sanctions and on the ability of bureaucrats to create the largely unfounded impression among those with clearances that if they divulged information they would be subject to prosecution. There was in fact no law covering classification, no law covering declassification, and no law to punish those who violated the procedures. Most people involved in the security system did not know that; Ellsberg did not know it when he copied the Papers; quite possibly the government didn't know it when it indicted him.

If Ellsberg had broken the law, then so had thousands of others who were not indicted; if he had not broken the law, then neither had Chomsky or Falk or Rodberg or the *New York Times*. The government's attempts to stop the newspapers from publishing, the wiretapping, the burglaries, the grand-jury investigations, indeed the entire line of government response, represented a search for something coercive to replace the good faith and general confidence on which the security system and the general commitment to law had once been based. Ellsberg's act called attention to the breakdown of that system—its abuse by the government and by those within it who were trying to serve their own ends—but it did not in itself suggest an alternative. Could one man ever possess the authority to declassify on his own initiative, and, if he did, what were its limits? How could anything be enforced if a sizable minority of the population no longer trusted the enforcers or believed in the objectives of the enforcement? It was hardly surprising, therefore, that the issues arising from the case would tax the legal system with questions it was never designed to answer. The Constitution never anticipated a government which marked millions of documents "Top Secret"; the Espionage Act did not contemplate the leak of political information to the newspapers, the grand jury was not meant to investigate this sort of "crime," and the entire structure had not been expected to bear the burden of wide and fashionable contempt for those who ruled.

In the end, however, it was the government which won—at least on principle, if not in specific cases. Eighteen months after the publication of the Papers, the Boston grand jury, which had still not heard testimony from many of the witnesses called before it, was discharged. And yet the constitutional protections which the recalcitrant witnesses had invoked had been narrowed considerably, especially by the

*Caldwell* and *Gravel* decisions. Neither journalists nor scholars (nor anyone else), said the Supreme Court, enjoyed any
special immunity; reporters could be called to testify and to
divulge their sources; congressional immunity extended only
to legislative business and not to incidental acts by members
of Congress which happened to take place in the confines of
congressional committees. Theoretically, therefore, Halberstam, Sheehan or, indeed, the entire staff of the *Times* could
have been called to testify. One of the scholars, Sam Popkin,
was ordered to appear, refused, and spent a week in prison
before the grand jury was dismissed. (The president of Harvard, Derek Bok, himself a former law school professor,
appeared unsuccessfully on Popkin's behalf.) That the government chose not to pursue the investigation with the additional armory of the *Caldwell* and *Gravel* decisions appeared,
on the whole, to stem less from specific legal limitations than
from Nissen's preoccupation with the case in Los Angeles,
and possibly from the government's reluctance to engage in
an open battle with the academic establishment. Dozens of
reporters were threatened with jail sentences in the months
following the *Caldwell* ruling for refusing to disclose their
sources, and one of them, William Farr of the *Los Angeles
Times,* spent seven weeks in a prison not half a mile from
the courtroom where Ellsberg and Russo were being tried.
The principle was established; next time the grand jury would
have fewer problems. Even more significant, however, was
the fact that between the time the Boston grand jury was
dismissed and the time of the Watergate eruption the entire
national climate had changed; somehow the accumulation of
political and legal developments of the preceding eighteen
months—in Vietnam, in the courts, and in the 1972 election
—made any single confrontation and decision seem relatively
minor.

v

On December 29, 1971, six months after Ellsberg was first
indicted, the grand jury in Los Angeles returned a supersed-

ing indictment charging Ellsberg and Russo with fifteen counts of conspiracy, conversion of government property (theft) and espionage.* Named as co-conspirators, but not indicted, were Lynda Sinay and Vu Van Thai, the former Vietnamese official whose fingerprints were on several pages of the copied documents. Thai, who had been abroad since he fell out with the Saigon government—he was in Paris at the time of the indictment—was hardly a major figure in the case, but he added an exotic quality to the charges, perhaps a touch of Oriental intrigue for the titillation of the jurors; during the trial Nissen would often refer to him as "the Oriental gentleman." Sinay, who was still living in Los Angeles and would later be described by the prosecution as "Russo's girl friend," might help suggest that, in addition to pilfering government secrets, the conspirators were prone toward sexually promiscuous behavior and therefore should not be credited with the saintly purposes which they invoked to explain their deed.

There was, nonetheless, something anticlimactic about the charges. Like those in the first indictment, they covered only the period in 1969–70 when the papers were copied; they did not involve the newspapers or the other major figures still under investigation, and thus seemed to reinforce the suspicion that the government was still finding it difficult to decide what crime, if any, had actually been committed. They also seemed to indicate a reluctance, at least for the moment, to take on the *Times* in a criminal case. (In Washington there were rumors that the Justice Department had made a gentleman's agreement with the paper: if the *Times* would play down the story after the Supreme Court decision there would be no prosecution. The rumor was denied all around, yet in fact the *Times* published only three installments after June 30, and a vast amount of material from the Papers did not appear until the Beacon-Gravel edition and the government's own subsequently declassified version

---

* For the text of the indictment, see Appendix B.

were issued.) The indictment involved only the eighteen volumes that Ellsberg had taken from Washington to Santa Monica, one other volume, the so-called Gurtov study on the Geneva Conference of 1954, which had been completed in Santa Monica in the summer of 1969 (and was probably the most innocuous part of the entire project from a military standpoint), and the Wheeler Report on the Tet offensive, which was not part of the Pentagon Papers at all. The eighteen volumes were presumably selected by the government because Ellsberg, in the view of the prosecution, had kept them in his personal control for more than a year, the Wheeler memorandum because it was regarded as the most portentous document cited in the indictment (a document written by the senior military officer of the United States for the President and the Secretary of Defense). It was difficult to explain why the Gurtov study was included at all. The common denominator for all of the twenty volumes was the fact that the FBI had found latent fingerprints belonging to at least two of the alleged conspirators on each of them.

Most significantly, the charges marked the formal end of the government's attempt to indict Gelb, Warnke and Halperin, and therefore to make a political case against the Democrats. Ellsberg later came to believe that the government was putting pressure on the judge to start the trial early in 1972 and thus to derive some political advantage before the election, but with the former Pentagon officials out of the indictment the possibilities for such a case had substantially diminished. The way the indictment was drawn, Ellsberg could be prosecuted only by demonstrating that he had violated the Rand regulations and his understanding with the three ex-officials. It was therefore a relatively limited case, focused legally and politically on the issues of classification, secrecy and free speech with which it was already associated. If there were any spies or traitors, they would include only Ellsberg and the relatively obscure individuals named in the indictment.

The new charges did, however, add the element of conspiracy, a popular item in the prosecutor's arsenal, in this case conspiracy "to defraud the United States . . . by impairing, obstructing, and defeating its lawful governmental function of controlling the dissemination of classified government studies, reports, memoranda and communications . . ." They also involved novel uses of the Espionage Act, and therefore unprecedented interpretations of its provisions, and they left ambiguous the question of whether Ellsberg and Russo had stolen tangible property (i.e., "documents") or whether the conversion involved something intangible ("information"). What the charges did, in effect, was take the confused strands of law and practice associated with the security system and tie them into a knot; they institutionalized disorder and thrust it into the hands of a judge and a jury: Criminal Case 9373 for the Central District of California, *United States of America v. Anthony Joseph Russo, Jr. [and] Daniel Ellsberg*. Since the separate strands seemed to involve the very essence of the relationship between press and government—including the potential power of censorship—the implications appeared enormous.

The core of the indictment, and hypothetically the most difficult element for the defense, was the conspiracy charge. Of the fifteen counts, it was the only one which linked the two defendants; more important, it would give the prosecution opportunities to present evidence and arguments inadmissible under the rules governing trials for specific, substantive crimes. Jessica Mitford, who covered the prosecution of Benjamin Spock and his fellow "conspirators" against the draft laws, once wrote that even though the law of conspiracy had been explained to her in considerable detail, and though she followed the explanation, she always had trouble remembering it: "The law is so irrational, the implications so far removed from ordinary human experience and modes of thought, that . . . it escapes just beyond the boundaries of the mind. One can dimly understand it while an expert is explaining it, but minutes later it is not easy to tell it back." Conspiracy had long been a prosecutor's favorite: for a century and a half it was used in the United States against political radicals, labor organizers, and opponents of government policy who could not be charged with specific offenses, and it was therefore a trademark of political trials. Conspiracy does not require a criminal act—all the means to carry out the conspiracy can be absolutely innocent; it requires only "intent" to carry out such an act and therefore can legitimately deal with the defendants' state of mind; the conspirators, moreover, do not have to be acquainted with all their fellow conspirators, or even to know of their existence, yet the acts and statements of every conspirator can be used against all the others.

More than any other important crime [wrote Abraham S. Goldstein in *The Yale Law Journal*] conspiracy impinges on the act requirement. It does so in ways significantly different from the other inchoate crimes. The law of attempts, for example, searches for the point at which criminal intent has proceeded beyond "preparatory" action and has reached "the commencement of the consummation" of the crime. The law of solicitations may substitute for this careful plotting of the line between intent and act, a context which indicates the probability that aggressive statement will be transformed into harmful action. In contrast, conspiracy doctrine comes closest to making a state of mind the occasion for preventive action against those who threaten society but who have come nowhere near carrying out the threat. No effort is made to find the point at which criminal intent is transformed into the beginnings of action dangerous to the community. Instead the mystique of numbers, of combination, becomes the measure of danger. Even when a statute requires an overt act "to effect the object of the conspiracy," as in federal law, it may be a completely innocent one which indicates little or nothing of the kind of injury to society which the conspiracy seeks to bring about. The agreement to accomplish the prohibited purposes furnishes, without anything more, the basis for criminal liability.

The statute under which Ellsberg and Russo were charged, Conspiracy to Defraud the United States (Title 18 of the U. S. Code, Section 371),* compounded the vagueness of conspiracy doctrine with the equally vague concept of "defraud the United States" and then, in Nissen's indictment, compounded them even further with the imputation of a "lawful governmental function of controlling the dissemination of classified Government studies, reports, memoranda and communications." There was, under federal law, no substantive crime called "defrauding the United States," nor was there any statute which specifically authorized the government to control the dissemination of classified government studies. The indictment therefore charged Ellsberg and Russo with intent to defraud the government by impeding a function that it could possess only by inference. Yet the government clearly had certain precedents on its side, most particularly *Haas v. Henckel,* a case in which the Supreme Court (in 1910) upheld the conviction of an Agriculture Department statistician who had disclosed confidential information to a co-conspirator for use in speculating in grain futures.

> The statute [said the Court] is broad enough in its terms to include any conspiracy for the purpose of impairing, obstructing or defeating the lawful function of any department of Government . . . Any conspiracy which is calculated to obstruct [the Department's] . . . efficiency and destroy the value of its operations and reports as fair, impartial and reasonably accurate, would be to defraud the United States by depriving it of its lawful right and duty of promulgating or diffusing the information so officially acquired in the way and at the time required by law or departmental regulations.

The *Haas* decision suggested that anything the government did was, in fact, a lawful governmental function. "To the

---

* See Appendix A.

extent that 'unlawful' conduct had been assimilated to the
civil law of fraud," said Goldstein, "it had come to embrace
both legal and equitable conceptions. In addition, regulations
and customs as well as statutes furnished standards of duty
and obligation. Perhaps the outstanding characteristic of the
phrase 'defraud the United States' after *Haas v. Henckel* was
that no matter how specifically one sought to define it, it was
necessary to leave the definition as open-ended as the functions of government in an expanding society." The decision
was later limited by the requirement (elaborated by Chief
Justice William Howard Taft in *Hammerschmidt v. United
States,* a World War I draft case) that "defraud" required
"deceit, craft, or trickery, or at least . . . means that are dishonest." But since Ellsberg and Russo had both signed statements in which they agreed to keep classified material
confidential, that limitation might not help them very much.
Violation of security regulations might itself be construed as
"deceit, craft, or trickery."

There were other problems. Conspiracy cases permitted
prosecutors to introduce evidence and pursue lines of argument that would be ruled out of other trials; they created an
aura of plausibility for the jurors from the mere fact that the
defendants are seen sitting together in court; and they tended
to create friction among the defendants (and among their
lawyers), since each could be impeached with the statements
of the others.

> When the trial starts, the accused feels the full impact of the
> conspiracy strategy [wrote the late Justice Robert Jackson].
> Strictly, the prosecution should first establish *prima facie* the
> conspiracy and identify the conspirators, after which evidence
> of acts and declarations of each in the course of its execution
> are admissible against all. But the order of proof of so sprawl-
> ing a charge is difficult for a judge to control. As a practical
> matter, the accused is often confronted with a hodgepodge of
> acts and statements by others which he may never have au-
> thorized or intended or even known about, but which help to

persuade the jury of the existence of the conspiracy itself. In other words, a conspiracy often is proved by evidence that is admissible only upon assumption that conspiracy existed. The naïve assumption that prejudicial effects can be overcome by instructions to the jury . . . all lawyers know to be unmitigated fiction.

In Case 9373, the government would therefore be able to use all the statements and acts of Russo and Ellsberg (and, indeed, of Vu Van Thai and Lynda Sinay) and attribute them to the defendants collectively.

By itself, however, the conspiracy charge, despite its breadth and imprecision, also represented an opportunity: what the government could do under the rules, the defendants could do also. They would be able to answer the prosecution's efforts to establish criminal intent with their own version of what they had in mind—might introduce testimony to impeach the classification system, might argue that there was no "lawful governmental function" in regard to classification, and might try to impress the jurors with the idea that they had merely copied information that rightfully belonged to the American public in the first place. What compounded the problem for the defense was the possibility that the jurors, feeling that the government was unable to prove its case on espionage and conversion, would convict on conspiracy simply because the defendants had violated the rules, broken some sort of trust. Since there was, at the time of the indictment, considerable doubt that the Espionage Act applied at all—it seemed to require intent to injure the United States (or aid a foreign power), or documents that could be so used—and since conversion might be hard to prove (the government, after all, still had use and possession of the copied documents), conviction on conspiracy might suggest itself as compromise. Conversely, the presence of the conspiracy count in the indictment also increased the chances of conviction on one of the other counts. Conspiracy had a nasty ring to it, but conversion—in essence appropriating

government property for personal use—fulfilled the requirements of a relatively minor crime for jurors who could be
persuaded that although the defendants had good intentions,
they had nonetheless broken the rules, if not the law. (In
Harrisburg, the defendants were acquitted on the conspiracy
charge, but two of them were convicted on the minor count
relating to the smuggling of letters in and out of prison.)
The conspiracy charge therefore raised the stakes on the
entire indictment, made the evidence hard to control, and
vastly enlarged the jury's options. In Los Angeles, where the
trial was to be held, there was no telling what a jury would
do. Under the law, conviction on all counts could mean
thirty-five years in prison for Russo, 115 for Ellsberg. More
important, a conviction on any count, if it were sustained by
higher courts, would give the whole security system the force
of law, enable the government to control any information by
stamping it "Secret" and, through the threat of prosecution,
reestablish the fragile order that Ellsberg had broken. The
indictment therefore seemed to affect the relationship between press and government far more substantially than all
the speeches of Spiro Agnew, all the subpoenas, and all the
threats of investigation.

# FOUR

# The Trial Before the Trial

THE defense complained bitterly about Los Angeles. The lawyers and the volunteers who came to work for the Pentagon Papers Defense Fund were certain that the government's decision to indict in Los Angeles was, more than anything, a device to secure a trial site that offered the best chances of conviction and would create the greatest hardship for the defendants. Nearly all of the witnesses would have to be flown out from the East; most of the attorneys and one of the defendants lived in the East, and the majority of the judges who were considered sympathetic in political cases occupied benches in New York and Washington. Southern California was the heartland of the military-industrial complex, a section of the country beholden to government contracts and defense employment, and the home of thousands of retired military officers. After a time, moreover (though none of them could be aware of it at the beginning), the place would also take its toll in more subtle ways, straining personal relationships between husbands in California and families in Boston or New York or Washington, enforcing

an artificial closeness as protection against the impersonality
and anonymity of the land of the rootless. People were
thrown together in incestuous tensions which exacerbated the
ordinary frictions of a case involving two very different defendants, more than a dozen attorneys and scores of consultants, volunteers, friends, groupies and assorted hangers-on.
They would live on an island of common concern and private
conflict separated from the rest of the world by miles of freeway and acres of parking lots. Sometimes their quarrels
would appear in the press or erupt in the corridors of the
courthouse, though for the most part they remained within
the confines of the offices they occupied in the rundown
building in downtown Los Angeles—fights between the so-
called Russo faction and the Ellsberg faction, fights about
the handling of the press, fights about housing, fights about
office responsibilities and, most emphatically, fights about
politics and strategy. The madness of Los Angeles could be
contagious.

Yet Los Angeles was altogether appropriate. This was the
home of the paranoid strain in American politics, the place
where fear of conspiracy grew as thick as orange trees, and
where reactionary ideology, CIA sabotage and political opportunism had fused to produce the Watergate style. It was
the home ground of Richard Nixon, Herbert Kalmbach, H.
R. Haldeman and Robert Mardian, and the place where,
during the campaign for governor in 1962, Nixon and his
future White House cronies had mailed out phony postcards
to a half-million Democrats urging them to vote for Nixon.
It was also, of course, the place where the Papers had been
copied—the scene of Ellsberg's alleged crime—and where
belief in the war received so much of its technological and
intellectual armament. Eventually all those things would mix
and turn full circle, conspiracies within conspiracies, Watergate, the Pentagon Papers, the felonies of Hunt and Liddy,
phony cables attributed to John Kennedy about the overthrow of Diem in Saigon, genuine cables from Henry Cabot
Lodge, the American ambassador, about his role in the coup,

Ellsberg taking files from Rand, Hunt and Liddy breaking into Ellsberg's psychiatrist's office to copy his file for someone in Washington. Each time the defendants' separate political agenda threatened to drive a wedge between them, the perfidy of the government would bring them together again; each time the trial was about to sink into a fog of meaningless words, the government would do something to remind us all who the real enemy was.

Hunt and Liddy traveled the low road; Rand was lofty and academic. Located a block from the ocean in Santa Monica, Rand had, as much as any American institution, turned war, coercion and sabotage into scholarship; it had contributed deeply to Vietnam, to the creation of the Pentagon Papers, to the belief that the resolution of impending failure or stalemate was still more information and more scholarship, and to an absolute severance of moral consideration from policy. Outside were the palm trees, the beach, the Pacific; inside were mathematical formulations for torture, and private safes stuffed with authenticated records of crop destruction and defoliation. From the perspective of Rand, Vietnam might have been an experiment in conflict resolution and crisis management for the benefit of classified scholarship in social science. Ellsberg's last major project for Rand, something on which he worked for nearly a year, was a study on "lessons from Vietnam."

His mind had never really left Rand. Vietnam had become monstrous not because information, however sophisticated, might always remain inadequate, because data by itself would always remain a trap, but because the wrong people controlled it, and he seemed incapable of understanding that his own sense of the horror of war could be told only in terms that went beyond statistics and analysis. He was another of the true believers, a cultist of information, another Midwestern transplant pursuing the golden dream and clinging to ultimates. He shuddered at the thought of being tried by a jury of his academic peers; they were the most likely to believe that he had betrayed them, an assessment that certainly applied to many of his former colleagues at Rand; he would rather be tried by the man in the street, who, in Ellsberg's estimation, had been the victim of the lies. During the course of the trial, Ellsberg would develop (or discover) a sort of neo-Marxist, neo-populist analysis of American policy and would see nearly everyone as a victim of the manipulation of what he belatedly came to call the establishment. In Los Angeles the risk was that the man in the street might also be a true believer, a man who, like the old Ellsberg, believed in secrets and in the importance of maintaining them, even a man who might believe that in the final analysis it wasn't the military which was guilty of failure in Vietnam, but the intellectuals who had studied and planned the policies. He might even agree with Ellsberg's idea that if there were any war criminals he, Ellsberg, was among them. Yet if the war was to be judged, if it was to be put on trial (as the defendants so fervently hoped), then there could be no more convincing test than Southern California.

It was inevitable that the legal confusion which led to the government's indictment of Russo and Ellsberg would follow the case into the courtroom. The charges in the indictment had resolved nothing; they were loaded with unresolved political and judicial questions—questions of statutory interpretation, constitutional precedent and applicable courtroom procedure. What was the meaning of the phrase "document . . . relating to the national defense" in the language of the Espionage Act? Was there a "lawful governmental function of controlling the dissemination of classified government studies" as charged in the indictment, and, if so, what were its limits? What property rights, if any, does the government have in information—the government is not allowed to hold copyrights as an author or a publisher— and therefore of what property had it been deprived? What were the legal foundations of the classification system, which was based on an executive order and not on statute, and what was the relationship between something stamped "Top

Secret" and the Espionage Law, which said nothing about classified documents? The crime in this case, if there was a crime at all, fell into a set of legal and constitutional fissures between words and phrases which had not contemplated an act such as theirs. Leonard B. Boudin, Ellsberg's chief counsel, was fond of the word "unprecedented"—later he would call it the most complicated case on which he had ever worked (certainly it was the most trying physically)— and in this instance "unprecedented" was appropriate. There had never been anything like it.

The central issues, complicated enough, were further complicated by the setting, and by the personalities involved. The case fell into a gray area between, on the one hand, the realms of high constitutional principle, portentous matters of state and great issues of free speech and, on the other, a wonderland of allegorical figures, hypothetical acts, spies and abstractions. Each stage of the proceedings became tangled in side issues: challenges to the jury-selection procedure, arguments about wiretapping (including the bugging of the corridors of the courthouse), appeals to higher courts, and, among other things, a controversy about whether the wife of one of the defendants would be allowed to sell health food sandwiches in the corridors of the allegedly bugged courthouse. Hollywood would become part of it, raising money for the defense (and, more significantly, congratulating itself for one of the swellest Beverly Hills parties of the season), converting freedom into show biz—John and Yoko, Ringo Starr, Barbra Streisand, Hugh Hefner—and then reconverting entertainment into cash for a perennially depleted defense fund that spent an average of seventy thousand dollars a month for more than a year. They would all perform: Ellsberg and Russo conducting press conferences on the steps of the courthouse, Russo smart-assing the prosecutor, Ellsberg reading data about the latest bombing figures in Vietnam, commenting on truce rumors, escalations, negotiations, Dan and Pat forever arm in arm before the cameras, Pat looking swoon-eyed at Dan while he was saying things she had heard a dozen times before, Dan forever certain about what everything meant—the trial and the war, rulings in Los Angeles, decisions in Washington.

What it would all conceal were profound changes in American mood and political behavior: first, the desire to forget the war and everything connected with it; beyond that, some deeper apathy about the issues that the events in Los Angeles were supposed to symbolize; finally, the corruption of the order and processes of the trial. The high constitutional matters seemed less important in the final stages of the trial than they had been at the start. The war front of executive power had moved beyond the issues of the trial and had corrupted their resolution, and the great faith in information—the justification for Ellsberg's act—threatened to turn to agnosticism and doubt. People knew about the Pentagon Papers, the bombing, wiretaps and government intimidation before the election of 1972, yet they had re-elected Nixon and celebrated the return of their prisoners of war. The Papers were only the history of a time long forgotten, the record of acts unrelated to domestic life, and the trial was a drama that belonged to another age, like a school pageant about Washington crossing the Delaware or Patrick Henry declaring "Give me liberty or give me death." It would, until the final revelations about Watergate, be mostly performance. Its significance, therefore, lay at least as much in what it revealed about where we had been as in where we were now. It would indicate a great deal about how the government regarded secrecy and used it—not necessarily the essence of power, but certainly the privilege and justification of power—and it suggested, almost to the end, that the government would continue to use that power in the same way no matter how this trial came out, and no matter how much information was available to its citizens.

II

William Matthew Byrne, Jr., had been on the federal bench barely three weeks when the *Times* began publishing the Pentagon Papers and not much more than a month when the first indictment was thrown on his calendar. The son of another Los Angeles federal judge—old Bill Byrne, a railroad worker in his youth, was a self-made man who had worked his way through law school—Matt Byrne had been executive director of the Scranton Commission on Campus Unrest, had served as the U. S. attorney in Los Angeles, where he had been David Nissen's boss, and was now regarded as a bright, personable and politically ambitious lawyer whose aspirations extended considerably beyond the United States district court over which he presided. It was difficult not to like Matt Byrne; he had something about him of the movieland hero playing the role of good-guy politician: ruddy, blond, with the hair just over the collar and with just a touch of the overgrown surfer, but with more than just the customary California veneer of alertness passing for intelligence. When Byrne was first chosen, in the normal draw of cases, to preside in this trial, Daniel Ellsberg went around New York telling friends that he had gotten a "good judge," maybe even a liberal. This would not be a Julius Hoffman trying the Chicago Seven or a Dixon Herman presiding in Harrisburg, not a hangman or an old backcountry curmudgeon. Byrne himself seemed to understand that the Vietnam War had been a major source of student alienation. "There would certainly be a reduction of the tensions that exist on the campuses today," he had written, "if the war were ended." More important, he recognized a certain legitimacy in protest, knew something about what had happened to American society in the sixties, and had read the literature of alienation and social division.

There was, nonetheless, something elusive about him. Politically and socially he was well connected—more connected than committed, it turned out. His professional friends included both Ramsey Clark and Richard Kleindienst, whose reputations as Attorneys General of the United States were symbols of very different attitudes about law enforcement. Although he was a Democrat, Byrne was, even in 1971, held in such high esteem by the Nixon Administration that he was on a list of those being considered to succeed J. Edgar Hoover as director of the FBI. (On his visits to Los Angeles, Kleindienst would usually get together with Byrne; both men insisted, however, that the meetings were discontinued after the Ellsberg case went to trial.) A forty-two-year-old bachelor, regarded in Los Angeles as a man-about-town who, in the words of a Hollywood columnist, went for "on people," he was also a Catholic who had been educated in Jesuit elementary and secondary schools (and then at the University of Southern California, where much of the region's professional mobility begins), a judicial conservative, an extraordinarily diligent worker, and a man who would do nearly anything, for reasons of judicial philosophy, to preserve a case for the jury. In the Ellsberg case there would be numerous questions which had no legal precedent: the judge would define the issues, determine how the jury was selected, instruct it at the end of the case, and rule on the materiality of evidence in dozens of situations which had never before arisen in an American courtroom. Many of the issues were legal and constitutional, but many more fell into a hazy area, again to be determined by the judge, between "legal" and "factual." It would have been a good opportunity to forge new law, to cut through a thicket of unresolved questions, even to throw out much of the indictment altogether on the ground that the laws, as applied, were overbroad and unconstitutional. But Matt Byrne was no more likely to do it than any other trial judge. He would do all he could to preserve the thicket, to pass the unresolved questions to the jury and to higher courts. He was a curious mixture of parish priest and amiable politician: part Irish Catholic, part California beach boy—a man devoted to the orderly management of his courtroom, a father in his own church, genial, personable, tolerant, courteous, who yet appeared incapable of making hard decisions. His best friends said that what he wanted most was to be loved.

David R. Nissen attempted to portray the case as simple

and straightforward: the only issue was whether the defendants were guilty of the acts charged in the indictment. It did not concern itself, Nissen said, with "United States military involvement in the defense of Vietnam," with the publication of the Pentagon Papers in the newspapers, with "the question of whether the public was 'entitled to know' about decisions in Washington," or with the legitimacy of the classification system.

> Like most defendants who consider themselves "heroes" [Nissen argued], their basic aim is to thwart any effort to try the issues raised by their indictment, and instead to transform the trial into a form of theater in which the defendants create new issues and new defendants to be tried in their place. Defendants have indicated in remarks to the media that this is their intention, that they plan to try "the war in Southeast Asia," the government's "classification system," the practice of information "leaks" from the Executive Branch, and "discriminatory prosecution" by the Government. . .

He regarded the evidence of Ellsberg's crime as all but overwhelming; there were fingerprint reports from the documents themselves, there was Lynda Sinay's grand-jury testimony, and there were a half-dozen security agreements in which Ellsberg and Russo acknowledged that they understood the regulations pertaining to the handling of secret documents and in which they pledged to obey them. No one was permitted, according to the regulations of the Department of Defense and the rules of the Rand Corporation (which were drawn in accordance with Defense Department requirements), to show classified material to any person without clearance and without a "need to know," to copy such documents or to alter them, to take them out of a secure area without proper authority, or to store them anywhere but in an approved facility. The regulations in the various security manuals were laced with warnings about violations of the Espionage Act and references to the proper handling of classified material according to Executive Order 10501.

Plainly the Pentagon Papers related to the national defense in the meaning of the Espionage Act—if they did not, Nissen believed, then nothing did—and plainly they were classified, had "Top Secret" stamped on every page. It would not be necessary, he would tell the jury, to "prove that the documents are vitally important," and he would not try to portray them as exciting or as representing "a disaster for the United States" if disclosed, although, when it came time to present evidence to the jury and argue the case, he would try to do just that. "The study was then [in 1969] and now useful for intelligence purposes," he would argue. It contained "some of the most closely guarded defense secrets produced by the United States—memos, National Security Council recommendations, sensitive communications, CIA reports, messages, plans and reports of negotiations through secret channels. Overall, the study gives an inner view into the workings of the defense establishment at the highest levels."

He had never tried a political case before, and he carefully avoided any political implications in the case before him. He probably had little if any suspicion that the White House burglars, Hunt and Liddy, had been receiving some of the same FBI reports on Ellsberg that he had, or that someone in the White House had commissioned an entirely separate "investigation" into the case. Later, when the disclosures came, he would call the burglars "dingalings" who messed up his case and who couldn't possibly have found anything useful to the prosecution. Yet he clearly relished his role of the heavy prosecutor of a crowd of Eastern liberal intellectuals, enjoyed its competitive challenge, and was often unable to hide his contempt for what he regarded as the incompetence of the legal celebrities who opposed him. He himself was uncontaminated by Harvard associations or elitist pretensions. He had his roots squarely in Middle America, in fundamentalist Protestantism, in a Midwestern church-affiliated college (Wheaton, 1954) where he played varsity baseball and where, while still an undergraduate, he was superintendent of the Salem Gospel Sunday School. After graduation he had served in Washington as a U. S. Army counterintelligence agent, received a master's degree in history from the University of Illinois, attended the University of Illinois Law School, and gone to work for the Department of Justice, first in Washington (in the Antitrust Division) during the Bobby Kennedy days, and later as head of the Criminal Division in Los Angeles. He did not drink or smoke, was regarded as a devoted family man, drove a Volkswagen, lived in a tract home in Orange County, and was active in the Church of Christ. Politics, it was said, mattered little to him; his concern was with the law, and that meant winning cases. His legal arguments tended to be brief —"methodical," someone called him, "an advocate to the core"—and he tended to scorn the complicated nuances of precedent and interpretation that the defense threw up; yet he was always carefully controlled, and the methodical was always there, in the angular gestures of the hands, the geometrically meticulous part in his straight black hair, the constant rearranging of the papers on the table before him, and his arrogant confidence in his own position. The defense lawyers strayed into court with their bulging briefcases and their stacks of documents; the prosecution, Nissen, Warren Reese, Richard Barry, marched in as a unit, usually in the company of two or three FBI agents, like a football team running from the dressing room to the field, suits pressed, shoes shined, papers carefully arranged in a three-drawer file cabinet that they wheeled into court every morning.

David Nissen's instinct was always to get on with it, and that instinct seemed to serve Matt Byrne's own impatience with the involuted inefficiency of a defense team more concerned with constitutional issues and legal precedent (and, occasionally, with academic posturing) than with the more mundane matters of getting the evidence in order, properly marking exhibits, and framing admissible questions. Nissen was not troubled by the ambiguities of language; he simply insisted that no word or phrase could possibly have any meaning other than the one that served his point. His argu-

ments before Byrne sometimes bordered on the insolent: the
judge, he implied, had his opinion, but David Nissen *knew*.
One could only imagine that Matt Byrne's tolerance was
based not only on an instinctive amiability but on a long
association in the U. S. attorney's office—mutual respect,
it was said, but no affection—which had accustomed him to
Nissen's manner and style and which had taught him that
David didn't mean any personal offense.

Nissen was a contender; the object of contention was to
win for his client, and the way to win was to use any means
within the uncertain bounds of what he believed he could
legally get away with. If he ever troubled himself with questions about what he really believed, he did not show it. Laws
were meant to be applied to concrete situations, not to general principles, and if the violations charged in the indictment led to a conviction, then the laws were proper and a
crime had been committed. It was obvious to him that Ellsberg had kept the documents in his possession for more than
a year without checking them into the Rand security system
(theft), that he had copied them without permission, and
that he had shown them to persons not entitled to receive
them (espionage). It was equally plain that there was a lawful governmental function of controlling the dissemination of
classified documents; the courts had consistently ruled that
executive orders defined lawful functions (even while the defense was asking how the President alone could make something a crime without congressional action), and it was
self-evident to him that the documents in the case did relate
to the national defense, one of the elements of proof required
by the Espionage Act, since they fell into a broad category
of material "relating to the military establishment, and the
related activities of national preparedness." National defense,
he argued in a pretrial brief, "embraces those military, diplomatic and all other measures directly and reasonably connected with the defense of our nation. It is *not* necessary that
[the documents] be vitally important, or that their disclosure
could or would be injurious to the United States." Moreover,

he argued, the defendants were precluded from challenging the classification procedure—although the fact that the documents were classified was clearly, in his view, evidence of their relationship to the national defense. "Defendants charged with impairing the governmental function of controlling the dissemination of classified government documents cannot defend themselves by claiming that the materials were not correctly classified. This would permit defendants now to challenge rules regarding the dissemination of classified material which they have been indicted for previously conspiring to circumvent." He argued, in other words, that although the defendants were charged with conspiracy to impede the lawful governmental function of controlling the dissemination of classified material, the basis of that function and the means in which it was carried out could not be challenged. When the defense demanded a bill of particulars specifying which portions of the Papers the government planned to use as evidence of relationship to the national defense, Nissen argued vehemently that no such specifics had to be supplied: the entire study related to the national defense; it was unreasonable and unfair to ask him to specify, because "it would require the government to disclose matters of strategy on the case." At most, he estimated before pretrial arguments began, it would take him two weeks to present his case.

Daniel Ellsberg had first consulted Leonard B. Boudin in December of 1970, three months before he delivered the Papers to Sheehan and six months before they were published. Boudin, who had helped defend Benjamin Spock in the Boston draft case and would participate in the Harrisburg trial, was probably the best-known civil-liberties lawyer in the country, though his experience was largely in appellate and not in trial work. During the period when Ellsberg had been thinking about staging a kind of war crimes trial—perhaps with himself as a "defendant"—he told a number of attorneys, Boudin among them, that he might have documents that could be used as evidence; he had also asked Boudin about the provisions of the Espionage Act and whether they could be applied to him if he disclosed the Papers, and Boudin replied that he wasn't certain, that he would have to do more research. Boudin had also been concerned with the provisions of another statute dealing with the unauthorized removal of documents from government files, but Ellsberg was never charged under its provisions. Boudin was then teaching as a visiting professor at Harvard, where he worked with a young law professor named Charles R. Nesson (no relation to Nissen, though their names would often be confused), who was also a constitutional lawyer and who had a reputation as one of the most brilliant students ever to graduate from the Harvard Law School. When the Papers were published, Boudin asked Nesson, who regarded Boudin as a kind of legal father-figure, to join him on the case; he knew it would be an extremely complicated and taxing defense, perhaps the most difficult he had ever worked on. In the succeeding months Ellsberg also engaged Charles E. Goodell, former U. S. Senator from New York, first as titular head of a defense committee and later as a member of the legal team (responsible primarily for making arrangements with former government officials to testify), Dolores E. "Dede" Donovan, a young graduate of Stanford Law School who had worked with a military defense committee in Vietnam and had helped Boudin in Harrisburg, and a number of Los Angeles lawyers who were used primarily to file motions and make other trial arrangements. It was Nesson who represented Ellsberg in the hectic days of June 1971 when Ellsberg was underground, who made the arrangements for his surrender to federal authorities in Boston late that month, and who would do most of the work on the factual elements in the case.

Russo, who had already changed attorneys after he was sentenced for contempt, changed again a few weeks before trial was scheduled to begin. He hired Leonard I. Weinglass, a thirty-seven-year-old movement lawyer who had been part of the defense team at the Chicago Seven trial, where Judge Julius Hoffman had cited him for contempt, and who had become a specialist in the defense of political activists. Russo regarded Weinglass as a more compatible attorney, politically and personally, than Michael Balaban. Weinglass would understand Russo's political objectives and would attempt to do more than present a narrow case aimed merely at the acquittal of his client. Russo also engaged two young attorneys, Jeffrey B. Kupers (for pretrial arguments), and Peter I. Young, another Harvard graduate, who feared that he might himself be indicted in connection with a grand-jury investigation of radical activities in Arizona; the charge, he had been told by other lawyers, was to be subornation of perjury and obstruction of justice—one of his former clients has told a government prosecutor that Young had counseled him to lie to the grand jury—but no indictment was ever returned. Boudin was apprehensive about them at first—he wasn't confident that he could work with this new breed of movement lawyers—but later came to be more impressed with them than they were with him. Although Russo came to regard Weinglass as a timid liberal, Weinglass managed to convert many of his client's political objectives into a legal context and thus make them admissible in Matt Byrne's court.

Only Boudin and Weinglass had much trial experience. Boudin's interests and orientation, moreover, were largely in the realm of constitutional law, and there would be occasions when his courtly absent-mindedness seemed to verge on open disdain for the mundane concerns of daily litigation. He refused to write out his questions, sometimes repeated himself, and encountered almost endless difficulty with objections from the prosecution. He was far from being an ideologue; he was a liberal and not a radical, a chess player, a man of warmth and charm who liked his comforts. Yet his concern with the subtleties of high-level legal debate, where he was often brilliant, and his casual references to Supreme Court cases in which he had participated became in themselves a kind of ideology, a view of the law as an eminently civilized and reasonable institution. His style, therefore, was as pronounced as Nissen's contentious absorption with witnesses, exhibits and the mini-details of cross examination—a quite different view of the law as an exercise. He and Nissen invariably talked past each other, and sometimes it was difficult to remember that they were part of the same case. Boudin was impressed with titles, credentials and academic records. He himself had gone to St. John's Law School in Brooklyn, he had never outgrown his Talmudic awe of prestige colleges and scholarship, and there were times when that awe looked like elitism. Early in the course of pretrial arguments Matt Byrne asked Boudin to stop referring to other lawyers in the case as Professor Nesson or Senator Goodell; everyone was a lawyer, and a plain "Mister" would be sufficient (except, of course, for his Honor), but the habit persisted: his client would always remain Doctor Ellsberg. At every turn Boudin would remind the jurors that the United States of America, in the guise of a WASP from the Middle West, was taking on a crowd of privileged intellectuals from the East, most of them Jewish. Yet Boudin also had a way of charming jurors: he entertained even while he fumbled, raising his glasses, walking around the lectern, turning a benign smile toward a witness, then becoming serious as he asked another question, humanizing the dead-serious, word-heavy contretemps of the case. In any popularity contest with a jury, Boudin would beat Nissen hands down.

The defense was suffused with ideology, often with conflicting ideologies, and was committed both by temperament and by legal necessity to a strategy that would cast the case in its most complicated light. Among Russo's friends were a number of people—including Katherine Barkley, Russo's young wife (who never used the name Russo)—who regarded the case as a magnificent opportunity to try the war and raise the issue of war crimes. Katherine, who had married Russo two weeks after his indictment (she had then known him about a month), called herself a Maoist, although she never quite clarified what that meant. She and many of Russo's friends planned an extensive Pentagon Papers Peace

Project which would publish fliers and a newspaper, produce films and television tapes, and organize demonstrations. The Peace Project would not be concerned with the legal defense but would be an auxiliary enterprise that took advantage of the attention that the trial was expected to attract. Under pressure from Ellsberg and his lawyers, and with the winding down of the war (and with the winding on, *ad infinitum,* of the trial), many of those plans were abandoned. Several issues of something called *The Pentagon Paper* were published, a tape was produced, and occasionally small groups of people with placards assembled outside the courtroom. By late summer of 1972, however, with the trial suspended pending an appeal to higher courts and with money running short, the auxiliary enterprises folded and the defense concentrated on the courtroom.

The conflicting ideologies and the divisions they produced nonetheless survived the demise of the Peace Project and the departure of those who had worked on it. The prime objective, presumably, was to win an acquittal for the defendants, but that objective was always associated with the intention of "educating" the jury and the public about the war and government secrecy, of raising what Russo regarded as "radical" issues (the Pentagon Papers, he would testify, were the most radical documents he had ever read), and of trying the war. There would be attempts to use the so-called "Nuremberg defense"—the proposition that a citizen's first obligation was to "international law," all domestic laws to the contrary notwithstanding, and that the Vietnam War was in violation of international law (which Byrne rejected)—and to have defense witnesses conduct what were, in essence, seminars before the jury on the crimes and duplicity revealed by the Papers (which Byrne, with some discomfort, did allow). Ellsberg and his attorneys were more concerned with constitutional questions and less interested in trying the war than were Russo and his friends. Ellsberg did not like the casual use of the word "imperialism," and by the end of the trial he was much more reluctant to talk about war crimes than he had been in his speeches and public statements two years before. Occasionally the differences among the "liberals" and the "radicals" would erupt into open conflict over the choice of defense witnesses, housing arrangements, office procedure and general approach. There were the liberal fat cats, Hollywood celebrities and other figures of political chic necessary to a defense that would eventually cost close to a million dollars; and there were defense intellectuals who had changed their minds about the war, among them Morton H. Halperin, the former Deputy Assistant Secretary of Defense, who had become the chief consultant to the Ellsberg defense; and there were Russo's movement friends who resented the idea that people like McGeorge Bundy and Arthur Schlesinger, Jr., whom they regarded as something akin to war criminals, should be called to testify on their behalf. By the end of the trial Russo had become convinced that Weinglass was not handling the case properly. Weinglass' "political analysis," Russo said, was closer to Ellsberg's than it was to his own. The strategy was too timid. Weinglass was not willing to push issues far enough, and he was acting "like a pacification chief" to control his own client.

The more serious problem for the defense, however, was not a reflection of the divisions between Ellsberg the academic and Russo the activist, but one of a common ambivalence shared by both defendants and their lawyers. How many witnesses could the jury stand? How could the defendants get across the positive reasons for wanting to disclose the documents (and not merely the argument that the Papers, if disclosed, would not injure the national defense)? How could the contents of the documents, the message as interpreted by Ellsberg and Russo, be made clear to the jury? How could the judge be persuaded to tolerate tactics designed to make this—whatever else it might be—a political case? And how could the jury be made to understand that the prime issue in this case was the issue of secrecy and free speech? The problem, finally, was to persuade the judge that the questions in this trial were so broad and complex that almost anything pertaining to the war and the classification system should be admissible.

### III

Pretrial arguments lasted almost six months, forcing Byrne, who had once expected to start the trial in March, to postpone jury selection half a dozen times. (Eventually there would be two juries, the first being dismissed after the extensive delay caused by the defense appeal to the Supreme Court on a wiretapping issue.) Such arguments were standard procedure in almost any major trial—it was what Jessica Mitford had called "going through the motions"—but in a case involving major constitutional questions and novel uses of the law they were likely to be at least as important as the presentation of testimony. They would not only shape the trial, determine what was admissible as evidence and, quite possibly, result in the dismissal of some charges, but, more important, delineate the legal and constitutional consequences of conviction, the nature of subsequent appeals and, in a larger sense, the political and social implications of the trial. Matt Byrne's court, Courtroom 9 in the Federal Building on North Spring Street, was an ideal setting for those arguments: a hermetic, brown-paneled, windowless, air-conditioned chamber that seemed totally detached from worldly concerns —an architectural abstraction which was acoustically misdesigned, a place alternately too warm or too cold (a clerk would constantly go to the thermostat to adjust the temperature), but a place also in which things like "the Constitution" or "free speech" could become independent realities seemingly severed from political pressure, compromise and the corruptions of daily life. Later, when the trial started, it would also become an appropriate place for extensive *explications de texte* about the Pentagon Papers themselves, perhaps a seminar room in some celestial university, or a chamber in the depths of the Vatican where questions of doctrine and heresy were picked apart by clerical scholars and papal inquisitors. The bench itself, a deep green leather chair, was at least thirty feet from the lectern where the lawyers stood to make their arguments and question witnesses, and at least twenty feet from the jury box, which was along the wall on the judge's right. The judge had constantly to remind lawyers and witnesses to keep their voices up. Usually those voices could be heard, though barely, since Byrne refused to use electronic amplifying systems, but it remained a constant mystery how any of the proceedings could ever leak beyond the heavy double doors that barred the room from the rest of the world. Against the noise of life outside in the corridors, in the newspapers, in conversations, the proceedings in the court always seemed artificial, as if exposure to natural air and light would immediately corrode them. After a time, life in the courtroom became a kind of addiction. As it ran on month after month, it started to limit, for many of us there, the only supportable reality, and to define life apart from life. Every trip outside required a readjustment. It was the government that would eventually connect the world in court with the realities outside, reminding us about them with suppressed evidence, with the felonies of the Watergate conspirators, and with its pervasive contempt of the routine processes of ordinary justice.

The arguments began in February, two months after the second indictment was returned, and continued through midsummer. With Boudin still occupied in Harrisburg, Nesson and Goodell came to Los Angeles to join Weinglass, Kupers and Young in pleadings for a bill of particulars, the detailed specifications of the government's indictment, and on a motion for discovery, essentially a request for a court order that the government provide the defense with material in its possession which was not otherwise available to it.

What the defense wanted, among other things, were (1) the specific passages in the Papers which government witnesses would cite as examples of material injurious to the United States under the terms of the Espionage Act; (2) those portions of the Papers which the government had used in the newspaper injunction cases to make its argument of potential irreparable damage; (3) internal government reports assessing the "damage" to national defense caused by the publication of the Papers and the potential damage, if any, which might have been caused by their hypothetical disclosure to unauthorized persons in 1969; (4) internal government reports and memoranda pertaining to the right of government officials and ex-officials to remove "from government files and to make copies of government documents relating to the national defense" and on the occurrence of leaks or disclosures, "authorized and unauthorized," of such documents; (5) transcripts of "background" press briefings by government officials; all material pertaining to the creation, handling and distribution of the Pentagon Papers; (6) all material in the government's possession which could be regarded as "exculpatory"—indicating, in other words, the defendants' innocence of the charges (in *Brady v. Maryland* the Supreme Court ruled that the prosecution in a criminal case could not withhold evidence indicating the defendant's innocence, and that if it did, a conviction could be overturned); (7) specifics on whether Ellsberg was charged with stealing "information" or "documents"; and (8) particulars of the government's view of the defendants' criminal intent, which, the defense argued, was required by both the conspiracy and the espionage counts. The individual items on the defendants' list, however, were not as crucial as Byrne's general response to their view of the case, and particularly to their hope that the contents of the Papers and the classification system could be made central issues in the trial. If Byrne could be made to understand that leaks of classified material were common practice in Washington, and if he could be persuaded that it was not simply the classification stamp that established the documents' relationship to the national defense, then there would be considerable latitude not only on the issues pertaining to the defendants' guilt, but in trying the war itself. This was when they would begin to try out the judge.

Nissen opposed every request. He argued that the defense

was not entitled to any of the information it wanted, and that if Byrne ordered the government to turn it over, to specify, to furnish details, "the defendants might as well move into the offices of the United States government." If the prosecution had "to produce all these documents, if every piece of paper has to be tracked down, there will be a paralysis of this trial." The Espionage Act, he said, "does not relate to damage to the United States" but only to information "relating to the national defense, which information the possessor has reason to believe could be used to the injury of the United States." The fact that the defendants had signed security agreements and that the documents were stamped "Top Secret" seemed to Nissen sufficient evidence to satisfy the law's "reason to believe" requirement. He argued, moreover, that if copies of all the documents cited in the indictment had to be turned over to the defense, the government would be disclosing material that was still classified. Although the Defense Department declassified and published most of the Pentagon Papers in the summer and fall of 1971, the four volumes dealing with secret contacts between the United States and North Vietnam in the mid-sixties had never been published. Neither had they been given to the *Times* by Ellsberg, who had turned his only set over to Fulbright. The pages of the Wheeler Report on the Tet offensive listed in the indictment were also still classified, although they had been published by the *Times* and were available in the Bantam edition of the Papers to anyone with $2.25. Nissen said he would introduce those documents to the jury "without publicity" and treat them in such a way as to protect their confidentiality. Nesson, with ample precedent on his side, said such a course was plainly a violation of the defendants' constitutional right to a public trial. He could imagine a situation in which the government brought documents into court under special guard or with special protection, a ritual of secrecy to impress the jurors. "This is the one thing that we fear more than anything else," he said. "The government has to make the hard choice between making these documents public and not using them in this case."

"That's a bridge we don't have to cross at this time," Nissen told the court. "If you don't protect the material now, then nothing you do later will make any difference."

In the first weeks of argument, Byrne had delighted the defense. He ordered the government to provide damage reports, if it had any, which showed that the disclosure of the Papers would have had little or no effect on the national defense in 1969. It was an order that would have a major impact in the trial. He further required the prosecution to choose between an "information" theory and a "document" theory on the theft counts (had they stolen words or paper?). He told the government to supply particulars on which sections or passages of the Papers the government would use to prove relationship to the national defense, and, most significantly, he indicated that the defendants would have ample latitude to discuss the Papers themselves, to get their contents (and thereby the war) before the jury. He also ordered the government to provide the defendants with a complete set of the twenty volumes cited in the indictment (including the still-classified negotiation volumes), although he qualified the decision with a "protective order" which prevented the defense from making the still-classified material public and required the defendants to provide the court with a list of those consultants and witnesses who would be shown copies of the classified documents. Nothing, he suggested, and would later say, would receive special handling once it was introduced into evidence. A few weeks after Byrne gave copies of the negotiation volumes to the defense, Jack Anderson published three columns based on their contents, disclosing that in 1966 the British had tapped telephone conversations between Aleksei N. Kosygin, who was then visiting London, and Leonid Brezhnev in Moscow pertaining to Soviet efforts to mediate between the United States and North Vietnam. Nissen immediately demanded a court investigation into possible violations of the protective order, suggesting that the defense had given Anderson copies of the documents. Among defense consultants who had been given access to the volumes were Tom Hayden, one of the Chicago Seven defendants, who had negotiated with the North Vietnamese for the release of American prisoners, and Robert Scheer, the former editor of *Ramparts*. Both were Russo's consultants. Byrne, however, was satisfied with defense assurances that they had leaked nothing.

What Nissen did not say—and what would later become clear—was that the prosecution had probably misled the State Department about Byrne's decision to treat the negotiation volumes like all other documentary evidence. An exchange of letters between the prosecutors and State Department officials, later introduced in court, indicated that the officials still believed that the negotiation volumes were receiving special treatment, even after they were introduced in evidence and were accessible to anyone who cared to come to the clerk's office in Los Angeles to read them. Senator Fulbright, meanwhile, was unable to get them released officially in Washington, despite repeated indignant requests to officials at Foggy Bottom. By mid-April, six weeks after pretrial arguments started, Nesson believed that Byrne was giving the defense more than he had expected. "We may have won the whole thing today," he said after Byrne ordered the government to particularize those parts of the Papers which it would claim related to the national defense; "he didn't have to give us all that stuff." And Russo was telling friends that, in his view, the government was getting ready to drop the whole case.

The optimism was premature. While Byrne was prepared to grant the defendants considerable evidentiary latitude in raising the issues that they considered important, he was unwilling to tamper with the indictment itself. Boudin had arrived in Los Angeles late in May convinced that portions of the Espionage Act as they had been applied in Nissen's charges were overbroad and unconstitutional, that there was no such thing as a lawful governmental function of controlling the dissemination of classified studies and documents, and that Section 641 of Title 18 of the U.S. Code (the conversion and theft law) could not possibly apply to information. The government, he believed, could not be deprived of information, since it was prohibited by statute from holding copyrights; if Congress had intended the law to be applied to information rather than documents or other physical objects, then the statute violated the First Amendment. Boudin and Nesson also hoped to persuade Byrne to hold a separate hearing on the matter of discriminatory prosecution on the ground that, since leaks of classified information were routine in Washington, Ellsberg and Russo had been singled out as political targets for disclosing information that was embarrassing to the government. Nissen claimed that there was no such thing as discriminatory prosecution. "No case has ever been made," he had said, pointing his finger at Byrne, "*none;* they have not shown me a case; there is no such case."

But Byrne had already rejected that assertion. "What are the courts talking about," he asked Nissen, "when they say they didn't prove their case of discriminatory prosecution?" In private conversations, Boudin declared that there was a better than even chance that before trial began Byrne would throw out the espionage counts as well as that portion of the conspiracy charge (Count One, Part 1) that accused Ellsberg and Russo of impairing the government's function of controlling classified documents.

The attack on the indictment was a brilliant performance, a constitutional case preliminary to the trial and an opportunity for Boudin and Nesson to do what they could do best. Byrne was reluctant to cut the arguments short, although he was often impatient with Weinglass (who, in pretrial arguments, was usually the one to raise the legally most radical arguments), and he was willing to do the work of reading the applicable cases and raising the difficult questions. When Boudin first arrived in his court, Matt Byrne seemed to ex-

tend to him a deference he had not shown the other lawyers
—the first team had arrived—and to raise questions to
demonstrate that he was as capable and well prepared as the
great man himself. Boudin returned the compliment with a
personal courtliness that contained more than a hint of elite
exclusivity. He and Byrne, he seemed to suggest, had a
special understanding and could conduct dialogue at a level
which others, for lack of experience or seniority or through
shortcomings in civility, could not attain. "Your Honor will
no doubt recall . . . As your Honor well knows . . . In the
Coplon case, as your Honor will remember . . ." He would
smile at Byrne with what Francine Gray, covering the Harrisburg trial, had called his "I-love-you-and-understand-you-
completely expression," raising his glasses above his forehead,
then dropping them to look at his notes, and suggesting that
no sophisticated person could possibly reason any way other
than the way he was reasoning now. Part of Boudin's effectiveness came from the sheer power of his arguments; part
of it came from the charm of a confidence man.

"This is the first case," he declared, "in which the government has proceeded on a charge of impairing the governmental function to disseminate classified data. But this is not
a lawful function of government under Section 371 [the conspiracy statute]; this is a form of information control." What
the government was attempting to do was to elevate the executive order on classification (10501) to the level of law; if
that were the case, he said, then "Congress would have dele-
gated to the executive the power to make crimes," an act that
would be not merely unconstitutional but unthinkable. Moreover, he said, Executive Order 10501 was not an order which
was obeyed; it was an "inherently violated *ad hoc* order"
which, if it defined anything, simply outlined a general house-
keeping function within the government (with violations
punishable by dismissal or other administrative sanctions),
and not a lawful governmental function subject to the conspiracy laws. Everyone in Washington knew that the executive order was violated daily, that government officials were

promiscuous in classifying documents without justification and were unwilling to declassify anything. If one page in a thousand-page document contained something that someone regarded as classified, then the whole document would be classified. ("The classification system," Goodell told Byrne, "is diarrhetic at one end and constipated at the other.") The defense, in preparing its arguments on discriminatory prosecution, had amassed dozens of affidavits from journalists and former government officials specifying how information was constantly leaked—how these leaks were themselves part of the system—and certifying that no one had ever been prosecuted for leaking information before. "In a remarkable number of instances," one of them said, "the classification system is designed to prevent an official from being embarrassed. There's nothing involving secrecy in the document. It's a personal thing. That's why the constant conflict between press and government is absolutely essential." There were no standards in the implementation of the executive order; in effect it gave the Administration unbounded latitude in determining what could or could not be released. If that latitude were backed with criminal sanctions, as implied in the conspiracy charge against Ellsberg and Russo, Boudin argued, "we are no longer in the area of national-defense information; we are no longer in the area of the question of criminal intent; we are no longer in the evidence of aiding a foreign power; we are in the area simply of information control."

"The courts have held that executive orders have the same force and effect as a statute," Matt Byrne replied, but he seemed troubled by Boudin's argument. Shouldn't there be a way to test the arbitrary nature of an administrative act in a court of law? he asked Nissen. What remedy did a person have if the way a document was classified was left entirely to executive discretion?

"Your Honor," Nissen replied, "my opinion is that individual court cases make rather bad places to cure the ills of the world, including all the arbitrary acts—"

"I am not worried about the ills of the world," Byrne shot

back. "I am worried about the Constitution of the United
States."

Boudin extended his argument about information control
to the theft charges. Even if Ellsberg had kept a set of the
documents in his personal possession for over nine months,
as charged by the indictment, what had the government been
deprived of? The government obviously had other copies—
there were complete sets at the Pentagon, at Rand and elsewhere, and a half-dozen former officials had copies in their
private possession. The government, he said, seemed to be
claiming that it had a property right not in documents but
in information, and that it had been deprived of the exclusive
right to have access to such information. If that was the basis
of the charge—if the government proceeded on the information theory on the theft counts—then the theft statute
(Section 641, Title 18 of the U. S. Code) would be an in-
formation-control law, and therefore unconstitutional. The
law had never been used that way. The government was not
allowed to hold copyrights; Section 641, moreover, said
nothing about information, least of all classified information.
Byrne, who had originally indicated that he would reject the
information theory, subsequently allowed Nissen to straddle
the issue—his informality often generated ambiguities and
debate on matters that seemed previously settled—and the
defendants were afraid that the uncertainty might eventually
land in the lap of the jury.

The defense was pinning its greatest hopes on its attack
on the espionage counts and on the possibility that Byrne
would conduct a separate inquiry on the matter of discriminatory prosecution. Section 793, Boudin reasoned, was
plainly designed as an espionage statute—Congress, he asserted, never intended it to cover release of information
outside the espionage context—yet nothing even remotely
close to espionage was alleged in the indictment. Much of
the argument was technical, involving the meaning of the
separate paragraphs of the law, the position of a comma, and
particularly the question of intent: Did it require "reason to

believe" that the material in question would or could be used to injure the United States or aid a foreign power, or did it simply require "general criminal intent" as Nissen insisted? Yet the "technical" questions had substantial constitutional implications. By the government's theory, Peter Young argued for Russo, "even innocuous information about the military" could be used as the basis of an indictment. Even Supreme Court Justice William Rehnquist, perhaps the most politically conservative member of the Court, testifying before a congressional committee when he was still in the Justice Department, had said that intent was required by the statute. The First Amendment right of the public to know was not affected by real espionage, Young argued to Byrne, and that was what saved the Espionage Law from vagueness and overbreadth. As used in this indictment, however, it would clearly be unconstitutional, since it affected free speech and press. Byrne again indicated that he was arrested by the argument, and particularly by the use of the words "willful" and "persons not entitled to receive" in the Espionage Act. He asked Nissen, who rarely bothered to argue constitutional points for more than a few minutes, what he thought they meant.

"In our view," Nissen replied, "persons entitled to receive are those authorized by regulation. Not entitled to receive is all others." He failed to see how First Amendment rights could be involved. "I have a lot of files in my office, and I don't see how anyone has a right to come up there to look at them." The right to see documents possessed by the government ("persons . . . entitled to receive") was determined by the department or official that controlled them.

The case of the defense for a special hearing on discriminatory or selective prosecution was its most ambitious and revealing assault on the indictment. It was buttressed by dozens of documents about the handling of classified information, the practice of leaking documents in Washington, and the manipulation of classified data to support administration policy. The defendants and their lawyers were certain that if Byrne were willing to hear the witnesses they were prepared to call he would understand that the government had singled out Ellsberg and Russo for political reasons, and would dismiss the indictment. Occasionally people had been reprimanded or demoted for leaking data, but no one had ever been prosecuted. The classification system itself was so elaborate that it could not function without the existence of a broad and informal system under which nearly everyone took classified documents home, showed them to people not entitled to receive them, perhaps copied them, and handled them in ways not permitted by the written regulations. If the written system were followed in practice, Nesson told Byrne, "it would bring government to a halt." Moreover, he said, every retiring government official takes files of documents with him, and many use them in their memoirs or contribute them to libraries, taking charitable tax deductions in return. In the State Department there was even an "old-boy rule" that permitted former employees to return and see the documents on which they had worked during their incumbency. Without that "rule," the files would be decimated.

What emerged from the disposition of those motions was a picture of a system which had decayed to the extent that its primary function was to protect government officials from embarrassment. Genuinely sensitive information was classified higher than "Top Secret" under procedures which were themselves classified and which provided for classification marks understandable only to those who had been cleared for them. Ordinary security classifications, said William G. Florence, a retired Air Force classification official who worked for the defense,

> are of such low value among the majority of individuals who handle classified material that they freely reproduce as many copies of classified documents as they wish. They also distribute copies of classified documents to suit their personal purposes . . . I often observed that the existence of a classification marking on a document constituted no restraint on officials at the

middle and higher levels in making copies of classified documents and using them for purposes for which they had no official authorization.

Florence also estimated, with some hyperbole, that ninety-nine percent of the 23 million documents marked "Confidential," "Secret" or "Top Secret," the three categories provided by Executive Order 10501, were improperly classified. Material was released selectively to buttress official policy or to reinforce the arguments of one agency which was in contention with another. "When I was in government," said one former official in a defense affidavit, "I witnessed many occasions when it was standard operating procedure to give out classified information in order to disarm our opposition. I not only witnessed it, I did it myself." The Air Force leaked material to embarrass the Army, the Pentagon released information to impede diplomatic negotiations supported by the State Department, and the White House showed reporters confidential documents which it believed would support its programs. The barrage of affidavits submitted by the defense included the following.

[A former CIA official] There is a great distinction between political secrets and state secrets. Most of what's classified is political secrets. There are areas of legitimate sensitivity that should be classified. They involve things like codes, communications, war plans, and real espionage. The rest is a bunch of baloney. It's policy posturing. People won't read it if it's not classified.

[A former member of the White House staff] The government couldn't operate without violating the security regulations. Everybody did it all the time. When you've got a hot item in front of you, you don't go to some declassification board that would take months to decide. You decide yourself. You know you're taking administrative risks, but that's the way it works. If your judgment is bad, you go. But everybody knows that most of the declassification has nothing to do with national security. You just don't want to embarrass your boss, so you give out the things that will really help.

[A former presidential assistant] After leaving office I wrote a book describing events while I was in government. In writing the book I relied extensively on classified documents, and incorporated substantial amounts of classified material, a fact which is evident from my book. I did not submit my book for any formal classification review. I have given my classified papers to a presidential library under a deed of gift showing that the papers were my personal property and access to them was subject to my personal control.

[A Washington journalist] On one occasion I was shown a photograph of the luxurious interior of a MATS plane. The photograph had the word "secret" stamped across it in large letters. Obviously the Air Force didn't want the Congress or the public to know how the taxpayers' money had been spent. People giving me classified materials are at all levels of government. I have received thousands of leaks from thousands of people, but I've never known one of them to be prosecuted. In several cases the government had to know who my source was.

Most of those practices were accepted elements of the Washington scene and would hardly be news (except, perhaps, to a jury). This led the defense to contend that Ellsberg and Russo had been selected for prosecution in retaliation for leaking embarrassing material. In Russo's case there was the added complication that he had refused to testify before the grand jury and had confronted Nissen outside the grand-jury room the year before about Nissen's refusal to obey Judge Ferguson's order to supply him with a transcript of his never-to-be-given grand-jury testimony; Russo was indicted, Peter Young would argue, "for persisting in his rights before the grand jury." The defense also felt it had grounds for suspicion in the government's great haste to indict Ellsberg on the eve of Supreme Court arguments in the newspaper injunction cases on the publishing of the Papers, in the refusal of the U. S. attorney in Los Angeles to sign the indictment, and in the fact that the FBI had investigated Ellsberg (and knew he had copied the documents) a year before the Papers were published. Ellsberg had been indicted, Charles Nesson said, only because he had violated the rules of the club and had exposed the practice of what Ellsberg called "immaculate deception" whereby press reports about progress in Vietnam, for example, were attributed to "official" but unnamed sources and could later be disavowed (although in the meantime they were allowed to serve as support for policies that the Administration was trying to push). The defense wanted Byrne to order the government to produce all internal correspondence relating to the origins of the case and particularly those which dealt with the prosecution's motives. Those affidavits, Goodell had said privately during arguments, "will make the judge think." If he could be made to understand how the system really worked, be persuaded to hold that hearing, he would have to throw out the indictment before the trial began.

Byrne ruled on those arguments over a period of weeks, often announcing decisions from the bench late in the afternoon and generally without explanation or formal opinion. He had not been persuaded either by the attacks on the separate counts or by the motion for a hearing on selective or discriminatory prosecution. Although he had ordered the government to submit to him *in camera* any government memoranda that pertained to the origins and reasons for the prosecution, those records were never made public, nor did they contain anything about the White House Hunt-Liddy investigation on the "prosecutability" of Ellsberg and his co-conspirators. A year later, when Hunt's grand-jury testimony was sent to Byrne, he would seize on the word "prosecutability" in the testimony and ask the prosecution whether the Plumbers' investigation was related to the government's decision to indict, but no explanation was provided. Byrne ruled that the defendants had not established that they represented a distinguishable class—most of the existing cases dealt with racial minorities—who, because of their identity as a class, had been selected as targets of legal action from which others were exempt. Nesson had tried to show that Russo and Ellsberg belonged to a political minority, opponents of the war, but, since no one else had been prosecuted, the class argument was rejected. Byrne also denied motions to dismiss the conspiracy and espionage counts on constitutional grounds, although he indicated that once the evidence was presented he might reconsider. He said, in essence, that the indictment and the statutes as applied in the indictment were not unconstitutional on their face but might prove to be unconstitutionally applied to the facts.

The most important of Byrne's rulings, those denying the motions for dismissal of the espionage counts, came in the first week of July 1972, roughly a week after the Supreme Court's decisions in the *Caldwell* and *Gravel* cases. "We cannot accept the argument," Justice White had said for the majority in *Caldwell,* "that the public interest in future news about crime from undisclosed, unverified sources must take precedence over the public interest in pursuing and prosecuting those crimes reported to the press . . . There is no First Amendment privilege to refuse to answer the relevant and material questions asked during a good-faith grand jury investigation." Justice White, in the majority opinion in *Gravel,* also declared that the congressional-immunity clause in the Constitution "provides no protection for criminal conduct . . . whether performed at the direction of the Senator in preparation for or in execution of a legislative act or done without his knowledge and direction . . . If republication of [the Pentagon Papers] was a crime it was not entitled to immunity under the speech or debate clause." Although neither decision bore directly on the issues involved in Byrne's rulings, each was related to the broader questions in the case, and especially to the way the court might "balance" the issues of alleged criminal conduct against the claim of First Amendment privileges. The decisions seemed to make clear the direction in which the court was going on the general issues related to the Papers. If Byrne was apt to follow the Supreme

Court returns, the decisions in *Caldwell* and *Gravel* provided unmistakable clues on how it would be likely to rule in the future. They also, of course, gave some clear indications about how the Court might respond to appeals in this case.

Byrne's decisions destroyed the defendants' optimism. "I might trade Byrne for Hoffman," Weinglass said after one ruling. "Hoffman wouldn't even listen, he'd just say 'Denied.' Here it'll look like the judge was fair." Pat Ellsberg was depressed, and Dan, who, like Boudin, had expected some of the espionage counts to be dismissed, was angry and began warning the press: "Sy Hersch [of the *Times*] can be prosecuted, Jack Raymond, who covers the Pentagon, can be prosecuted. Everything he prints is leaked. They've been doing weather modification in Vietnam for seven goddam years—I was there, and I didn't know it, no one knew it." What Byrne had done, he suggested, was clear the way for government prosecution of anyone who leaked a story and anyone who printed it. "Even now," said Mark Rosenbaum, a third-year Harvard law student who did legal research for the defense, "this indictment will be copied. They can try it again, no matter what happens."

IV

On June 13, the first anniversary of the publication of the Papers by the New York *Times,* the defense staged a party at its office at 125 West Fourth Street in Los Angeles. Pretrial arguments were still under way, and the selection of the first jury would not begin for another month. There was champagne, a cake in the shape of a pentagon, and a great deal of joking.

Admittedly there wasn't much to celebrate. The Boston grand jury was still sitting and might well return another set of indictments, Byrne had not ruled on any of the substantive issues in the case, and the war was going on. There were, moreover, the festering divisions within the defense. The Ellsbergs, their lawyers and their consultants were living at Bunker Hill Towers, a downtown upper-middle-income housing development (with swimming pool, tennis courts, and "health club") which had been erected on the cleared site of an old Chicano neighborhood. Most of Russo's friends, as well as Tony and Katherine themselves, were living near the beach and among the freaks in Venice or Santa Monica, or in communes, and many of them resented Bunker Hill and those who lived there; it was the product of urban renewal and therefore the consequence of another instance of exploiting the poor. (Later Tony and Katherine would also move into Bunker Hill, but the political divisions that it symbolized never disappeared.) Yet the party that evening indicated that the defense had become more or less a fully functioning operation.

Through Boudin, Ellsberg had met Stanley K. Sheinbaum, an independently wealthy organizer of liberal causes who had helped raise funds for *Ramparts,* was instrumental in securing the release of deposed Greek Premier Papandreou from prison and was a major fund raiser for George Mc-Govern in California. Sheinbaum had taken over financial and organizational responsibilities for the Pentagon Papers Defense Fund the previous fall and would manage not only to keep his disorderly troops functioning but to find sufficient funds—through mailings, lecture appearances by Russo and Ellsberg, meetings, and Hollywood parties—to keep his operation more or less solvent. Although Louis Marx, Patricia's father, refused to have anything to do with Ellsberg, Patricia herself managed to raise or borrow enough against trust funds to contribute an estimated $50,000. Other major sources would include Max Palevsky, a Southern California liberal who had made a fortune in Xerox, Carol Bernstein, the widow of a New York investment broker, and a much publicized $250-a-couple gathering of Hollywood celebrities where Barbra Streisand raffled off songs for as much as $10,000 each, among them a rendition of "People" over a special telephone hookup for a Bar Mitzvah party in Beverly Hills. Sheinbaum would often complain that press reports indicating the trial was going well for the defense were discouraging contributions, but as the case progressed to its Watergate climax Matt Byrne's courtroom became an increasingly fashionable place, and the jurors would spend the dull moments trying to pick out the celebrities: George Segal, Eva Marie Saint, Jack Nicholson, Jane Fonda, Roman Polanski, Lee Grant . . .

Russo and Barkley avoided the Hollywood connection, it was not their thing either in principle or in style, and they refused to attend the Streisand extravaganza. What they helped attract to the effort, however, were the services of dozens of volunteers, people who worked for little or nothing in clerical jobs, research, and office help. The turnover among them would be enormous, there would be endless meetings to deal with someone or something, to resolve clashes between the need to give orders and the demands for participatory democracy, yet a number of people who worked for the defense at the beginning would still be around at the end. For them the party was a kind of beginning: Teri Simon, who had taken a year off as an undergraduate at the University of Pennsylvania, would do much of the office work; Adam Bennion and Paul Ryder, students who had dropped out of college through a combination of boredom and devotion to the cause, spent most of the next year comparing documents to determine what material in the Papers had been published elsewhere before the Papers were copied; Marcia Meyers, who had been teaching part time in Berkeley, did much of the research on the jury; Rosenbaum, the Harvard law student, did legal research; and Robert Sachs, who had worked for Goodell when he was in the Senate, handled the press and was the person on whom, in the absence of any help from the prosecution, the reporters covering the trial came to depend.

The most important member of the team, however, apart from the lawyers and the defendants, was Morton Halperin. Halperin had taken a leave of absence from the Brookings Institution (where he had been a fellow since leaving the government) to become the chief consultant and resident authority on matters relating to the Department of Defense. Halperin, who had worked for Kissinger and was not embellishing his own short-run career prospects as a defense intellectual by his activities in Los Angeles, often explained that he had made his decision because "the government had gone too far" in prosecuting Ellsberg, and because he believed that the covert activities of the government—many of them unknown to presumably responsible senior officials— were jeopardizing not only civil liberties but the regular conduct of foreign affairs. (He suspected, even then, that his telephone was tapped: "It was constantly breaking down, and there were repair trucks outside all the time.") But plainly he had also been bored since he left government; the heady days when, as Deputy Assistant Secretary of Defense, he studied the daily cables from Vietnam were over, and he sensed that there might be more excitement in Los Angeles. It was Halperin who devised the defense strategy that suggested that the documents Ellsberg copied were not government property at all, although he never was willing to claim outright that they were private property belonging to himself, Gelb and Warnke. When the *Times* and the *Washington Post* later implied that he had made such a claim (and Warnke immediately called him to protest), Halperin wrote a letter to the newspapers denying it.

The party that evening didn't last long. The tension and anxiety undercut the celebration. Ellsberg, his shirt sleeves rolled up, was showing people a telegram he had just received from New York stating that his publisher had proposed his book of essays, *Papers on the War,* for a Pulitzer Prize (which he would not get, although the *Times* did get a Pulitzer for publishing the Papers) and talking about how the publication of the documents had helped demythologize secrecy: people were reading the Papers without being turned to stone. Yet he was clearly discouraged by the continuing war. Since the North Vietnamese offensive in the spring, the bombing had escalated; there had been as many people killed by bombing in Vietnam in the first five months of 1972 as in all of 1971. "The last twelve months," he said later that week, "illustrate that the President is unconstrained by the law, the Constitution, or by humanity," and he wondered whether "we have a coup in our future, or whether ours has already taken place." The executive branch had "slipped free of the constraints of the Constitution," and a time was at hand which he compared to the 1760s and 1770s, a turning point when people would face the choice between going along with "government by expert, government by decree, and government by lies" and having "a second birth of life." At the time it seemed like standard Ellsberg rhetoric and the press wasn't paying much attention—he often complained that even the reporters covering the trial never interviewed him—but later, when I found the notes from that week, the words seemed dangerously prophetic. He had uttered them roughly twenty-four hours after the burglars working for Hunt and Liddy had been caught at the Watergate.

V

When they first entered the courtroom, they looked like a couple of busloads of tourists from Indianapolis who had lost their way to Disneyland: white, middle-aged, old-aged, pinch-faced, obeisance-repressing-anger, the last revenge of the Puritan in America. Until the full force of their presence really struck, they seemed like the objects of some grand judicial joke, a malicious conspiracy of judges, jury clerks and prosecutors to even accounts with defendants who had taken up too much of their time with legalistic nit-picking. They kept coming through the double doors of Matt Byrne's court, filling the spectator section under the eyes of a pair of solicitous ushering marshals: flinty women with blue hair, retirees from Orange County, wives of executives at North American, RCA and Lockheed, an even one hundred people of whom six were black and perhaps ten were under thirty, a roll call of WASPs thinly sprinkled with Chicanos and census-defined "others": Abata, Allen, Andersen, Anderson, Arroyo, Arvizu, Asta, Bahena, Baldwin, Benwell, Berkey,

Bracci, Brazile, Buckenhizer, Campbell, Clearwaters, . . .
Vaughan, Walls, Warenburg, Washington, Wiegand, Weitz,
Wight, Worden, Wyatt . . . From these people the defense
and the prosceution, exercising a limited number of peremptory challenges, would select a panel of twelve jurors
and six alternates.

For three weeks, while other pretrial arguments were still
in progress, the defense had been challenging the selection
procedure. The names in the jury wheel, they argued, did not
reflect the composition of the population of the Central District of California—Los Angeles and surrounding counties
—from which the jury was to be drawn. The people on the
jury list were older, whiter, more conservative, more established than those on the list of registered voters. The defense
had produced statistics and affidavits to prove the contention
and had even persuaded Byrne to hold a brief hearing and
call witnesses on the way juries were selected. (The major
witness was one Jody Mody, jury clerk for the Central District.) Eighteen-year-olds would be allowed to vote in 1972,
but the jury wheel had been made up long before most of
them had registered. The defense wanted a new panel called
which would include the new voters, but that would have
been administratively impossible even if it had been judicially
ordered; there would be no new jury list until fall. Even
people between twenty-one and twenty-nine were statistically
underrepresented; studies of other juries had shown younger
people to be, in general, less prone to believe policemen and
prosecutors, less biased against defendants and more likely
to be sympathetic to opponents of the war. They represented
the age group that was subject to the draft and service in
Vietnam, and, needless to say, the generation that had been
most vocal in opposing them. Byrne wanted to know whether
such a group constituted a "cognizable class"; the courts had
thrown out a number of convictions by juries from which, for
example, blacks or other minorities had been excluded or on
which they were underrepresented. The defense lawyers
argued that they did, but were not able to prove it to Byrne's

satisfaction. The man who had been staff director for the Scranton Commission on Campus Unrest, and who seemed more than a little offended when the defense tried to identify and explicate for him the literature of student protest, could not be persuaded that the young constituted a distinct social group whose exclusion from the jury might be prejudicial to the defense. After the panel of jurors first appeared in the courtroom Weinglass told Byrne that the grounds for the challenge to the panel had become apparent in physical terms. "This," he said, "is not a cross section of the community." *We move for an autopsy,* said a note making the rounds of the press table.

Another jury issue: the matter of *voir dire,* the interrogation of potential jurors. The defense asked that lawyers on both sides be permitted to ask questions. In the federal courts, the judge has the option of permitting such a *voir dire*—Judge Herman had allowed it in the Harrisburg trial—but most judges ask the parties to submit questions, select from among them, and conduct the *voir dire* themselves. The official purpose of the *voir dire* is to elicit from members of the panel indications of bias which might constitute bases for challenges for cause and provide information for peremptory challenges (for which no cause need be stated). In a number of cases, however, particularly Black Panther cases in state courts, the defense has used the interrogation as a way of "educating" jurors by constantly reminding them how racial or other bias could influence a verdict, by suggesting, through questions, that membership in the Black Panther Party was not evidence of any crime, and by subtly challenging the jurors' sense of fairness to the point where some, at least, were ready to bend over backward to demonstrate their racial tolerance. More significantly, a *voir dire* conducted by the parties can be used to establish a rapport between lawyers and jurors that is impossible if the judge questions them and thereby increases the unstated feeling that they are *his* jurors, dependent on *his* decisions. The defense also wanted Byrne to order the government to turn over all its sources of jury information, and particularly data which the defendants believed had been culled from military records, FBI reports and income tax returns—all of it available only to the prosecution. Boudin was certain that the government had extensive dossiers on potential jurors in political cases and that the U. S. Attorney's Office maintained a jury book with the verdicts and individual votes of previous juries on which they had served. Byrne rejected all the motions: he would ask the potential jurors about other cases on which they had sat, but he would do the questioning himself.

For its part, the defense was scarcely helpless. The defendants had accepted the volunteered services of sociologists and psychiatrists who would observe the behavior and evaluate the answers of the prospective jurors during the course of the questioning: were they weak or strong, authoritarian or tolerant, and how would they react with each other? They had even begun to organize an informal "network" of people who could do "research" on the potential jurors in the communities where they lived. Something of the sort had been tried in Harrisburg, where a number of people, among them Jay Schulman, a sociologist who formerly taught at the City University of New York, began systematic studies of jury selection and what was, in effect, a sociology of the jury room. It had been found, among other things, that "nonverbal behavior (eye contact, body orientation, facial expressions, dress) could provide important information." Schulman had come to believe that all resources of the government would not provide information as useful as that which could be gotten through careful observation of potential jurors during the *voir dire* and extensive research in their communities.

In Los Angeles, the network would not become fully effective until the selection of the second jury in January, when the defense got lists of people who had worked as McGovern volunteers and who could, in many cases, be called on to do something for Ellsberg, Russo and the cause of free speech. Even for this first jury, however, there were enough workers to check the voter registration cards of people who had been called for jury duty; in California those cards contained not only the individual's party affiliation but also his record, if any, in signing initiative and referendum petitions. Had he supported the petition for the restoration of the death penalty or the recall of Governor Ronald Reagan or the legalization of marijuana? It was a matter of public record, and one could go to the local registrar of voters and look it up. The network would also try to find people who knew or worked with the potential jurors and who (presumably in absolute confidence) would tell more about him. Others would be sent to look at the streets and neighborhoods where potential jurors lived and to report on their general class, income and political characteristics. Since the list of names that were called for any particular panel—the hundred-odd people from whom a jury was to be drawn—was not available until the first day of the *voir dire* (which, in this case, would last perhaps two to three weeks), the research would ideally include all persons in the jury wheel for that particular term of service, a total of more than three thousand names.

The *voir dire* (which Byrne pronounced "voir dyer") was more a ritual of fairness than a probing attempt to elicit information and discover bias. Byrne questioned them both in groups and individually while the lawyers sat silently and took notes. Arguments, suggestions and challenges for cause took place out of the presence of the jurors. A group of eighteen people would be called at random from the panel of one hundred seated in the courtroom and would be placed in the jury box for general questioning: employment, residence, military service, education, and personal connections, if any, with the defense, the prosecution or other agencies of law enforcement. Then, with the other panelists out of the room, each venireman was called individually and questioned on his opinions about the war, his knowledge of the case, and his experience, if any, with clearances and security. When the questioning was completed, Byrne would entertain challenges for cause—which, as it turned out, were limited to overt expressions of bias toward one of the parties. Then peremptories would be exercised in an alternating pattern—two for the defense, one for the prosecution. (Since there were two defendants, Byrne had given them fourteen challenges to the prosecution's six.) When the peremptories were exhausted, those people who had been called and had not been excused would constitute the jury. Byrne could have been more perfunctory (some juries are selected, more or less blindly, in a couple of hours); on the other hand, he was less searching than he would become later in his examination of the second jury, but he consistently managed to instruct potential jurors, through the form and phrasing of his questions, on the kind of answers he wanted. Could they be fair and impartial to both sides? Could they accept the law as he instructed them? Did they understand that the indictment was only a formal charge and not evidence of guilt? He made it clear, both with statements and questions, that he wanted a jury that had formed no opinions about the defendants, about the Pentagon Papers, or, if possible, even about the war, and that if anyone had such an opinion he should drive it from his mind in considering the issues in this case. The essence of the process was something which the lawyers call rehabilitation, but which, in style and substance, was reminiscent of confession and absolution. If a person acknowledged some opinion (most did not), he would become, in effect, the drunk or the adulterer in the confessional booth, and would be asked if, for the purposes of this trial, he could forget his errant ways.

Venireman Walls had heard something about selling the Pentagon Papers to the newspapers; he himself was for winning the war in Vietnam with a victory. Could he still be completely fair and impartial? Yes, he could. Would he tend to favor the side in this trial that seemed to agree with his views? Yes, no, perhaps. Could he be fair and impartial to both sides? Yes, he thought he could.

Venireman Shapland believed it was a shame we were over there. He didn't know whether it was right or wrong.

Could he decide this case without reference to that opinion? Yes, he could.

Venireman Gomer believed that the disclosure of the Pentagon Papers was indicative of another government foul-up; government security was loosening up, but he had no opinion about the Papers. He also felt that we should end the war over there but shouldn't surrender or just get out. Did he feel he could be fair in his decision to both sides in this case, despite the fact that one side might disagree with him on the war? He thought so.

Venireman Grunewald knew something about the security system; when documents were entrusted to you, you had a right to use them only if you had a need to know. He himself had a "Secret" clearance, and he believed he could be a good judge of what was going on. He had formed no opinion of the guilt or innocence of the defendants.

Venireman Knapp believed that the Pentagon Papers were government papers, secret papers that should not have been taken; his neighbor had told him that they had disclosed some papers that he didn't think should be disclosed, but he didn't pay any attention to it—his sprinkler system had been flooding out. He could come to a just decision.

Venireman Silver felt he had some knowledge of security regulations; he had worked with blueprints for a missile component which had to be locked in a secret cabinet every night and logged in and out. Did he feel that his experience would influence his decision in this case in any way? He would be more influenced by what he heard in court than by what he had heard before.

The questioning became a game: what did the judge want? Some were afraid they were supposed to know something and would fail the test; others learned quickly that the less they knew, the fewer opinions they had, the easier the test would be. Byrne, amiable through a hundred repetitions of identical questions, was teacher, father, confessor, with a charm that endured fatigue, the edge of a cracking voice and the tedium of a thousand uncertain answers. Most of the prospective jurors had never read the Pentagon Papers or, with the possible exception of a headline somewhere, even heard of them. Many, indeed, barely acknowledged reading a daily newspaper. They read the funnies or "Dear Abby" or *Reader's Digest* or the *San Diego Valley Tribune;* or they worked in their gardens, or took care of too many children, or watched television, or manned a cash register in an all-night discount store, or directed the activities of a club or helped elderly neighbors get where they wanted to go, or pleaded to be excused because the daily hundred-mile drive from home to the courthouse and back was too much. In Los Angeles, an inability to handle the freeways is itself a crippling infirmity.

Yet they had, many of them, one thing in common: personal association, or association through wives or husbands or children, with the defense industry of Southern California; and for a time the reiteration of names and titles became a joke almost as monstrous as the reiteration of faces on the day they first entered the courtroom—North American, Douglas, Jet Propulsion Laboratory, Lockheed, General Dynamics, Navy, Army, engineer, B-1, draftsman, security clearance, systems analyst. The defense therefore found itself in a double bind: it wanted people able to read and understand the Papers, some three thousand pages of material (Nissen, Weinglass had said, "just wants them to be able to read two words: 'Top Secret' "), yet the educated members of the panel were almost invariably connected with the defense industry. Those who conformed to populist biases, the hypothetical man in the street, acknowledged little reading and seemed to display (or feign) an apathy under Matt Byrne's questioning that shocked even the defense. "We want a civilian trial," Boudin told the reporters outside the courtroom, "not a court-martial." If this continued, the defense would move to strike the panel, move again for a more searching *voir dire,* or move for a change of venue, a trial site away from Los Angeles where they would have a chance to get a better jury.

The answers often came painfully, like those of school-children who wished they had learned their lessons more thoroughly; again one was afraid to fail the test and wished for more facility. During the individual questioning each sat alone in the jury box not knowing what was wanted, knowing only that a lot of strange people were listening and taking notes and looking one over. Yet the anguish also came, it seemed, from a genuine feeling of being trapped, of failing convictions and uncertain commitments: We shouldn't with-draw and leave it as if . . . shouldn't fight a war that can't be won . . . should have decided to win it . . . shouldn't have been there in the first place . . should get out honorably . . . Most of them wanted the war to end, but hardly one favored immediate withdrawal, and for everyone who had a son of draft age there were at least two who wore prisoner-of-war bracelets. Several had a general idea of what the Pentagon Papers were about—one called them the "security papers"—but only one acknowledged having read any part of them; he had rushed to a newsstand in Hollywood to buy the *New York Times* on the Sunday when the first story appeared, believed that the country had profited from their publica-tion, and was soon excused for cause. Among the over-whelming majority—assuming they were reasonably honest in their answers—Daniel Ellsberg and the Papers had caused not a ripple.

Midway into the second week of the *voir dire,* Boudin, Nesson and Weinglass tried to mount another attack on the procedure. All persons with extensive connections to the mili-tary or to defense industry, they argued, should be excused for cause—Boudin was "appalled" by "the depth, intensity and scope" of military families and backgrounds and the range of military experience—and those who had experience with the security system or who held clearances should be questioned much more extensively. Such people had been indoctrinated on what the "law" was and what the regulations required, would be witnesses rather than jurors, and would, more likely than not, be embarrassed with their superiors if they returned a verdict of acquittal. The jury in this case, Boudin argued, would come in "loaded with preconceptions and misconceptions." The questions Byrne addressed to them were "not questions which produced facts . . . [but] only generalized statements of acquiescence" that they could be fair. The defense had affidavits from people who were afraid that merely testifying as witnesses for Ellsberg and Russo would jeopardize their clearance and therefore their livelihoods; this fear would obviously affect the jurors as well. Nissen, Boudin said, was in a hurry to get the trial started because his witnesses were about to go on vacation—it was now mid-July—and he objected to what he regarded as pressure from the prosecution to get the trial under way. (Byrne had in fact been talking about extending the hours of court— which normally ran from 9:30 A.M. to 4:30 P.M., with an hour and a half for lunch—but that probably reflected his own impatience rather than any pressure from Nissen.) They were operating at "breakneck speed" which was turning the selection of the jury into a matter of form. He could not continue at this pace, he told Byrne, alluding to his heart problem—he had a heart pacer—but even the younger lawyers were having difficulty. Nissen, chin on hand, listened silently through most of Boudin's argument, observing only that when it came to security regulations the jurors were "near-illiterates in the field." If what they knew constituted expertise and therefore grounds for disqualification, "then everybody who's been in the service is a walking expert."

Byrne rejected the complaints. He was asking the questions as fairly as he could and would take as much time as necessary. Yet the arguments seemed to have effect: his questions became more searching, and, over Nissen's objection, he agreed to ask the veniremen (with great diffidence, as it turned out) whether they would be able and willing to read the materials in the case, a question that many assumed had something to do with physical rather than educational liabilities. (Among those who said they could was a retired furniture craftsman who spoke broken English, read no newspaper and acknowledged that his formal education consisted of six years of grammar school in Italy. The defense wanted him excused for cause—he would obviously be unable to understand the documents—but Byrne found no reason to comply. He became Juror Number One.) Byrne's questions about the effects of instruction in the classification system (for those who had any) also became somewhat more extensive, though in the end he would always return to the injunction to "search your hearts and your conscience to see if you can be fair and impartial jurors in this case." He excused two men who confessed that they might not be able to disregard their previous experience in the security system. Those who indicated that they could be removed from the jury only through the exercise of peremptory challenges Byrne would "rehabilitate" wherever possible—fairly, impartially, it seemed, regardless of whether the individual in question seemed to hold views favoring the defense or the government, though the mode of his questions seemed consistently (for those who wanted to sit on this jury) to invite evasion rather than candor. Those who searched their hearts and consciences most deeply were also the ones who would have the most doubts about their ability to disregard their prejudices and therefore the most difficulty escaping challenges for cause. Perhaps there was no other way, perhaps it could only be played as a game. In an ordinary criminal case political views might not make much difference; in a case such as this, where so much was involved, it would be nearly impossible to get a jury that was simultaneously honest, literate and unbiased by previous experience and opinion.

The final selection of the jury devolved on a series of moves and maneuvers, a chess game determined by the sequence of peremptory challenges established by the judge in advance: government, defense, defense, government, defense, defense, defense, government, defense, defense . . . The defendants, in consultation with their lawyers and psychiatrists, operated on the general principle that it was better to fill the jury box with people they regarded as weak and apathetic than to get one or two strong people who would ultimately go against them and take the rest of the jury along. At the same time it was important to exercise challenges in such a way as to seat at least one person who would be almost certain to hold out for acquittal, to go, at the very least (given the composition of the panel) for a hung jury. Information gathered by the network hadn't yielded much: the members of the panel were, for the most part, as uncommitted out of court as their answers indicated during the course of the *voir dire*. One man who was thought to have registered as a member of the Peace and Freedom Party in 1968 turned out to be a case of mistaken identity. A woman about whom the defendants knew nothing, and who therefore made them apprehensive, was peremptorily challenged by the government; she had been born in Holland, and perhaps Nissen, using the records of the Immigration and Naturalization Service, knew something more; perhaps he was merely guessing. The defense challenged those with extensive experience in the security system and those who were currently employed as professionals in the defense industry; the government challenged those who had expressed strong antiwar views or who looked too young and freaky, and, in one case, a woman who was obviously rebelling against an authoritarian father who had spent all his life in the military. The key person for the defense, finally, was a woman named Sally Gordon (the wife of a retired laundryman), whose sister had expressed sympathy and support for Ellsberg and Russo and whose Jewish-mother demeanor immediately appealed to the defense. As the cycle of challenges went, the defense, by giving up its next-to-last peremptory, was able to get her on the jury without giving the government another opportunity to remove her.

It was, nonetheless, a weak jury, four men and eight women, among them the Italian furniture craftsman, a Disneyland Hotel piano player's wife who believed the United States should get out of Vietnam "with honor," a housewife who thought it was "hard to know" whether she could be fair and impartial (then later said she could), a mechanic's wife who believed the United States should not be involved in Vietnam but whose opinion, she told Byrne, was "not strong enough to march on," a custodian for a rubber company who said he read the sports pages first (but who would later tell Russo that, as a fellow Italian American, he was sympathetic), a retired mailman and mailroom clerk, a Japanese-American civil engineer who worked for the County Road Department and had no views on Vietnam, a sheet-metal worker's widow who had read about the Pentagon Papers in the newspapers but never took what she read in the papers as fact, a furniture salesman's wife who wished the war were over "and the boys would come home," a retired postal clerk's wife who read *Reader's Digest* and had no opinion on the war "at this time," and Mrs. Gordon, the Jewish mother. According to the charts kept by the psychiatrists, the men on the panel had no particularly strong views on the war or the Papers, but neither did they seem to have any hostility toward the defendants. They were characterized as happy-go-lucky types. No one on the panel was regarded as highly persuasive or tenacious: the government had removed people, particularly women, with dovish views; the defense had challenged people with heavy commitments to the defense industry or with hawkish or authoritarian attitudes.

Ellsberg, true to his growing populist inclinations, tried to remain reasonably optimistic: Perhaps they wouldn't read much of the Pentagon Papers, but the "contradictions, lies and omissions" about the war didn't need much elaboration. If he had been on that jury four years earlier he would have voted for conviction, but it was precisely the evidence that the defense was about to present that had changed his mind. Among others on the defense, however, the gloom increased with each passing day. Halperin was calling it a tragedy, and when Mrs. Gordon informed the judge that she was nervous about sitting after having received some anonymous calls, there developed a growing feeling that the case was out of control. Byrne persuaded her to stay on, but

that decision only seemed to amplify the feeling among
defense lawyers and consultants that this jury, combined with
Byrne's rulings on the pretrial matters, had created a situation
that bordered on desperation. During the same week that
Mrs. Gordon asked to be excused, the defense received word
that John Paul Vann had been killed in Vietnam. Vann, who
had developed a reputation as a tough and honest military
officer and was perhaps the most knowledgeable American
in Vietnam, had remained one of Ellsberg's closest friends
(though they differed on the war) and was expected to be an
important defense witness in Los Angeles. Vann, the maverick colonel, knew about the falsified data and the self-decep-
tion. His death was a serious blow not only to Ellsberg
personally—he wept on hearing of it—but to the cause of the
defense. There was something spooky about the whole thing,
Rosenbaum said—the jury, Mrs. Gordon, Byrne's rulings,
Vann's death: a sense of fragility that produced a despair
bordering on fear. Something was needed to mitigate that
feeling and to restore the morale of a defense team that had
become increasingly prone to internal fights, depression and
fatigue. They had all begun to think that the very best they
could hope for was a hung jury, and even that was no longer
a certainty. Boudin believed that with this jury there was a
good chance, at the very least, of conviction on theft.

VI

Their opportunity came, almost literally, through the back
door: an unannounced and seemingly furtive *in camera* submission from the government to the judge that was, in hindsight, the turning point in the case. On July 24, the prosecution, pursuant to a standing court order to disclose any wiretapping of the defendants, their lawyers or their consultants
—among them Halperin, Hayden and Scheer—informed
Byrne, without notice to the defense, that there had been an
"interception" of a conversation by someone covered by the
order. The defendants learned of it from Byrne when, in
response to a defense complaint about what they regarded

as the insufficiency of an affidavit denying electronic surveillance, he announced that the *in camera* material had been filed. The affidavit, based on an "investigation" of government records, said there had been no surveillance except as "may hereafter be disclosed to the court." Although the prosecution was not required to give the defense the contents of the filed material until the judge could rule on its relevance, it had an obligation to notify the opposition that something had been submitted, and Byrne was stunned that no notice had been given. The prosecution had just learned of this "overhear," Nissen explained, and there had been no time to let them know.

Boudin and Weinglass wanted Byrne to stop all proceedings at once. They were in the process of selecting the last jurors, and opening statements were scheduled to begin within two days. "This is an incredible development," Weinglass told Byrne. "We've been kept totally out of it . . . We're supposed to operate on some kind of level of trust . . . We're totally cut out of this process; we don't know whose line has been tapped or who has been subject to electronic surveillance." Under a Supreme Court ruling in *Alderman v. United States,* Byrne was required to hold an immediate hearing to determine the legality of the tap and, if it was judged to be illegal, to determine whether information derived from the tap could have tainted the evidence in the case or prejudiced a lawyer–client privilege of confidentiality. It was not up to the judge to determine whether the tap material related to the case, Boudin said; the judge alone could not make such a finding. Even "an apparently innocent phrase, an apparently chance remark . . . or even the manner of speaking," Boudin argued, quoting from a Supreme Court decision, could provide important information. Only the lawyers in the case could properly judge what might be relevant, and under *Alderman* they had a right to see it. In any case, the government's behavior in this instance was "so shocking" and "shameful," the government's affidavits denying surveillance so dishonest, that the indictment should be dismissed.

Nissen objected to any disclosure or any interruption of the proceedings. A third party could have been overheard, he said, and disclosure could jeopardize "the installation" and therefore be highly prejudicial. The government's affidavits were in full compliance with the court's orders, and he objected to Boudin's remarks impugning his honesty.

BYRNE:     There is some concern about the meaning of the affidavit [denying surveillance directed against the defendants, lawyers and consultants], and so we have an understanding [that] the government's investigation discloses that there has been no electronic surveillance directed against any of the individuals [covered by the order]. Is that correct?

NISSEN:     That is what we said, your honor.

BYRNE:     Is that correct?

NISSEN:     Everything in the affidavit is correct. The answer to that question is "yes."

BYRNE:     That there has been no electronic surveillance conducted at any of the places [of residence or business of the people listed in the order]?

NISSEN:     That is what we said and that is correct.

BYRNE:     And the only electronic interception that there has been, and has been disclosed *in camera,* is that some individual or individuals were overheard on a surveillance being conducted against someone else, or at some other place, is that correct?

NISSEN:     That is the only thing it could be, although the affidavit says . . . that they have not been overheard at all except as hereafter disclosed.

BYRNE:     All right, but is that what your investigation has revealed?

NISSEN:     Yes, sir.

Byrne ruled within twenty-four hours. He had examined the *in camera* material and found that there was just one interception "on a single date" and that nothing in that interception "could conceivably be related to the attorney–client

privilege" or be in any way material to the case. There had
been no violation of the Fourth or Sixth Amendment rights
of the defendants (regarding, in one instance, the prohibition
against illegal searches and seizures and, in the other, the
right to counsel) and he refused to disclose the name or function of the person who had been overheard. Later the defense
learned that the material dealt with an attorney, probably
Boudin, who had regular dealings with the Chilean Embassy
and the Cuban mission to the United Nations and who did
legal work for both. Byrne also refused to stay the proceedings until the defense had an opportunity to go to the Ninth
Circuit Court of Appeals to request an order requiring him
to hold a hearing on the wiretap. The judges for the entire
Ninth Circuit, he informed the defense, were currently meeting in Los Angeles at their annual judicial conference. "If the
Court of Appeals finds merit they will stay it."

The decision to appeal stemmed largely from desperation.
The defense lawyers had doubts that the appeal would succeed, but the move might delay the trial long enough to force
Byrne to dismiss the jury and select another. The Supreme
Court was in recess and would not reconvene until October;
unless it met in emergency session, any appeal from a circuit
court decision could not be heard until then; if the court
ordered a stay pending the outcome of such an appeal, the
trial could be held up for at least three months. More significantly, the move also seemed to offer an opportunity to
recapture the initiative. Boudin was exasperated with Byrne
(though he never expressed it publicly) and was looking for
something that would chasten him. It was not that Byrne was
thought to be biased in the sense that he favored one side,
but that he simply had too much ambition and too little experience to make the proper decisions. Most judges were influenced by "community values," and most felt that the
government, as a party to a case, was on a "higher level."
Byrne was caught by that. For weeks, Boudin felt, they had
been losing, and even the slim chance of winning on this
issue, of beating Byrne in a higher court, of getting the jury

dismissed, anything, drove them to work all night to prepare their motion and draft the necessary papers.

Their hopes rested on Justice William O. Douglas, who, since the death of Hugo Black, had been the leading civil libertarian on the Supreme Court. Douglas, who had jurisdiction for the Ninth Circuit and was empowered to issue stays and other temporary orders on behalf of the Supreme Court while it was in recess (each justice of that Court is responsible for one circuit), was himself attending the judicial conference at the Sheraton Huntington Hotel in Pasadena. Even if the circuit court refused to stop the trial, or if it denied the appeal, Douglas might be persuaded to act. The defense would request a writ of mandamus, basically an order from a higher court commanding Byrne to hold the hearing they wanted. It was an unusual procedure, since appeals courts rarely stop litigation once it has begun; the normal course is to wait until a trial is completed and then appeal on the ground of judicial error in the lower court. But Douglas, sensitive to issues of wiretapping, might issue the stay until the Supreme Court could hear the case.

The bet paid off. Douglas' willingness helped persuade two other judges of the Ninth Circuit, of which he was technically a member, to join him in signing an order stopping the proceedings in Byrne's court until a three-judge panel could rule on the appeal. The panel quickly denied the appeal, ruling that there was nothing material to the case in the wiretap and that therefore Ellsberg and Russo lacked standing to pursue their appeal. But Douglas was still in town and was available for an immediate appeal to the Supreme Court.

There ensued an improbable scene at the Pasadena hotel: the judges, in their pink and lavender jackets, yellow shirts, white slacks, standing around the hotel patio with their pre-dinner drinks; the defense lawyers, Boudin, Nesson, Weinglass and Donovan, in search of Douglas, wandering through the crowd in their rumpled business clothes like cinema Bolsheviks casing a palace reception; and the reporters, a seedy quartet who had chased the lawyers up the freeway from downtown Los Angeles, hanging around the Sheraton Huntington lobby trying to persuade themselves that the whole thing was really taking place.

"Yakima?" one of the lawyers said. "Yakima? You've got to be kidding."

"He wants us to come to Yakima," said a rumpled business suit, the hastily drawn papers still in his hand. "He'll hear arguments in Yakima tomorrow at four-thirty."

"Yakima," said another rumpled business suit. "Where the hell is Yakima?"

Douglas, who had become noted not only as a civil libertarian but as a mountain climber and as something of a curmudgeon, told them he was on his way to his summer retreat in Goose Prairie, Washington, near Yakima, which is twelve hundred miles from Los Angeles. The defense lawyers were asking him to take an extremely serious step, he informed them, and he wanted to hear arguments from both sides. There was a small courtroom in the post office building in Yakima which was (for him) a convenient place to summon the lawyers: Nissen, Reese and Barry for the government—who, when they failed to get a commercial flight, went by Navy jet; Boudin, Weinglass and Young for the defense. The defense lawyers also had trouble making their travel arrangements—Nissen hadn't offered them a ride—and they finally flew by commercial jet to Seattle, then by chartered plane to Yakima.

For an hour in the Yakima courtroom, Douglas heard the arguments. Nissen contended that stopping trials midway was chaotic (a jury had just been sworn), that lawyers couldn't simply go running to an appeals court "every time they get a ruling they don't like," and that appealing trial court decisions piecemeal could be justified only in an extreme situation where the trial judge clearly exceeded his authority. Boudin argued that this was just such a situation, that, in fact, Byrne lacked authority *not* to order a hearing on the wiretap evidence. In the background was the Supreme

Court's own increasing suspicion of wiretapping by the government, in a series of decisions which, despite the Court's four Nixon appointees and its law-and-order reputation, made any evidence from an illegal tap (which seemed to include almost any tap not authorized by court order) inadmissible and permitted defendants to challenge an entire prosecution if the government's case had been contaminated "by the fruit of the poisoned tree." Whether the tap in question was in any way proscribed by prior decisions was at the time uncertain—Nissen had said it was justified on grounds of "foreign intelligence"—nor was it clear whether an order stopping the trial at this point (and on these grounds) was legally proper.

Douglas felt it was. A day later, having contemplated the matter on the heights of Goose Prairie (and, it is believed, having called some of his fellow justices), he ordered the trial stopped until the full Court could decide whether to hear the appeal. Using a public telephone, since there was no phone at his home, he called the clerk of the Supreme Court and dictated his opinion:

> The constitutional right . . . pressed here is the right to counsel guaranteed by the Sixth Amendment. That guarantee obviously involves the right to keep the confidences of the client from the ear of the government, which these days seeks to learn more and more of the affairs of men. The constitutional right of the client, of course, extends only to his case, not to the other concerns of his attorney. But, unless he can be granted standing to determine whether his confidences have been disclosed to the powerful electronic ear of the government, the constitutional fences protective of privacy are broken down . . . I am exceedingly reluctant to grant a stay where the case in a federal court is barely underway. But conscientious regard for basic constitutional rights . . . makes it my duty to do so.

The order, of course, raised more questions than it answered. Could the Supreme Court vacate the stay without convening in emergency session? Could it be done by phone?

Should Justice Rehnquist, who had been in the Justice Department when this prosecution was initiated, disqualify himself? Could the jury be held for several months until the trial began? The government, represented by Solicitor General Erwin N. Griswold, regarded the stay "as an impermissible interference with the proper course of criminal proceedings" and wanted it vacated at once. It would be wholly unprecedented and improper "to keep this jury on leash indefinitely." There was even a possibility that if the trial judge discharged the jury during the expected delay, "the United States will have forever lost its right to a trial of this indictment." In response to Griswold's plea, Chief Justice Warren E. Burger polled other members of the Court by telephone to determine whether they wanted to convene in a special term, but they declined, and so, on August 9, having instructed the jurors again (as he had every day they appeared in court) not to discuss the case or read about it in the newspapers, Byrne excused them until October. The case, tangled in legal questions from the beginning, had come to a dead stop.

No one celebrated. Boudin, who was delighted to get away for a while from Los Angeles, a place he hated, explained that they had done the only thing possible, yet no one regarded the stay as a victory. Russo was angry and Ellsberg was ambivalent. There were other things to do, Ellsberg told the reporters. He would go on a speaking tour to talk about the war and the bombing of the dikes in Vietnam, and try to help defeat Richard Nixon. Every week of the trial, the United States had dropped explosives equivalent to one Hiroshima bomb on Vietnam; a million tons had been dropped since June 13, 1971, the day the Pentagon Papers were published; in World War II all the belligerents combined had dropped only two million tons. But he had also been counting on this trial as a way of telling the story and resisting the war and the government. "This," he said, "is not a satisfactory way to complete this trial."

Later Ellsberg would deny that he had opposed the appeal to the Supreme Court and that he had been furious with his

lawyers for pressing it, yet there was never a time during the
entire proceedings when he appeared more despondent, a
man closer to the verge of defeat. The nation's equilibrium,
he told me just before he left for his speaking tour, "is very
precarious. People are on the edge of hysteria." He himself,
he confessed, had never felt as much fear as he had a few
weeks before when the people who were called for the jury
testified on the extent of their involvement with the military
and the defense industry. Now all he could foresee was more
bombing and mining, and it was possible to believe that
Nixon would use nuclear weapons in Vietnam before the
next four years were over; Ellsberg had seen documentary
evidence in 1969 that had persuaded him that the United
States would bomb the North all out and mine its harbors
before 1972. The only hope, therefore, was McGovern, who
would have a mandate to get out. "The country and I are
about to drift apart; we can't understand each other except in
terms of madness. The country is being judged in this election; the country is up for judgment." Why did everyone
think he was crazy when he spoke of war crimes?

There were other complaints among the defense: the
stay was a cop-out, a technicality. They had come to expose
the war and the government, and now the defense itself had
deprived them of the chance. At the moment when it mattered most, just when Nixon was up for reelection, the forum
would not be there, and one would have to go elsewhere to
resist the war. Among the young volunteers there was even a
suspicion that the government had found the wiretap to suit
its own convenience—it was all a trick by the Administration
and the Justice Department to get the trial postponed. Russo,
who usually managed to get directly to his point, told the
reporters that this was a government that wanted to destroy
the Bill of Rights, that Nixon was an international outlaw,
and that this wiretap, like many others, was the responsibility
"of the same people who tried to bug the Democratic National Committee. They've done a lot more bugging than
they'll admit to." (Russo's broad rhetoric, as it turned out,

was not exaggerated.) And there was also the general let-down of an aborted effort, leaflets that could not be published, films that could not be made, demonstrations which would never take place. A whole collection of movement refugees had drifted here for another action that had been taken away from them; for them, as for so many others, Ellsberg and Russo, though in jeopardy of long prison sentences, were sometimes vehicles, public platforms for the greater cause, and therefore objects (even like Vietnamese, or draftees, or prisoners of war) to be used in the struggle. The war and the government could dehumanize all of us, no matter which side we were on.

The stay remained in effect until November, when the Supreme Court declined to hear the appeal. Byrne meanwhile had kept the jury intact, even though the defense had offered to waive the constitutional guarantee against double jeopardy in order to encourage him to dismiss the jury and thus strengthen its own case for a full Supreme Court hearing. (Since the jury had already been sworn, the trial was technically under way. In the absence of a waiver of double jeopardy, the declaration of a mistrial and dismissal of the jury at that point would have raised questions about whether the defendants could have been tried again.) Even after the long delay, with the likelihood that the jurors had heard enough to blame the defense for it, and despite the chances that the jurors had been exposed to all varieties of outside influence about the case, Byrne was determined to proceed with the same panel. No jury had ever been held out this long.

In the meantime, moreover, a number of officials, among them Vice-President Agnew, had made public statements about the case; Robert Dole, the chairman of the Republican National Committee, had publicly accused Ellsberg of stealing government documents (he compared him, unfavorably, to the Watergate burglars); and *Time* magazine had disclosed that Bernard Barker had been hired by Hunt to bring a group of Cubans to Washington in May 1972 and attack Ellsberg as a traitor at an antiwar rally on the steps of the Capitol. Secrecy itself had become a campaign issue. Prophetically, Boudin accused the government on November 30 of a "pattern of misconduct" (a phrase he was to use frequently in the following months) that tied Watergate directly to the Ellsberg-Russo trial: Mitchell, Mardian, Liddy, Hunt and Barker were inseparable, he said, whether they were acting as political campaigners or as the government of the United States. Not only did Boudin want Byrne to declare a mistrial and dismiss the jury, he now also asked for a full hearing to determine the government's involvement in the attack on Ellsberg and in political espionage involving his clients. He had no idea at the time, of course, about the burglary of Ellsberg's psychiatrist's office or about the other White House activities in the case. ("If I hadn't heard it," Nissen said in reply to Boudin's charges, "I wouldn't have thought it possible." Boudin, he claimed, was simply trying to delay the trial even longer.)

The defense, in the face of Byrne's refusal to dismiss the jury, appealed to the Ninth Circuit Court again, was again denied a writ of mandamus, but received an opinion from the court—an overt message to Byrne—that "it would be foolish" to try the case before a jury that had been at large so long. It was the chastening that Boudin wanted, in effect a reprimand from a higher court. Byrne responded immediately, called the jury in, and discharged them. "You couldn't have found a better group of people," said juror William F. Abata, the rubber-plant custodian, rising unannounced from his seat in the jury box, "or a fairer group of people."

# FIVE

# The Rituals of Secrecy

I

IN September 1972, with the trial suspended, Charles Goodell went to the Pentagon to see his old colleague from the House of Representatives, Defense Secretary Melvin Laird. He wanted to inform Laird that if the trial in Los Angeles were resumed there would undoubtedly be disclosures that would cause the government some difficulties, particularly in the Department of Defense. Goodell was certain that there would be testimony about those higher than Top Secret classifications whose very existence was regarded as extremely sensitive by the government.

Laird called in J. Fred Buzhardt, general counsel for Defense and an old political friend of Senator Strom Thurmond of South Carolina, who explained that Goodell was confused, that he was talking about access categories, not a classification system. The discussion quickly bogged down in semantics about the difference between a classification system and special categories of access within that system. Obviously an individual with a Top Secret clearance would not be entitled to see everything that was so classified, Buzhardt said; there

was also the "need to know," which would be established by
the relevance of the material to the individual's duties.
Goodell countered that there were categories of access beyond
Top Secret which necessitated quite separate clearance procedures and involved investigations presumably more searching than those for an ordinary Top Secret clearance. It would
be revealed, he suggested, that the Defense Department, the
National Security Agency, the CIA and other agencies of
the federal government were honeycombed with separate
security systems, codes, and categories of restricted information; the fact that such systems were even maintained (let
alone the information itself) was not supposed to be known
by the Congress, by the public or, in many instances, even by
the senior civilian officials of the very agencies which maintained them. Goodell further informed Laird that during the
course of the trial the still-classified negotiation volumes
would almost certainly become public and that a number of
other items considered sensitive by the government were
likely to be discussed. Goodell did not ask Laird to propose
that the prosecution of Ellsberg and Russo be dropped;
he just wanted to let him know what was involved. Laird
thanked him, and Goodell left. A few weeks later Goodell
checked with Laird again, but there were no further developments. The prosecution would go on.

What Goodell did not tell Laird was that six months earlier
he and other members of the Ellsberg-Russo defense team
had had a series of cloak-and-dagger meetings with an Air
Force lieutenant colonel named Edward A. Miller, Jr., who,
as a member of the Office of Security Review in the Pentagon, had written a series of reports evaluating the sensitivity
and relevance to the national defense of the Vietnam study.
They had found Miller through Senator Gravel's office, where
he had gone looking for a postretirement job—he would
retire in July—and they had arranged to see him at a series
of clandestine meetings in Washington-area parking lots. The
reports had been commissioned by the Pentagon General
Counsel's Office (headed by J. Fred Buzhardt) in response to

a request from the Department of Justice issued the previous December. Miller gave copies to the defense lawyers a few months after they were written and agreed to testify about them at the trial.

Miller's reports concluded that the volumes of the Pentagon Papers he had been asked to review were harmless from a national-defense point of view, and, moreover, that many of the documents in them should have been declassified years before. Miller was not an expert, except perhaps on the procedures of declassification, but he had submitted the documents to the appropriate government agencies, had received back lists of "exceptions" to declassification, and had then checked those lists against material that had already been published or had, for other reasons, become dated. "We do not believe," he had written in reference to one of the volumes, "that any of the classified sources should retain security markings, and that, had they been submitted for security review even as long as ten years ago, all would have been declassified without difficulty." In his opinion, he wrote about another volume, "none of the material should be classified, nor would it have qualified for classification in 1969." In another instance, he noted that the State Department had objected to declassification of portions of the volume dealing with the overthrow of Ngo Dinh Diem as President of South Vietnam in 1963:

Some task force reviewers objected to mention of how, even inadvertently, the U.S. supported the plotters, on the grounds that U.S. relations with other governments would be damaged. The argument centers on the premise that friendly governments might conclude that the U.S. will freely interfere in their internal affairs in the same manner that it did in SVN. This point has validity only so far as similar conditions to those existing in SVN in 1963 exist in other friendly states. The simple fact that other governments might be suspicious of the U.S. as the result of the anti-Diem plot revelations does not seem sufficient grounds to deny U.S. involvement, because press speculations and memoirs of participants preceded by years the "Pentagon Papers."

Miller did not regard any of the volumes covered by the Ellsberg indictment as sufficiently sensitive to prohibit their disclosure in 1969. He believed the objections of the various agencies were marginal or covered information that had, in substance, been long in the public domain, often in documents published by the government itself. More significantly, he also believed that someone in Defense was trying to suppress his reports. He had seen an internal Defense Department memo from someone higher up in the Office of Security Review or in the Office of Public Affairs (which supervised OSR) which referred to instructions that his evaluation of the Pentagon Papers should be removed from the files. He had also told the Ellsberg-Russo lawyers that other people in the Office of Security Review, which was responsible for reviewing material for declassification, and possibly others in the Pentagon, had worked on the Vietnam study in connection with the prosecution of Russo and Ellsberg. By the time Goodell saw Laird and Buzhardt, the lawyers had already contacted a number of former high officials in the Kennedy and Johnson Administrations, among them McGeorge Bundy, Arthur Schlesinger, Jr., Theodore Sorensen and John Kenneth Galbraith, who were prepared to testify that disclosure of the Pentagon Papers (even in 1969, when they were copied) could not have been injurious to the national defense. But Miller's memos represented the first solid indication that someone within the government who had been assigned to evaluate the Papers for the Department of Justice had reached the same conclusion. Fortuitously, Miller had retired in the meantime and was now working for the Center for Defense Information, an independent organization in Washington which reviewed national-defense policies and budgets.

David Nissen, in the meantime, had been trying to sharpen and revise his case. He had maintained from the beginning that everything in the Pentagon Papers related to the national defense, but, in response to Byrne's orders, he had been forced to specify the passages he intended to use or about which he expected to elicit expert testimony. "Someday in this courtroom," Byrne had said to him, "you are going to tell the jury and try to urge upon the jury that 'this document relates to the national defense and let me show you where it does' and you are going to say 'it relates here and it relates there and it relates here and I am to call witnesses A, B, and C to show you it relates to national defense there.' " Nissen had been "firmly convinced" that the court had a "misconception about the character of the documents and the manner in which they will be dealt with," but he had nonetheless complied with the court's demands and listed some four hundred pages or passages he expected to use. During the fall, he revised and changed them, preparing a new list substantially different from the bill of particulars he had given the defense before the break in August.

The change was prompted by the assignment of Brigadier General Paul F. Gorman, a career Army officer, as chief consultant to the prosecution. Gorman, who had been Leslie Gelb's deputy on the Pentagon Papers Task Force and had written one of the volumes himself, was now the assistant commander of the Fourth Infantry Division at Fort Carson, Colorado. A graduate of the U. S. Military Academy and the holder of a master's degree in public administration from Harvard, Gorman had taught history at West Point, had served in Vietnam with the First Infantry Division, had done a tour of duty in 1969 as a military liaison officer to the U. S. negotiators at the Paris peace talks, and regarded himself familiar with "virtually all kinds" of intelligence. When he was later asked to state his profession, however, he would simply tell the jury, "I am a soldier." He would also testify that he did not want to become involved in this trial—he had privately told acquaintances that he thought the Army would be made to take the blame for the prosecution, and that its reputation would suffer—but he had been persuaded (or ordered) to do so. Gorman was regarded as a briefer, a man who had conducted hundreds of chalk talks, pointer in hand, for other officers, members of Congress and officials of the Administration, and his assignment to the prosecution seemed to indicate that the government's case would be presented as a series of "dog and pony shows"—military officers in full uniform briefing the jury on the contents of the Papers. But that never happened; Nissen, it seemed, was having more trouble with his case than the defense.

Gorman's suggestions and counsel caused Nissen to produce an entirely new list of exhibits for the case, leading the defendants to charge that the Administration planned to use the trial as a forum to stage an affirmative defense of the Vietnam War and to emphasize, perhaps even try to glorify, the need for secrecy in negotiations. Of the six hundred-odd items on the new list, each of them a page in the Xerox copy of the Papers, and each of them a slide to be projected in the courtroom, 390 were not on the original bill of particulars (one entire volume, Nissen told Byrne, had been left out through a "typographical omission"); and more than three hundred which had been in the original bill had been dropped. Much of the new material came from the still-classified volumes dealing with secret "contacts" with Vietnam during the Johnson years; a great deal also covered the earliest years of the French Indochina War, American estimates of the Communist threat, and elaborations of the domino theory. There were extended references to the necessity for secrecy in planning and negotiations, a discussion of the Strategic-Hamlet Program of 1961–63, and assessments of the importance of Cambodia in the defense of Vietnam. It was, Ellsberg said at the time, "the beginning of a revisionist history of Vietnam, one way for Nixon to say, 'I am the protector of your good name and your good conscience. No one died in vain.' " The government would try to show, at the very least, that the people who made the Vietnam decisions were sincere, that secrecy was necessary, and that Nixon's trip to China and the Kissinger–Tho negotiations then in progress were indications of that necessity. The inclusion of press conference statements by Lyndon Johnson and other items from the public domain which were reproduced in the Papers was obviously not intended to impress the jurors with the military sensitivity of the documents, nor was there any reason, in Ellsberg's view, for adding material about Cambodia if the Administration wasn't trying to justify its own invasion in 1970. "All these things were added to justify Nixon's policies." The government was now trying to play the same game as the defense—using the trial to make a political case.

The suspicion was incorrect, or only partially correct, and Ellsberg later conceded that his conclusion had been hasty. Gorman had simply induced Nissen to emphasize those elements in the documents which he knew best and about which he could most easily testify—Gorman himself would be Nissen's key witness on the Papers—and that was in turn a reflection of the problems that Nissen was having with his case. He found it hard to get people who were willing to testify on the national-defense aspects of the Papers; either they thought that the documents contained little that could injure the United States if disclosed or they believed that their testimony, by pointing to sensitive matters relating to United States intelligence, would in itself constitute a breach of security and contain information useful to some foreign power. One employee of the National Security Agency, which was charged with intercepting and decoding foreign communications (and which was apparently engaged in routinely tapping a large number of telephone calls between the United States and foreign countries), would later indicate that the Justice Department had been told that the Papers did in fact contain material derived from "communications intelligence" —interceptions of foreign communications—but that NSA would not disclose, even to the highest officials in Justice, what that material was.

Nissen also had difficulty with the State Department, which, through most of the trial, remained under the impression that the negotiation volumes would be subject to some

sort of protective order and be discussed only *in camera,*
certainly not be discussed in detail in open court or be accessible to the public in the clerk's office. Although those volumes presumably contained some of the most effective material in Nissen's case, Nissen never called anyone from State
to testify about them; as far as that department was concerned, the volumes were still classified and therefore could
not be discussed in open court. Nor could he get anyone from
the CIA. One senior official was reportedly prepared to testify, but a number of other people in the agency, believing
the documents in the Papers to be innocuous, had threatened
to volunteer as defense witnesses if the agency became involved. At the very end of the trial there was a rumor that
Nixon himself had issued a call for volunteers to testify as
rebuttal witnesses, but the only person with diplomatic experience to testify, Philip Habib, then U. S. ambassador to
Australia, talked only in the most general terms about the
need for confidentiality in negotiations and never specified
what portions were particularly damaging. Nor did he disclose who had asked him to testify. What did become clear
was that the Byzantine systems of secrecy within the government had, from the beginning, frustrated the government's
own efforts to prosecute those who had violated them.

II

The screen, twelve feet wide and ten feet high, had been
set up by the prosecution attorneys, with the help of attendant
FBI agents, to face the bench at the left center of the courtroom, with its back to the spectators. It blocked the view of
half the people in the room, including nearly all of the press.
No one other than the judge, the lawyers and the jury could
see what was projected on the screen, and more than half the
audience would be unable to see the prosecution table, the
witness box or the judge.

"We have carefully planned out our opening statement,"
David Nissen explained. "If the court takes away the screen,
you take away our opening statement." He planned to use a

number of slides with his statement, he said, and had placed the screen where the material would be readable.

"It's readable from my office," Matt Byrne replied, and he ordered Nissen to move the screen against the wall to his left, opposite the jury box.

Would the court inquire of the jury if they could see? Nissen asked.

The room, which had been crowded with spectators (among them a dozen uniformed members of the Vietnam Veterans Against the War) ever since the marshals opened the doors at 9 A.M., now erupted with derisive laughter and catcalls. Byrne quickly stopped the outburst: he expected the spectators to extend complete courtesy to all parties. Then he called in the jury, and the trial was ready to begin.

The date was January 17, 1973. It had been six months since the beginning of the selection of the first jury, and over six weeks since the hiatus ended. The first anniversary of the indictment under which the defendants would be tried had long passed, Richard Nixon had been reelected by a landslide, the Vietnam peace settlement was imminent, and the trial of the Watergate burglars had started in Washington. More than ever, this trial now seemed to be a footnote, and Ellsberg a footnote to a footnote. Yet the mood in Courtroom 9 that morning was expectant, as if portentous things were about to happen, things that went beyond the war and even beyond the constitutional issues that were supposed to be at stake. It was as if it were known that the case was somehow connected to a government and to government practices that were suspect for reasons beyond ordinary politics. It was no longer a gray mood. The defense was more buoyant—Byrne had had his comeuppance from the Ninth Circuit Court of Appeals—and the spectators, nearly all of them partisans of the defense, expressed something that verged on the festive, like the moment before the kickoff at the big game. Even Nissen seemed to respond; his humor took in the symbolism of the screen, and he joked about it with the reporters, but some of his assurance had apparently left him. He had been gently chastised by Byrne for his last-minute changes in his case and for his failure to give the defense adequate notice of what was, in effect, a new bill of particulars, and he seemed, since the selection of a new jury, no longer as certain of himself or his case.

The jury had been chosen more quickly than the first panel —the procedure had taken less than two weeks—although Byrne's questions had been more searching and probative than those he asked during the first *voir dire*. A new term of jury service had begun, the new voters were on the rolls, and the attacks on the methods used to select the first jury in the case (and challenges by defense lawyers in other cases) had produced conscious efforts within the district to make the names in the jury wheel more representative of the community. During the arguments the previous summer, the lawyers representing Ellsberg and Russo had demonstrated that Jody Mody, the jury clerk, had excused virtually anyone who claimed hardship (legally, excuses were supposed to be granted only by a judge, but in practice the jury clerk usually acted on her own authority); this time excuses had been issued more parsimoniously, and the panel from which jurors were selected included many more black people, more Chicanos, more people under thirty, and fewer with extensive connections to the military or to the defense industry. Although the defense lawyers renewed their earlier challenges to the procedure, and although they asked again to conduct their own questioning, the demands were less desperate, the veniremen were much more to their liking, and the judge was more responsive. Byrne indicated that he would add questions to the *voir dire* that he had not put to the first group, among them several dealing with their views of government information policies: Had the government, in their opinion, withheld too much information from the public, or had it disclosed too much? Would they have any bias for or against people who had spoken out on U.S. military activities in Southeast Asia? Would a verdict, either way, cause them any embarrassment with their employers or associates? He informed the jurors that they might have to read hundreds or "maybe thousands" of pages of material, made fewer attempts to "rehabilitate" doubtful jurors, was more sparing in giving them clues about the kinds of answers he wanted, and conducted a more confident search for information. Byrne had obviously learned from his experience with the first panel —there had also been an important appeals court opinion regarding Judge Hoffman's jury selection in the Chicago conspiracy case—and, since his chastisement by the Ninth Circuit Court, he had appeared more responsive to the positions of the defense.

The defense lawyers were also more confident of their own decisions, had more information from the "network" (who had, for example, interviewed a bowling partner of one of the jurors and the co-workers of another, and learned that one had a "hippie daughter" and that another had been "horrified by the bombing of Bach Mai Hospital in Hanoi") and had notes on the responses of veniremen in jury selection in other cases in the district, some of them the same people who were called for this jury. At one point Nissen remarked that he would be happy to trade all his information with the defense; he also objected strenuously to some of Byrne's *voir dire* questions: they would mislead the jurors into believing that this was a trial about the war or about the government's information policies, which, he said, it was not. When the final jury was selected, the defense was visibly delighted. There were two men, one black, one a Spanish-speaking native of Costa Rica, and ten women of whom two were black. None was a college graduate. Three of the six alternates were also black, and one was a long-haired law student. Russo called it a "Third World jury."

Cora C. Neal, a widow with three grown children, who worked as a draftswoman for General Telephone. She knew, she said, that "the Pentagon Papers were stolen . . . from the Pentagon" and that they related to Vietnam. She had also told Byrne that she didn't like the war but didn't know what to do about it. She was a registered Republican who, it later turned out, had voted for McGovern.

Jean E. Boutelier, a native of Australia and a former nurse, who was married to a municipal employee. The war, she believed, should be ended as quickly as possible; she had no opinion about the withholding of information, had heard something about the Pentagon Papers and wondered "what was behind it."

Donna R. Kelpe, the wife of a precision machinist and the mother of three children, the oldest of whom was eighteen. She read no newspapers and worried that she would appear ignorant. She had no strong opinion on the war, but she didn't like to see people getting killed, "their people or our people, either one."

Joan B. Duhigg, the wife of a medical representative for Abbott Laboratories and the mother of three children, aged twelve, ten, and eight. She wanted the war to be over but hoped it could be done "in an admirable way." She had also heard that the government had withheld information.

Dulcey V. Embree, a former jazz pianist, black, who once had her own band, "Frances Green and Her Rhythm Queens," and who was the widow of a carpenter. She did not read the papers and never thought about the war. Some members of her social club had mentioned it, but she never talked about it.

Annie M. Saunders, a black postal employee and the wife of another postal worker, whose fifteen-year-old son was in a juvenile home. "If we're fighting for what we think is right, well, maybe those people are fighting for what they think is right," she told Byrne. The government must be withholding information, "because I don't know why our soldiers are fighting in Vietnam."

Margaret C. Kashube, the wife of a shop foreman for a Chevrolet dealer, and mother of two children. She and her husband had both been active with the American Legion, but the Kashubes and the Legion had "had a parting of the ways." She believed, nonetheless, that the war was not being fought "the way a war should" and that the country had "to work awfully hard not to lose face."

Lupe Vasquez, a seamstress for a sportswear manufacturer, and a widow, who had heard that someone had broken into the Pentagon and stolen papers. She didn't believe women liked wars, but had no strong opinion on the war herself.

Phyllis E. Ortman, the wife of a darkroom foreman for an aerial mapping company and mother of a six-year-old daughter, who wished "the war would be over," assumed that the Papers had something to do with military activities, but thought they had been written more than ten years ago. Her answers to Byrne's questions came painfully, though she would later turn out to be an articulate woman who decided, at the end of the trial, to try to write a book about her experience.

Monellis Pittman, a black assembly-line worker at a Ford Motor Company plant who read both local papers every day and who believed the Pentagon Papers "had been taken from someplace, mostly Washington, and had something to do with military defense." Pittman, who served on a local United Auto Workers negotiating committee, believed that "we sometimes get involved in war" to step up the economy. Having been in the military himself, however, he knew "there are some things you just don't tell the public."

Darlene Y. Arneaud, twice divorced, who was raising not only her own two children but also five nephews on welfare payments. "My country right or wrong," she said in response to one of Byrne's questions. "I support my country, but they could be wrong."

Wilfred R. Baltadano, a veteran of the Marine Corps who had been seriously wounded in Vietnam and was now a student at the University of California at Irvine. "We were on a search-and-destroy mission," he explained in the *voir dire,* "when darkness was approaching, and we had to get back to the command post, because we don't want to walk around in the dark . . . Our lieutenant asked a platoon of tanks to give us a ride back. I was on the third tank, the first tank stalled and the tank I was on went to its assistance . . . it went off the road and it hit a seven-hundred-fifty-pound bomb, one of our bombs. It demolished the tank, thirteen men died, and I got out." When he first went to Vietnam, he said, "it was just as a soldier, obedient to what I was being told, and as far as I was concerned, I was doing the right thing." Since he returned, however, he had changed his mind. "I can't condemn the government for its actions; by the same token, I can't condone their actions, either, so I leave it to our elected officials to do their best. . . . It should have been over a long time ago; we could have ended it one way or another." What he knew for sure was that the military often withheld accurate information on casualties.

Baltadano's recitation of his military experience and his views on the war had created the one genuinely dramatic moment in two weeks of *voir dire*. The defense lawyers regarded him as something of a risk; his ambivalence about the war bothered some of them, and the combination of his Vietnam experience and his intelligence were likely to sway many of the uncommitted. Baltadano and Pittman would clearly become the strong voices on the jury. Yet it would obviously be impossible to remove him; there were no grounds to challenge for cause, and a peremptory challenge of a wounded Vietnam veteran (by either side) was out of the question. In any case, it was the Baltadanos that the defense was ostensibly trying to reach; they were the symbols of the age.

David Nissen promised the jurors that his case would be unemotional and undramatic. There would be no documents and no witnesses to litigate the war, no discussion of how it should be ended, and no testimony about the information policies of the government. "Such matters," he said, "are immaterial." He wouldn't even try to prove that the documents in the case were vitally important, that they were exciting or that, if disclosed, they would represent a disaster for the United States. Yet he also managed to advise the jury that the Papers contained "some of the most closely guarded

defense secrets produced by the United States," recommendations of the National Security Council, "sensitive communications . . . CIA reports . . . messages and plans . . . negotiations
through secret channels"; he laced his opening statement with
acronyms and alphabetic agencies—NSC, USIB, JCS, DOD,
MACV, BIR, DOS, CINCPAC, AMB—and told the jurors
that the Papers provided "an inner view into the workings
of the defense establishment at the highest levels." Permitted
two hours for his opening, he devoted much of the time to
summarizing the origins of the Papers, describing how, in
the government's view, they got from Washington to Santa
Monica, specifying the overt acts of the crime, and, with the
aid of a series of charts projected on the screen, summarizing
the indictment and the specific documents it covered:

*Count 6*
    Ellsberg——conveys——1 Study
              (to Thai)

*Count 7*
    Russo——receives——9 Studies
                 Wheeler Memo

He explained how Ellsberg had obtained possession of the
documents—he was acting as a courier for Rand and, in
direct violation of the regulations, failed to turn them in to
the Rand Top Secret Control officer—and how Ellsberg and
Russo had gotten Lynda Sinay, "at that time a girl friend of
defendant Russo" and still a close friend of both defendants,
to assist in copying them. Russo knew that they had been
stolen, and that Ellsberg had taken them for "purposes not
permitted"; Ellsberg knew what he was passing, knew to
whom he was passing it, and knew that the receiver was not
entitled to have it. The government would show, moreover,
that the cost of producing the Papers far exceeded one hundred dollars per volume (a requirement of the theft charges),
that the volumes were classified government property, that

they were "duly classified" by a person authorized to classify them, and that they related to the national defense. If these documents did not relate to the national defense, then "no documents in the world" could.

Despite Nissen's references to the possible usefulness of the documents to a foreign power, his elaboration of the functions of the defense-establishment alphabet agencies, and his description of "closely guarded secrets," his presentation was even less emotional than promised, a deliberate underplaying of a case that Leonard Boudin was about to describe as one of the most significant ever to be litigated. If Nissen meant to impeach Ellsberg and Russo as fanatics or to suggest that Ellsberg was an unstable person with, as Howard Hunt later put it, "a rather unusual life style," he gave no indication; nor did he attempt any personal contact with the jurors, make any effort to create rapport, to charm or to seduce (as the defendants, facing the jury, had already started to do). With his flow charts, his elaboration of the functions of various government agencies (which, in itself, constituted a short civics course for the benefit of the jurors) and his diagrammatic analysis of the indictment, Nissen's presentation cast the trial in the mold and style of an antitrust case, a corporate price-fixing caper without drama, humor, victims or tangible damage, committed by defendants lacking any discernible character or motives. Yet perhaps that was the only possibility in this case; the more dramatic or important he made it, the more he would play to the defense, to the argument that this was a political prosecution, and to the idea that free speech itself was at stake. It had to be styled, as much as possible, as an ordinary case, just another crime, a routine matter. Its very form had, in some way, to be furtive and underplayed. To make it big and brassy and dramatic was to invite defeat.

Boudin, of course, played to the jury, clearing his throat, fussing with his glasses, wandering beyond the lectern, straying well beyond the narrow confines of Nissen's definition of the case. He presented his opening statement now; Leonard

Weinglass reserved his statement on behalf of Russo until the defense opened its case. Boudin wished to remind the jurors that there were no charges of real espionage here, no military secrets given to an enemy, no classified data delivered to a foreign government. It was, rather, a case about a war whose origins, in the view of the defendants, had been concealed from the American people, and it involved documents which showed that at least two Presidents had refused to give Congress information as to why the country was at war. They would present witnesses, among them former ambassadors and other high government officials, who would testify that these Papers contained not military but political secrets, policy secrets, which had been kept from the American people; they would show that Ellsberg had lawful possession of the documents and had not violated instructions, that the information did not, and could not, belong to the government, that the Papers should never have been marked classified, that much of the material in them had already appeared in books and newspapers, some of it leaked by the government itself, and that the classification system was a method of executive control which was used to conceal information from Congress. Ellsberg, Boudin told the jury, wanted to get the information in the Papers to Congress because they revealed, as the jurors would learn during the course of this trial, that the Congress and the public had been misled by the executive branch. They would get, for the first time, an inside look at how Presidents and Secretaries of State really operate to deceive the American people. There would be no great differences between the prosecution and the defense on the "mechanical facts" of the case, he said, there were only differences in interpretation, but those differences, he suggested, were monumental: who owned these Papers, did Ellsberg have lawful possession, were they connected to the national defense, and, most significant, was there, in their disclosure, a chance of injury to the United States, or were there great advantages to the nation?

Since the purpose of an opening statement is ostensibly to

tell the jury what each side hopes to prove with its evidence, Byrne occasionally stopped Boudin (as he had stopped Nissen) when his statement moved into the realm of argument; yet Boudin succeeded, during his two hours, in raising virtually every issue that the defense considered important: the war, the classification system, government secrecy, and the deception of the American people. Toward the end Boudin, obviously fatigued, began to run down, and some people in the defense felt he could have been stronger, yet he had managed to broaden the case to the very limits of its possibilities.

Nissen was furious. Although he objected several times while Boudin spoke, he reserved his anger for a formal response submitted four weeks later attacking not only Boudin's presentation but, more significantly, Byrne's definition of the issues and his earlier rulings on what would be admissible as evidence. Byrne had indicated, ever since the arguments in the spring of 1972, that he would allow considerable latitude on the issue of national defense, and that he would, among other things, regard potential injury to the United States (or aid to a foreign country) as one of the elements required for a definition of "relating to the national defense." In a statement from the bench on the eve of trial, he had amplified that ruling. Among the issues in the case, he had told the lawyers, is the question "Are the documents the type that require protection in the interest of the national defense in that their disclosure could adversely affect or injure this nation or be to the advantage of any foreign nation?" Another issue, he had said, was whether the documents were "confidential and the type that their disclosure could reveal information that was not at that time publicly available." Those rulings and the latitude that Byrne had allowed Boudin in his opening statement seemed to promise a corresponding latitude on evidence as the trial went on.

For several weeks, Nissen's impatience with his old boss had been rising. During the *voir dire* Byrne had asked what Nissen regarded as improper questions having nothing to do with this case, he had later chastised Nissen (though gently) for the last-minute changes in his list of exhibits, and he was now permitting arguments that Nissen regarded as highly prejudicial. Boudin's statement, Nissen told Byrne in a formal memorandum, "ranks among the most outrageously improper ever permitted in a court of law . . . an almost endless string of grossly improper remarks," among them attempts to "try the war, to try other persons not on trial" (such as people in government who leak information or fail to declassify documents), to discuss "post-offense irrelevancies" (such as the delivery of the Xerox copies to Fulbright), and to "try the information policies of the government." But his attack on Boudin's opening was only a preface to an attack on the court itself. Byrne's earlier rulings on the applicable statutes in the case, he said, rendered "superfluous and completely redundant" portions of the Espionage Act which supported his broad definition of national defense as "all matters directly and reasonably connected with the defense of our nation." To his knowledge, he said, "not a single court has ever defined the term 'related to the national defense' as meaning something which if disclosed would injure the United States or aid a foreign country." Moreover, he said, Congress never intended to protect only those documents which a jury

might find could injure the United States or aid a foreign country. The Congressional purpose was obviously to permit those bearing the responsibilities for national defense to exercise their best judgment concerning what could or not be safely disclosed . . . To require proof at a public trial [as Byrne had ruled] of how national defense documents could have injured this country or aided another would in many cases render trials for [Espionage Act] violations more damaging to the country than the violations themselves. A document's relation to the national defense may appear obvious to everyone, and yet its potential for injuring the United States may be unknown and unapparent, except to those with special knowledge and information. To require such potential for injury to be spelled out at trial by disclosing this special knowledge and information would create hazards that would render [the Espionage Act] a dead letter.

The only purpose served by "such an erroneous interpretation of the statute," Nissen went on, would be to protect Byrne against possible reversal on an appeal by rendering a conviction unlikely.

Since the Government cannot appeal from any ruling of the Court in trial, regardless of how erroneous or unfairly beneficial to the defendants or injurious to the Government, and since the defendants would have no appeal from an acquittal, the Court would be safe from reversal by a higher court. However, such considerations should not be allowed to impinge upon the public's right to a fair trial, even though that right lacks any means of enforcement.

Nissen also took issue with the court's ruling that the question "Were the documents lawfully classified under Executive Order 10501?" would be one of the issues of the case, and that the question of whether the documents were in fact "classifiable" would be among those which the jury would have to consider. Those were matters, in Nissen's view, that should not go to the jury; the mere fact that they were classified (properly or not) was the only thing that the jury could properly consider.

It is little wonder that the defense was ecstatic over the Court's statement of "issues." A parallel situation would exist where a Government automobile is stolen from a Government agency which purchased it under an executive regulation allowing acquisition of autos for only certain purposes. No doubt the thief would be delighted to be told that at his trial he could litigate the "issue" of whether the Government should have purchased the car. The defendants are likewise delighted in this case to be given the special privilege of litigating not the issue of whether the documents were duly classified and guarded by those having authority to do so, but instead the question of whether the documents *should have been* guarded and classified. The defendants have already been permitted unprecedented privileges to place everyone on trial but themselves. The Court's creation of the concept of "classifiability" will constitute another giant step in that direction and will simply privilege the defense to try the classifying authorities. The Court's ruling on "classifiability" is perfectly "safe" for the Court since the Government lacks the right to appeal from any adverse ruling ... However, as the foregoing [shows], the ruling is wrong. The Government hopes that the Court will prefer to be right rather than safe.

By the time Nissen submitted his memorandum—nearly a month after opening arguments—it had become clear that his case was in trouble. He had been informed about the unwillingness of the National Security Agency to tell the Justice Department about the material in the Papers it regarded as sensitive, he had failed to get State Department witnesses to testify about the diplomatic volumes, and he had been caught by the defense and the court in an attempt to suppress evidence which indicated that the disclosure of many of the volumes in the Vietnam study could not have injured the United States. He hoped that his memorandum might influence Byrne to restrict the defense in the presentation of its case and to curb Weinglass when he made his own argument. "The Government is confident," he said, "that the next 'opening statement' of defense counsel will at least rival the first one in its degree of impropriety . . . Plaintiff respectfully requests that the Court deal with defense misconduct when it occurs, without forcing the Government to make repeated objections." Nissen began to speak like a loser.

Nissen's testiness seemed to run beyond the substantive issues of the case—Byrne's rulings, Boudin's arguments, his difficulties, whatever they might be, with other agencies of the government—to reflect a personal sense of embattlement, the voice of a man who regarded himself as a victim. If the defense lawyers often saw Byrne as just another prosecutor in black robes, it was even easier to imagine Nissen, in the context of this courtroom, as a besieged minority, the representative of a somewhat outmoded underclass confronting an alien judge, alien defense lawyers and a hostile press. Whatever their differences, Byrne, Boudin and Nesson had more in common, in terms of class, than Nissen had with any of them, smart folks traveling the elite circuits and representing the views of current fashion. Perhaps he was still a hero to his superiors in Washington, doing the work of the righteous in the cause of law and order, but in Courtroom 9 he was the villain, the man the spectators wanted to hiss—hissin'-Nissen-Nixon—and a man who, as the case progressed, would seem increasingly determined to play the role, to demand punishment for offenses and behavior beyond the requirements of his case, the premeditated bad boy in a trial that seemed to thrust the part upon him.

### III

From the first day of testimony the subject was secrets: the secrecy of the Papers—their markings, their cables, their memos—the celebration of secrets, the disclosure of secrets, and, ultimately, the revelation of the secrets about the government's handling of the trial itself. The totem was a plain brown carton, something the delivery boy might have brought from the supermarket, containing the blue-covered Xerox copies of eighteen of the forty-seven volumes of the Papers that Ellsberg and Russo had run through Lynda Sinay's machine, the eight pages of the Wheeler Report, and the so-called Gurtov study on the Geneva Accords of 1954. Properly introduced and identified by their custodian at the Department of Defense, Assistant General Counsel Frank A. Bartimo (who would return to the witness stand on matters more embarrassing to the government), the carton became the symbol of the secret, the container of a sacred and unspeakable text too powerful for ordinary mortals to behold. Although Nissen had told the jury in his opening statement that they should not rely on the word of experts, that they themselves should judge the portentousness of the contents, he immediately proceeded to put his experts on the stand: Lieutenant General William G. De Puy, the former commander of the First Infantry Division in Vietnam and inventor of the search-and-destroy mission, now assistant to the Army Vice-Chief of Staff; and General Gorman, the government's chief consultant. Neither appeared in uniform, but both made the most of their military experience, deluging the jurors with acronyms, code names and references to clandestine intelligence operations. De Puy would testify about the Wheeler Report; he had accompanied General Wheeler to Vietnam on his mission to assess the situation there in the weeks after Tet in 1968, and had helped write the memorandum. Gorman would be the prosecution's expert on all the other documents.

The point, orchestrated with extensive details, was simple: if a foreign government knew what we knew (or if it knew what we knew about what it knew) it would be in a better position to direct its counterintelligence activities, understand our intelligence system, and plan more carefully in the future. Gorman, looking like nothing so much as a prelate—open-faced, cherubic, pontifical—conjured up a hypothetical "foreign intelligence analyst" who, he claimed, would have enjoyed an "intelligence windfall" had the Papers fallen into his hands, a hypothetical foreign government which could have interfered with the Paris negotiations or in other diplomatic efforts to secure peace if it were to possess the documents, and a hypothetical North Vietnamese general assessing hypothetical American plans for hypothetical operations by studying the discarded plans of other operations in other circumstances. The men who planned and executed the Tet attack, De Puy told the jurors, were the same men who ordered the attack in the spring of 1972; the Wheeler memorandum stated that the initial attack in 1968 nearly succeeded in a dozen places—"it was a very near thing"—and that if the enemy were to synchronize an attack in the same areas with an offensive in the highlands, "MACV, the U.S. Military Assistance Command in Vietnam, will be hard pressed."

This was therefore telling the North Vietnamese what action they could take "that would be the most telling." (Wasn't Tet itself a synchronized attack, Weinglass asked him on cross examination, and hadn't General Giap, the Vietnamese commander in the victory over the French and now North Vietnam's Defense Minister, written about "synchronized attacks"? Yes, De Puy answered, they might have known many things, but this confirmed it.)

More important than the information in the Papers, however, was their scope and source. The two generals tried to explain to the jurors that even if a great deal of the information contained in the Papers had already been published elsewhere, the range of the documents, their origins, and the "Top Secret" classification stamp itself would make them invaluable to the foreign analyst. This was not something attributed to an anonymous Pentagon source or an unconfirmed report in a newspaper or a hint by a Washington columnist. This was the Real Thing, an "authoritative survey of the war in Vietnam labeled with the highest classification that this government has." The whole was greater than the sum of the parts, the documents, because of their source and classification, more important than separate pieces of data, the "Top Secret" stamp itself certification of their importance. "These volumes, taken together," Gorman said so frequently that it became an incantation, and a joke among the reporters, "would be principally useful for two purposes: to augment the intelligence capabilities of the foreign analyst, and to influence international relations."

Together, Gorman and De Puy took the jurors through several hundred pages in the documents, explicating the text on the slides that the government had prepared. They represented, in Gorman's view, "the product of the National Intelligence Board and other similar high government agencies" and dealt collectively with the deployment of military forces and with arrangements to decrease the level of forces. They told "all about what the United States attempted to do . . . American strategy . . . governmental planning to conduct the war . . . and to bring it to an end." Although the defense objected vehemently, Gorman repeatedly pointed out that the sources listed in the footnotes—the cables, the CIA assessments, National Intelligence Estimates (NIE's)—were still classified. (If Gorman referred to them and pointed out that they were classified, the defense maintained, the cited documents should be produced to determine their contents and the propriety of their classification; there were several thousand such documents; although Byrne refused to have them produced, he instructed the jury that classification itself should not be regarded as evidence of relationship to "national defense.") The foreign analyst could use those materials to assess the capability of United States intelligence and improve his own counterintelligence operations: JCS, MAAG, Deptel, OCB, DIA, Eyes Only, TS, NODIS, LIMDIS, EXDIS, 201-Group messages, 500-Group messages, ciphers, telephone intercepts . . . Some of the documents could be used by the foreign analyst to identify certain American agents and to determine that certain clandestine operations took place "under military cover" in the years following the 1954 Geneva Accords. Even though many of those agents had been identified before and others retired, the Papers still offered a "documented insight into American intelligence operations," the personalities of those involved, their instructions, and the way they operated. Here was a tempting look into the realm of the spook, a shadowy world made darker still by Gorman's allusions, and by his suggestion that there was a lot more there than he could tell, and more than anyone in the courtroom could possibly know.

There was also the matter of diplomacy, another shadowy realm full of potential for compromise, embarrassment and premature disclosure. In 1969, as in the period covered by the contact (negotiation) volumes, "the United States in Paris and elsewhere was attempting to talk to the North Vietnamese to reduce violence and bring our prisoners back," Gorman said. Former Ambassador Lodge's own position in Paris as a negotiator could have been compromised by the

disclosure of the details of his involvement in the overthrow
of Diem in 1963. Matters of this kind have to be protected
by secrecy because disclosure could be used to "curtail communications" and embarrass governments. Moreover, the
documents themselves pointed out how the North Vietnamese
repeatedly warned about leaks to the press—many of which,
it turned out, had been deliberate disclosures by U.S. officials
in Washington—and how disclosure of those contacts could
impede or destroy the effectiveness of third-party contacts.
(By 1969, of course, the U.S. was negotiating directly with
North Vietnam in Paris and needed no third-party contacts.)
There were references to telephone intercepts, to meetings
where "M told B that A and M vouched for K" (the K
being Henry Kissinger), to American ability to detect the
installation of missiles through aerial and satellite photog-
raphy, and to the British bug on Kosygin's call to Brezhnev
from London:

> Here you see that an American by the name of Cooper received
> information from the British Foreign Office . . . that the Premier
> of the Union of Soviet Socialist Republics had sent three Presi-
> dential cipher telegrams, referring to the code used by the
> Soviets, from his delegation in London to Moscow, and that,
> according to a telephone intercept, Kosygin called Brezhnev
> and said—and then there is a quote of what he said.
>
> Then, following on down, you can see the entry that this had
> been submitted to the National Security Agency for—this prob-
> lem had been submitted to the National Security Agency, and
> we have a report from the National Security Agency that the
> North Vietnamese transmitted a 201-group message from Hanoi
> to Moscow at a given time, and a 500-group message to Hanoi
> from Moscow at another time.
>
> Now, the "Thompson was informed" refers to the ambas-
> sador. That is communications intelligence. It is communica-
> tions intelligence gathered from an ally, the British, by an
> American.

The defense lawyers objected to any references to communications intelligence, which was governed by a special classification system which was itself classified and unavailable in court. The Papers contained no communications intelligence, no markings (according to defense consultants familiar with the procedures) indicating such information. They would suggest, moreover, that the Russians and the North Vietnamese understood American intelligence capabilities, and, through their own witnesses, they would indicate that the Russians wanted their telephone conversation overheard, had taken few precautions against it, and had used it to indicate their earnestness in pressing North Vietnam to negotiate. Gorman, nonetheless, continued to talk about communications intelligence. The four negotiation volumes provided

the wherewithal for a foreign analyst to forecast how the United States would behave in a given set of circumstances in 1969, the material with which to manipulate the American decision-making process in the National Security Council or elsewhere at the top of the American government, to bring into jeopardy the very channels of communications whereby we were attempting to collect information about the settlement of the conflict or to convey messages to the North Vietnamese about our attempts to reduce violence in Vietnam . . .

He emphasized, however, that it was the totality of the material, its scope and its classification that made it of particular interest to the foreign analyst. The foreign analyst would see that this material had been labeled by the United States "Top Secret Sensitive" and that it had come from the Office of the Secretary of Defense. "That would be worth reading, no matter what."

The defense subjected both generals to extensive cross-examination, showing them excerpts of books, newspaper clippings and government reports covering material similar to those portions of the Vietnam study about which they had testified. Nesson had planned to use a second slide projector and screen to compare passages, but the mechanics quickly overwhelmed him; at one point the projector, loaded with slides of material that had not yet been introduced into evidence, began to run forward (and then back) automatically, projecting articles and headlines in manic succession, a staccato of old leaks about troop requests, battlefield conditions and strategic plans. The projector was abandoned. The defense lawyers would also have difficulty marking and introducing exhibits (about which Byrne was a purist) and framing what Byrne regarded as admissible questions, permitting Nissen on occasion to turn a line of questioning into a shambles, and sometimes leading Byrne, in exasperation, to take over the questioning himself. They managed nonetheless to press both government experts to admit that in many instances the material in the Papers was dated, that situations had changed, and that much of the military information, though hardly all, had previously been published. Boudin, cross-examining Gorman, also managed to impeach to the satisfaction of the defense, if not of the jurors, the general's expertise in the field of diplomacy. What books, Boudin wanted to know for openers, had Gorman read in the field of international relations?

"I'm having a problem recalling titles," Gorman replied.

"I'll take authors for a beginning."

Gorman hesitated. There was a book on the Crimean War by Cecil Woodham-Smith, a three-volume French series, *La Guerre du droit,* about World War I, a Chinese text on warfare written before the time of Christ, and something called *The Art of War* . . .

"What books have you read in the field of international relations?"

"All those books deal with international relations."

Boudin meant international relations "as of today," material pertinent to Vietnam. What had he read?

Gorman replied that while he was attached to the U. S. delegation at the Paris peace negotiations he had "a closet stacked high with captured documents . . . transcripts of interrogations . . . intelligence analyses." He had read hundreds of documents pertaining to Vietnam.

Gorman acknowledged that the facts of many of the third-party contacts with North Vietnam had long been public knowledge, that transcripts of National Security Council decisions were not necessarily useful to a foreign analyst, that many of the volumes dealt with military operations prior to 1965 (and therefore with a buildup of military forces rather than, as was the case in the indictment period, with phased withdrawal), that one entire volume dealt with contingency plans for a situation that had long ceased to exist, and that the code word indicating communications intelligence appeared nowhere in the Papers. Gorman told the jurors, in response to a question from Weinglass, that he was not allowed to tell what the word was, but he acknowledged that it did not appear. He also acknowledged that at least one of the volumes about which he testified, *U.S. Involvement in the Franco–Viet Minh War, 1950–1954,* could have been made available to the public in 1969 without harm to the national defense. Weinglass took him through a reading of passages indicting the South Vietnamese government and questioning its base of popular support (the beginning of the defendants' political case against the war), citations of American complicity in sabotaging the Geneva Accords, and documents describing the failure of the United States to respond to Ho Chi Minh's requests for assistance during the Truman Administration. Among other things, he had Gorman read a cable that Ambassador Lodge sent Johnson in May 1964:

I much prefer a selective use of Vietnamese Air Power to an overt U.S. effort perhaps involving total annihilation of all that has been built in North Vietnam since 1954 because these would surely bring in the Chinese Communists and might well bring in the Russians. Moreover, if you lay the whole country waste, it is quite likely that you will induce a mood of fatalism in the Viet Cong. Also, there will be nobody left in North Vietnam on which to put pressure . . . It is . . . a relatively simple matter to go out and destroy North Vietnam. What is complicated but really effective is to bring our power to bear in a precise way so as to get specific results.

Such passages, Gorman suggested, were themselves harmful to the national defense. They indicated that the South Vietnamese might be "simple tools or instruments" of American officers, advertised U. S. impatience with the inability of the Saigon government to run its own affairs, called attention to friction in the alliance, provided information that could be used to compile dossiers on Allied officials, suggested American complicity in the Diem overthrow, and could be used for North Vietnamese propaganda. Information stamped "Top Secret" could always be used for something.

WEINGLASS: Would the contents of this volume [*Aid for France in Indochina, 1950–1954*], if released in 1969, result in an injury to the national defense of the United States or an aid or advantage to a foreign nation?

GORMAN: Yes.

WEINGLASS: It would?

GORMAN: Yes.

WEINGLASS: And, briefly, could you explain in what way?

GORMAN: This volume, like the one before it, details the modus operandi of the National Security Council, the Joint Chiefs of Staff in dealing with the developing military crisis in Indochina. This volume, to a greater extent than the other one, depends upon the records of the Joint Chiefs, of the Secretary of Defense, and of the National Security Council. This information, not available in any other form, and— I'm sorry; may I go back and correct that statement?

BYRNE: Yes.

GORMAN: These records were not available in any other form, and, therefore this document would be useful in and of itself in 1969 in order to inform an analyst of how the United States had reached these military decisions which bore upon our policy as the military situation in Indochina developed to crisis proportion in early 1954 with the battle of Dien Bien Phu.

WEINGLASS: And 1954 is fifteen years removed from 1969?

GORMAN: Yes.

WEINGLASS: And the military crisis you are referring to in 1954 is the French military crisis?

GORMAN: Yes.

WEINGLASS: And the French were not in Vietnam in 1969?

GORMAN: No.

WEINGLASS: They had been out of Vietnam for fifteen years?

GORMAN: The last of their forces were withdrawn in 1956.

WEINGLASS: So it is thirteen years. And in your opinion, despite that fact, the information contained in that volume could be of injury to the United States in the hands of a hypothetical foreign analyst?

GORMAN: That is possible.

WEINGLASS: When you say "That is possible," do you have anything in mind other than conjecture?

GORMAN: I would have to conjecture . . . Suffice to say, the North Vietnamese continually harked back to the events of 1953 and 1954. To them that concatenation of events was the model, the type of events that was going to bring them to ultimate victory in 1969. They, more than any other nation, are fond of alluding to Dien Bien Phu, "the Dien Bien Phu in the sky" that they talk about as having occurred in Hanoi last December. This record, drawn from the files of the top level of the United States, could be useful to them and disadvantageous to us. It is entirely possible, for example, that a foreign analyst, coming into possession of this kind of material, could produce a volume of propaganda . . .

Through most of his testimony, however, Gorman remained the well-prepared briefer, turning in the witness chair to address the jury, returning again and again to his basic text about the total scope of the documents ("these volumes, taken together"), speaking in measured cadences and proliferating clauses, and eluding apparent contradictions by returning to the refuge of his starting point. And that point was that it did not matter what had been published before or how much the situation had changed; what mattered was that the government itself had created this text, had given it value, and, through the imprimatur of classification, had created a legitimacy beyond the information it contained. This was revealed truth.

De Puy, who testified just before Gorman, had taken a similar approach, but he confronted the defense lawyers with different tactics. A short man with the face of a fox, who was regarded as one of the Army's intellectuals, he had been Westmoreland's closest adviser on strategy. "He believed that massive fire power and American mobility were the answer, that the enemy simply could not stand up in the face of it," Halberstam had written in *The Best and the Brightest*. "He had a tendency to establish contact and then pull back his troops and pound the area with air and artillery, a tactic which lowered his own losses, increased civilian casualties and led to vastly inflated casualty lists." On the second day of De Puy's testimony Russo had handed him a press handout in the courtroom (which Nissen immediately passed on to Byrne, accusing Russo of harassing his witnesses) which charged De Puy with "direct responsibility for the deaths of hundreds of Vietnamese." De Puy, it said, "is a principal war criminal and should be brought to trial; unless he is, the law has little meaning as far as justice is concerned—it simply functions as an instrument of repression." Shrewd, ambitious, De Puy was regarded by many people in the defense as the toughest witness they were likely to face. They believed Gorman to be a decent and reasonably honest man. They did not think the same of De Puy. What they did not know was that De Puy had been poorly prepared, that he had had only a few brief interviews with Nissen, and that he was angry about it.

In his direct testimony he had relied on several "examples" from the Wheeler Report, particularly the following.

> The enemy has been hurt badly in the populated lowlands, is practically intact elsewhere. He committed over 67,000 combat maneuver forces plus perhaps 25% or 17,000 more impressed men and boys for a total of about 84,000. He lost 40,000 killed, at least 3,000 captured and perhaps 5,000 disabled or died of wounds. He had peaked his force total to about 240,000 just before Tet, by hard recruiting, infiltration, civilian impressment and drawdowns on service and guerrilla personnel. So he had lost about one fifth of his total strength . . .

Those figures, De Puy had told the jury, would give the enemy an estimate of how good the American and South Vietnamese intelligence was; he wouldn't have made any of the information in that report available to the enemy.

Weren't those same figures, elaborated in more detail, included in a report by General William C. Westmoreland dated June 30, 1968, and published by the Government Printing Office for public sale at six dollars a copy early in 1969? Indeed, the defense lawyers asked, hadn't De Puy himself helped prepare Westmoreland's report for publication?

Some of the information in that passage did appear in the Westmoreland Report, De Puy replied, but he had cited the passage only "as an example." The whole page was important; the passage was sensitive in the context of the page, and the page in the context of the entire excerpt of eight pages. "I do not think you can compare the two documents. One is an official action document written by the Chairman of the Joint Chiefs of Staff; it gives the North Vietnamese his view of the attack. The other document contains all sorts of information about the Vietnam War. It is not an official action document and it does not give the point of view of the

JCS. One is protected, the other not." The fact that it was classified drew attention to its importance. "The data were used in the Wheeler Report to illustrate the message. It's the message that was important."

It was the message that the defense was primarily interested in. The whole purpose of the report, they believed, and clearly its most significant portion, was a request of the Joint Chiefs for an additional 206,000 troops for Indochina above the 525,000 already authorized by Johnson. The request, attributed to MACV (Westmoreland), had leaked two weeks after the Wheeler mission returned from Saigon and had been published in a front-page story in the *Times*. The Wheeler Report asserted that the forces now authorized for Vietnam were, in Westmoreland's view, insufficient:

> Forces currently assigned to MACV, plus the residual Program Five forces yet to be delivered, are inadequate in numbers . . . To contend with, and defeat the new enemy threat, MACV has stated requirements for forces over the 525,000 ceiling imposed by Program Five. The add-on requested totals 206,756 spaces for a new proposed ceiling of 731,756, with all forces being deployed into country by the end [of the 1968 calendar year]. Principal forces included in the add-on are three division equivalents, 15 tactical fighter squadrons and augmentation for current Navy programs . . .

The defense believed that the entire Wheeler mission had been cooked up in the Pentagon, quite possibly by De Puy himself, not as a fact-finding trip to assess the situation after the major Tet attacks, but as a pretext for the troop request. Westmoreland had not, in fact, asked for 206,000 additional troops, but only for units that he had requested earlier, which would have totaled about 25,000 men. The report therefore suggested that, despite his prior optimism, Westmoreland had been unable to handle the situation in Vietnam. Westmoreland would later come to believe that the "request" attributed to him had had a lot to do with his dismissal as commander in Vietnam, and he would become obsessed by the feeling that he had been double-crossed not only by Wheeler but by De Puy, his onetime aide, who, in his ambition to rise in the military hierarchy, had abandoned his former commander. Many of the troops requested were not meant for South Vietnam, according to subsequent rumors, but as strategic reserve units available for other situations, including military operations in Cambodia, Laos and North Vietnam. It was a conspiracy by the generals to deceive the President, Ellsberg said. The rejection of the request was one of the indications that the escalation of the ground war in Vietnam had come to an end.

De Puy denied everything. The troop request was not an important element of the Wheeler Report, he said. After a few weeks had passed and the request hadn't been granted, "it became a non-event which was not of much interest to anyone." To his knowledge the request was only for troops to be used in operations in South Vietnam; in any case, it had merely been a request from MACV that Wheeler was passing on to Washington. (At the next recess Nissen complained to Byrne that he had seen Ellsberg mouthing the words "You're a liar" in De Puy's direction.) De Puy was aware that reports of the troop request had appeared in the press, but those were ascribed to anonymous sources—they talked about "officials"—and the American public was skeptical about things like that. "Officials," he said, "are not General Wheeler."

Unlike Gorman, who really seemed to believe the tenets of secrecy he expounded for the jury, De Puy behaved more like a secret agent under interrogation, evading questions, admitting nothing but the obvious. He acknowledged reluctantly that the headline the defense showed him might have been a genuine *New York Times* headline, but the article which accompanied it, he said, "refers to the Wheeler trip; it is not about the Wheeler Report." He conceded, after extended questioning, that "some of the same numbers" appeared in both the Wheeler and the Westmoreland reports, asserting casually that he did not review published sources containing similar data in forming his opinion on the damage that disclosure of the Wheeler Report might have caused. In each instance he seemed to be saying that he knew that the information in the document was marginal, that the North Vietnamese might have known all of it long before Ellsberg had copied the document (there was no evidence, of course, that they ever saw it), that specific bits of data didn't matter. What mattered, rather, was the principle: this was General Wheeler's report, and no one had any business seeing it. The defense, in presenting its own case, would later produce testimony from a CIA intelligence analyst indicating that the figures about enemy troop strength in the report—the 84,000, the 67,000, the 240,000—were themselves highly dubious, that they were drawn from MACV order-of-battle reports which some people in the CIA privately regarded as inaccurate, if not actually fabricated, and that they reflected a fundamental misassessment of the number and character of the various enemy units in Vietnam.

The defense would not learn of the existence of the CIA witness for nearly a month after De Puy had left the stand, yet it is unlikely, even if they had known, that his evidence would have altered De Puy's basic position. The point, after all, was General Wheeler and secrecy, not accurate data. Anything that the Chairman of the Joint Chiefs said in the course of his official duties that was regarded as sufficiently sensitive to merit classification assumed importance far beyond the value of the information involved. The stamp itself was a way of creating value; it evaluated the innocuous or the inaccurate to a position of significance not only for the purpose of concealing bureaucratic mistakes or manipulating public opinion, but for the illusion of power it helped create.

Ordinary public information was not worth considering at all; it was hardly even real information. It became valuable only when it was created by the government and legitimized by classification. The priesthood maintained its position by seeming to know things that ordinary people did not, or could not, or should not know; the idea that information improperly disclosed might contain nothing of vital military importance was therefore all the more threatening. Even if it did not involve any embarrassing political secrets, the very absence of military secrets suggested that there was nothing in the black box, no special knowledge, no magic to justify the claims of the priests. The *information* was important because they had created it or had access to it; *they* were important because of the information they possessed.

IV

The mechanical facts of the government's case against Ellsberg and Russo, as Boudin pointed out, were never in doubt; yet David Nissen still had the unenviable responsibility of proving them to the jury's satisfaction. More difficult still, he had to do it without opening a Pandora's box of fact and innuendo suggesting that the security system was something less than an honorable, and generally honored, way of keeping military secrets from Moscow, Peking and Hanoi. Given the situation and the witnesses available to him, the job turned out to be nearly impossible.

There was, to begin with, the problem of the security system itself. The theology, doctrine and practice of secrecy had always been different matters. The regulations were clear, but given the volume of documents routinely marked "Confidential," "Secret" and "Top Secret"—the three categories of classification established by the executive order—and the complexity of the regulations covering access, storage and downgrading, there was simply no way for most agencies to function without procedures that were often so loose and informal as to make a mockery of the regulations outlined in the executive order, the Defense Department's Industrial Security Manual, and the various corporate security manuals required by Defense for private firms handling classified government material. The executive order itself severely limited the kind of information that could be marked "Top Secret" to that "which could result in exceptionally grave damage to the Nation" (armed attack, breaks in diplomatic relations, or compromise of data "vital to the United States") and suggested that material improperly stamped, or stamped without proper authority, was not, in fact, classified at all. The government, in effect, acknowledged that interpretation when it later proposed revisions in the Criminal Code that would impose criminal sanctions on the disclosure of any stamped document, no matter how the stamp got on it.

In the case of the Rand Corporation, the problem was further compounded by the conflicting claims of secrecy and scholarship, and by Rand's ambivalent self-image: on the one hand it was a defense contractor often indistinguishable from the Air Force or from the Defense Department; on the other it imagined itself to be an institution committed to research and scholarship, a budding institute of advanced studies, perhaps even an embryonic university. Rand's formal system conformed to all the regulations—the requirement to log material in and out of the Top Secret Control Office, a procedure establishing "need to know," pink "access sheets" attached to all documents marked "Top Secret"—but there also existed a corresponding informal system which encouraged employees to bootleg papers from the government to Rand, permitted them to take classified documents out of the building, and tolerated informal handling of classified material outside the structure of the formal system. Although he would later deny it, Rand president Henry Rowen himself had made the arrangement with Gelb, Warnke and Halperin to store a set of the Pentagon Papers outside the formal Rand system.

Nissen attempted to limit testimony and exhibits to the written regulations delineated in the manuals; the defense tried to restrict evidence to a description of the system as it functioned in day-to-day practice, and particularly to the procedures followed in the handling of the Vietnam study. Both efforts were only partially successful, and so the jury was treated to a string of witnesses and a group of documents —manuals, receipts, inventories, access sheets—indicating that the Papers had been classified with little reference to the formal requirements (and that Gelb himself did not understand the regulations), that they were sent to Rand under the special arrangement between Gelb, Warnke and Halperin (on the one hand) and Rowen (on the other) which provided that access and distribution "shall be approved" by two of the three senders, and that "all papers referred to herein" (which also included private papers belonging to Warnke and the late John McNaughton) "should be available" to the three senders on seventy-two hours' notice. The agreement itself was kept so confidential that not even Richard H. Best, Rand's senior security officer, was informed of it. The three former Defense Department officials regarded Rand as a convenient place to store the Papers—it contained properly secure facilities for such material—but they also regarded Rand's own system as too liberal for material whose very existence was supposed to be secret and over which they wanted to retain personal control. The Rand witnesses, including Best, Jan Butler, Rand's Top Secret Control officer, and Rowen, who has been eased out as president shortly after the publication of the Papers, therefore found themselves enmeshed in a deepening set of contradictions reflecting, on the one hand, their attempt to describe the minutiae of the formal rules, and, on the other, the facts of the agreement covering the Papers, Rand's failure to log them into the system, and the absence of the required pink access sheets which listed the names of the people allowed to read the material attached. Despite his professed inability to recollect the agreement on the witness stand, Rowen acknowledged that Ellsberg had shown him some of the volumes and that he had failed to register any complaint about the absence of the pink sheets. Ellsberg had maintained that he had been instructed not to log the Papers in and that he was supposed to keep them in his own safe at Rand, and there was nothing that the Rand witnesses said which indicated otherwise. He had violated an agreement with Rowen, and with Gelb and Halperin, but they had violated the formal regulations of the government.

Despite defense objections, Nissen was able to introduce the appropriate security manuals and the acknowledgments signed by Ellsberg and Russo certifying, among other things, that they understood that "it is the policy of the Government of the United States to control the dissemination of Restricted Data and other classified defense information in such a manner as to assure the common defense and security," that "the provisions of the Espionage Act, Title 18 U.S.C., Sections 792, 793, 794, 795, 797 and 798, prescribe penalties for the disclosure to unauthorized persons of information respecting the national defense," and that they had read the Rand manual, which further elaborated the statutes and penalties covering disclosure of classified material to unauthorized persons. The Industrial Security Manual defined "official information" as "information which is owned by, produced by or is in the control of the United States Government" (thereby repealing the First Amendment) and required specific warning to those who had access to such information not to show it to people without a "need to know." At the time the Papers were copied, Best testified, Russo's clearance had expired; Sinay and Thai never had a clearance, and none of the three had ever been given authorized access to the Papers. In response to Boudin's questions on cross examination, he conceded that there was nothing in the Industrial Security Manual or the Rand manual that permitted the kind of arrangement that Gelb, Warnke and Halperin had made with Rowen, but when pressed he merely pointed out that the agreement was "neither consistent nor inconsistent" with the manuals. He had never seen such an agreement before, and he was unaware of the existence of the documents at Rand until just before Ellsberg had turned them in during the spring of 1970. They had not been found in the course of Rand's semiannual Top Secret document inventories and had never been missed because they had never been recorded into the system. (Ellsberg claimed that during several of the inventories—safes were routinely examined every six months—he had stored the Papers in Rowen's own safe.) Even after Ellsberg had turned them in and Rowen had ordered them properly logged, it took Jan Butler, for reasons never explained, more than six months to do the job. Butler, who acknowledged that she and Ellsberg had been personal friends, also testified that Ellsberg's "violation" of the formal Rand regulations never prompted anyone to question his security clearance, to cite him for infractions as provided by the manual, or to deny him access to Top Secret documents.

What they presented was not the image of an efficient, secret, sinister organization committed to scenario gaming, systems analysis and policy research, but something more nearly resembling a chaotic collection of individuals each pursuing his private interests and trying to preserve his separate empire with the government's money. War itself was a toy, and death could be abstracted into data. Yet the boom in those enterprises seemed at an end, and they were now anxiously seeking contracts in civilian areas to hedge their commitment to military research. All they wanted was a chance to continue the game, and in the light of day they turned out to be forgetful, frightened people who knew that something had gone terribly wrong. Rowen, who had been an Assistant Secretary of Defense before becoming president of Rand, had been reduced to a professor of management at Stanford, Butler had been given another job, and Rand itself had been forced to yield custody of all its classified data to the control of the Air Force. Although the company had survived Ellsberg's leak and the intensive investigations which followed it, the fragile charm of "modern" military strategy based on scientific research had been tarnished—had started to go even before the Papers were published. Ellsberg simply dramatized the demise and forced the keepers of the mystery of military science into self-serving denials and contradictions to save themselves. Rand, Vietnam and the euphoria of science had failed together, and their representations in court now sounded more like the pleas of survivors than the assertions of confident people in a going, significant enterprise.

At the end of the trial the jurors would regard the witnesses from Rand as the least sympathetic and the least credible. Most of the jury regarded them as liars.

Nissen had other problems. Because there had never been a budget for the McNamara task force or a formal contract for the services of the researchers who worked on it—they had all been borrowed from other government jobs—he never managed to introduce evidence establishing the cost of the study to the government or the value of the allegedly stolen documents. He had difficulty with his FBI fingerprint expert, one Deemer E. Hippensteel, who, with the aid of photographic enlargements, testified at great length about his examination of the documents, explaining about "intervening ridges," "branching ridges" and "bifurcated ridges" but managing also to suggest that at least some of the conspirators had handled the documents in such a way that they could not possibly have read them. Nissen also encountered memory lapses on the part of two witnesses who had been counted on to help establish the conspiracy case and, in the process, to suggest a little about the defendants' extracurricular interests. Yvonne Svenle Ekman, Ellsberg's old girl friend and the object of extensive material in Howard Hunt's files, testified that she had seen Dan rushing off with an accordion file to copy some documents but couldn't recall whether she had warned him not to involve his children; and Lynda Sinay, now the wife of a manufacturer of burglar alarms named Stewart Resnick, couldn't recall any of the conversations she had had with Dan and Tony at the time of the copying. They had told her that Dan was expecting to leave Rand and that he had certain documents in his safe "that he had authored or co-authored that he wanted to take with him," but she could never remember whether it was Dan or Tony who told her or whether she knew some other way. She recalled the copying (her eyes getting bigger, sweetly reminding Nissen that she was Mrs. Resnick, not Miss Sinay, forgetting what she had told the grand jury, casting soulful glances at the defense), recalled when the cops came in response to their inadvertent tripping of the burglar alarm—"a nervewracking experience"—recalled the visit of the person Nissen described as "the Oriental gentleman" and who, she later learned, was Vu Van Thai, but whom she had never met and would never meet again, yet not recalling who had given her instructions, not recalling any conversation about where the documents came from, not even recalling the conversations after Nissen showed her her own grand-jury statements.

"Have you recently suffered some reduction of memory?" Nissen wanted to know.

She remembered knowing, remembered being told, but couldn't recall with whom the various conversations took place.

Didn't she recall telling Nissen that one of them had told her "it was a joint enterprise"? Did she recall talking about that to Nissen in his office just a few days before she took the stand?

"No, I don't," she replied. "What did I say?" More than a year before, Nissen had threatened her with perjury charges, telling her on a second appearance before the grand jury, "This is your last chance." She had been frightened then, had believed that she might have misstated facts, and had been told by a lawyer that "they were going to get me." Later, much later, when she read her testimony, she learned that she had been telling the truth all along, but by then she had probably also learned that no one had ever been sent to jail for a faulty memory. Now, as she testified, it was patently clear that she was trying to help her old friends Dan, who, she said privately, had been "like a big brother," and Tony, the man who "thought he could save me from political error, thought he could save my soul." The jury would know she was forgetting selectively, was covering for them, but they would also wonder what kind of conspiracy could include a curly-haired Jewish princess, an "Oriental gentleman" who appeared once, seemingly by accident, and managed to leave fingerprints on a study of negotiations long since concluded, and a defendant who wanted to deliver the loot from his theft to a Senate committee and was willing to involve his young children in the crime.

V

Frank A. Bartimo, assistant general counsel in the Department of Defense, had been called by the government as a routine first witness. He was a short man with straight black hair and the self-effacing air of a career bureaucrat. His function, as official custodian of the volumes of the Pentagon Papers involved in the case, had merely been the identification of the allegedly stolen goods, and his appearance was to last no more than a few minutes while Nissen took him through the motions of properly introducing the evidence. Yet before Bartimo was finished in Los Angeles he had made a half-dozen trips to the witness stand, had been sent back to Washington to search his files for missing documents, and had inadvertently triggered what became, in effect, a second trial, a trial within a trial, in which the defense, out of the presence of the jury, prosecuted the government for what turned out to be a flagrant pattern of suppressing evidence and concealing witnesses. As Byrne became increasingly exasperated and then visibly angry, he called a half-dozen officials of the Defense and Justice Departments to testify in Los Angeles, producing a mounting collection of reports, analyses and studies that the government at first denied even existed.

The second trial proceeded in counterpoint to the first: Gorman or De Puy in the morning or early afternoon, Byrne's special hearing in the late afternoon and, as the evidence began to accumulate, during increasingly long interruptions of the regular testimony. Frequently the jurors were sent home for four-day weekends or sat for extended hours in the jury room playing cribbage or dominoes, discussing the trivia of the courtroom (Was that woman with the short gray hair Leonard Boudin's wife or Daniel Ellsberg's mother? Which were Ellsberg's children? Who was the woman next to Pat

Ellsberg?) and wondering what it was they were not allowed to hear. Toward the end of the trial, when the connection between Watergate and this case produced headlines in the *Herald Examiner* and the *Los Angeles Times,* and when Bill Carter, one of Byrne's law clerks, led them out of the courthouse through the basement, they would know. But the earlier episodes puzzled and sometimes angered them: they were supposed to make the decisions in this case, yet obviously they were being excluded from something of importance. Matt Byrne told them that it was a "legal matter" and of no concern to them.

What Bartimo had revealed on cross examination—his direct testimony had lasted less than ten minutes—was that on instructions from his boss, J. Fred Buzhardt, he had initiated the work of a task force in the Defense Department to review the national-defense aspects of the Papers. The testimony came hesitantly, uncertainly; it had been a long time, and he had seen a lot of documents. He could not recall the names of the participants in the task force, nor was he clear at first what the work entailed, but he believed the analysis had been done "at the suggestion of the Justice Department." Since the defense lawyers, through their own sources, already knew about the reports prepared by Colonel Miller (though they did not tell Byrne or Nissen), and since the prosecution had not responded to the court's orders to turn over exculpatory damage reports and other Brady material indicating the defendants' innocence—there were no such reports, Nissen insisted—Weinglass and Nesson pressed Bartimo for details and demanded that Byrne launch a full inquiry not only to protect the rights of the defendants but to assure compliance with the court's orders. What they did not know at the time was that there had been several studies and several sets of reports and that what Bartimo had started talking about was not what they were looking for. His task force, he recalled, had been primarily concerned with the sources of the leaks to the press—"these documents," he said, "were all highly classified . . . and here it was spilling out across the nation"

—but his testimony, perhaps because it was fragmentary and therefore even more suggestive, would lead to something which, for their purposes, was a great deal better. Pressed by Byrne, who often took over the questioning himself, Bartimo admitted that in addition to the investigation into the source of the leak "there were other evaluations made, which I know from hearsay."

"What other evaluations made?" Byrne wanted to know.

Bartimo seemed to recollect that it was something "requested by Justice of individuals," but he could not recall what it was or whether he had ever seen it. "As I recollect, there were memoranda setting forth various parts of the documents . . ."

"What was the physical form that you saw them in?" Byrne asked, turning prosecutor. "Was it in a bound form or in a looseleaf folder?"

"Typewritten paper."

"Just loose?"

"My recollection is that they were probably one page or possibly two pages with a paper clip or staple."

"When you went back to Washington this last weekend [Bartimo had been sent there to search his files], did you ask anybody about those?"

"No, I did not."

"Why?"

He had gone back to look for the reports that he had talked about in his first appearance on the stand, those dealing with the source of the leaks.

Had Nissen seen those? Byrne asked.

Nissen had not, but Bartimo had turned over to him some other documents, because the court seemed to be asking for such things.

BYRNE:    Have you ever seen any prepared by Mr. Buzhardt, other than what you submitted to me *in camera*?

NISSEN:   Yes. The document submitted to you *in camera*, and possibly other letters and things, but nothing

|         | of the type the court is inquiring about, and I had not seen them— |
|---------|---|
| BYRNE:  | I want those documents. |
| NISSEN: | Your Honor . . . I don't know what you are talking about, and I don't know what he is talking about. |
| BYRNE:  | I don't either. It seems to me— Well, I won't comment on it at this point. . . . You know what I am talking about now, don't you? What I want is any study, analysis, survey, report prepared by the Department of Defense, regarding these documents, "these documents" being the so-called Pentagon Papers, the Joint Chiefs of Staff Report, the Gurtov study, as to whether they in any way caused—their release could, would, did, or possibly could, would, or did cause injury to the United States or damage [*sic*] to a foreign country . . . Do you understand? |
| BARTIMO: | I understand. |
| BYRNE:  | I would like you to stay here, sir, tomorrow so I can get the report from you as to when those documents will be available and what they are, and then I may have some additional questions . . . |

The documents came in installments—memos, letters, analyses. One set was delayed for more than a day because the government regarded it as so sensitive that it had to be delivered by a special courier traveling on a military plane, and much of it dealt with material that Byrne did not consider exculpatory or relevant to the case: analyses tracing the source of the leaks, and material relating to the declassification of the Papers in the weeks after the *Times* had published them. But the most significant documents did not come from Washington at all; for more than a year they had been sitting in Nissen's own files on the thirteenth floor of the courthouse: official reports commissioned by the Justice Department and written by officials in the Departments of State and Defense which concluded that nine of the twenty volumes involved in the case, and portions of several others, could not have in-jured the United States or helped a foreign nation if disclosed in 1969. The Defense Department reports were written by William Gerhard, an employee of the National Security Agency who had been assigned to the Office of the General Counsel and had received his instructions at a meeting in Bartimo's office in December 1971 which Bartimo attended. (Miller had also attended the meeting.) Gerhard had turned his reports in to Bartimo's boss, J. Fred Buzhardt, who, more than a year before they surfaced in Los Angeles, had for-warded them to John L. Martin at the Internal Security Division at Justice, Nissen's immediate superior in Washing-ton and the man who, as it would turn out, had been sending FBI reports to James McCord at the Committee for the Re-election of the President. Martin had sent his copies to Nissen, and they had been sitting in Nissen's office long be-fore Byrne had issued orders to submit such material to him *in camera* to see if it could be considered exculpatory and was therefore to be turned over to the defense. A number of the volumes, Gerhard believed, might impair the national defense if disclosed in 1969. But nine of the twenty could not. The suppressed studies concluded, among other things:

> It is not . . . possible to identify material in the Gurtov study which, in 1969, related to the national defense or would have caused injury to the United States if disclosed.

> Taken as they are from U.S. documents for the early 1950's these and similar statements printed in this volume [*Aid for France in Indochina, 1950–1954*] did not, it is felt, adversely affect in any significant way U.S. national defense in 1969, nor do they today.

> Since virtually all the information presented in this volume [*Re-Emphasis on Pacification, 1965–1967*] has been in the pub-lic domain prior to 1969, it would be difficult, if not impossible, to assess the contents of the volume as having any effect what-soever on national defense as of 1969.

D.O.D. review of this volume [*Phased Withdrawal of U.S. Forces, 1962–1964*] does not show that its compromise would in any way affect national defense interests in 1969 or today.

Despite fairly extensive use of intelligence reports and classified D.O.D. and State Department cables, disclosure of the information disclosed in this volume [*Origins of the Insurgency, 1954–1960*] would not have affected national defense interests as of 1969 or today.

Nissen insisted that the reports did not constitute Brady material; they were merely "one man's opinion—a single person that does not represent the Department of Defense, was not acting for the Department of Defense, except at our request, was never approved by the Department of Defense, and never used by the Department of Defense." The documents in his files, he said, could not possibly indicate that the defendants were innocent of any element of the offenses charged.

NISSEN: The fact that somebody I have talked to or have not talked to but has been requested to review something for me, and that he comes back with a statement that your Honor wishes to interpret as you do, which I think is unfounded, doesn't mean that that is something that shows that anyone is innocent of an offense. The documents have not changed. They are perfectly available for the defendants to review in any way they want to.

BYRNE: What documents?

NISSEN: The documents that are being reviewed, your Honor. It is not like a hammer and tool mark, where they are linked together, and someone analyzes the physical evidence and says "This mark made that." We are talking about evidence, and the evidence is the document.

BYRNE: We are talking about the availability of exculpatory evidence. We are talking about the availability of a

witness who could be called by the defendants who is
an employee of the Department of Defense, who has
called the Department of Defense and told the Department of Justice that that particular document that
is the subject of this particular count does not relate
to the national defense. Now don't you think that is
material and exculpatory evidence . . . ?

NISSEN:    Your Honor, I not only don't think so, I know so . . .

The disclosure of the Gerhard reports, which Byrne immediately turned over to the defense, raised more questions than
it answered. Through their questions, the defense lawyers
made it plain that they knew something about the Defense
Department analyses and the meetings in Bartimo's office at
the time they were commissioned (most of it from Miller)
that went well beyond paranoia or guesswork. Bartimo acknowledged that he might have received a request from Justice for analyses like those that Gerhard and Miller made,
but he couldn't be sure, and he couldn't recall any meetings
in his office at the time they were requested. It was difficult
for him to distinguish between the work that had been done
in the civil suits concerning the Pentagon Papers—including
a suit by a group of Congressmen to have all the documents
declassified—and the criminal case (leading Byrne to ask
the assistant general counsel of the Department of Defense
whether he was a lawyer). Bartimo didn't recall any Colonel
Miller on his task force, and he didn't remember any memo
(which the defense had already obtained from Miller) outlining the work to be performed by Gerhard. "Just ask me
and I'll tell you," he said to Nesson, "the truth, the whole
truth and nothing but the truth." But much of the time he
couldn't remember.

In response to defense demands, Byrne called Martin, Gerhard, Buzhardt, Miller and Charles Hinkle, the director of
the Office of Security Review, the Pentagon department
which analyzed documents and congressional testimony by
Defense Department officials for declassification. Miller had

been assigned to OSR, and if anyone could testify about the disposition of his reports Hinkle was the person. The defense suspected that Gerhard had been instructed to evaluate the same volumes of the Papers that Miller had already done after Defense or Justice had found Miller's reports unsatisfactory, that they were useless in building a case for the prosecution, and that someone ordered them removed from the files. They also believed that the twenty volumes were selected for analysis not because they were the most damaging to the national defense but because they were the only ones on which the fingerprints of Ellsberg's co-conspirators had been found. Martin confirmed that the Justice Department had asked someone to redo at least one report "because the first didn't have enough depth," but, in trying to explain why they were not turned over to Byrne long before, he would say only that he did not regard the studies as "damage reports" (as specified in one of Byrne's orders) and that he had left it to Nissen to decide what constituted Brady materials. "It is Mr. Nissen's decision to decide whether it falls within an order of the court." He simply got whatever Nissen asked for. Nissen, on his part, had merely forwarded copies of Byrne's orders without further specification.

Byrne's inquiry into the analyses quickly became entangled with testimony about other studies of the Pentagon Papers—the declassification reports, the civil suit, and the newspaper injunction cases—and the Defense Department officials called to testify did little to help him out. The government was losing its collective memory with the deftness of a crowd of Mafiosi testifying before a congressional committee. What did become clear was that Byrne's orders to the Justice and Defense Departments to search their files for damage reports and Brady material had been systematically violated, and that even after Bartimo had started to testify, and Byrne had restated and further specified his orders, no thorough searches had been conducted. Copies of Miller's reports were eventually found at the Office of Security Review and the Office of the General Counsel, but only after it was apparent that the defense already knew they existed. Miller testified that he had seen the memo that Hinkle had allegedly written for the file stating that he had been called by Jerry Friedheim, the director of the Pentagon's Office of Public Affairs and Hinkle's superior, and had been instructed to get Miller's reports "out of the files as if they never existed." Hinkle had told him about the call, Miller testified, and had informed him that the instructions originated with Buzhardt. Miller, however, did not have a copy of the memo, nor was he able, on cross examination, to recall what it looked like.

Buzhardt and Hinkle denied everything. They suggested that no one, in fact, had ever asked Miller to write any reports. "I presume," Buzhardt said, "that the author was aware that someone was working on these [volumes] and voluntarily did them on his own." He never had a conversation with Friedheim about suppressing those reports and had never expressed any interest in them. Just the day before, Buzhardt testified, he had asked Friedheim about the allegation and Friedheim had answered, "Hell, no, and anybody that says you did is a damn liar." Hinkle had sent copies of Miller's reports to Daniel Henkin, then Assistant Secretary of Defense for Public Affairs, and therefore Friedheim's boss. (Gerhard to Buzhardt; Hinkle to Henkin; Nesson and Nissen: would everyone refer to these people by their first and last names, Byrne requested, so that the court reporter wouldn't get confused?) Henkin had immediately returned them to Hinkle with an acknowledgment (Hinkle to Henkin to Hinkle); they "appeared to be some person's opinion as to the contents of some of the volumes of the forty-seven-volume study," Buzhardt recalled, but there certainly hadn't been any instructions about having them removed from the files. He hadn't asked for the stuff, and Bartimo hadn't asked for it.

Hinkle supported him, but with a conspicuously poor memory. He had sent Miller's reports to Henkin because he thought "Henkin should be aware" of them, but there had never been any conversation that he could recall about suppression. The reference to "one man's opinion" in the covering memo was his, but he merely regarded that as a "truism" about "the nature of any security judgment." He had, in fact, not read the reports.

"Weren't you in fact saying to your superior, 'Look here, here are some reports which exonerate, but somebody else could have an entirely different judgment, I think you should be aware of them'?" Nesson asked. "Isn't that what you were saying?"

"No."

"Do you put this sort of truism on every report that you forward?"

"I don't recall. Rarely."

"Would it be customary for staff members in your office to volunteer, without assignment, to do reports such as these?"

"Not normally."

"Does it ever happen?"

"I don't recall that it ever happened, no."

"Mr. Hinkle, have you ever received any instruction or suggestions at any time in your tenure at the Office of Security Review to suppress any materials produced in your office?"

"Not to my recollection."

"It has never happened?"

"Not to my recollection."

"So, then, it would be an extraordinary thing, an unusual event, if it were to happen; is that correct?"

"I—In that context, I suppose."

"Once in a career, once in eighteen, nineteen years?"

Nissen objected, and Byrne took over the questioning himself. Did Hinkle know today whether he had ever received such instructions?

He did not recall.

Did he deny that Friedheim ever gave such instructions? Weinglass asked.

He did not recall.

"Do you deny that Secretary Laird ever gave such instructions? . . . Do you deny that President Nixon ever gave such instructions?"

Nissen objected. Improper.

"I want to see how far we have to go," Weinglass explained.

"You've gone far enough," Byrne said.

Miller, it developed, had turned in some of his reports to Bartimo's office and had given others directly to Gerhard, who had used a few in writing his own analyses but who found most of them unsatisfactory for the job he had been assigned at the original meeting in Bartimo's office. (Miller had also given a complete set to Hinkle, the set that Hinkle sent to Henkin.) Gerhard himself, however, failed to do the job that Nissen wanted done. Gerhard's expertise, as an official of the National Security Agency, was in communications intelligence, information derived from the interception of foreign communications, but Gerhard refused, for security reasons, to list or assess the communications intelligence material in the Papers. At first he regarded the omission itself as a privileged matter: his reports did not say that no such assessment had been made. It was only on the eve of his appearance in Los Angeles that he had checked with his superiors and had received clearance to inform Nissen that the material the prosecution most wanted could not even be discussed.

While Bartimo, Buzhardt and Hinkle suffered their lapses of memory, Miller managed to get himself trapped in a series of contradictions and by Nissen's suggestion that perhaps he believed his reports "deserved further notice." He could not recall the wording of the suppression memo, admitted that he had never discussed it with Hinkle, though they had discussed the instructions Hinkle had allegedly received, and could not remember whether Hinkle had in fact received an order or only a suggestion. In the military, he explained, there isn't much difference between a recommendation and an order. He also acknowledged that he had volunteered to work on the original declassification review of the Pentagon Papers in the weeks following their publication in the press, although his analysis of the volumes relating to this case had been made pursuant to the meeting in Bartimo's office at which he had been asked to participate. Gerhard was to coordinate the work, and Miller was to furnish all his studies to him. Nissen also managed to suggest that Miller had himself stolen government documents when he took a set of his reports from the Pentagon; hadn't he done that in an effort to get a civilian job after he retired, and hadn't he created the suppression story as a way of inflating his own importance, particularly when he was job hunting among Senators like Mike Gravel? At one point the insinuations became serious enough for Byrne to stop the interrogation and advise Miller of his constitutional rights to counsel and his Fifth Amendment rights against self-incrimination.

Miller survived the assault, although the reality of the Hinkle memo began to fade: he had never copied it because it was not his and, unlike the reports on the Papers, had never been part of his own files. In the context of other instances of suppression, however (and there were more yet to come), Miller's story was at least consistent. When Nissen, Hinkle and Buzhardt asserted that the Miller and Gerhard reports were merely the opinions of individuals—one man's opinion, the work of a volunteer, unofficial documents—they were, in effect, arguing that the government which had created the secrets could also determine their use and the way that the country might be damaged by the disclosure. The assessment of secrecy was a bureaucratic decision subject to institutional definitions. It was not the information in the Papers that was the most sensitive—certainly not the military information, and perhaps not even the possibility of political embarrassment—but the principle of secrecy itself. Bureaucrats who are required to take individual responsibility for their acts (as on a witness stand) tend almost inevitably to lose their memories and look for cover, but the collective attempt to conceal information was, most significantly, a way of protecting the integrity of the institution and asserting the principles of secrecy which justified it. The institution would find it inconceivable that someone would reveal its secrets without some self-serving motives of his own: truth was not a consideration, because truth was defined by the institution itself.

The defense wanted the case dismissed. The prosecution had concealed "vital data" from the court and the defense counsel, data to which they were entitled under the Supreme Court decision in *Brady v. Maryland* and under Byrne's own orders:

> The defendants have spent over a year in a most involved and expensive defense, against a devious and deceptive prosecution, only now to be told that the government had officially researched and produced evidence to clear them of most of the charges against them. We do not know what further evidence will turn up tomorrow or a year from tomorrow which will further expose the government's bad faith and further confirm the defendants' innocence. . . .
>
> In the name of the government, Mr. Nissen's conduct—we know and say nothing about his two colleagues—has violated standards established by common decency and now embodied in the standards of the American Bar Association. . . .
>
> The conduct of the officials of the Department of Defense and Justice in this case is the antithesis of that obligation to the defendants and devotion to our democratic institutions. The conduct is so gross and prejudicial as to require the dismissal of the indictment with prejudice. Such conduct, in our view, calls for additional sanctions. It is our hope that in addition to dismissal of the indictment, the Court will take appropriate disciplinary steps against those responsible for the concealment of material evidence . . . and will convene a grand jury to determine whether the conduct of the government officials which

here has jeopardized the freedom of the defendants has violated
the criminal laws.

This was unlike those cases where evidence had been lost or
accidentally destroyed, Boudin argued. It was, rather, an
instance of "deliberate, contumacious, knowing and dishonest defiance of a court order." Their examination of
witnesses had been "hopelessly compromised"; De Puy's
testimony had been completed and it would take at least a
month to prepare for a proper cross examination of Gorman
(who was then still on the stand), a delay that would certainly prejudice the jury against the defense. There was,
moreover, no certainty that "a government that has engaged
in such conduct in this instance will stop at another." (Nissen, yawning, was examining his fingernails as Boudin
spoke.) Boudin would also ask that, in the event there was
no dismissal, the defense be permitted to make a new opening statement before the jury, that Byrne explain to the jury
the reasons for the delay in Gorman's cross examination, and
that the story of the suppression be made clear. The record
of the suppression was an admission by the government of
the importance of the evidence suppressed, and was therefore
material to the jury's evaluation of the facts in the case. Peter
Young, arguing for Russo, called it "trial by ambush."

The defense lawyers conceded that there were no precedents. In most similar cases (as in *Brady*) the disclosure that
the government had withheld exculpatory evidence came up
on appeal. Byrne ruled that there were no grounds for either
dismissal or mistrial. At the appropriate time, he suggested,
the defense would be able to use the reports in its own case
or in the impeachment of government witnesses. Eventually
he would also preclude the government from offering evidence on the national-defense aspects of the Gurtov volume,
thus effectively dismissing one count of the indictment. Earlier he had asked Nissen whether he wished to present an
argument on the defense motions; when Nissen replied that

he would stand on the record, Byrne snapped back that "the record, Mr. Nissen, isn't too favorable." It was the most serious sanction he imposed.

Five days after Boudin argued his motion for dismissal, Nissen submitted a "Notice of Information Which the Court May Consider 'Brady Material' " which appeared, at first, to be a legalistic parody on the judge's rulings on the Gerhard and Miller reports. "In accordance with the Court's statement that the views of anyone favorable to the defense on any issues involved in this case are 'evidence of innocence' under the rule of *Brady v. Maryland*," the "notice" said, the plaintiff, the United States of America, was hereby advising the defendants of the following.

> 1. A Mr. Samuel A. Adams, Route 4, Box 240, Leesburg, Virginia, has expressed the view that he has information which would rebut statements of Government witness William De Puy as reported in a newspaper.
> 2. A Mr. Chester Cooper, 7514 Vale Street, Chevy Chase, Maryland, has expressed the view that testimony of Government witness Paul Gorman as reported in a newspaper was untrue.
> 3. David A. Munro, 802 Bluebird Canyon Drive, Laguna Beach, California, has expressed the view that the Government's prosecution in the . . . case is a criminal conspiracy, meeting secretly and acting illegally.
> 4. A person whose name and address are unknown has expressed the view that Government witness Paul Gorman is responsible for the cruelty and poverty in the world and that he persecutes any person that tries to improve the world.

In response to questions by Nesson, who called the "notice" a "funny attempt by the government on a matter which to us is extremely serious," Byrne declared the document not to be "what I consider *Brady* material," nor did he think, when pressed, that it was a "matter for humor" (although Byrne himself had tried to make a joke of it). What neither he nor Nesson knew was that Samuel A. Adams was a re-search analyst at the CIA who had been trying for two weeks to contact the prosecution and the court to offer testimony on what he believed were fabricated figures in the Wheeler Report. Adams had read a story in the *Times* about De Puy's testimony dealing with the number of troops the Communists had committed to the Tet offensive. On January 24, while the hearing was going on in Los Angeles about the Gerhard and Miller reports, he had sent a memo to the Office of the General Counsel of the CIA asking that his allegation be brought to the attention of the Justice Department, attaching to it documents he had prepared earlier outlining what he regarded as evidence that MACV had produced false data on Communist troop strength and charging violations of the Uniform Code of Military Justice. "The statistics," he said, "were derived from numbers which had been deliberately fabricated in late 1967," presumably for the purpose of making the situation in Vietnam look more optimistic than it was. A week later, having received no reply but still determined to go through proper channels, Adams sent another memo to CIA general counsel Lawrence Houston, stating that if the CIA would not forward his material to Justice he would do so himself. This prompted a series of exchanges between the CIA and John Martin at Justice and, two days later, a request from John K. Greaney, CIA assistant general counsel, that Adams prepare a memo summarizing the facts as Adams saw them.

> Pursuant to that request [Adams said in an affidavit], I prepared on the same day a Memorandum for the Record, entitled 'Possible Exculpatory Evidence,' and delivered it to Mr. Greaney. Mr. Greaney told me it would be sent to Los Angeles shortly, and that the Prosecutor planned to show it to the Judge so the Judge could decide what to do with it. I indicated to Mr. Greaney that I would accept whatever the Judge decided, and I had no intention of contacting the defense independently.

The prosecutor did not show Adams' memorandum to the judge, nor did he tell Byrne that Adams had any connection with the CIA, that he had "conducted research on our adversaries in Indochina" from 1965 to 1972, or that Adams believed that "the fabrications alleged . . . bear directly on the reported testimony of General De Puy." Martin had sent Adams' materials to Nissen; all Byrne received was Nissen's "notice" of February 7. On February 9, two days after Byrne's colloquy with Nesson about humor, Adams was informed by Greaney that Byrne did not regard Adams' information as exculpatory. Nissen quoted Byrne to Martin, Martin told Greaney, and Greaney gave Adams a copy of a memo he had written for the record:

On February 8 Mr. John Martin, Internal Security Division, Department of Justice, called to inform me of his telephone conversation with Mr. David Nissen, Assistant U. S. Attorney in charge of the Ellsberg prosecution in Los Angeles. Mr. Nissen had discussed with Judge Byrne in camera the written statement prepared by Samuel Adams . . . to determine if the Judge considered this to be exculpatory material within the Judge's previous ruling. Judge Byrne did not consider this to be exculpatory material and, therefore, would not require Samuel Adams' name to be given to the defense. Based on the Judge's ruling, there is no requirement for Mr. Adams to testify at this time.

The defense, and Byrne, learned about Adams by accident. A week after Adams had received Greaney's memo (apparently satisfying him to the point where he decided not to pursue the matter), the defense pressed Byrne for more information about Chester Cooper, who had also been mentioned in Nissen's "notice" and whom they knew to be a former CIA analyst who had worked on Bundy's staff. The defense asked Byrne to order Nissen to submit *in camera* whatever information he had on Cooper (since that might also be *Brady* material), and Nissen responded by filing not only the Cooper material but the Adams documents as well. That same evening, Nesson ran into a *New York Times* reporter at a party, related to him the story of Nissen's "notice," and was told that Adams worked for the CIA. He also learned that although Adams was regarded as a maverick in the agency, he had a reputation as an extremely capable intelligence analyst. A direct descendant of the colonial Adamses and a graduate of Harvard, he had been in charge of estimating the strength of Vietcong units in South Vietnam, and had for several years been waging a one-man campaign within the CIA against senior military officers who, he believed, had consistently falsified figures on enemy troop strength. Two months earlier he had sent a memo to the inspector general of the CIA asking him to forward a complaint to the Inspector General of the Army charging that senior officers at MACV had ordered the head of the MACV Order of Battle Section to hold down the estimates of enemy strength:

> MACV used several devices to keep overall OB within prescribed bounds. One method was to remove from official lists at least two large classes of persons who had been in the OB for over six years. A second method was to employ "conservative" methodologies. However neither device was enough to keep the OB below the paper number.
>
> So MACV used a third method . . . Whenever it began to come clear that one component was about to rise, orders would pass to lower arbitrarily another component to conceal the gain. Say, for example, the CIA managed to argue successfully for a higher number of Component B. Colonel [Gaines] Hawkins (the Head of the Order of Battle Section at MACV) would thereupon order the MACV officers in charge of Component C or Component D to dock their numbers a requisite amount . . . I do not know who . . . originated the instructions to Colonel Hawkins to manipulate the components of the Order of Battle. . . . I have heard speculation and what I consider strong circumstantial evidence that the originator was

General William Westmoreland, then head of MACV. But on this I have no first hand information.

His campaign had never gotten anywhere, except to make Adams himself into a pariah within the CIA; he had already been shuffled to a lower-status job and would eventually be forced out. But for the defense in Los Angeles he represented not only an opportunity but also another example of government attempts to suppress evidence and conceal information.

Within minutes after Nesson learned Adams' identity, and before anyone knew the contents of Nissen's latest *in camera* submission, Morton Halperin had called Adams at his home and made tentative arrangements to see him that weekend. Adams, on his part, was surprised that the defense had his name; he knew nothing about the transactions in Los Angeles and assumed that he would have no further part in the case. Still adamant on going through channels, he refused to give his materials directly to the defense and insisted that his meeting with Halperin take place in the presence of Lawrence Houston, the CIA's general counsel. He did, however, give Halperin an affidavit on his attempts to contact the court and on his exchange with Houston and Greaney. Two weeks later he testified in Los Angeles, becoming eligible, a reporter said, "to join Miller in some leper colony."

The disclosure of the government's attempts to conceal Adams from the defense coincided with the conclusion of the government's case, producing, within a week, separate defense motions for a directed verdict of acquittal, dismissal of the case, dismissal of certain counts, and removal of Nissen from further participation in the trial. Nissen, in a masterpiece of obfuscation, asserted that Greaney had been confused: Greaney had assumed that the exchange between Byrne and Nesson "out of the presence of the jury" was an *in camera* discussion and therefore reflected an *in camera* submission of the Adams documents. If the defense lawyers didn't intend to follow up on Adams, Nissen said, "we certainly don't intend to push them"; they could have learned everything merely by getting in touch with the otherwise unidentified person named in his "notice." He also asked Byrne to sanction him personally for his continuing refusal to turn over the Adams material to the defense even after Byrne ordered him to do so, so that he could appeal the sanction to higher courts. He wanted Byrne to believe that he, Nissen, regarded the court's interpretation of the *Brady* rule quite preposterous, though he never explained why he worked so hard to keep information from the court and why, by not submitting the material *in camera,* he failed to give the judge an opportunity to make his own decision. "That guy," said a reporter in the press section, "has balls." When Byrne indicated that he would follow a different course, that he would strike all evidence pertaining to the Wheeler Report if the material were not turned over, Nissen complied. Byrne declined, however, to hold Nissen in contempt, to dismiss the indictment (though he would acquit on two counts, one against Ellsberg and the other against Russo, on which he believed the government lacked sufficient evidence) or to remove the prosecutor from the case. Nor would he allow the defense to inform the jury of the government's attempts to suppress evidence; he regarded that as a matter of law and therefore not to be considered by the jurors. The government, he suggested caustically, had analyzed *Brady* "inconsistent with the way I analyzed *Brady,*" but that did not constitute sufficient grounds for other sanctions. He ordered Nissen, Martin and Greaney to submit affidavits on the transactions regarding the Adams matter in which Greaney accepted responsibility for the confusion but where he categorized as "absolutely false" the allegation that an attempt had been made "to persuade a witness not to testify." Nissen acknowledged nothing except what Byrne already knew; the most revealing point in his affidavit was that after he "had advised the Court" of his conversations with Martin, "defendant Daniel Ellsberg approached me in the Courtroom and called me a 'despicable liar.' "

# SIX

# Trying a Forgotten War

TONY RUSSO never believed that the defense had been political enough. Daniel Ellsberg, he once said, "was continuously going beyond points I thought he wouldn't go" (the voice of a teacher speaking about a pupil), but as the trial progressed he became increasingly concerned that there was so little discussion of the political nature of the prosecution, so few attempts to connect this case with a broader attack on American society, and so much emphasis on the negative aspects of the Papers—proving they were innocuous from a military point of view. It seemed to be, he said, "a fight within the establishment."

Occasionally he tried to politicize the trial: he issued his press release charging General De Puy with war crimes, he made statements attacking the government from the courthouse steps, and he pressed for more witnesses who would call attention to the political significance of the Papers. The way the newspapers were presenting the trial, he felt, there seemed to be no reason for leaking the Papers in the first place. On one occasion he altered an exhibit standing on an easel in the courtroom on which a witness had listed the various Vietcong units that made up "the enemy," by adding "The People" to the list of units arrayed against American forces; on another he had a shouting match with Halperin, who, as much as anyone, had become the central figure in the management of the defense and whom Russo regarded as an agent of the old Pentagon establishment. He wanted to press Byrne more: until they had been threatened with contempt charges they really hadn't gone far enough to challenge the legitimacy of an unjust system. There was too much thinking, Katherine Barkley said after the trial, about "what favors we could get from Byrne," too much collaboration, and therefore too much acceptance of the conditions under which they were being prosecuted. On the day the trial started, Russo had issued a statement on the case, and Katherine would distribute it again the day after the trial ended:

> Far more is at stake here than the liberty of two men. Dan is charged with giving the Pentagon Papers to me. I am charged with receiving them. Congress and the newspapers received the documents too, but the executive chose to prosecute me for receiving them instead. The newspapers won Pulitzer prizes and Congress goes its merry way, oblivious to our need for peace at home and in Indochina.
>
> The Pentagon Papers case marks a constitutional crisis. The government is on trial; history will find it guilty of trying to abridge freedom of speech and of the press. Christmas has already found Nixon guilty of genocide.
>
> The 1972 Christmas battle of Hanoi-Haiphong was America's version of Dien Bien Phu. Sitting Bull haunts the continent and one more American president has lost his reputation to Ho Chi Minh.
>
> The Pentagon Papers belong to the American people. Secrecy is the death of democracy. Truth is on the side of the Revolution. The trial will be won. Vietnam is one.

Katherine herself began to withdraw. It was Daniel Ellsberg's trial, not Tony's, and it was shot through with elitist thinking that the jurors would be incapable of understanding the political issues, with the fear that they were getting bored, and therefore with an inability to "develop a political over-view" of the issues. She had had her own confrontation with Byrne: in response to complaints from the operators of the courthouse snack bar, he had ordered her to stop selling health food sandwiches in the corridors of the courthouse, and she had responded with a letter to the judge in which she said she was doing it to raise money for Russo's defense; if he would grant Tony's application for financial help from the federal government (Russo, they argued, was legally a pauper) there would be no need to do so—"The government has unlimited resources while I have to panhandle for the week's food." Yet she also knew that by the time the prosecution had rested its case, Russo, in the opinion of his lawyers, was pretty much in the clear: the government had failed to make a strong conspiracy case; it had succeeded only in portraying Russo as a person who had been present at the copying, not as a spy or a receiver of stolen goods. "I knew that Tony wouldn't go to jail," she said later. The trial therefore was an opportunity to make a political case, and that opportunity was being missed. Dan had wanted his day in court, and he was getting it, but that meant accepting the legitimacy of the process, the legality of the indictment, meant conceding the propriety of the whole corrupt system. Before the trial started she and Tony had contemplated certain concessions of their own: Tony would cut his hair and wear a jacket to court, and they would both wear dime-store wedding rings for the benefit of the jurors. But the idea of the rings didn't last long, Katherine's appearances in court became increasingly infrequent, and her garb—barebacked dresses, and shawls—seemed increasingly a declaration of determined noncompliance with the conventional decorum of the obedient and faithfully supportive wife.

Patricia was the person who played the wife's role to the point where, in public, she seemed to have no independent life or desires whatever. She appeared unfailingly at Dan's side for his statements to the television cameras on the courthouse steps, the adoring smile directed at Dan, the head cocked in rapt attention—had been so unfailing that one reporter suggested to Bob Sachs, the press representative for the defense, that he produce a photographic cutout of Patricia that could be held up next to Dan for his appearances, thereby sparing Pat the trouble. Dan often spoke of her importance in his life, her influence in his decision, yet she appeared to be the very model of the unliberated woman, a person of intelligence, charm, wealth and connections who had herself spoken on her husband's behalf, but who had no distinct career of her own, no views, no attitudes, nothing that could be distinguished from Dan's. After the trial was over, she said, she hoped to resume her budding career as a radio reporter, and perhaps to have children, but those desires appeared to be responses to questions that required some sort of answer, and not the compelling desires of an independent woman impatient to get started. But within the private meetings of the defense, and particularly through Dan, she asserted herself, becoming the conservative force, the voice of restraint, the person who opposed "radical" witnesses, and who seemed to be embarrassed by Dan's hesitant association with the scruffy elements of the Vietnam Veterans Against the War who occasionally appeared in the courtroom and with whom Russo was so visibly comfortable. Patricia had no need to sell health food sandwiches in the courthouse.

The defense had planned a three-part strategy. In the first part they would refute the government's contention that the Papers contained vital military information that could have been used to the injury of the United States; in the second they would try to demonstrate that the Papers were not properly classified and that the documents Ellsberg copied did not belong to the government; and in the third they would present an affirmative elaboration of the political significance of the Papers, and thereby an attack on the war and the illegitimacy of the U. S. position in Indochina. It was the division among those parts—the emphasis to be placed on each—that generated the arguments.

The list of defense witnesses was enormous, and the political associations among them offered a little for everyone: the knights of Camelot, McGeorge Bundy, Schlesinger, Sorensen, Galbraith; the dovish members of Congress, Fulbright, McCloskey and Ernest Gruening, the former Senator from Alaska who had voted against the Tonkin Gulf Resolution; the government professionals, present and former, Allen S. Whiting, a former State Department intelligence analyst, Gene La Rocque, retired recently as a Navy rear admiral and now head of the Center for Defense Information, Sam Adams of the CIA, Halperin, William G. Florence, a retired Air Force classification official, and Chester Ronning, a retired Canadian diplomat who had been one of the contacts between Washington and Hanoi; the "radicals" Tom Hayden, Howard Zinn, Richard Falk and Don Luce, the former head of the International Voluntary Service in Vietnam and the man who had led U. S. Congressmen to the tiger-cage prisons; and the defendants themselves. The defense had also asked McNamara and George Ball (who, as an Assistant Secretary of State in the Johnson Administration, had opposed the escalation of the war), neither of whom wished to testify and whom the defense was reluctant to subpoena against their wishes, and United Nations Ambassador Arthur J. Goldberg, who also declined, but who, to the amusement of defense attorneys, offered to argue their summation before the jury. Russo's insistence had led to the inclusion of Zinn and Hayden—some members of the defense feared they would be too radical, and that the case was already too long—but he was unable to block the appearance of Bundy, whom he regarded as a war criminal. They also considered the idea of calling Vu Van Thai, and he came to Los Angeles prepared to testify, but ultimately they decided against it. Nissen had never managed to make the "Oriental gentleman" real, and they felt there was no reason to have him materialize and thus risk his elevation into a flesh-and-blood spy. Fulbright would also be dropped from the list, although he had indicated his willingness to appear. They would show, Weinglass told the jurors, that "while the military facts were known, much was not known," and that while there were some voices in this country who tried to tell the real story, the government, hinting that it had information not available to the average citizen, had been quick to rebut them as misguided, dishonest or unpatriotic. They would tell the story of two defendants who had come to the realization that what the government needed "wasn't merely the talents of its young men, but their courage as well."

It would become, as Weinglass said, "a battle of experts." Our admiral against their general, our intelligence analysts against theirs, political secrets against military secrets. But the defense escalated the battle not only in numbers but in prestige, enlisting the fallen stars of the Johnson and Kennedy Administrations, and mustering for the jury armories of credentials, positions held, Presidents advised, summits attended, intelligence analyzed, cables read, negotiations conducted, reports drafted, plans drawn. Collectively they had been privy to secrets "higher and tighter than Top Secret," had used classified documents in writing their books, could speak about Kennedy and Khrushchev at Vienna, about the times "John Kennedy came to my house," about the Berlin Wall and the Cuban missile crisis, about the interrogation of German generals after World War II, about missions to Saigon, about a whole generation on the fringes of history.

The case was simple: most of the information in the documents had long been out of date; it was, Bundy said, "the first cut of history," and useful only in the same sense that "one would find useful *The Congressional Record,* State Department bulletins, the public papers of the Presidents, or the files of major newspapers." Secret information tended to have a very short life; it was overtaken by events or it became public. Bundy could confirm, for example, that the most important element of the Wheeler Report was the leaked recommendation for 206,000 additional troops, which would have been of interest to an intelligence analyst in March 1968, when the report was a "live document," but by 1969 *The Congressional Record* or the *New York Times* would have been far more useful; the rest of the report, even in 1968, was limited in its usefulness, because it was an argument to a conclusion. He could also confirm that the order-of-battle figures in the report had been used repeatedly by McNamara, Wheeler and others in congressional testimony. Every government was interested in the character, policies and way of doing business of the senior officials of another country; in the case of the Pentagon Papers, however, even that element had become a matter of historical interest and not much more, since there had been a change of administration and there were new policies and new personnel, and in any case the North Vietnamese already had this kind of information coming out of their ears. If he had to choose between the whole file of the executive branch and *The Congressional Record* in gathering intelligence about the United States, he would choose *The Congressional Record*.

The significance of the argument lay in the style in which it was made, Bundy's undiminished confidence, Schlesinger's arrogance, participants transformed into critics and scholars, characters stepping out of the play to review the script. Their presence on the witness stand was not so much atonement—there was little of that—or even a reflection of the changed perspectives about the war, as it was an indication that the voice of authority can survive its own errors, and that the speaker with multiple credentials can step into new frames from which he can see himself as a totally distinct personality in a separate arena. Schlesinger, testifying about a volume dealing with plans for a phased withdrawal of troops in 1962, 1963 and 1964 (plans quickly aborted), concluded that it would have been of great advantage to the United States if it had been publicly known (Nissen's objection was sustained: the issue was not "advantage to the United States") and that it would now enable "the historian to understand President

Kennedy's attitude about the war," thus turning himself from the participant whose "in" box was filled every morning with intelligence reports to the historian assessing the events and decisions in which he had himself participated. As a general proposition, Schlesinger said, material from the past can shed light on the present, but there were great differences between "interest," "use" and "advantage." The American plan for withdrawal in 1963–64 would have been of no use whatever to the North Vietnamese in assessing how the United States would conduct its withdrawal in 1969 (and therefore of no use in any scheme to circumvent a truce agreement); speaking as an intelligence expert, he said there was no analogy between the two situations, since in the one case 16,000 troops were involved, and in the other it was a matter of some 500,000.

Nissen wanted to know whether the North Vietnamese might have derived some advantage from the information in the volume that under the 1963 withdrawal plan "radio research units" would be among the last to leave.

That would be no surprise, Schlesinger said. Units of this sort were always the last to leave. In any case, there had been a revolution in communications; the technology had changed radically.

Did he know precisely what the North Vietnamese knew about American intelligence capabilities?

He was not God, he said.

Byrne often allowed them to run on, turning the testimony from the conventional forms of courtroom interrogation into an extended seminar—disquisitions on the documents, personal recollections, theories of information, historical analyses. There was a vast difference, they suggested, between genuine secrets and what appeared in the Papers, between real intelligence—for example, the high-altitude photographs of the Russian missiles in Cuba—and what Galbraith, assessing one volume, called a "tedious account" of a great deal of administrative detail which, even if one had the patience to read it, could not possibly be useful. Their contempt for what the generals regarded as sensitive was often monumental. It was simply assumed at the White House, Bundy said, that any information in the hands of the South Vietnamese "would quickly become known to the Communists, and that included MACV order-of-battle figures." The fact of classification, moreover, was of no interest; one judged the value of a document by its content, not by its classification (a statement made in such a way that one could only conclude that any person who thought otherwise was an idiot). He wished to make it clear that there was no comparison between the intelligence situation of the North Vietnamese and that of the United States; one was a tightly closed society, the other among the most open in the world. The American intelligence community was therefore "looking for scraps and pieces in a desert"—of course we would like to have a North Vietnamese Wheeler Report—while the foreign analyst was trying to find the relevant data in a vast amount of information. (Everything was grist for the mill, Schlesinger said; the problem was glut.) Schlesinger and Bundy had surveyed the scene from the Olympian heights. They had used people like Gorman for errand boys, and, although they never mentioned them, they made it clear that the preoccupation of the generals with mini-secrets, National Security Council memos and obsolescent op-plans was simply the myopic failure of bureaucratic clerks suffering from a crippling (though perhaps understandable) lack of perspective. Anyone would know that the sort of information contained in the Papers would rapidly become known to the North Vietnamese. Everyone knew that a National Security action memorandum, or any other document that had presidential approval, didn't necessarily tell a foreign power anything. There was nothing like the voice of authority.

Perhaps inevitably, the testimony began to drift to an analysis of the information the defense considered politically significant. Bundy was restrained; he adhered to the issue of military secrecy. Schlesinger and Galbraith did not. Although Byrne attempted to prevent the witnesses from talking about how the disclosure of the volumes could have been helpful to the United States, and although he ordered the jury to disregard such references when they were made (the issue was injury to the United States), the message came across. His rulings, moreover, began to teach the defense lawyers, and particularly Nesson, how they could get things in: one merely asked the witness to read certain portions, or to summarize them, or to explain what they meant. The Papers were all in evidence, and the experts could discuss them. Galbraith talked about attempts (as indicated in one volume) to keep the corruption of the South Vietnamese government from the American taxpayer, the preference of the United States for a military government in South Vietnam, the ineffectiveness of the Saigon generals, MACV's suspicion of the press, and Lodge's collaboration with the government in Saigon to restrict press coverage of its failures and corruption. The fact that the Strategic Hamlet Program was not working, he said, was well known to the Vietcong—"they were in a better position to know what was happening than the authors of this report"—and there was nothing in the volume discussing it that would have told them anything; it would, however, "have been positively advantageous" if the information had been known to the American people. (The jury would please disregard that.) Schlesinger, who acknowledged that he had played virtually no role in the formulation of Vietnam policy—his responsibility in foreign affairs did not include Vietnam—nonetheless lectured the jurors on Kennedy's determination to end American involvement in the war; if Kennedy had lived, he seemed to suggest, there would have been no escalation, no Tonkin Gulf. Release of this material, he said, "would not have been of injury to the United States. In fact—" And then the judge stopped him.

The defense lawyers hoped they could get Galbraith to testify on the use of leaks by administration officials; he had given them extensive affidavits on the way classification was used to conceal embarrassing information—he had thought of doing it himself—and how material was given to the press when an official regarded it as helpful, but Byrne quickly stopped that line of testimony. It was clear that his involvement with Vietnam decisions was marginal, that he had no expertise in military operations in Indochina—Nissen let him stumble over the acronyms—and that he had been poorly prepared for his testimony. When he appeared on the stand, moreover, he appeared tired and, unlike Schlesinger (and unlike himself), uncontentious, bored and, at times, depressed. Yet he also managed to convey an impression that the details of all this material did not really matter, a magnificent intellectual *hauteur* suggesting that only petty minds could be concerned with such trivia. When Nissen asked him for his grounds for saying that the 1963 plan for withdrawal had been a pretext, his reply that he, Galbraith, had great doubts it was going to happen was in itself the most conclusive proof that the statement was correct. It was true because Galbraith said it was true.

The attack of the defense on the military value of the Papers often tended to overkill. The jury heard at least four times about the 1965 landing at Danang of U. S. Marines (the first regular American combat troops in Vietnam), and would hear more from government rebuttal witnesses. They would be told again and again that while the landing had been represented by the Administration as a response to an invitation from the Saigon government, it had in fact been hurriedly arranged at the request of the U.S. government while the troops were already under way, and that while Gorman had testified that the volume contained contingency plans for the introduction of American ground forces in the event of a North Vietnamese or Chinese Communist attack, the very landing of the Marines had rendered those plans obsolete. They would be told, moreover, that the entire operation had been rehearsed beforehand in a battle exercise staged at Camp Pendleton, California, which simulated action in an unnamed country where the people wore conical hats and black pajamas and where the political geography could correspond only to Vietnam. (The witness who described the exercise was Representative Paul McCloskey, who had then been a reserve officer in the Marines and had played the role of the American ambassador to the mythical country.)

The jurors would also hear multiple witnesses on pacification, strategic hamlets, and the Wheeler Report. Admiral La Rocque, the very first defense witness, had testified about the Wheeler document, calling it so vague and ambiguous that it would have been impossible for any foreign analyst to determine what Wheeler was thinking (did he believe, for example, that enemy morale was going up or down?), so full of bureaucratic double-talk that some of it was "absolutely unintelligible." Bundy and Halperin testified about it, and Adams discussed it a fourth time, conducting another seminar on how the data it contained had been collected, what it meant, and how the order-of-battle figures had been fabricated: one thing the Wheeler Report would tell the North Vietnamese, Adams said, was that "General Wheeler apparently didn't know what was in his own order-of-battle figures." The CIA figures set the enemy forces at 500,000, while MACV "continued to bump along at 240,000." In any case, the Vietcong would have known those figures, because, among other things, a Vietcong agent had been an adviser to President Thieu on American policy. Adams offered little evidence to corroborate his assertion that the figures had been deliberately fabricated (the defense had interviewed one of Adams' sources, the Colonel Gaines Hawkins who had helped prepare the order-of-battle figures, but was fearful that he would not confirm Adams' charges), but he managed nonetheless to make the MACV data appear highly suspicious. As the figure for one category went up, the figures for others would automatically go down. There had never been accurate body counts, for example, because no one wanted to risk his life counting corpses. Tet, the CIA had concluded, could not have occurred if there had been only 240,000 people in the enemy order of battle: the director of the CIA had fought for higher figures in the National Intelligence Estimate, but ultimately "he threw in the sponge."

The Vietcong might list someone as a "political cadre" or a tax collector, but that did not mean he wasn't part of a military force or that he didn't carry a weapon. "Not all these guys are in uniform; there are a lot of people out there trying to do you in with pungee sticks."

The heart of the case against the military significance of the Papers depended on two witnesses: Halperin, the former Deputy Assistant Secretary of Defense for International Security Affairs, and Allen S. Whiting, the former assistant to the director of the Bureau of Intelligence Research at the State Department. Together they would be able to talk extensively about the papers—Whiting about intelligence, Halperin about everything else; together they had enough credentials in intelligence analysis, defense planning, and strategic problems to overwhelm any jury. Whiting had helped prepare National Intelligence Estimates, had forecast how the North Vietnamese would react to American bombing, had reviewed bombing-target lists, and had been personally involved in Vietnam questions since 1963. Although he was still in his forties, his hair had turned prematurely gray; it had happened, he said, in a two-year period between 1963 and 1965, when he saw what was happening to Vietnam policy and when he witnessed the decisions and processes that produced it. (Quoting Lyndon Johnson—off the stand—to explain his own position: "We were six months pregnant before we knew we'd been fucked.") Since leaving State he had taught at the University of Michigan, had served occasionally as a consultant to Kissinger, and still held clearances "higher than Top Secret," although he was not permitted to disclose what they were. When Nissen, trying on cross examination to impeach his expertise, asked him how long he had actually been in Vietnam, Whiting responded that he possessed information considered so sensitive that the government could not risk his capture by the enemy and therefore restricted his travel. When he had gone, he said, he had traveled under "high security."

There was nothing in the documents that could be of any

advantage to a foreign government, Whiting testified. He had read Gorman's testimony, had examined all his examples, and had placed himself in the role of the hypothetical foreign analyst. The material was useless: it was dated and contained little that would be helpful in assessing American intelligence capabilities. Among other things, the technology had changed radically; it was now possible, for example, to use electronic devices to identify passing vehicles and human beings, and, with the use of infrared sensors, to detect body heat and the ashes of fires. By 1969, moreover, there were far more U.S. and allied agents in the country than there had been a few years before, there existed new capabilities in photographic reconaissance from drone aircraft, and the documents obtained from defectors and prisoners had been superseded by better and more recent documents. Everyone knew our general capabilities in the area of communications intelligence—they knew, for example, that we knew what their radar showed—but there was no way, given the logistics of the war, to develop effective counterintelligence techniques. Complicated code patterns depended on machines, and the Vietcong forces in Vietnam were men of "little education" who required simple communications.

Whiting's testimony became a seminar on the politics of intelligence. National Intelligence Estimates, he explained, were "analytical essays" summarizing lower-level intelligence judgments, but they contained nothing to indicate where the information for those judgments came from. They were documents prepared by committees composed of representatives of different agencies and were therefore the results of a bargaining process: "You want agreement on your points so you don't protest too much on his points." The first NIE on what North Vietnam would do if the war were escalated by the United States (March 1964) "predicted a stalemate at best" in the event of escalation. Then the military came in with an optimistic estimate, pressed for its position, and changed the picture. In the summer of 1963, MACV had said that some indicators showed that "we were winning the war"; a State

Department analysis of the same indicators said "we were losing the war." The documents were full of the language of prediction—in effect, implications of scientific accuracy—yet the predictions were often political statements; the question was always who was analyzing the data. From 1962 to 1966, the analyses of the State Department had been superior to the analyses of the Department of Defense. What Whiting was suggesting, and what Adams had already said, was that in the bargaining among the CIA, the State Department and the military, the military generally prevailed, and the military was generally wrong. The intelligence evidence indicated that Westmoreland's famous opinion that he saw the light at the end of the tunnel in November 1967 was incorrect. If Adams' suspicions about the figures were accurate, MACV had purposely manufactured the grounds for the optimism.

Halperin, however, was the central figure, the chief strategist for the defense, its key witness and, as it turned out, ultimately the prime focus of government suspicion. A former defense intellectual at Harvard and a Kissinger protégé, he had lectured at the Army War College, the Naval War College and West Point, had been a consultant at Rand, the Hudson Institute and the Institute for Defense Analyses, and had served as a special assistant in the Pentagon before becoming Deputy Secretary of Defense at ISA. Halperin's activities in the Pentagon and at the National Security Council had seemed to cut squarely across the issues and documents involved in Los Angeles; he had written summaries on the Wheeler Report for McNamara, had been involved in the Pentagon Papers Task Force from its inception (and by now probably knew the Papers as well as any man alive), and had worked with Kissinger on the first National Security Council study of Vietnam after Nixon's election. In each of those instances, a major document or an important piece of information in a document had leaked (the troop request in 1968, the Pentagon Papers in 1971, NSSM-1 in 1972); in each of those instances Ellsberg had also been involved. Like Ellsberg, Halperin had become disenchanted with the war and excessive government secrecy; unlike Ellsberg, however, Halperin had never become a public crusader. He often explained that he became involved with the defense through a combination of boredom and commitment, but it nonetheless remained hard to determine just where that commitment lay.

Halperin demeaned the Papers. They had been classified "only Top Secret," which, contrary to what Gorman said, was not the highest level of classification; they did not contain information about North Vietnamese codes or any other militarily sensitive information (since such information was unavailable to the task force), and they did not, in fact, "present an authoritative view of the thinking at the highest levels." Almost all the documents quoted (again answering Gorman) were documents "which received wide circulation in the government" and were therefore the sort of material that would almost inevitably leak to the newspapers within a few days. The most sensitive statements at State or at the Pentagon were not reduced to widely circulated memoranda; at most they went to two or three people, and often they were simply communicated by word of mouth. Anything that was widely circulated was, in fact, a form of internal government propaganda: people wrote memos not because they believed what was in them but because they wanted to score points. The study, therefore, was hardly authoritative. "It was not formally adopted by the Secretary of Defense . . . and did not represent the views of any senior official of the U. S. government." If any foreign analyst concluded from these documents that he knew what was believed at the highest levels he would have seriously misled himself.

The significance of the Papers, Halperin suggested, lay in the difference between what the government believed (or, given his analysis of the memos, what people in government wanted each other to believe) and what the Administration wanted the public to believe. It lay, for example, between the understanding in Washington after World War II that Ho Chi Minh's government was legitimate and popular and the public statements that he was merely a Communist agent; in the falseness of the attempt to make it appear that the introduction of the Marines at Danang had been requested by the Saigon government; in the reluctance of the Administration to admit publicly that the role of American troops had been changed from an advisory to a combat capacity; in the significance of Bundy's memorandum urging the government to avoid premature publicity about the changing role of U. S. forces; in an accidental disclosure that the mission had changed; and in the "private understanding that it would be a long war" as against the public statements to Congress that the war was being won. There were several consistent themes in the volumes: apprehension of a neutralist government in South Vietnam, fear of negotiations, and the use of bombing to scuttle talks that might produce negotiations.

Halperin's testimony contained, throughout, an implicit contradiction between his depreciation of the documents as internal propaganda (and, in any case, not the reflection of high-level official views) and his imputation of credibility to the same documents when he discussed the matter of official duplicity. Did they represent the thinking of the government, or did they not? What Halperin's testimony suggested was that the government wasn't thinking anything, that while there was in fact collusive duplicity in misinforming the public and the Congress, there was at least as much duplicity within the government in assessing information and determining policy. Halperin said that he had never seen a document which someone wouldn't consider embarrassing, that he had seen little that didn't require concealment from someone else in the bureaucracy. The author of the volume on pacification, for example, had been assured that Robert Komer, a former member of Bundy's staff, would not see it; the volume "was uncomplimentary to Komer's activities in pacification." Accordingly Komer, when he asked for it, was refused access. It was for such reasons that the entire study was marked "sensitive"; this was why its very existence was regarded as secret, why he, Gelb and Warnke had made their special arrangement with Rowen, and why McNamara wanted the work to proceed in absolute confidentiality. The style that produced the Papers, therefore, was also the style that had produced the war.

The controversies and animosities among and within government agencies remained a fixed backdrop to the testimony. Beyond that, however, there also developed further elaborations of the "fight within the establishment"—career generals against disenchanted defense intellectuals, loyalists against converts, the users of intelligence against the analysts. There were suggestions, moreover, that if the former analysts felt, as Nissen implied, that their work had not received sufficient attention, there was a corresponding tendency among the users of information to reshape it to conform to policy positions they had already taken, that, as the conditions of war and the criteria of success became increasingly abstract, the temptation to fudge data became increasingly strong, and that military intelligence had become a weapon of general-staff propaganda: phony body counts, the use of the Wheeler Report as a cover for a predetermined attempt to recruit more troops, the false MACV figures to justify Westmoreland's optimism. In trying to impeach the witnesses for the defense, Nissen (presumably with Gorman's advice) attempted to transform those controversies into suggestions of personal animosity, self-aggrandizement, disloyalty and collusion. Had Miller stolen government documents, had Whiting been harboring "an antipathy toward the military," had they all been coached by the defense lawyers and prepped with extensive analyses of the testimony of the government's witnesses? He directed a series of questions at Whiting implying that Whiting did not really believe that defeat in Vietnam was necessarily injurious to the United States.

Would the capture of a South Vietnamese regiment be detrimental to U. S. national defense?

It depended on the context, Whiting replied. In principle the interests of the allies and the United States were both separate and convergent.

Then what did relate to the national defense?

The defense of the interior of the United States, treaty commitments, U. S. bases abroad, the guarding of United States intelligence. We had no treaty with South Vietnam.

Would South Vietnam be important to the national defense without a treaty?

That would depend on the stance of the President. It was the President who had deemed South Vietnam to be vital to the national defense of the United States.

Nissen's cross examination focused on minute questions, particularly those concerning the motives, affiliations and relationships of the witnesses. Subtly, yet consistently, he suggested that the government professionals and ex-professionals who appeared for Russo and Ellsberg—Miller, Adams, Whiting, La Rocque and Halperin—were either victims of paranoid delusions or the voices of various forms of political disaffection whose judgment was warped by their hatred of the military. Didn't Adams regard General De Puy as part of the military conspiracy that had falsified order-of-battle figures? (Adams said yes; he thought it was "okay to be somewhat dishonest, or a little dishonest, or reasonably dishonest, but not to go whole-hog dishonest.") Wasn't the Center for Defense Information which La Rocque headed, and for which Miller worked, an organization established to challenge defense policies and new weapons systems, and not merely to "analyze"? Hadn't La Rocque himself come out against the Trident submarine? (He had not, La Rocque replied; the Center had merely suggested some alternatives.) Hadn't Melvin Gurtov, who testified on the volumes of the Papers he had written, helped organize a defense fund for Ellsberg and Russo? (He had made statements and given interviews endorsing what they had done.) These were all proper questions seeking to show the bias of witnesses, but they accumulated, first inferentially and later overtly, into an argument that the defense was a much larger conspiracy of alienated military officers, liberal intellectuals and (when Hayden, Zinn and Luce took the stand) militant radicals who had been negotiating with the enemy. Nissen treated the Camelot people gently—Bundy, in any case, was too much for him—but his arrogance with other witnesses, particularly the defrocked defense intellectuals, could become overwhelming. He had a tendency to point toward witnesses with his index finger, a preference for the repeated and contemptuous use of the word "sir" (a long-time favorite of junior officers and prep-school students) and a manner—reinforced by the use of contact lenses—of cocking his head slightly back and looking over his nose. He questioned them extensively on their meetings with the defense—where had they taken place, who was present, what was discussed?—and examined them on their notes, reinforcing the image of collusion: if he was asking all those questions he must know something.

What had La Rocque done with the rough notes he had prepared on the volumes when he first read them?

He had destroyed them.

How?

He had torn them up and flushed them down the toilet.

Was that what he ordinarily did with notes he no longer needed?

It was an old Navy practice. You tear them up in little pieces and flush them down the toilet.

Nissen also questioned Adams extensively about his notes and about his differences with the military and with his own superiors at the CIA. Some of them, Adams said, had agreed with his view of the order-of-battle figures, but they had finally made their compromises and yielded to the military.

In other words, Nissen said, they had disagreed with him. What did Adams believe made for competence in an intelligence analyst?

Experience, hard work, the ability to think, imagination, and, "above all, honesty."

Wouldn't the United States be in a better position to know allied troop strength in Vietnam than the Communists? Couldn't the Wheeler Report have told them something about that?

The Communists knew better than the South Vietnamese how many troops the South Vietnamese had. There was a great deal of padding at the lower levels. It was a common practice among commanders so that they could get their kickbacks. An officer who had only twenty-two men in his command would list thirty-three, collect pay for thirty-three and pocket the difference.

But they could have gotten General Wheeler's views.

That would have been practically useless; it probably would have confused them, since it would have indicated that Wheeler didn't know how many troops he had. It might have been interesting to fill out their files.

~~What did he mean?~~

He imagined they were just like us. They would take the document, open the drawer, and shove it in.

Nissen concentrated his attack on Halperin. It was Halperin, he suggested, who was the real center of the conspiracy, the figure connecting the various elements, the link among the leaks. What Nissen tried to insinuate was that Halperin, Ellsberg, or McNaughton, for whom both had worked, had originated the idea of the Pentagon Vietnam study, that Halperin had recruited Ellsberg for the project, that they had colluded both in the leak of the Papers and in leaking the Wheeler information three years before, and that Halperin had arranged the storage of the Papers with Rowen to make it possible to leak them. Hadn't Halperin violated all his own security acknowledgments that he would not take classified documents when he left the government, and hadn't he, or Ellsberg, or someone—probably several people—arranged to set up the task force in an effort to expose the government or the military? Nissen asked Halperin about a dinner party at his home in the fall of 1970 attended by Neil Sheehan and the Ellsbergs, and he pressed him repeatedly about contradictions in the statements to the FBI in the months following the publication of the Papers.

Didn't he tell the FBI that the task force documents were

government papers and not private papers, and that he acted as a government official in shipping them to Rand?

He didn't recall.

Hadn't he asked Ellsberg to work on the analysis of the Wheeler Report?

Warnke had asked Halperin to do some work on alternative Vietnam strategies, and Halperin had asked Ellsberg to join a group working under Gelb on the analysis. They did have access to the Wheeler Report.

Hadn't he refused to answer FBI agents' questions about the leak of the troop request when they were investigating the Pentagon Papers?

The agents told him that the questions about the Wheeler leak had been submitted by someone at the Department of Defense; he did not see how they related to the investigation they were conducting.

When he left Kissinger's staff, in September of 1969, hadn't he been given an oral exit interview in which he had stated that there were no Top Secret documents under his control?

He had. (Later the Army sergeant who conducted all such interviews testified that he recited the same material to every person; he could not recall Halperin.)

By whose authority had he taken the Papers?

He hadn't taken them, he had had them deposited.

By whose authority?

No specific authority. He had agreed that all classified documents would be returned at the conclusion of his service at Defense, and he told the government that he had no such documents in his possession when he left. But no one took that to mean personal possessions. Government officials took all sorts of papers with them. It was standard practice for people who left government to take with them papers they had written or on which they had worked.

Halperin, who spent three days on the stand, obviously enjoyed the performance. He had difficulty finding examples, in response to Nissen's questions, that bore directly on his contention about the "themes" in the Papers: the volumes involved in the trial contained little that stated specifically (and necessarily out of context) that the United States feared a neutralist government in Saigon or that demonstrated—except inferentially or through statements by North Vietnamese officials—that the United States used bombing for the specific purpose of destroying the possibility of serious negotiations. But Halperin weathered the attack. He could be as cool as Nissen, could make much of his expertise, and could, in a sense, vindicate himself both with his "radical" critics in the Russo camp and with his old colleagues at Defense. Yet there remained the uncertainty of his own motives, of the roles he had played and of his loyalties. Halperin always denied that he had anything to do with the leaks, and there was certainly no evidence that he had conspired with anyone. Beyond those considerations, however, there remained the question of where his own conversion had led him, and by inference the larger questions of style and loyalty.

It had been people like himself and Ellsberg who had created the intellectual systems of the war, who had assessed the intelligence, written the memos, and, in some instances, manipulated the generals. When the war turned sour they turned from planning to analysis, employing the same techniques of scholarship, writing the assessments in the Papers in similarly disembodied voices, and studying documents very much like the ones they themselves had written. It would even be possible for some who had recommended policies of "sustained reprisal" and urged against "premature publicity" of the escalation of the war to testify in the cause of exposure. And while the Bundys repaired to esteemed positions at the Ford Foundation or the Council on Foreign Relations, of which Halperin was also a director, the generals and politicians, though hardly blameless, became the patsies. It was at least possible to understand how someone like Gorman or De Puy or Westmoreland, however brutal or dishonest, could decide that he had been screwed—screwed in the first instance by being put in a militarily impossible situation, and then screwed again by the subsequent disdain of the intellectuals who had helped put them there in the first place.

It would also be possible to understand how those who remained in government—the "hacks," "time-servers," and "wiretappers"—might regard people like Halperin as enemies. They might easily suspect that the latter did, in fact, constitute an establishment in exile, at Brookings, at Ford, at Harvard, and that someday they hoped to be back.

II

There had never been much chance that the trial in Los Angeles could become the kind of showpiece about the war that some members of the defense team, if not the defendants themselves, often dreamed about. The daily ritual on the courthouse steps—statements by Ellsberg, Russo, Weinglass or Nesson—produced material for the evening news, but it started no movements and generated only limited interest: perishable comments that were aired and forgotten. Ellsberg, despite his brief career as movement hero, was unable to elevate his own prosecution to the symbolic importance that the defendants felt it deserved, nor did he have the capacity or the inclination to convert his notoriety into a position of continuing leadership. There had always been an inherent contradiction between Ellsberg's putative martyrdom (expecting to go to prison "for a long time") and the assertion that he had violated no law, the claims of civil disobedience as against the profession of legal innocence. In the early months of pretrial argument he talked about the First Amendment and Tom Paine, spending much of his time on lecture platforms extolling their virtues, often before audiences who were at least as aware of them as he was; later he discovered the neo-Marxist analyses of writers like C. Wright Mills and G. William Domhoff—power elites and ruling classes—and would try to discuss them with people who were familiar with them as if that argument had just been invented. Foreign policy, he concluded, had always been controlled by the

establishment (the familiar old establishment of Ivy Lea-
guers, bankers, WASPs and members of the Council on
Foreign Relations), and he would patronize those naïve
enough to suggest that perhaps that establishment had lost
some of its clout, that Vietnam and Nixon appeared to represent the breakdown of old forces and the rise of something
new. Yet the analysis, however accurate, led to nothing new,
and to no apparent awareness that he himself was, in some
way, part of that establishment or at least one of its bene-
ficiaries. Each day while the costly defense of Ellsberg and
Russo was proceeding in Courtroom 9, handcuffed prisoners
in hundreds of routine criminal cases were led through the
corridors by federal marshals and were represented by court-
appointed lawyers who were as likely to bargain for reduced
sentences as to offer a serious defense. Unlike Russo, Ellsberg did not use his exposure to attack the system. His appearances before the cameras were commentaries on the trial
or the war (and later on Watergate), reactions to bombing
or peace negotiations or the extension of the war into Laos
and Cambodia. He was always articulate and sometimes
brilliant, yet the analyses seemed always to come from a platform in space, reactions based on what had happened in the
courtroom or on what he had read in the papers. Ellsberg
appeared to be outside the frame of the action, playing the
role of the Greek chorus, analyzing events and commenting
on the actors. He was what he had been, and seemed to be
still searching for something to become. His acts had given
him credentials in the past, not in the present.

There were other problems. Officially the war was over,
and if there remained echoes in Laos and Cambodia, most
Americans preferred not to hear them. At the same time the
constitutional issues in the case had been temporarily eclipsed
by other events; repression, intimidation and the unchecked
assertion of executive authority had moved to new fronts. The
simmering Watergate affair had produced broad claims of
executive privilege, the Paris negotiations were used, among
other things, to celebrate the virtues of secret diplomacy, and

the most urgent battles over the First Amendment were being fought at the jailhouse door. All those things related deeply to the trial in Los Angeles, but more as analogies than as matters directly connected. Executive privilege was like the secrecy system; the prosecution of newsmen was like the prosecution of Russo; Watergate was like Vietnam. The trial was still being covered by a faithful group of newspaper reporters —Gene Blake of the *Los Angeles Times,* Sanford Ungar of the *Washington Post,* Martin Arnold of the *New York Times* —and by a handful of writers from the wire services, the networks and the underground press, and there were still days when it was difficult for spectators to get seats in the courtroom, but by the time the defense put its "radicals" on the stand, national attention had diminished to the point where only five percent of the clients of those wire services were using the stories they received on the case. Late in March, Theo Wilson, who had been covering the trial for the *New York Daily News* since it began, was sent to cover the return of the prisoners of war. There also came a day when the *Times* sent Arnold off to cover a minor earthquake. The real story was in the end of the war, in the rising price of meat, and increasingly in Watergate. The events in Courtroom 9 seemed to be ancient history.

Yet the case would be made, if only for the benefit of the jurors in this hermetic chamber, would be shouted into the wind, would, if possible, be recorded for the benefit of a history as remote in the future as the war seemed to be in the past; that was the only reason that they were here, the only chance to make their case. The problem was how to make it. Halperin believed it would be a mistake to call the "radicals" and suicidal to put the defendants on the stand: they might just talk themselves into jail. The trial had already gone on long enough, the jurors were becoming impatient, and in the view of the defense lawyers the espionage charges had been beaten. Calling Howard Zinn or Noam Chomsky or Tom Hayden would simply remind the jurors that the defendants were associated with the extreme Left, with long hairs and with apologists for Hanoi. What, the jurors might ask themselves, was Jane Fonda doing, whose side was she on, when she claimed that no American prisoners had been mistreated? Compounding the problem was the necessity of refuting the theft counts, which the defense, by midtrial, had come to regard as the most difficult of the charges to answer. Despite testimony that many of the documents Ellsberg had copied were in some sense "private property" and that he had had authorized possession of them, there had been no authorization to copy, no evidence that the Wheeler Report had ever been anything but a pilfered copy (stored at Rand) of an official government document, and no conclusive proof that Gelb, Warnke and Halperin were themselves acting legally when they shipped their documents to Rand. Nesson would say later that he had always believed that the inclusion of the espionage and conspiracy counts had been a serious mistake by the prosecution—had made it possible for the defense to "contaminate" the entire government case with the history of the war and the record of government deception. A simple charge of theft would have precluded any reading of the documents themselves and any discussion of the contents, and could have been based on the simple allegation that Ellsberg had misappropriated government property.

The defense lawyers resolved to take advantage of the possibilities of contamination. They tried to overwhelm the jurors with unrelated testimony about government suppression of evidence (Adams, Miller, Gerhard) and about the political contents of the Papers themselves. The record of suppression might reinforce the record of deceit on Vietnam and prejudice the jurors sufficiently, or impress them enough with the moral justification for Ellsberg's act, to acquit on all counts. Trying the war therefore became, at least in the minds of some members of the defense team, a tactical as well as a political imperative.

The attempt to generate testimony on suppression failed. Byrne allowed just enough into the record to create a disjointed, confusing story which told the jurors (if they could assemble the pieces) that Gerhard had given his reports to the Justice Department and that Justice had shipped them to Nissen, that Miller had turned his reports in to someone at the Pentagon, and that Nissen had failed to mention them in the prosecution's case. They would never learn (or even suspect, judging by their comments after the trial) that the government had been under a court order to make such documents available to the defense, and that the prosecution had denied for a year that they existed. Nor would they get any idea of the government's machinations to conceal Sam Adams. Nissen managed to get on the record the fact that it was the government which had given Adams' name to the defense; the defense lawyers were never able to frame questions eliciting the fact that the prosecution had submitted the name in such a way as to conceal his identity and the significance of the evidence he had offered to present.

There had been a similar failure in the effort to try the classification system. William G. Florence, the retired Air Force classification official who had been advising the defense (and who called himself a "security consultant"), testified that the hypothetical foreign analyst would ignore the "Top Secret" marking because he would know that a great deal of material was overclassified. Florence had gone through the documents, challenging them against the criteria of classifiability established by Executive Order 10501 and searching for "anything that could have been prejudicial to the defense interests of the United States" (and would therefore merit classification in 1969), but he had found nothing. "It is my considered conclusion," he said, "that the troop movements in South Vietnam were not for the protection of the United States—the troops were there for a political purpose." Byrne, however, refused to permit testimony on the classification system itself—the issue was only the classifiability of these documents, and not the use or abuse of the system in general practice. Nissen, moreover, managed to impeach his testimony—confusing enough already—with questions suggesting that Florence himself had been penalized for violations of the regulations and that he was therefore "bitter against the government." (It had been, Florence had explained, a political effort by others in the bureaucracy to get him for his honest application of the executive order.) When Nissen was finished there was no redirect examination, and the defense was happy to get Florence off the stand.

The political case was far more successful. The attack on the war and the explication of the political significance of the Papers had never made headlines; Ellsberg had rarely been able to do that while the war was officially still going on, and there was no reason to expect more solicitous attention from the press now. Everyone knew about the war; the war was over. Everyone knew about the Papers; the Papers were boring. Yet within the confines of the courtroom, the political case seemed to satisfy even Russo's extravagant expectations. Byrne, as liberal on evidentiary matters as he was conservative on other legal questions, permitted Zinn, Luce, Chomsky and Hayden to testify as experts; he tolerated monologues that sometimes exhausted patience, and he allowed discussion of matters relating to Vietnam which had only a faint connection with the contents of the documents. They would begin with the text of a volume, shift to their own experience, then go on to elaborate conclusions, setting out the case that had been made by radical critics of the war since its beginning: the repression of the Buddhists, the "war of the Saigon government against the independence movement," the popularity of the National Liberation Front, the involvement of the United States in the Diem coup, the attempt of the United States "to win its objectives in Vietnam through military force rather than negotiations," the government's fear that if negotiations began, world pressure for a peace settlement would build, and the use of diplomacy by Washington "to create a political effect, to create an image." Ironically, the evident distance between the courtroom and the war—in time, space and atmosphere—seemed to contribute to the defense's case, made the implicit passion of the testimony more persuasive, and amplified the horrors of the war.

There were two kinds of military activity, Zinn explained. One was in defense of a country, the other was offensive intervention in countries thousands of miles away. No one could explain the linkage between Vietnam and the national defense of the United States. (Speaking softly now, addressing the jury as if he were telling a fairy tale of infinite sadness.) There was an element of national defense which was often overlooked, and that was the morale of the people of a country: how did people feel about their country, was there a sense of community, did people believe the government was representing them? There were a lot of Americans, he believed, who felt their government was lying to them; they were distressed by the killing of Vietnamese, and they found it impossible to understand how that killing was vital to the United States. "Our troops, of whom we like to feel proud —we see on television those troops burning villages." "National" meant the whole nation; the question was not whether something was injurious "to some people, or to some politicians" or whether something was embarrassing. Maybe there were corporations interested in rubber, tin and oil, but they did not constitute the national interest. The war was not about the national interest of the United States but about special interests.

It was a simple, consistent story: the brutality of the Saigon government, the determination of the Vietcong, the American fear of negotiations. Zinn had been regarded as a test. The defense lawyers, still beset by conflicting pressures, had agreed that if the historian was effective they would call the others, and when he passed they proceeded to expand the argument to the bounds of legal possibility and, with Nissen's inadvertent help, beyond anything they could have expected in a court of law. Hayden, who identified himself as an "organizer, a teacher and a writer," described a career in which "I tried to educate myself and other people and bring them together to struggle to change society . . . control their own lives . . . and shape their destiny." He recounted the history of his private negotiations with the North Vietnamese (primarily for the release of American prisoners) : trips to Paris, trips to Hanoi, visits to Cambodia and Laos, meetings with Madame Binh and Xuan Thui, the NLF and North Vietnamese negotiators in Paris, conversations with Premier Pham Van Dong in Hanoi about "the aspirations of his people" and the negotiating terms of his government. David Nissen objected vehemently to the qualification of Hayden as an expert witness on diplomacy, but Byrne overruled him. The co-founder of Students for a Democratic Society was allowed to testify as an authority on foreign relations.

Hayden took the jury through each of the "tracks" of the contact volumes: Pinta-Rangoon, Marigold, Sunflower, Packers, Killy, Aspen, Ohio, Pennsylvania, each a code name (as he explained to the jurors) for one of the third-party efforts to establish contacts between Washington and Hanoi. The volumes indicated, he said, "that America's diplomatic allies found the U. S. position on negotiations more rigid than that of the North Vietnamese," that it was the United States which was afraid of talks, and that the direct negotiations in Paris which began in 1968 were prompted by the Tet offensive and Eugene McCarthy's victory in the New Hampshire presidential primary. (In what volume did that appear? Byrne wanted to know. The witness would please restrict his testimony to the contents of the volumes.) Each time the North Vietnamese had shown signs of softening their preconditions for direct talks, the United States would intensify the bombing. It was not the leaks which had jeopardized negotiations, it was the bombs: the United States had been committed to a settlement through military force, not through negotiation. Pham Van Dong had believed that through the entire period of third-party contacts—the American "peace offensive"— the United States was engaged in "image building" in response to world pressure. American diplomacy had been a vast effort in "stage management."

The political argument was always consistent: special interests as opposed to a genuine national interest, the brutality and corruption of a puppet government, the determination of the U. S. government to exert its will by force, the systematic deception of a people that would not have supported the policies had it known the truth. Even if the jurors were to discount Hayden's testimony as the statement of a revolutionary (or, more likely, as the words of Jane Fonda's husband), it would nonetheless survive in the context of what others had said, by its inner consistency, and in the trappings of scholarship with which it was surrounded. Chomsky, who testified on the political history—"something we would call aggression if another country was carrying it out"—reinforced the contention that the United States was fearful of "the neutralist option," that it had used bombing to stop the erosion of morale in its client government, and that it was the fear of a neutralist or Communist government, not invasion from the North, which prompted military intervention. The testimony thus became cumulative: they had begun to explain the war and had started to make a political case that would never be answered by the government.

Nissen attempted to impeach this testimony not by cross examination on its substance but through exposure of the associations and activities of the witnesses. Who had paid for those trips to Hanoi, what organizations were involved, who had accompanied them, what contacts had they had with the defendants, what rallies and demonstrations had they attended, what relationships did they have with members of the defense? But the questions seemed to reinforce the consistency of the position and the reasonableness of the argument: the witnesses were associated with people like themselves—war resisters, demonstrators, activists: Hayden and Weinglass, Zinn and Chomsky and Ellsberg, the Berrigan defense, rallies in Boston, fund raisers on Cape Cod. The very fact that the activities were so public, and that Zinn, Chomsky and Hayden could discuss them without embarrassment, gave the entire position respectability. They were not furtive Bolsheviks with bombs, but writers, college professors and scholars persuasively professing a concern with human beings. They enjoyed the benefit of a distant association with the people from Camelot: Bundy, Schlesinger and Galbraith had been witnesses for the same side and spoke, in some senses, for the same cause. The makers of war and the resisters of war were lying down together.

It was Luce who caused Nissen the most difficulty and who most undercut the implied charges of revolution and treason. Luce was the Christian who in response to each question about his associations and organizations mentioned another church board, another missionary society, another group of Methodists. He had spent thirteen years in Vietnam, first as an agricultural worker with the International Voluntary Service, then as a journalist for the Board of Social Concerns of the United Methodist Church, the World Council of Churches, and Dispatch News Service. In 1971, after he led a group of visiting American Congressmen to the tiger cages, he had been thrown out of the country, and he was now director of something called the Indochina Mobile Education Project, a traveling exhibit on Vietnamese culture and the effects of the war on Vietnamese life. He had been a supporter of U.S. policy in Vietnam until 1965, had not gone there as a political activist but as someone who had, among other things, been testing sweet potatoes in the Vietnamese climate, and he had occasionally met with the U. S. ambassador to discuss agricultural problems in the country. It was only when he became aware of the brutality of pacification, the uprooting of people from their villages and their resettlement in refugee camps, and the repression of the religious sects, that he had changed his mind. He had resigned from IVS in 1967 to speak out against the bombing of villages and the forced resettlement of the village population. The real brunt of the war, he told the jury, was being borne by the peasant farmers.

Hadn't he also gone to North Vietnam? David Nissen asked. How and with whom was the trip arranged? With what officials did he confer?

He had made the trip. He had gone with a Canadiansponsored group of priests and ministers to learn what was going on in the villages—in the northern part of Vietnam. They had conferred with officials in the Ministries of Health, Labor and Education, and had spoken with the mayor of Haiphong.

Hadn't he been invited to attend the funeral of Ho Chi Minh?

He had attended a funeral service in southern Vietnam. Ho Chi Minh was a hero in all parts of the country. He had gone as a journalist.

Hadn't his articles been published in the official organ of the NLF?

His articles and letters had been reprinted in many places, including South Vietnamese newspapers sold on the streets of Saigon. He had never sent anything to the NLF to publish.

Nissen showed him copies of the articles, among them a long piece he had written on the visit to the tiger cages. The South Vietnamese government and the American advisers from AID had lauded the prison at Con Son as a model of progressive penology: the prisoners were growing their own gardens, raising their own food, and being treated with dignity. Luce, who had heard otherwise, took a group of visiting Congressmen to see it and through a combination of circumstances, including the prestige of the visiting legislators, managed to find something else. The article had first appeared in the *Manchester Guardian* and was later reprinted in *Life*. After Nissen had finished his cross examination, Weinglass asked that it be introduced in evidence. Byrne declared that he couldn't see its materiality, but Nissen did not object. (If he had objected, the jury might have assumed something worse.) Weinglass asked Luce to read it to the jury:

> The tiger cages are small wooden compartments. Inside each cage is a wooden bucket for sanitary purposes which is emptied once a day. The cages are not quite five feet across and about nine feet long. There were three prisoners in each one. To see

them we climbed up a stairway and looked down on the prisoners through an opening at the top which is crossed with iron bars. There were 60 or 70 cages in the building.

"Donnez moi d'eau," one prisoner said in French.

"I'm sorry I cannot speak French," I answered in Vietnamese . . . "but I can speak Vietnamese. This is a congressional team from the United States who have come to look into prison conditions in Vietnam."

"We are thirsty. We are hungry. We have been beaten," one said and the chant was picked up.

"I am here because I spoke for peace. This is all Vietnamese want. We only ask for peace," said another.

As we walked down the aisle above them, the prisoners pointed to sores on their bodies. One man showed us his hand. Three fingers were missing.

"They cut off my fingers when they arrested me," he said. Then he turned his head and showed a big scar on his head.

None of the men could stand up. Until a few days ago, they said they had been shackled to a bar that went across one end of the cage. The bars had just been removed (although the bars were still left in a few cages), but the slots to put them back in were still there.

"We will be shackled again in a few days," one said as he crawled around the cage using his hands to move himself.

One of the prisoners pointed to the scars on his useless legs and said, "We were shackled here for months. We are hungry, thirsty and sick. Please give us some water."

"I am a Buddhist monk and I spoke for peace in 1966. I am here for no reason except wanting peace. I have been beaten. I have been shackled. But I still speak out for peace."

Above each was a bucket of lime.

"What is this for?" we asked Colonel Ve.

"The lime is to whitewash the walls," the Colonel said.

"No! No!," the prisoners shouted. "It is thrown on us when we ask for food."

The floors of many cages were covered with lime.

"When it is thrown on us, we cough and spit blood. Many of

us have the disease of the lungs and it is so difficult to breathe when the lime is thrown on us."

"There are other cages. You must see them, too," we were told. "There are cages with women. We hear them screaming and they are near. Right over there."

We climbed down the stairs and went to the adjacent building. Here was another double row of cages identical to the ones in the men's side. The women ranged in age from fifteen years old to one old, blind lady who must have been nearly 70. . . .

Many of the women were obviously very sick. Some had T.B., some had eye diseases; most had skin diseases. Those who were in the worst condition lay on the floor of the tiny cages while others fanned them with odd bits of cloth.

"How old are you?" I asked one beautiful young girl.

"Eighteen."

"Why were you arrested?"

"I was in a peace demonstration."

"Are you a Communist?"

At this the girl laughed at what seemed to her an irrelevant question.

"No, I am not a Communist. I am not concerned about politics. I am concerned about peace."

"Will you salute the flag?" the guard who was standing beside me demanded.

"No! No! I will not salute your flag which represents all the things you have done to me . . ."

"Then you are a Communist and should be killed." . . .

Luce read on. There were about five hundred people in the cages; they were hungry and thirsty, and many showed signs of having been beaten. The AID official who accompanied the party on the visit told them that they had no business interfering in internal Vietnamese affairs. It *was* their business, one of the Congressmen replied; the United States was paying for this.

When Luce finished reading—it had taken some fifteen minutes—there were no further questions. It would be a short day in court: that afternoon Matt Byrne had an appointment with John Ehrlichman in San Clemente.

### III

On April 9, the defense called Anthony J. Russo to testify in his own behalf. It was eighteen months since he had gotten out of prison after his confrontation with Nissen and the grand jury, and he had developed a measure of poise and control over his deepening anger that he lacked in the first weeks of his notoriety. His statements were often still brittle with movement jargon—rhetoric about American imperialism and war crimes, facile Marxist distinctions, absolutist expressions of class conflict—but they were now the statements of a seasoned campaigner, informed by a comprehension of complexity, and not those of an overgrown member of the youth rebellion. He seemed to understand the irony of his own position as a secondary figure in the trial, even to accept it, and to have developed a staying power for political activities that would go well beyond this case. Sometimes he still showed a propensity to make smart-assed remarks—"I said to myself, 'My goodness, that document is Top Secret; we should be more careful.' "—but he displayed a measure of control and grace that he had rarely shown in his statements for the cameras or on the platform. He had made his compromises with the trial and with its forms. In two hours Weinglass took him through his entire story: the ready admission that he had helped in the copying, his education, his job at Rand, the experience in Vietnam, and the relationship with Ellsberg. Nissen's cross examination took a day.

As a participant in the Viet Cong Morale and Motivation Project conducted by Rand for the Department of Defense, Russo had administered interviews with Vietcong prisoners, producing sixty thousand pages of transcript and dozens of reports. Among its objectives, he testified, was to assess for the Air Force the effect of antipersonnel weapons; over half the bombing tonnage in Vietnam consisted of such weapons, and it had been his hope that the report would lead the Air

Force to stop using them. Instead, he said, "they escalated." He subsequently left the project because "the results were being altered . . . the results were being used to promote the Air Force . . . lies were being told right and left." He had disagreed with the major conclusion of that study, that air-power "was doing a good job," and had asked to have his name taken off. Subsequently he was transferred to the economics department at Rand and assigned to another project, a "highly mathematized lie" which concluded that the United States was fighting on the side of poor people, when in fact it was clear that the United States was fighting on the side of the rich. He had found that it was "the spirit of the people . . . that kept them going against the greatest technological onslaught in history." In the U. S. crop-destruction program, ostensibly designed to deny food to the insurgents, the Air Force, through defoliation, had denied a hundred pounds of rice to the civilian population for every pound denied the Vietcong.

Russo recounted the story of an interview with a Vietcong "education cadre," a man who had specialized in educating young people, "the strongest man I ever met." The French had wiped out his village many years ago, and since his capture he had been tortured. Russo had thought until then that the Vietcong were "indoctrinated fanatics," but, he said, people who are indoctrinated or brainwashed will break down under extreme stress, and this man would never give up. During the course of the interview they had "built up rapport," and the prisoner had sung songs and recited poetry for his interrogator. Russo began to quote the lines for the jury, then broke down, and tears came to his eyes. Byrne had the clerk bring him a glass of water, and Russo continued. "He was the strongest man I ever met."

Russo had first met Ellsberg in Saigon in 1965, but they saw little of each other until 1968–69, when they were both at Rand in Santa Monica. Russo didn't know that Ellsberg had a copy of the McNamara study, or that he had worked on it, until the day he was called about finding a Xerox machine. But through the spring and summer of 1969 they talked constantly about Vietnam. "We learned a great deal from each other. I was telling him about the village experiences I had . . . I was saying that I had seen a very definite pattern of lying, alteration of facts. Dan said he had had the very same experience." One morning Ellsberg called him and said, "You know that study I told you about?" "I said, 'Yes.' He said, 'I want to get it out. Can you arrange for a Xerox machine?' " That night they met at Lynda Sinay's office and began to copy.

What documents had Russo copied? Nissen asked. Did he recall the specific volumes? What was he referring to when he said "the Pentagon Papers"?

The most radical document of this age.

The fact was that he didn't recall what document he copied, wasn't that true?

Exhibit 6 had his fingerprint on it, but it was not charged in the indictment; he supposed he had copied that one too. Maybe his fingerprints didn't appear on some of those other exhibits, but maybe he also copied them. It was possible that he Xeroxed every one of them.

Did he read any of the documents while he was copying them? He wasn't just there to "sit at a desk, talk on the phone, eat cake or things of that kind," as he had claimed?

It was very possible he had read portions of the volumes. "Those are very interesting documents." He wouldn't deny that he did it. It was an honor.

Wasn't he aware that Ellsberg had no authority to possess these documents at Lynda Sinay's office? Did Ellsberg say anything as to who allowed Russo to possess the documents or who had permitted him to copy them?

The agreement to keep secrets about crimes that had been committed was a criminal thing. Russo knew that the documents came from Rand. "Any American who knew what we did would consider it his official duty to get the Papers to Congress and the American people." (The jury would please disregard that remark.) The duty of an American citizen was total under the Constitution. (The jury would please disregard that too. The question had to do with authority from Rand.) He was pretty sure that they didn't have any kind of bureaucratic slips or permission from Dick Best, but in Saigon he had seen government officials give out materials stamped "Classified" all the time. They leaked information when it made them look good. When it didn't, then they applied the rules.

But they did discuss the fact that the documents being copied were not supposed to be shown to anyone without a clearance and without a need to know?

He thought every American who cared about his country had a need to know. They had removed the classification stamp because it was very confusing. The marking could scare someone unless he knew how meaningless it was. (The jury would please disregard that also.) They wanted to get the documents to Senator Fulbright, to the Congress and ultimately to the American people because they had a need to know. (What was done with the copies, Byrne subsequently ruled, was immaterial and should be disregarded. The copies were not part of the case.)

Had he ever been a delegate to the International Commission of Inquiry into American War Crimes in Indochina?

He had. He had gone to Copenhagen the previous summer as an expert witness on war crimes to testify about villages in central Vietnam that were completely wiped out by bombing and shelling.

Had he ever attempted to influence a witness in this case— had he handed General De Puy a press release?

He had. He believed General De Puy to be a war criminal.

Doctor Ellsberg. The defense called Doctor Ellsberg.

For weeks he had been preparing for his testimony, sitting at the defense table writing notes on a yellow legal-size pad. Occasionally he would look up to listen to a witness or to watch Nissen—he had become fascinated, he said, with the prosecutor's hangups with power—but much of the time he was preoccupied with his notes. He wanted to tell the story completely, to explain himself and his relationship to the war, to talk about the secrets, the conversion, everything. On the day Russo took the stand, the crowds had started to return—the marshals would line them up along the wall in the corridor while they waited for seats—and now they were larger than ever. The peripatetic reporters also began to come back, there were more cameramen waiting in the spring heat outside, more courtroom artists crowding the front row facing the witness stand and the jury box, anticipating the final virtuoso performances of the principals and carrying with them the heady aroma of significance.

Doctor Ellsberg. Place and date of birth, education, scholarship, honors, theses, military service, conferences, special studies, Harvard, Society of Fellows, Cambridge, Rand, Pentagon, task forces, study groups, nuclear war, Bundy, McNamara, Kissinger. Ellsberg the scholar, Ellsberg the seeker, Ellsberg the ubiquitous presence in crisis, consulting, advising, observing, concluding, telling the story of two decades at the peepholes of power in a manic stream-of-consciousness, Pentagon jargon, personal recollections, and irrelevant asides. (Why can't the son of a bitch hold still? You couldn't get a decent drawing in time for the evening news with him jerking his head around all the time.) In his first hours on the stand, he seemed unable to describe his activities—what in fact had *he* done?—and became rather like some impotent deity who had floated from crisis to crisis, task force to task force, omniscient but powerless: "Task force on presidential command . . . named the sole researcher . . . took me to SAC . . . plans for general war . . . no President or Secretary of Defense had ever seen . . . in which decision-makers at a high level . . . might want to take action . . . gave a briefing . . . in which I set forth for him certain problems . . . in drafting alternative options . . . to subordinate commanders . . . in patterns of high-level decision-making in international crises . . . to form the basic national-security policy of the United States . . ."

It began as pretentious fumbling, an evocation of plans, operations and secrets to overmatch anything General Gorman had stashed in his closet. Ellsberg, seemingly, had been everywhere and seen everything. He had visited nearly every command post in the Pacific in a study of the nuclear-command structure and communications networks (what if the President, in the event of nuclear attack, could not communicate with his commanders?); had studied plans for general war, evaluated missile gaps, participated in two working groups on the Cuban missile crisis (two of the three, he pointed out, which reported to the executive committee), worked on NATO policy, written speeches for McNamara, participated in the planning of the Vietnam bombing campaign at the Departments of State and Defense, read the cable traffic on Vietnam—two stacks of paper daily, each seven feet high—and had spent two years in Vietnam himself. Yet the testimony was disjointed, an avalanche of unfocused questions and undisciplined, self-serving responses (interrupted by a staccato of objections from the prosecution) stringing together names and titles and allusions to an endless series of higher-than-secret operations. He had reported to McNamara, Bundy, Katzenbach, Harriman, Nitze and Vance, drafted questions for Kissinger, selected problems for the personal attention of McNaughton, told Bundy about the things he couldn't learn from the cables, drafted a speech for General Ky, and, while a student, written studies on "The Theory and Practice of Blackmail" and "The Political Uses of Madness." When he went to Vietnam in 1965 he discovered that he had a highly marginal role on General Lansdale's team—he had gone as "an apprentice" in political warfare—and so he had gone into the countryside on his own initiative to compare the reporting of officials with "what I could learn from my own eyes and ears."

"He hasn't discussed his duties yet," Nissen objected.

There was an increasing divergence between the reality one saw with one's own eyes and ears and what was being reported—

"Just what you did in furtherance of your job functions," Byrne said.

He had gone to a village in Long An Province; it had been occupied by the Vietcong. There was a bridge nearby, and under the bridge there was a regiment of the Vietnamese Army. When the village was occupied not one squad of the ARVN came out from under the bridge to try to retake it. Instead the village was mortared and shelled; by occupying the village the Vietcong had caused the ARVN to destroy it.

Nissen objected again.

There were schools built of cement where you could put your hand right through the walls. The cement, supplied with American funds, was sold on the black market by the South Vietnamese district chief, and the walls were so weak they blew away in the wind. Ellsberg had reported to his superiors about that. There were instances where South Vietnamese Rangers had rampaged through villages, holding the villagers at gunpoint and raping the women. He had gone up in a plane with a forward artillery observer, and during the flight they had spotted two figures in black pajamas running from the plane. Repeatedly the pilot turned to fire at the figures, and the question arose as to the identity of the people he was firing at. He told Lansdale that the pilot had said that there were nothing but VC in the Plain of Reeds; he told Lansdale of his concern that humans were being hunted like animals.

He should just give the general nature of the report, Byrne said.

There was an incident that he thought particularly significant. An American soldier was bayonetting a canteen he had found lying on the ground. His commander had requested permission to burn a house suspected of being a Vietcong hiding place; the canteen was a substitute for the Vietcong. He told Bundy about some of these things, informed him of the ARVN's low level of performance and of the Vietnamese government's corruption, about which nothing was being reported to Washington. The only antidote was to talk to people privately and unofficially and bypass the channel of command. The official reporting screened out embarrassing information; the bosses at higher and higher levels seemed to be less and less well-informed. He showed McNamara copies of some of the reports he had made and told him how when he drove around the roads in Vietnam the kids would run up and shout "Okay" or "Number one," and how he recalled reading that in World War II the kids had learned a few words of Japanese to call to the soldiers; it made him feel very strange to think he was following in the footsteps of the Japanese invaders.

The last portion of the answer would be stricken.

When he left the stand at the noon recess, he broke into tears. He had started to talk about color photographs he had taken from the air of the effects of defoliation; the recollection of a countryside where one side of a river was lush, the other a desert, had overwhelmed him. But there was also the tension and the suspicion that the great performance had not started well. (His father had come out from Detroit, his children were there, and the fashionable liberals from Hollywood were occupying seats in the rows reserved for friends of the defense.) Nesson had told him at a recess an hour earlier that he would have to be more lucid, would have to curb what one member of the defense team later called "that egocentric shit." There had been too many names, titles and academic degrees, too much Harvard. That afternoon the defense asked Byrne for an early recess because Boudin was exhausted and was to be examined by his cardiologist. The recess was extended for several days and the defense team used the time to work with Boudin and Ellsberg to try to get the testimony into better shape.

Ellsberg returned to the stand the following Monday (the day, it turned out, when Watergate prosecutor Earl J. Silbert learned about the burglary in Beverly Hills of Ellsberg's psychiatrist), recounting the story of the transportation of the Papers from Washington to Santa Monica, the arrangements with Rand and the copying at Lynda Sinay's office; on each of the two trips, he said, he had taken as many documents as he could fit into a satchel. He had become more focused and disciplined during the recess, and Boudin's questions were sharper. The artists stopped complaining: Ellsberg was sitting still. Byrne had ruled that Ellsberg could talk about intent (to make copies) but not motive (to get information to the American people), but Ellsberg nonetheless managed to make his version of the motive clear; he was allowed to tell the jury what he had told Russo and the Ellsberg children: he wanted to get the information to Congress. After each copying session he took the documents back to the safe in his office or, if he didn't return them immediately, kept them in his home overnight ("while I slept briefly"). He did not intend to retain them or give them to someone else, and none had been lost, destroyed or defaced. (Later Nissen asked him about some marginal marks: had he written the word "wow" or the word "Hitler" next to a passage about Diem? These words, he acknowledged, were his.) He asked Russo and Sinay to participate only because he needed access to a copying machine and because they would help get the work done faster. Neither of them knew that he had the documents until he called Russo, nor did he have any intention of making copies when he first picked the documents up in Washington. In any case, not a page of those documents could have injured the national defense. "If I had believed it could, I would not have done what I did." After ten years of work in the executive branch he knew that their disclosure could not harm the national defense.

The Papers, he told the jury, revealed "four realities of Vietnam": the French effort would have failed much earlier without American help; the Saigon governments were narrowly based, corrupt, and supported only by the military that we supported; the majority of Vietnamese wanted to end the war; but the war was not going to end with a military victory for the United States when a majority of the population was so dedicated to removing foreign influence from Vietnamese soil. A lot of Americans took their "realities" from what the President said; they assumed that the President had special information. It was important, therefore, for people to learn that the President knew what everyone else knew; the explanation for failure was not good intentions and bad information—the intentions were not that good—and the explanation for continuing the war was not special information. Although the President had all the responsibility for the war and had kept the realities from the public, the documents indicated that there were no "supersecrets" known only to him. The war would not end, he realized, until Congress had the same information and began to share the responsibility. After the trial Ellsberg would say that he never regarded the Papers as all that important, that he disclosed them "because that's what I had," but this was the first time he depreciated their significance: more important than the secrets in the Papers was the absence of even greater secrets. The Papers exposed the government's deception of the American public, but, he now suggested, they also revealed the lack of positive information justifying the continuation of the war. He had been bothered by a published suggestion that he was as infatuated with secrets as the government; that, he countered, might have been the old Ellsberg, but it did not represent his views now. At the very end of his direct testimony—at the end of a legal process that had lasted almost two years—he had come to the point of acknowledging publicly that the Papers were not tablets handed down from Moses.

Nissen tried to attack the details of the story: Had Ellsberg stopped somewhere on his way from Washington to Santa Monica? Had he ever kept documents out of his safe longer than overnight while he was copying them? Had he, in fact, intended to copy the documents as early as August 1969, the time when he brought the second installment from Washington, and had he mentioned his intention to disclose them at a conference of war resisters in Philadelphia a month before the copying began? Nissen's questions also succeeded in suggesting that Ellsberg himself believed that what he was doing might be illegal, that he regarded the contact volumes

as so sensitive that he refused to release them to the newspapers, and that he was himself responsible for the Mc-
Namara study—that it was his idea, and therefore just possibly he had been thinking about exposing the evidence of
"war crimes" ever since 1967.

Ellsberg often responded with a smirk; he knew what Nissen was up to, and he wasn't going to be tripped up. He had
stopped in Denver on his trip from Washington; he did
occasionally keep some of the volumes in his home over the
weekend while they were being copied; but he never had any
intention of disclosing them until the day he called Russo.
The security manuals did forbid access to classified information to persons without a clearance, but it was not an easy
matter to determine what was classified; he had "given consideration" to his signed security acknowledgments when he
copied the Papers, but they made no sense since they mentioned statutory penalties for disclosing classified information which did not exist. In no respect was the Rand manual
ever followed "either at Rand or outside" (the remark would
be stricken), nor did he ever believe that the contact volumes required protection in the interest of national defense.

When Thai came to Sinay's office, had Ellsberg told him
that he was copying the documents?

He had told him he intended to give them to Congress,
that he would probably lose his job and his clearance and
probably wouldn't be able to see him much. Thai had replied
that being patriotic was a complicated matter; he doubted
that giving the material to Fulbright would have a strong
effect and didn't believe that Congress would make the documents public.

Did he believe that the Papers contained evidence of war
crimes?

He was not a lawyer; he thought they contained evidence
of illegal actions. The high-level-planning documents were
evidence of the same kind as those used at Nuremberg. They
indicated clear-cut planning to conduct a war in violation of
our commitments. He thought that international lawyers . . .

Byrne stopped him: there would be no discussion of legal questions. Any mention of what the law provided was not a matter of evidence for the jury.

Hadn't he spoken of a conspiracy by high-level officials of the United States to wage war?

He had spoken of the conspiratorial style as against conspiratorial intent. He thought they probably meant the best for the country, but there was a conspiratorial manner—the lies, the efforts to mislead the Congress and the public. He had been part of it himself in a "lowly" way. They knew a lot of people were going to die; if the majority of the American people had known that, they wouldn't have supported it.

IV

The defense decided not to call Fulbright. Since Byrne had ruled that evidence pertaining to the disposition of the copies was immaterial, most of what they wanted Fulbright to discuss would be inadmissible. Although he could have testified as an expert on the contact volumes, there had already been ample testimony, redundant testimony, on the Papers. The defense did, however, call Richard A. Falk, professor of international law at Princeton. Falk had contributed a chapter to the second volume of *Washington Plans an Aggressive War,* a series of essays written by members of the Institute for Policy Studies on Vietnam (his colleagues had assumed he had seen the Pentagon Papers before they were published), and he himself had been under investigation by the grand jury in Boston. The lawyers wanted Falk to testify that the Papers contained evidence of violations of international law, which, according to the standards applied at the Nuremberg war crimes trials, not only permitted disclosure but required it. International law, they argued in a brief, was part of "the supreme law of the land"—presumably higher than domestic statute law—and the defendants, according to the Nuremberg precedents, could have been indicted as war criminals, for they had both participated in Vietnam. The effort to disclose the contents of the Pentagon

Papers was therefore a "reasonable and effective manner of ending their participation in the prosecution of war and, thereby, ending their legal accountability. As 'superior orders' embedded in domestic law are no defense against a prosecution for the violation of international law, the defendants were entitled to ignore competing legal claims, to the extent they existed, inhibiting the disclosure of the information contained in the Pentagon Papers."

Byrne and Boudin knew that the argument had never been recognized in an American court—that international law was a pretentious myth and that its invocation was fatuous. Boudin confessed that he knew of no American case "directly in point." It was therefore a ritual performance—the last of many—conducted in a virtually empty courtroom (out of the presence of the jury) for the satisfaction of knowing it had been tried. Byrne rejected the argument (it would, among other things, require the jury to make a determination on violations of international law), and Falk, who had already been sworn, left the stand. At 11:10 A.M. on April 19, the defense rested.

# SEVEN

# Watergate West

I

THE WORD arrived April 26 in a brown envelope which
Nissen handed Byrne: a copy of a memo from Watergate
prosecutor Earl J. Silbert to Assistant Attorney General
Henry E. Petersen. Byrne refused to accept it *in camera* and
ordered it turned over to the defense the next day. It read:

> This is to inform you that on Sunday, April 15, 1973, I re-
> ceived information that at a date unspecified, Gordon Liddy
> and Howard Hunt burglarized the offices of a psychiatrist of
> Daniel Ellsberg to obtain the psychiatrist's files relating to Ells-
> berg. The source of the information did not know whether the
> files had any material information or whether any of the infor-
> mation or even the fact of the burglary had been communicated
> to anyone associated with the prosecution.

Byrne ordered Nissen to begin an immediate investigation
to determine whether "the legal or constitutional rights of any
of the defendants or any other individuals are possibly involved." He wanted to know what else Silbert had learned—
"all the facts surrounding the occurrence of the burglary . . .

and whether the information obtained, if any, has been used by anyone in the preparation of the prosecution of the case," including, among other things, the initial decision to indict. Since the memo was dated April 16—Nissen said he knew no more than what was in the memo—Byrne also wanted to know why it had taken ten days to reach him.

Nixon himself had held it up, but neither Byrne nor the defense would learn that until after the trial was over. On the weekend of April 15, White House Counsel John W. Dean III, in mounting panic, had gone to the prosecutors to negotiate for immunity and told the Justice Department of the involvement of senior White House aides in the Watergate coverup; Petersen and Attorney General Richard Kleindienst immediately relayed Dean's story to Nixon, meeting with him that Sunday after a White House prayer breakfast. Nixon told Petersen to proceed with the Watergate investigation but (according to the Nixon statement of May 22) "to confine his investigation to Watergate and related matters and stay out of national security matters." Two days later, when Petersen received Silbert's memo, he called Nixon, and Nixon told him, "I know about that. That's a security matter; you stay out of it. Your mandate is to investigate Watergate." After telling Silbert to "forget it," Petersen began to "ponder the situation" and to discuss with aides the question of whether disclosure of the burglary was exculpatory material which had to be turned over to the Ellsberg defense. On April 25, he decided that this was not the case in which to test the question—the case was too political and they might well lose on the issue—and so he went back to Kleindienst and asked for help.

> We spent most of the day talking about this [Petersen testified later at the Senate Watergate hearings] and he solicited some independent opinion and concluded that I was right, that indeed it should be disclosed. I told Mr. Kleindienst that the President had told me to forget about this but that nonetheless I thought we should go to the President, and if he was unhappy

about it we'd simply have to take the consequences, and Mr. Kleindienst agreed to that. . . . He went to the President, and the President agreed.

Nixon later claimed that he didn't learn about the burglary until April 25 and that he then directed "that the information be transmitted to Judge Byrne immediately." Yet Nixon had in fact known about the burglary at least since late March, when Dean and Ehrlichman had discussed it with him. (Subsequently he acknowledged that he learned about the burglary on March 17 and that the April 25 date was wrong.) More important, Nixon had known for almost two years that this had been a political prosecution and that a special unit had been operating out of the White House to investigate Ellsberg. Having rationalized the activities of the Plumbers with "national security," he had now tried to use the same argument to rationalize this suppression of evidence, and the Justice Department had, at least for a week, been willing to accommodate him. There was even a hope at Justice that Byrne would receive the Silbert memo *in camera* without informing the defense; a number of people at Justice were livid with anger when Byrne ordered the memo turned over.

The defense reacted uncertainly, displaying a mixture of jubilation and apprehension. Ellsberg did not want it known that he had ever been in psychoanalysis, and the disclosure made him nervous. (The first public mention of Fielding's name did not come from the defense but in a leak published by *Time*.) Shortly after the burglary was revealed, Ellsberg also told other people on the defense that the revelation of the burglary would have no effect on the case. Later in the day, however, he regained his composure, although he still remained ambivalent. "I wish I could say as a citizen that I'm surprised," Ellsberg told the reporters. "How can I be surprised just because the Administration breaks the law? The law stops at the White House fence." Yet the defense lawyers began to feel that if the burglary did not lead to dismissal of the indictment, it would at least rescue the trial from the doldrums, justify what they had been saying about the government and the reasons for prosecution, and put the case on the front pages as a major exhibit of the government's crimes. The Pentagon Papers were wearing thin—material from another era, records of past perfidy; only the rhetoric of the defense had linked Vietnam, the Papers and what Senator Sam Ervin of North Carolina would come to call the Gestapo mentality of the Nixon Administration. The burglary fused the two eras, made history whole, and at last turned the trial into the showcase that the defendants had always desired. That afternoon, Byrne gave the jurors extensive instructions not to read headlines, ordered the newspaper racks removed from the sidewalks around the courthouse, and told the clerk to lead the jury out through the basement. They were not supposed to know what was going on, yet now they would know because at last the case had exploded beyond the confines of the courtroom, beyond the constitutional issues, beyond free speech.

A week before, the government had started its rebuttal case. Nissen had called, among others, Lloyd R. Vasey, a retired Navy admiral who testified about the military sensitivity of one of the volumes, retired Marine Corps General Victor "Brute" Krulak (to disparage McCloskey's testimony about the Marine exercise preparatory to the landing at Danang), and General Alexander M. Haig, Jr., Kissinger's deputy (and, within three weeks, Haldeman's successor at the White House), who appeared in full uniform to testify that Halperin's role at the National Security Council had been marginal. Russo pursued Haig out of the courthouse to hand him a copy of a summary of the Pentagon Papers; when Haig refused to accept it, Russo gave it to an aide, who threw it on the sidewalk. Nissen also called a covey of Rand officials and government clerks to cast doubt on mini-details of defense testimony (Ellsberg's stopover on the trip from Washington to Santa Monica, Halperin's security acknowledgments, Gelb's understanding with Rand), and there were rumors that he was preparing to summon Wheeler or West-moreland, a senior State Department official, and other government "experts," but none of them ever appeared. His case had started to run down. Vasey and Krulak were so transparent that they became jokes among the press—"This man has no eyes," the notes said, "this man is not alive"—and the testimony from the Rand people seemed only to reconfirm the contentions of the defense. When the news of the burglary broke, the rebuttal case, which was being sustained by rumors about important witnesses to come, faded to total obscurity. Reese and Barry, Nissen's two co-counsel, who had been sitting silently at the prosecution table for nearly four months, were assigned the task of examining the last witnesses. The government seemed to have given up.

On April 30, Monday, someone set up a row of dominoes on the prosecution table. Each of the dominoes was marked with a name: Hunt, Liddy, Ehrlichman, Haldeman, Nissen, Martin, Mardian, Mitchell, Byrne and Nixon. Earlier that morning Nesson had received a call from Halperin, who had returned to Washington, about an article in the *Washington Star-News,* and Nesson immediately called Byrne's clerk to ask for verification. Was it true, Nesson wanted to know, that Byrne had had a meeting with Ehrlichman and Nixon to discuss a high-level government appointment? (Russo and others on the defense would be furious with Nesson; why give Byrne an opportunity to prepare an explanation, why not spring it on him in open court?) The clerk said he would mention it to the judge. When Byrne arrived in court he said he wanted to make a statement.

A few weeks earlier, Byrne said, he had received a call from Ehrlichman "about a future assignment in government." He had met with Ehrlichman and told him he couldn't consider another assignment as long as the trial was going on. The only discussion pertaining to the trial itself dealt with its duration; he told Ehrlichman it would last perhaps another month. During the course of his meeting (at San Clemente) he also had a one-minute meeting with the President, exchanging greetings, nothing more. Byrne did not mention that there had been a second meeting with Ehrlichman two days later (in a park in Santa Monica), that the job discussed was the directorship of the FBI, or that Kleindienst had been sponsoring him for the post for nearly two years. When L. Patrick Gray III, who had been serving as acting director since J. Edgar Hoover's death, became implicated in Watergate (in response to a request from someone in the White House he had destroyed the "political dynamite" from Howard Hunt's safe) Byrne's name came up again. There would be two versions of the story, and they would be told in pieces over a period of months. Byrne insisted, as he had in court, that he had been unequivocal in telling Ehrlichman that he could not consider any new job until the trial was over, and that the second meeting in Santa Monica (which, it later turned out, Byrne had asked for) was merely to confirm his prior decision; Ehrlichman maintained that Byrne had shown a strong interest in the job from the beginning, that Byrne knew why he had been asked to come to San Clemente, and that the judge had used the meeting in Santa Monica to restate his interest.

Now someone, perhaps Ehrlichman himself, had leaked the story of the meeting in San Clemente, either to strike back at Byrne for turning over Silbert's memorandum or to block his appointment as FBI director. The old hands at the FBI wanted an insider for the job. In the Byzantine games of political leaks, any number could play.

Whose dominoes were those? Byrne asked Nissen.

"They're not ours," the prosecutor replied. "We don't own them; we're not playing with them."

What information had the government turned up on the burglary? Byrne asked. There must be some information that constituted the basis of Silbert's memorandum. What was the source of Silbert's information?

They were following the court's instructions, Nissen said. The matter was being worked on diligently. He would try to submit something later.

Boudin had information. The psychiatrist had confirmed that there actually had been a burglary, that the FBI had attempted to interview him before the break-in occurred, that a few days before the burglary the cleaning people had seen two men inside Fielding's office taking photographs "of the walls," and that two others, believed to be Cubans, had left a valise inside the office a few hours before the burglary took place.

Perhaps, Byrne suggested, the defense would provide *in camera* a copy of the psychiatrist's records so that he could determine what information could have been obtained.

Impossible, Boudin replied. Those records were privileged and Ellsberg was not going to waive that privilege. What was required now was an immediate hearing to determine whether the Ellsberg indictment was part of a general political espionage operation on the part of the executive branch. Some evidence had already been destroyed; there had been material in Hunt's safe marked "Ellsberg" and "Pentagon Papers," and Ellsberg had been the target of an attack organized by Hunt on the Capitol steps the previous spring. The Attorney General had been wearing two hats; it was no longer possible to take the word of the government. Dean, Gray, Hunt and Liddy "should be required to appear here tomorrow morning," Mitchell, Kleindienst, Mardian, Haldeman and Colson should be called, the products of the entire FBI investigation of the case should be turned over and the electronic-surveillance orders broadened to cover the White House and the Committee for the Re-election of the President. They could no longer rely on statements and affidavits; the only way to get information was to bring people into the courtroom and put them on the stand. "We don't trust the government of the United States as represented by the executive branch. . . . Maybe if we proceed immediately with this investigation we may avoid further destruction of evidence."

The implication of Byrne's conversation with Ehrlichman dawned slowly. Boudin alluded to it in his argument that morning, citing the canons of judicial ethics about conflicts of interest and judicial impropriety, but he did not press it. It was only later that the defense lawyers, largely at the insistence of Weinglass, would seize on it as their most powerful weapon. Yet Byrne was obviously caught; in a chaotic case involving an endless series of crucial decisions from the bench, Byrne had appeared, at the very least, as a person untouched by overtly conflicting interests and subject only to the vaguest charges of overweening personal ambition. Now he himself had been implicated, had become associated with the core of the White House conspiracy, and had acknowledged his involvement only when he had been found out. (At the very moment that he made that acknowledgment, the wire services were carrying the story that Dean, Kleindienst, Haldeman and Ehrlichman had resigned.) If he held his hearing now he would have to take testimony from the man who had offered him a job barely a month before; if he did not, his own complicity (let alone the questions of White House involvement) might never be resolved. Had any member of the defense team offered Byrne a job, Weinglass said later, they would all be in jail.

Byrne wavered, responding to Boudin's argument by expanding his orders to the government. The investigation, he told Nissen, was not limited to the alleged burglary; he wanted all information pertaining to any investigation by any official agency or "any nonofficial agency," all leads to any other kind of investigation, any investigation performed by the White House, anything similar to what Hunt and Liddy had done, any investigation of any kind pertaining to the Pentagon Papers, Ellsberg and Russo. If the government had any doubts about anything, it should turn it over. He could not specify all of it because "I may not be imaginative enough." He did not, however, order the hearing. He took the request under submission; perhaps he would conduct a hearing before the case was submitted to the jury, perhaps after the trial, perhaps not at all.

The information arrived in grudgingly small installments: Hunt's grand-jury testimony on the break-in, inventories of the contents of his safe (including a pistol, electronic equipment, and the Ellsberg folders), Ehrlichman's statement to the FBI that he had not authorized the burglary (and had told the Plumbers, on hearing of it, never to do it again), an affidavit from Egil Krogh, chief Plumber, taking responsibility for the break-in, denials from Colson and Haldeman that they knew anything about it (also made in statements to the FBI), though both obviously knew about the Plumbers' unit, Hunt's testimony about his work in trying to fabricate the cables implicating Kennedy in the Diem assassination and his attempt, with Colson's encouragement, to foist them off on a writer from *Life*, interviews with CIA officials about the provision of disguises and cameras to the Plumbers, and affidavits from Justice Department officials, including Martin, Petersen and Nissen, that no evidence from the Plumbers' investigation had been used in the Ellsberg prosecution and that they were unaware of the burglary until they received Silbert's memo.

Byrne, pressed by the defense, became increasingly impatient; he wanted something that afternoon, the next morning, wanted Nissen to call Washington at the next recess, wanted to know why it wasn't coming faster. He became visibly angry at the apparent inability (or unwillingness) of the government to provide data. He himself had been taken—they had found his weakness—and his Irish was up.

Nissen said the court should be satisfied, they were doing everything they could: "Today the court said there weren't many answers in the box we provided to you. I want to tell the court that I don't put answers in boxes. I put what the court asks for in a box."

"I don't find the envelope of 'Eyes Only Mr. Hunt' in there," Byrne replied.

"Well, and the reason you don't is because it is not there."

"Well, let's get it there."

"Yes. And your Honor will recall that you mentioned to me yesterday—"

"Mr. Nissen, I realize the reason I didn't get it is because it wasn't there, and I don't really require your simplification of the issues on that. If we spent a little more time getting it there than we do trying to simplify the issues, I would appreciate it."

"Certainly. It was not meant to be disrespectful, your honor. I was merely trying to explain to the court that your feelings about how rapidly this should get here are not in accord with what is physically possible. . . ."

As the investigation proceeded, Byrne's courtroom became an open pipeline for Watergate news; even after Byrne had ordered the marshals to reserve extra seats for the press, the reporters were sitting on each other's laps waiting for the arrival of documents. Nissen would deliver the latest installment from Washington, Byrne would examine it and, in most instances, order it turned over to the defense, and the defense would immediately make multiple copies and distribute them to the press.

The defense did not, however, disclose the contents of Hunt's "Ellsberg" file, which included the psychiatric reports, lists of people Ellsberg had called, old FBI interviews with Yvonne Svenle, and a "chronology" Hunt had prepared on Ellsberg's life and career. At the request of the defense, Byrne ordered them held *in camera.* In their rush to get the documents, the reporters also missed items filed with the clerk which the defense chose not to hand out, among them portions of Hunt's grand-jury testimony discussing Ellsberg's "bizarre life style" and "peculiar sexual practices." As a consequence it would be more than two months before the public learned what the Plumbers had been looking for and to discover that the White House investigation was more concerned with data useful in discrediting Ellsberg than with finding leaks of Top Secret documents.

Nissen wanted Byrne to put some restriction on what was turned over; it was likely to have an adverse effect on the cooperation of witnesses if everything they said to an investigator was certain to appear in the newspapers the next day. Byrne acknowledged the validity of Nissen's point, but he rejected the request after Boudin argued that the defense was conducting its own inquiry and that the publicity would produce more leaks and more information. Almost everything that had been learned in the first days of Nissen's inquiry, Boudin said, had come from the newspapers; if the *Washington Post* and the *Star-News* could get information, "why doesn't Mr. Nissen get it?" In the meantime the defense had also learned, partly through its own inquiries, partly through the press, that the Beverly Hills Police Department had ascribed the burglary to a small-time second-story man and purse snatcher named Elmer Davis; in the course of another investigation, the police had succeeded in getting Davis to "confess"—though he had never been prosecuted for it—and had written off the case as solved. Later it turned out that Davis had been in prison at the time of the burglary.

II

Part of the difficulty with Byrne's "investigation" was telling who was investigating whom. At one point Boudin, in exasperation, told Byrne he couldn't understand why an investigation was necessary at all: all he had to do was order the government to produce the pertinent records in the case, material that presumably already existed somewhere within the government. But who, Byrne asked, was the government? Legally, technically, it was a single party; an order to Nissen as the government's attorney was presumably an order to every agency and every employee. But the government, long before Watergate, had undergone adaptive mutations to preclude the execution of such an order; the processes of bureaucracy and internal secrecy were designed as much to serve the purposes of intra-agency and interagency deception as they were designed to mislead the public and the Congress. The Vietnam War, the Pentagon Papers, Watergate, the trial, all suffered the consequences of such secrecy and deception. As a consequence, the investigators were investigating each other, prosecutors sending out FBI men to interrogate people who had, until recently, been their superiors, agents interviewing presidential assistants in the White House, the entire government ordered to turn upon itself. They were all as capable of lying to one another as they were of deceiving judges, defendants and the public.

What Byrne's inquiry produced was a second-generation cover story. Krogh, in his affidavit, took sole responsibility for authorizing the burglary. Ehrlichman told an FBI agent that he knew that Hunt and Liddy were conducting the investigation for the White House and were going to the West Coast to follow up on leads—there was "information available that Ellsberg had moral and emotional problems" and that "Hunt and Liddy sought to determine full facts relating to these conduct traits"—but he denied all prior knowledge of the break-in; Mardian, interrogated by an agent, refused to say anything, claiming some sort of lawyer–client privilege, although he did not then say who his client was; Colson told the agents that Dean had told him not to discuss the Ellsberg investigation at all, "as it was a national-security matter of the highest classification"; and Haldeman denied all knowledge of everything. The inference to be drawn from these statements was that the Plumbers had worked more or less independently, had cleared the burglary with no one higher than Krogh (a man known never to do anything without checking with superiors), and that all White House personnel above them had been dismayed, if not shocked, when they learned of the break-in. The existence of the 1970 intelligence plan, the story that newsmen and members of the National Security Council staff had been wiretapped, and the degree of Nixon's own involvement in the matter would not become clear until later. Many of the details would never be disclosed.

The arrival of the information in Los Angeles reinforced the growing atmosphere of legal chaos: the case was out of control, in spite of the residual formalities of the courtroom. The defense lawyers, oscillating between exasperation and euphoria, issued often contradictory demands covering the entire spectrum of judicial remedies. They continued to ask for a hearing, moved for dismissal of the indictment, and told

Byrne that it was a travesty to continue with the normal business of the trial, the government's rebuttal case, while the questions raised by the disclosure of the burglary remained unanswered. At one point Byrne had declared that he would not allow the case to go to the jury as long as the investigation was incomplete, and had warned Nissen that the government had a positive responsibility to prove that the indictment and the prosecution were not tainted by illegal evidence; but in the meantime he had started to back away from that position: the defendants had a right to be judged by this jury, he said, and he ordered the proceedings to continue.

On May 4, in an attempt to increase the pressure, the defendants instituted a boycott, arriving in court without their normal clutter of files, papers and briefcases, and announced that they would no longer raise objections to Nissen's questions or participate in cross examination. "The defendants," Boudin said, "are not compelled to try two cases at once." There was no way to do it "physically or psychologically"; a totally different case had developed, a case against the United States government, and it was farcical to carry on with normal business. Byrne proceeded to raise his own objections to questions he regarded as improper, while the defendants and their lawyers sat silently at their table. He also asked both parties to provide him with "points and authorities" pertaining not only to a formal motion to dismiss but also to a motion for mistrial, reminded them again to complete their suggestions for jury instructions, and declared that the investigation of the burglary and White House involvement in the case remained of paramount importance. Byrne, himself enmeshed in the surrounding chaos, was busily considering everything.

The defense made its first formal motion to dismiss on May 1, amplified it three days later, and continued to press it—often by sheer reflex rather than premeditation—until the end. Although the arguments, written and oral, emphasized the obvious matters of government impropriety—the withholding of evidence, the attack on Ellsberg in Washington,

the burglary, and the general involvement of the White House
—they also raised, with increasing insistence, the issue of
judicial misconduct. Weinglass was certain that Byrne had
been set up by the White House, that Ehrlichman, anticipating the disclosure of the burglary, had, with Nixon's approval,
called the judge to San Clemente in the hope of influencing
him enough—through his vanity or his ambition—to make
him reluctant to disclose the facts of the break-in once he
learned them. Although Byrne's fairness was never questioned
—he had turned Silbert's memo over—there still remained
the issue of the "appearance of fairness."

> We do not see how the effect of the San Clemente incident can
> be mitigated [the defense argued in a brief]. The conduct of the
> President . . . has compromised the judiciary to the point where
> a fair trial is impossible now or in the future. It would have
> been infinitely wiser if the Judge had refused to visit San
> Clemente in the midst of what may be the most important
> political trial in our time. If he did go, we would have wished
> that he had advised counsel for the defense in advance of that
> meeting, or certainly after he discovered that the purpose was
> to offer him a Federal appointment. . . . That no disclosure was
> made before the issue was raised by the defense is perhaps an
> indication that judges, like the rest of us, have human failings.
> But it is those very human failings which make it improper for
> the case to proceed. . . . The White House, by initiating this
> meeting, has irretrievably compromised the court.

There was at least "the appearance of a possibility," Weinglass told Byrne, that Ehrlichman knew his name would come
up in connection with this case. Ehrlichman brought to the
trial "the inextricable wedding" between Watergate, "the
most invidious national scandal in the history of this re-
public," and the prosecution of Russo and Ellsberg. "This
trial cannot continue to withstand those facts."

There were other situations where a sitting federal judge
was offered a promotion, Byrne said.

If Ehrlichman's record were unimpeachable, Boudin replied, that would be true. But it was hard to believe he didn't have a "base motivation." When the White House engaged in this kind of malfeasance "I'm not saying the government should fall, but this case should fall."

The offer from the White House did not influence the judge, Byrne said.

That didn't matter, said Boudin. This would be a warning to future Presidents and their assistants.

"Nothing has occurred in any way at all to indicate bias by the court."

Nissen thought the whole argument was absurd; he said nothing on the issue of judicial misconduct (although he occasionally yawned while the defense lawyers argued) and told Byrne that there were absolutely no grounds for dismissal. The only way the disclosures relating to the burglary could bear on the issue of dismissal was if the improper acts of the burglars "in some way impacted" on the prosecution. So long as he could show the court that his questions, his material, his evidence did not come from the burglary or other illegal acts, which he was prepared to do, there were no grounds for dismissal or the declaration of a mistrial. They should let the case go to the jury and, if necessary, conduct a post-trial hearing. The arguments about the burglary were becoming "the typical daily rain dance" and proved nothing. "I will be able to certify to the court that no tainted evidence was used." Unexpectedly, however, he closed his rebuttal case a week earlier than anticipated. A few days before, he had announced that he would have three or four more witnesses; after he finished with Philip C. Habib, a career foreign-service officer (the witness boycotted by the defense), Nissen announced he was finished.

Did that change the government's evaluation of the case? Byrne asked him.

It did not. They were not considering a motion for dismissal.

Byrne formally rejected the argument of judicial impropriety—there was no bias and therefore no basis for dismissal

on those grounds—but the defense lawyers continued to
press him. Playing to what they regarded as Byrne's sensitivity
about his own role and his negative reflex about appeals to
the Ninth Circuit Court, they began to raise the possibility
of taking the "appearance-of-fairness" argument to the higher
court. On May 6, a Sunday, they decided to send Peter Young
to San Francisco the next day to file notice of an appeal.
Russo, angry that he was not consulted, objected. He did not
want the trial stopped by another mandamus hearing or
thrown out simply on the grounds of judicial misconduct.
There were more important issues; if at all possible, he
wanted a verdict from the jury. Peter Young therefore did
not go to San Francisco, and the motion was never filed, but
the possibility of such action was suggested again and again
in the course of other arguments. No hearing, Nesson argued
on May 8, was "going to be adequate in this case." If the
situation involved anyone but the President of the United
States, "he would be called to explain why he held up" Silbert's memo. "When you were called to San Clemente and
offered the hand of the President, you were told where Mr.
Nixon is at . . . Now it's time to show where the judiciary is
at." The evening papers interpreted that as a suggestion that
the defense might try to subpoena Nixon to appear in Los
Angeles. But more significantly, it was another reminder to
Byrne about his own compromised situation. On the same
day, Boudin mentioned the possibility of asking Byrne for a
recess in the trial to permit the defense to perfect a motion
for a writ of mandamus from the Ninth Circuit Court.

The defense continued to ask for a hearing, but by May 8
(ten days after the original disclosure) those demands had
been eclipsed by the reiterated arguments for dismissal. In
the confusion of motions, arguments and daily disclosure,
however, the position of the defense became equally confused. For a few days the lawyers gave serious consideration
to a formal motion for mistrial; until they began to suspect
otherwise, they were confident that a declaration of mistrial
under existing circumstances precluded any subsequent gov-

ernment attempt to retry the case. Simultaneously there developed among the defendants a growing apprehension that Byrne would find some limited grounds for dismissal and that they would therefore lose not only the opportunity for a judgment on the original issues in the case but also the chance to punish the government for its misconduct. Russo was particularly concerned that the disclosures relating to the burglary would eliminate any possibility of a decision on the Papers and the matter of government secrecy. The government might get off the hook on both, losing its case on what might be explained away as a "technicality" without being exposed or chastised for its crimes. While Boudin was dropping hints about the Ninth Circuit, Russo wanted to win the case in Courtroom 9, preferably with the jury. On the afternoon of May 8, Ellsberg, looking for a copy of an evening paper, was stopped outside a saloon on Fifth Street by a patron, taken inside, and introduced as a celebrity. The betting odds, he learned, had gone from four-to-one against him to three-to-one in his favor on the day the burglary was disclosed, and to ten-to-one in his favor by May 6; now it was impossible to get anyone to put money on the government at any odds. The question was no longer whether they would get off; they were arguing only about the means.

Byrne kept asking for precedents: what case could the defense cite permitting a judge to dismiss a prosecution before the conclusion of the trial? He frequently reminded the defense lawyers that while they had been arguing, the investigation of the burglary had continued to turn up fresh information—that therefore the inquiry was justified—but that it had produced nothing to indicate that the indicment or the evidence used by the prosecution was in any way tainted by illegal acts. "There may be misconduct," he said, "but the court lacks authority to dismiss" because no taint had been shown. Boudin replied by arguing that in this case the "taint of behavior" was itself so gross that the whole thing should be thrown out of court. He acknowledged that the precedents all involved concealment or destruction of evidence, but, he said, "the totality of misconduct" in this case had been so severe that the court should simply say "enough is enough." When in the history of the United States had the President himself been involved in the inception of a criminal case, when had a government ever used "black squads—Plumbers" and when had the President himself attempted (as reported in that day's newspapers) to obstruct the delivery of evidence to a court? If the materials in this case "don't strike the conscience of this court," Weinglass added, "then I can't imagine what would." There was, in any case, "an inherent power to do justice." The authority of the courts was ample:

"Each time we talk about 'Is there a precedent?' " Boudin said. "Surely I need not remind your Honor that precedents are set by judges, and your Honor is such a judge."

"I understand," Byrne said.

"And in the days to come, other judges won't have to ask me whether there is a precedent," Boudin added with a smile, "because I will be able to refer to your Honor as having established one."

The burden of proof was on the government, it had destroyed evidence, it had engaged in conspiracy; it was not up to the defense to prove that the evidence destroyed by Gray pertained to this case. "What kind of judicial proceeding is this in which you have to flush this kind of material out of the government?" They would take no further steps relating to the original case until Byrne acted on a dismissal or on a hearing; they would, in effect, expand the boycott, and would not prepare to argue any motion for acquittal on the issues in the case until Byrne acted.

They should not take the motion for acquittal lightly, Byrne said in reply; crucial matters were at stake. Yet by the time he said it he himself had begun to lurch, putting off arguments, then scheduling them again, talking about hearings, suggesting that the jury should get the case, then sending them home for a five-day weekend, trying to keep control of the chaos, searching for a way out. The jury's appearance in court on May 8 would be its last.

III

Byrne's "out" arrived on May 10 in the form of a memorandum from Acting FBI Director William D. Ruckelshaus to Henry Petersen citing an investigation he had started May 4 to interview "present and retired FBI personnel" to determine whether the FBI had been bugging the telephones of "unidentified newsmen."

> A preliminary report which I received last night [May 8] indicates that an FBI employee recalls that in late 1969 and early 1970 Mr. Ellsberg had been overheard talking from an electronic surveillance of Dr. Morton Halperin's residence. It is this employee's recollection that the surveillance was of Dr. Halperin and that Mr. Ellsberg was then a guest of Dr. Halperin.
>
> I have no information concerning the substance of the conversation nor has the investigation to date been able to find any record of such a conversation. The investigation, of course, is not complete and further facts bearing upon the wire taps may be uncovered . . .

The logs of those taps would turn up, but not soon enough to affect this trial. The installation had been prompted by Kissinger after the leaks in 1969 and carried out on orders from the White House over Hoover's objections; Kissinger had received periodic summaries of what had been overheard. Since the installation was regarded as particularly sensitive by someone in the government, the normal indexing procedures were not followed, and when the tap was removed early in 1971 Hoover gave the logs to Deputy Director William Sullivan, presumably a trusted aide, for safekeeping. Late that summer, however, Sullivan got in touch with Mardian and informed him, according to Mardian's subsequent testimony, that Hoover might use the logs to blackmail the Administration (which had been contemplating a forced retirement for the director). On instructions from Mitchell and Nixon, Mardian had them picked up from Sullivan at the FBI and delivered them to Ehrlichman for storage in

Ehrlichman's White House safe. Although Mardian insisted that he had no idea of what the logs contained, their removal from the FBI at a time coinciding almost precisely with the beginning of the Ellsberg prosecution also suggested that someone in the government, wary of possible court orders to disclose wiretaps involving Ellsberg, had conveniently removed them. (A few hours after the trial ended, the logs were found.)

Byrne was furious. They had played him every way possible. In his amiable reluctance to make tough decisions and go beyond narrow precedents, he had failed to punish the government for suppressing evidence and concealing witnesses, had tolerated the glacial progress of the investigation of the burglary, and had allowed his ambition to compromise him with a gang of White House conspirators. Now they were messing with him again. His own power was limited to the case, and his taste for the dirty business, for the big trial which he would conduct so fairly, was nearly exhausted. He had been a prosecutor long enough to understand the procedures and requirements of electronic surveillance: where were the logs, how long had the installation been in place, why was there no record of the taps either at Justice or at the FBI? To start an extensive investigation now, with another investigation still dragging on and producing a few more scraps each day, was to make a mockery of the court and a joke of his proud patience. Yet to seize on this new disclosure as the ground for the dismissal was, likely as not, to play again into the government's hands. Had he been a tougher man, he might have ordered his own hearing, might have called them all to testify in his court: Ehrlichman, Mardian, Mitchell, Hunt, Dean, Haldeman, the whole gang. Yet his own record was compromised: he would have to investigate dealings in which he had himself been a participant. There were, moreover, so many other investigations already' scheduled or under way that another might be regarded as nothing more than a complicating grandstand exercise in a legal situation that was badly snarled already.

The disclosure of the tap, he told the lawyers, "may or may not" put the case in a different light, but it was impossible to proceed on the legal ramifications until more facts were known. Yet it also seemed clear that he would not wait long for those facts to be produced. He had made up his mind; Nissen was given an hour to check with Washington and inform the court of details.

Nissen returned an hour later. He had tried to contact Ruckelshaus, Petersen and other people at Justice, but could reach no one. After the luncheon recess, he returned to report that the records had been missing since July or October 1971.

Were there other surveillances for which there were also no records? Byrne asked. He wanted to know where the investigation stood, yet he seemed reluctant to press it. He had started drafting an opinion.

Nissen didn't know whether anything was missing. It appeared that something was missing. But even if they had all the information on the tap, those things were not crucial. The court should require the government to demonstrate, as it could, that it had "an independent source for each and every witness and each and every item of evidence."

Byrne, who had heard demands and arguments for dismissal for the preceding ten days, taking them under submission, said that if the defense was prepared he was ready to listen to argument.

Boudin said he was ready to argue the case for acquittal. The defense, suspecting that the government had "found" the tap as a pretext for stopping Byrne's investigation and ending the case, had reversed itself.

The matter of the wiretap had now intervened, Byrne said, and he wanted to hear the lawyers on the motion to dismiss.

Boudin said that inquiry should be made of W. Mark Felt, an FBI official who had been mentioned in the press in connection with the taps of newsmen, and of Robert C. Mardian and John Mitchell. There should be a hearing. There had been no investigation into the wiretapping to determine "how these things work." It seemed to him that among the White House, the Attorney General and the FBI, "one appears to have been the subject of robbery by the other."

"My power," Byrne replied, "is limited to the cases before me." They could make motions; he could rule on them.

It was very strange, Weinglass said, that in a period of four days the FBI was able to come up with an unnamed agent who remembered an overhear after more than two years, and that his recall coincided with the President's possible involvement in this case. There was a serious question whether "this court was dishonestly dealt with." In order for the court not to fall victim to such manipulation, Byrne should investigate why "this agent wasn't found until now." The legal precedents did call for dismissal, but dismissal would leave a lot of questions unanswered. Weinglass was certain, though he did not make it explicit to Byrne, that the overhear of Ellsberg on Halperin's phone had been "discovered" to stop the investigation; once Ehrlichman had failed in his attempt to influence Byrne on disclosure of the burglary, the government had to stop the trial by any means possible to prevent even more embarrassing revelations. It was giving Byrne the wiretap as a pretext to dismiss.

Nissen rejoined that the wiretap was no basis for dismissal. According to the logic of the defense, he said, if the tapes and the logs could not be found, the defendants would be "forever immune from prosecution." If another prosecution were to start next month against one of them he could claim immunity on the basis of the missing tapes. Such reasoning would exempt them both from any prosecution by the federal government. No court in its right mind (Nissen told Byrne) would order something turned over which didn't exist. The remedy was to have a hearing to show that the prosecution's sources of information had nothing to do with the taps or the Fielding burglary. He seemed so confident of his position that Ellsberg would later charge that the Justice Department

had known about the burglary and the wiretaps from the very
beginning and had carefully constructed its case to make
certain that no charge of tainted evidence could ever be
proved.

On the morning of May 11, Byrne heard the arguments
again. With the jury gone, he permitted the overflow of reporters to sit in the jury box while Boudin, Weinglass and
Nissen repeated what they had been saying for more than a
week. There was not much left that hadn't already been said.
Boudin explained that there was no alternative to dismissal,
though there was no mandate "to dismiss this case today"
and certainly no reason to limit a dismissal to wiretapping
alone. He was arguing reluctantly, preferring now to deal
with the motion for acquittal. Byrne could dispose of that
first. (With Rosenbaum's help Boudin had prepared a lengthy
argument for an instructed verdict of acquittal.) But Byrne
was reluctant to hear it; he was ready to dismiss. He told
Boudin he was considering the break-in, the wiretapping and
what "the effect of that has been on this trial." They would
have to "resolve now whether it has become impractical or
impossible to go forward because of the government's conduct."

After the noon recess he asked Nissen whether the government had any additional information.

There was nothing, said Nissen, but they hoped to have
something shortly.

Byrne declared that he was ready to rule. He recognized
that the defendants wanted a ruling on the motion for a judgment of acquittal before the ruling on dismissal. He believed,
however, that "the motion for judgment of acquittal would
not be dispositive of all of the issues and counts that are
involved in this case, and that only by going to the jury for
determination of some of the issues would the defendants
have an opportunity to be acquitted on all counts." He was
telling the defendants that if they wanted the case adjudicated
on substance they would have to take their chances with the

jurors. He would not order an acquittal on all issues or all counts. If they wished to proceed on that basis it was their right to do so.

Could they have a moment to confer? Russo asked.

They could, Byrne said, and there was a short pause while the defense people huddled around their table. Russo still wanted to go to the jury for acquittal, but was talked out of it by Ellsberg and the lawyers. Then Boudin told Byrne that they pressed their motion for dismissal based "upon the totality of government misconduct, including the suppression of evidence, the invasion of the physician-patient relationship, the illegal wiretapping, the destruction of relevant documents and the disobedience to judicial orders."

Byrne proceeded to read from a yellow pad. His face was flushed, and occasionally he stumbled over words, stopping once as if distracted, and being stopped another time by Boudin, who asked that something be repeated.

Commencing on April 26, the Government has made an extraordinary series of disclosures regarding the conduct of several governmental agencies regarding the defendants in this case. It is my responsibility to assess the effect of this conduct upon the rights of the defendants. My responsibility relates solely and only to this case, to the rights of the defendants and their opportunities for a fair trial with due process of law.

As the record makes clear, I have attempted to require the government and to allow the defendants to develop all relevant information regarding these highly unusual disclosures. Much information has been developed, but new information has produced new questions, and there remain more questions than answers.

The disclosures made by the government demonstrate that governmental agencies have taken an unprecedented series of actions with respect to these defendants. After the original indictment, at a time when the government's rights to investigate the defendants are narrowly circumscribed, White House officials established a special unit to investigate one of the defendants in this case. The special unit apparently operated with the approval of the FBI, the agency officially charged with the investigation of this case.

We may have been given only a glimpse of what this special unit did regarding this case, but what we know is more than disquieting. The special unit came to Los Angeles and surveyed the vicinity of the offices of the psychiatrist of one of the defendants. After reporting to a White House assistant and apparently receiving specific authorization, the special unit then planned and executed the break-in of the psychiatrist's office in search of the records of one of the defendants.

From the information received . . . it is difficult to determine what, if anything, was obtained from the psychiatrist's office . . .

The Central Intelligence Agency, presumably acting beyond its statutory authority, and at the request of the White House, had provided disguises, photographic equipment and other paraphernalia for covert operations.

The government's disclosure also revealed that the special unit requested and obtained from the CIA two psychological profiles of one of the defendants.

Of more serious consequence is that the defendants and the Court do not know the other activities in which the special unit may have been engaged and what has happened to the results of these endeavors. They do not know whether other material gathered by the special unit was destroyed, and though I have inquired of the government several times in this regard, no answer has been forthcoming.

Though some governmental officials were aware of the illegal activities of this unit directed at the defendants, and thus at this case, neither the Court nor the defendants nor, apparently, the prosecution itself was ever aware of these facts until Mr. Silbert's memorandum, and then not for some ten days after it had been written.

These recent events compound the record already pervaded by incidents threatening the defendants' right to a speedy and fair trial. The government has time and again failed to make timely productions of exculpatory information in its possession, requiring delays and disruptions in the trial.

Within the last forty-eight hours, after both sides had rested their case, the government revealed interception by electronic surveillance of one or more conversations of defendant Ellsberg. The government can only state and does only state that the interception or interceptions took place.

Indeed, the government frankly admits that it does not know how many such interceptions took place or when they took place or between whom they occurred or what was said. We only know that the conversation was overheard during a period of the conspiracy as charged in the indictment.

Of greatest significance is the fact that the government does not know what has happened to the authorizations for the surveillance, nor what has happened to the tapes nor to the logs nor any other records pertaining to the overheard conversations. This lack of records appears to be present not only in the Justice Department, but in the Federal Bureau of Investigation, from the response forwarded by Mr. Petersen yesterday that the records of both the FBI and the Justice Department appear to have been missing.

The matter is somewhat compounded also by the fact that the documents have been missing since the period of July to October 1971.

The FBI reports that, while the files did once exist regarding this surveillance, they now apparently have been removed from both the Justice Department and the FBI files. As I stated, it is reported by the FBI that the records have been missing since mid-1971.

There is no way the defendants or the Court or, indeed, the government itself can test what effect these interceptions may have had on the government's case here against either or both of the defendants. A continuation of the government's investigation is no solution with reference to this case. The delays already encountered threaten to compromise the defendants' rights, and it is the defendants' rights and the effect on this case that is paramount, and each passing day indicates that the investigation is further from completion as the jury waits.

Moreover, no investigation is likely to provide satisfactory answers where improper government conduct has been shielded so long from public view and where the government advises the Court that pertinent files are missing or destroyed. My duties and obligations relate to this case and what must be done to protect the right to a fair trial.

The charges against these defendants raise serious factual and legal issues that I would certainly prefer to have litigated to completion. However, . . . the defendants have the right to raise these issues when they desire. They desire to raise them now, and it is my obligation and duty to rule on them now. However, while I would prefer to have them litigated, the conduct of the government has placed the case in such a posture that it precludes the fair dispassionate resolution of these issues by a jury.

In considering the alternatives before me, I have carefully weighed the granting of a mistrial, without taking any further action. The defendants have opposed such a course of action, asserting their rights, if the case is to proceed, to have the matter tried before this jury. I have concluded that a mistrial alone would not be fair.

Under all the circumstances, I believe that the defendants should not have to run the risk, present under existing authorities, that they might be tried again by a different jury.

The totality of the circumstances of this case which I have only briefly sketched offend "a sense of justice." The bizarre events have incurably infected the prosecution of this case. I believe the authority to dismiss this case in these circumstances is fully supported by pertinent case authorities . . .

I have decided to declare a mistrial and grant the motion to dismiss.

I am of the opinion, in the present status of the case, that the only remedy available that would assure due process and the fair administration of justice is that this trial be terminated and the defendants' motion for dismissal is granted and the jury discharged.

The order of dismissal will be entered; the jurors will be advised of the dismissal, and the case is terminated.

Thank you very much, gentlemen, for your efforts.

When he finished his reading, Byrne rose from the bench and strode out of a courtroom which, on his last words, had erupted with cheers and applause. A standing ovation for the judge, the defendants, the lawyers; embraces, tears, Nesson standing with a cigar at the defense table, Patricia glowing her way out of the courtroom, Boudin telling a reporter that the decision was "appropriate, necessary, eloquent, justified and dispositive," cheers for something which, if it wasn't justice, was at least a desperate gesture of restitution. Ellsberg and Russo, running from studio to studio to make the rounds of the evening television interviews, continued to reflect their ambivalence between the sense of elation and the sense of fraud. "The issue of government misconduct," Ellsberg said, "is the issue of the Pentagon Papers." The jury had been cheated of an opportunity to make a judgment— not a single one of them would have voted for conviction— but this, he seemed to suggest, was equally good. Now, he said, looking at Pat, he was planning "to make love in every climate on earth." Russo, for his part, was planning to do something about impeaching the President. David Nissen should go to jail; he was a good example of "the kind of fanatic, the kind of zealot who will lie for the President." Russo had wanted the case to go to the jury and had opposed the mandamus, but he was satisfied.

In the confusion following Byrne's decision, Nissen and his colleagues disappeared upstairs, where they would remain "in conference" for the remainder of the afternoon. On the way, a reporter caught Warren Reese and asked him about the possibility of an appeal. "It's over," Reese replied. "It's dead." Two hours later he and Barry, who had spent almost two years on the case, the silent partners of the prosecution, left the federal courthouse, Reese on his way back to the U. S. Attorney's Office in San Diego, Barry on his way back to Des Moines. Under his arm Barry carried a stack of framed diplomas and certificates, among them something he called his "John Mitchell certificate," a commission appointing him an assistant United States attorney and signed by the former Attorney General, who, just the day before, had been indicted on charges of conspiracy in New York.

In the courthouse elevator, meanwhile, an attorney asked a reporter what had happened and was told the news. "Son of a bitch," he replied. "The government spends ten million dollars and some guy screws it up." Another reporter, managing to make his way to Matt Byrne's outer office—for two days Byrne had been under guard following a telephone threat to his office—found his secretary and clerks speaking in hushed tones, the waiting room outside the sickroom. The judge would not see anyone; perhaps later. An hour after he finished reading his decision he would be back in a nearly vacant courtroom working on another case, but he would continue to maintain his silence; he could not discuss the case or the White House offer.

# EIGHT

# Silent Verdict

I

STANLEY K. SHEINBAUM, chief fund raiser, adminis-
trator and counselor of the Pentagon Papers Defense Fund,
wandered through the crowd like a suburban father who had
finally managed to get his youngest and most difficult child
through a better-than-average college. There was no point
in playing host: the crowd, which spilled from the living
room and the kitchen of his rented Beverly Hills house to
the patio lawn and into an adjacent building, managed itself,
a great swarm of people—jurors, lawyers, defense workers,
reporters—who had been thrown together, some of them
for more than a year, and who would never see each other
again. In the bedroom, a small group had joined Daniel
Ellsberg to watch the news on a large color television set
(George Putnam, the right-wing newscaster, at ten; NBC,
CBS and ABC at eleven), and in the living room Russo,
Boudin and Nesson were listening to the observations of the
jurors above the noise of the crowd and the rock music on
the phonograph. And so Sheinbaum remained at the edge of
the celebration, occasionally answering a reporter's question

about the cost and watching with the tolerant eye of a man who knew more than he could say and infinitely more than could ever be printed. For eighteen months he had kept raising the money, coping with neuroses and political ego trips, holding the internal animosities under control, and now, at last, thank God, it was all over. The great cruise was at an end.

The jurors had learned the news that afternoon, some of them within minutes after the decision was read. Byrne and his clerks had called them to say they did not need to return to court, and to thank them for their services; the press had called, trying to establish a "verdict," the defense had called to invite them to the party, and they had called each other. Eight had come to the party, seven regular jurors and one alternate, and they had begun to indulge what they had so long been denied: the chance to talk about the case. Cora C. Neal, the heretofore stone-faced first juror, had arrived with her daughter, hugged Ellsberg and Boudin, and shouted, "I'm not mean." Now she was collecting autographs and gossip, and disclosing that she had favored acquittal ever since the government rested its case. On a sofa, Phyllis Ortman, a bouffed blonde, was being interviewed by a television reporter—her picture would make all the papers the next day —and outside Monte Pittman, the dapper black auto worker, was telling someone that Nissen had struck him as "a cocky little guy." They had all known that the trial had become involved with Watergate, had suspected it since the day Silbert's memo was turned over—Ortman's husband pointedly told her that evening that she wouldn't be able to read about Watergate anymore—but they had been honest (or uncurious) enough not to learn the details, had even ostracized one alternate who started bringing newsmagazines to the jury room and telling them that the case was certain to be thrown out.

By the time they arrived at the party, the television newscasts had already reported that the majority of the jurors were leaning toward acquittal—seven for acquittal, two for conviction, and three doubtful—yet even that seemed less than certain. One woman had told a fellow juror that she would not attend a "Communist party," and of the eight who did come one stood in a corner of the patio all evening, maintaining a sanitary distance, torn between her conclusion that the government had failed to prove its case and her feeling that the defendants were guilty, while another would make it abundantly clear that she was certain Ellsberg and Russo had done something wrong and that, depending on the judge's instructions, she might have voted either way. Some of them had come to celebrate or watch the celebrants or meet the celebrities they had observed in court for nearly four months, others simply to break the enforced silence. Yet if any of them had been seriously radicalized, if they were now ready to march, they failed to express it. What they expressed most frequently was regret for the lost opportunity to deliberate and reach a verdict. They had become a community without the means to deliberate on the matter that held them together. Officially, they had lost their voice.

The voice would always remain indistinct. They had not heard summations from the lawyers and were never instructed by the judge, and the questions to be resolved would therefore remain unfocused. The judge, one of them said, was "sort of like God," and it became clear in the week after the dismissal how crucial his instructions would have been, that in a word-cluttered case as complex as this only the court could have provided the frame and language for a definitive resolution. Although the majority were prone to acquit on all counts, there were enough reservations on issues and personalities and enough potential holdouts (at least on the theft counts) to make it likely that they would have seized on Byrne's instructions to resolve any inner ambiguities and external conflicts. Had he instructed them on the theft counts as the prosecution asked, theft as any misuse or misappropriation, they would have voted almost evenly on conviction; had he accepted the interpretation of the defense, that theft required "substantial deprivation," a majority would have favored acquittal. David Nissen would say later that, given the instructions he expected from Byrne, the best he could have hoped for was a hung jury: the judge, he believed, would have framed the issues in such a way as to leave little chance for conviction and therefore no possibility for reversal in higher courts. Byrne, he thought, was protecting himself. Yet there remained at least the possibility that the doubts and the holdouts would have produced a compromise that included conviction on one or more counts of theft.

There was not much question on espionage or conspiracy. The government had simply failed to make its case. In separate interviews and in a taped five-hour seminar at UCLA a week after the dismissal in which eleven of the twelve jurors and four of the six alternates participated, it became clear that the defense had destroyed the prosecution's arguments about the national-defense importance of the documents. Darlene Arneaud, the divorced woman who was raising seven children on welfare payments, and Jean Boutelier, the Australian-born nurse, continued to have misgivings: Wasn't there somthing there that could have harmed the national defense? Why hadn't Ellsberg gone through proper channels to have the Papers declassified? Where did one man get the right to do that on his own? It frightened her, Arneaud said, that people could take material from the government without anyone knowing it—plans for a nuclear warhead, or a cure for cancer. Yet those arguments were overwhelmed by elaborations and versions of the points the defense tried to get across: the public had a right to know, the Papers contained political, not military, secrets, and the country had been deceived. Their views would continue to reflect diverse responses to witnesses, lawyers and defendants—class and style and sex were obvious elements in their attitudes—but they seemed, most of them, to take it for granted that the Pentagon Papers contained nothing that could have harmed the national defense. At least seven and probably as many as nine would have voted for acquittal on espionage on the first ballot; among them were the two male jurors who were re-

garded by the defense (probably correctly) as representing
the strongest voices on the panel. Wilfred Baltadano, the
wounded Vietnam veteran, had his doubts about Ellsberg's
sincerity—only time will tell, he said, whether Ellsberg "was
a superpatriot," there was "a shadow of a doubt about him"
—but he was sufficiently certain about the Papers to wonder
whether he himself would have gone to Vietnam if he had
known what was in them.

Most of the women were partial to the defense—some of
them from the very beginning—and sympathetic with Ellsberg, but, in many instances, were put off by Russo and
"Jane Fonda's husband." Ortman, Neal, Kelpe and Duhigg
were certain they would have acquitted on all counts, certain
enough that they would probably have held out against the
doubts of people like Boutelier and Arneaud. They had
learned the "lessons" the defense tried to draw from the
Papers, although they were not necessarily ready to join any
movement. "I always thought we were the good guys," Kelpe
said in an interview. "I thought we were in great hands, the
great United States." Now she was no longer sure.

Neal: "I couldn't believe what I was listening to. . . . I
don't think we were informed on what was going on, I
couldn't believe it. . . . Now I know why some of these kids
didn't want to go."

Duhigg: "It changed me from being a very apathetic citizen into a concerned one. . . . When the prosecution stopped
their case, I was just amazed; they really hadn't proven anything to me. . . . Lodge's involvement with Diem, when that
was first read to us, you sat there and said, 'Oh, that's ter-
rible.' It hit a lot of us that way. . . . Later, after we read
about how the troops went to Danang, we heard about Cambodia, and one of the jurors said, 'You gotta be kidding.
Here we go again.'"

Ortman: "They ruined two people's careers for nothing.
. . . You sit through a trial like this and you learn that not
everything you've been told is true. . . . I just couldn't believe
the lack of compassion that exists in the military. I was be-

coming disillusioned before the trial; this just kind of confirmed it. I didn't think we were the good guys necessarily, but I didn't know the extent of how bad we were. . . . The American people had a need to know this."

Kelpe: "By the end of the prosecution's case, I thought they hadn't proved a thing to me. . . . Maybe if we'd had a verdict it would have helped in some way to revise the classification system. . . . I couldn't believe the extent to which people had been lied to and deceived."

To the end, however, many of them remained uncertain about the issues. Several didn't understand "what all these counts were for," one alternate believed the defendants to be "guilty of copying" but not guilty of conversion or espionage, and another was prepared to interpret the law "different from the judge" if that was how he saw it. They had had similar responses to many of the witnesses, and had frequently made remarks about them in the jury room or at lunch. They thought most of the Rand officials were liars, liked Chester Ronning, the avuncular retired Canadian diplomat who testified for the defense on his role as a third-party contact (and who had made virtually no impression on the press), and they tended, with some exceptions, to like Ellsberg and dislike Russo. One of the exceptions was Baltadano, who believed Russo was sincere and thought his tears on the witness stand credible; he knew "those people didn't want us over there."

Yet even those who had come to understand something about the uses of secrecy and the record of deception could not, in many instances, break their reverence for authority or their awe of witnesses who tried to impress them with the importance of those secrets. The "lesson," therefore, had been incomplete and, even with the added evidence of Watergate, remained a relatively isolated perception about government. Baltadano maintained some ironic distance: he was amused by the attempt of the defense to portray Ellsberg and Russo as people with working-class backgrounds and was suspicious of Haig's appearance in full uniform. Kelpe suspected that Gorman and De Puy had been ordered by the government to give the testimony they gave. But for the most part deference to the authority of "these intelligent men" remained intact. Most of the jurors were simply incapable of going outside the frame of reverence, of breaking the barrier between what they recognized as evidence of misjudgment, dishonesty and deceit and a lifetime of training in respect for people in official positions of authority. They regretted their inability to deliberate a verdict—for several of them it would have been a way to send the government a message—but except for general declarations about their new appreciation of the need to be aware (if not wary) of what the Administration was doing, and something, in one or two instances, about "maybe raising your children a little differently" there was no new resolve to act, no certain expression of anger, and no indication of conversion. The jury, Russo said on the day after the dismissal, was "the most legitimate party in the courtroom," yet without the chance to deliberate and without a verdict they had no role, no way to confront the cathartic moment that might have driven the message home, not only in Washington, but among themselves.

## II

The party, which continued into the early hours of the morning, dissolved into a bleary downtown press conference where whatever it was they were celebrating the night before would be explained. Sheinbaum, who had gone to bed before the party was over, declared that the $900,000 raised by the defense—they were still $75,000 short—had been "the best money spent in this country in a long, long time. . . . For the first time it is we who are on the aggressive, the peace movement is on the aggressive, and the other side on the defensive." There would now be lawsuits against the government, a civil suit not only on wiretapping (such a suit had already been filed), but, Boudin explained, on a "much broader spectrum of illegal activities . . . to obtain redress."

Russo was about to rush off to Chicago to attend a meeting on the impeachment of Nixon, Weinglass had already left to meet with a group of Indians he was representing in connection with the case at Wounded Knee, and Ellsberg, congratulating the press (which, he said, had "performed more honorably" than any other institution), was preparing to appear before an *ad hoc* Senate subcommittee to testify on secrecy. He had a close relationship with the press, he explained, but for now it was over. "I'm going back to my wife."

Nesson, more eloquently, suggested that the trial had "contributed something to a reawakening of spirit in this country." It was the end of an era, "our case was one page in the last chapter," and he could now look for a time "when we get back to something that looks like warmth in this country." Yet no one was able to express what, if anything, the trial had accomplished, what had changed in the country, what "reawakening" meant. Ellsberg later suggested that there was a new public interest "in the criminal behavior of Presidents," an acceptance of the idea "that the President can be a lawbreaker." He had therefore contributed to a deflation of the awe and magic of "secret" documents and, in some measure, to a reduction of the excessive prestige of the presidency. The papers did not deal with Nixon—that was "an enormous limitation"—but the curtain had been pulled aside, the safe had been opened "to show there was not much there" that justified such extremes of secrecy. Ellsberg might also have said that, as much as anyone, he had set off the chain of events that ultimately led to Watergate, that in that sense he had done something bordering on demonic genius.

When the Papers were published no one had suspected the consequent "panic" in the White House. Ellsberg was certain it had been a pretext for political attacks against Democrats whom the Administration had hoped to associate with him, and an opportunity to justify increasing political repression. For a time after the trial he even managed to suggest that in some way he had been an unwitting instrument of the Administration, which, he believed, had been watching him ever since the FBI investigation in 1970 and waiting for him to do exactly what he did—had allowed him to do it in anticipation of a politically beneficial scandal. But the evidence indicated that the attempt to use Ellsberg had been an afterthought entrusted to a gang of second-level political operatives and B-movie spooks who fumbled their way through bungled burglaries and phony cables too transparent to peddle. If they were lying in wait for Ellsberg, they were shockingly ill-prepared; Hunt had been hired on July 6, three weeks after the *Times* began to publish, Liddy on July 12. No one at the White House, except possibly Kissinger, knew what was in the Papers, and no one, apparently, knew enough about Ellsberg, even after all those months of surveillance, to make whatever they could possibly have found in Fielding's files superfluous.

The entire record of the administration—its design to tie the Democratic Party to violent demonstrations and the demonstrations to the Communists, the enemies list, the political use of the Justice Department, the burglaries, the wiretapping, the National Intelligence Plan, the forged documents —constituted clear evidence of some vast hope to establish permanent and unchecked control of the American political system, and it cannot be discounted by references to the incompetence with which the White House sometimes tried to carry it out. Nixon maintained his personal interest in the Ellsberg case even after its partisan political possibilities had all but vanished, and he occasionally asked Kleindienst how it was going. The President of the United States hated Daniel Ellsberg. But the assertion that the entire design grew from a premeditated strategy leaves too little to paranoia and to the facts of political life in an age where allegiance to government and country can no longer be taken for granted, where symbolic expressions of civil disobedience are common, and where there no longer exists an establishment substantial enough to mediate serious problems before they reach crisis proportions.

For a President and an Administration with compulsive

needs to control an hermetic environment—a man who sat before open fires in his White House fireplace with the air conditioning running, a man who never removed his coat in public, an Administration which programmed every second of applause at its national convention—the idea that there were things in the executive branch that they could not control had been too threatening to tolerate. Gary Wills wrote that a man obsessed with the need to have enemies and to regard himself as an embattled underdog would always manage to create, or invent, threats to his position:

> He had to be protected 24 hours a day; and he had to have enemies to be protected from. Only thus could he lead, or gain confidence; hold together his coalition of fears and grievances. He huddles over sustaining fires of grievance, even when grievances have to be conjured up . . . Others may think there is no enemy. But his old bruises ache to signal each change in political weather. It is only a matter of time before the press or some other evil monster strikes . . . But now the bitterness does not find a useful public channel, to mobilize in others a supportive hate of Commies or the press. He needs, above all, a useful public enemy.

Ellsberg was a useful public enemy, and Nixon even managed to use him in his speech to the returned prisoners of war long after the case was dismissed and the involvement of the White House in the case was known. By conjuring up an enemy and then slaying him, Nixon could satisfy psychic and pragmatic needs simultaneously; by drawing up lists of enemies to be screwed, the White House could satisfy its fantasies of retribution and dominance, a crowd of amateur voodoo doctors manufacturing dolls and sticking pins into them. Their collective needs required control, absolute control, and the country was just divided enough to furnish the raw material of which public enemies could be made. The chain reaction in which demonstrations, protests and leaks prompted such things as the Plumbers, burglaries and Watergate constituted a form of self-destruct mechanism for an

Administration too obsessed with enemies and too compulsive in its need for control to maintain it.

But that was only part of the story. Although Ellsberg was sorry that the Papers did not deal with Nixon, it had never been his intention just to get Nixon, or any other President. The argument had always been that secrecy and deception were endemic, since executive power had become overgrown. The focus now, however, was on Nixon: had Nixon authorized the burglary of the psychiatrist, had he participated in the cover-up of Watergate? By implication, civil institutions were intimately involved—the White House, the presidency, executive power and privilege—but the style and character that produced Watergate, the Plumbers and the scandals were Nixon's own. Quite possibly, were he to be impeached, and perhaps in any case, Watergate might infuse a modicum of courage into the Congress and reduce the arrogance of the White House, although even on that score the early signs were uncertain. The government might, in the future, be more circumspect in its prosecution of political dissent. Maybe, as a consequence of the disclosures and Nixon's mounting discomfort, there was a new sense of freedom, even exhilaration, at least among the liberals. No President, it was said, would ever try such things again.

Yet while all this was under discussion and, in some instances, being acted on, institutional forms of secrecy, espionage and repression seemed to be assuming new legitimacy. In the months following Watergate, the CIA and the FBI were both subject to extensive congressional rescue operations, often conducted in closed session, designed to separate them from the smear of White House scandal. The chairman of the Senate Armed Services Committee, John Stennis of Mississippi, called for legislation to restrict the power of the CIA, and the acting chairman, Stuart Symington of Missouri, promised to "eliminate anything that will allow the CIA to run a war." To do that, however, required fundamental restructuring of the agency—breaking up, among other things, the inner systems of secrecy—and a corresponding assumption of continuing responsibility beyond anything that the Congress had been willing to exercise before. There was, moreover, the unresolved question of the climate in which the agency operated. A member of the House of Representatives familiar with the CIA suggested that the real issue was not the law under which the CIA operated but whether the country wanted the kind of "capability" that the organization provided: "Do we want to be involved in this kind of thing?" Secret wars were conducted under CIA auspices (and criminal suspects could be beaten up in the police station) precisely because the civil authorities needed "deniability"; the dirty work had to be done in such a way that the Administration (the Attorney General, the President, the mayor, the Secretary of State) could deny diplomatic or political responsibility and the public would be spared the onus of moral complicity. That was part of the social function of secrecy: the need not to know.

The Congress had always been mesmerized by claims of "national security," had usually been happy to yield to the executive branch when they were made, and showed a limited indication of serious disenchantment even now. Nixon's nominee for director of the FBI, Clarence Kelley, was confirmed by the Senate without a whisper of dissent, even though he had given the Judiciary Committee only the vaguest assurance of accountability and though two of his predecessors as candidates for the job had been manipulated by the White House for political purposes; the new director of the CIA, William E. Colby, was scheduled for easy confirmation though he himself had been accused, while an operative in Vietnam, of slanting intelligence data and submitting misinformation, and though he was criticized for his role as head of the American advisers with Operation Phoenix, the "pacification" program that led to the killing of an estimated 20,000 South Vietnamese; and J. Edgar Hoover was canonized (even among some liberals) for bucking Nixon and the White House on the matter of the 1970 intelligence plan. In the fashionable wave of reaction against dirty political tricks, it seemed, the victim and the culprit were of more concern than the practice. For the White House to do such things against the Democrats or Daniel Ellsberg was obviously bad form. For the FBI to do it against Panthers or the Vietnam Veterans Against the War, or for the CIA to do it against Laotians or Chileans, was another matter. If the Army had in fact given up its dossiers on political figures as it claimed, state and local police, with funds from the Justice Department, were more active than ever in assembling computerized dossiers on schoolchildren and other "potential" criminals.

What seemed to matter were legitimacy and professionalism: Hunt and Liddy, as David Nissen said, were "dingalings" messing around in things which were none of their business and collecting data so useless "they should have sent it to the Russians." The charge was unprofessional conduct, and the remedy was to make certain that henceforth secret agents and organizations were not enlisted in the cause of partisan service. But the elaborate structures of secrecy and covert operation within the executive branch and the casual acceptance of a vast, permanent establishment of war and espionage were not seriously challenged. Congressional response to Watergate and to the Plumbers reflected an overwhelming tendency to keep those operations intact, to protect secret organizations from public exposure and open congressional scrutiny. The fact that the CIA and the FBI were involved in "political" activities by the White House was, if anything, conducive to an attempt to separate them even more sharply from supervision and control by persons responsible to elected officials. Ironically, therefore, the reaction to the attempt to "use" the CIA and the FBI would probably make it even more difficult to restrict and control them in the future.

What seemed most likely on the morrow of "victory" in Los Angeles was that the country, impeachment or not, would learn still another lesson in toleration and apathy: people would become further inured to the idea that there were things worse than secret domestic intelligence plans, political trials and lists of "enemies" to be "screwed" by the Internal Revenue Service. Even after Nixon himself acknowledged he had authorized an intelligence plan that provided for burglary, wiretapping, mail covers and harassment of political enemies, the Senate Watergate Committee, the press, and the public continued to be bemused by the question of whether Nixon had known about Watergate and had participated in the cover-up. Impeachment did not become a serious issue until the so-called "Saturday-night massacre" when Nixon ordered the firing of Watergate prosecutor Archibald Cox and when the two senior officials of the Justice Department were forced from office. The President's own vulnerability seemed to rest not on a record of systematic attempts to invade civil liberties and employ police-state methods—on constitutional crimes—but rather on his participation in ordinary felonies: obstruction of justice, tax evasion, and the appropriation of public funds in improving the real estate at San Clemente and Key Biscayne. And as the country entered the first chaotic months of the energy crisis there was the growing possibility that what the Congress and the public most desired was a strong, centralized administration—any administration as long as it was honest—and that government secrecy and civil liberties were not serious issues. At the end of 1973, Henry Kissinger headed one of the lists of the most respected men in America.

The "victory" in Los Angeles proved that Ellsberg and Russo had been right about the government; like the Pentagon Papers, it provided documentation to persuade the late and the reluctant about something that had been suspected for years; but it also seemed to prove that they had been wrong about the country, that it would still be possible for people to say the defendants had gotten off on a "technicality"—as if the prosecution itself had not been an expression of the very thing that finally led to dismissal—and that if people now read the statements of the President with greater suspicion, they still seemed unable or unwilling to act.

The entire conspiracy was based on "deniability," a collusion in feigned ignorance, deliberate ambiguity and formally withheld information. What the person up the line was not explicitly told could not be used to implicate him later in charges of criminal conduct or ethical impropriety: Mitchell claimed he did not tell the President of what he called "the White House horrors" because it would require Nixon to crack down on the culprits and therefore impair his chances for reelection; the Justice Department and the CIA "misunderstood" each other about what the prosecution told Byrne about the availability of a CIA witness; Colson refused to allow his friend Hunt to tell him what he had been doing over the weekend of the burglary. Yet the message was abundantly clear not only in the inferences that came down from the top but also in the choice of personnel, in officially certified decisions (e.g., the National Intelligence Plan) and in the accepted record of the past: phony campaign ads and illegal practices were nothing new in Richard Nixon's political career. Two sets of instructions were communicated on the same frequency: do what is required by any means necessary, but don't tell me about it. Now the country and the Congress seemed to demand the same deniability: if it could not be proved that Nixon was explicitly informed of the Watergate burglary or the cover-up, if there was no explicit evidence that he had lied in his public statements, then he was presumably in the clear. The only crime of which he could be convicted was lying on television. Yet while the Senate Watergate Committee was pursuing its redundant questions and arguing about the evidence of the President's tapes, the Pentagon admitted with relative impunity that with the President's encouragement it had systematically deceived the public and Congress about the bombing of Cambodia before the invasion of 1970, and that it had later given the information to a select group of Senators to make certain it would not fall into the hands of people who opposed the policy. Every day new Pentagon papers were being written faster than they could be leaked.

There was no resolution; the classification system and the modes of government secrecy remained as pervasive as ever. If the Administration had no official-secrets act, neither did violators of the classification system have any assurance they would not be subject to a long and expensive trial and possibly to prison. The great purge of expiation and cleansing was on, and there were even people to suggest, as did Mary McCarthy, that Watergate was somehow the great attempt to atone for Vietnam, a form of national self-flagellation for sins past. But there was nothing in that to indicate that it wouldn't all go on, that the CIA (or, for that matter, the Pentagon) would go out of the business of clandestine war, or that it would cease to furnish alumni, along with cameras and disguises, for more plumbing in the future. Ellsberg and Russo had victory in preventing the government from doing worse, and Boudin had his "precedent" from Byrne in the broad language of the dismissal; perhaps, if he or anyone else ever had a case like this again, he could cite Byrne's opinion to the judge. But the government had not been punished, and the clear inference would always remain that the transgressors in the case were Hunt and Liddy (or "the White House") and not the Justice Department, the Pentagon or the CIA, all of which had helped suppress evidence and conceal witnesses. The defense had not broken the system of secrecy and deception, and had not stopped the government. It had helped stop this Administration.

The most significant unresolved issue transcended administrations and institutions of government. For a generation, the country had become increasingly European, particularly in its conduct of foreign policy. The Atlantic Ocean, once the great barrier against the practices and involvements that earlier Americans escaped and presumably abhorred, had evaporated as a significant factor in decisions of war, peace and diplomacy, and the luxury of absolute distinctions between war and peace was no longer possible. Kissinger's position as the country's senior manager of foreign policy symbolized the rise of a Clausewitzian view of war as diplomacy-carried-on-by-other-means, which, in the decade before Watergate, sustained increasing recourse to invocations of "national security" and growing temptations within government to establish some American version of an official-secrets act. Combined with the imperial pursuits, particularly in Indochina, of a series of national administrations, and the corresponding divisions in American society, those elements could generate within any administration a desire for devices and techniques that would circumvent constitutional provisions covering the conduct of war, the maintenance of political and diplomatic secrets, the protection of civil liberties and the imposition of governmental authority. The Nixon Administration tried to solve those problems by pretending that there was a continuing state of war which seriously endangered the country, and then compounding the pretense with its paranoid inability to distinguish between overblown considerations of "security" and domestic politics.

But the particular practices of the Nixon White House which became associated with Watergate were the excrescences and not the whole of the problem. No foreign correspondent who covered the Ellsberg trial ever managed fully to understand the constitutional issues because none of them could comprehend situations where the government was not assumed to have the legal right to withhold whatever information it considered secret. As long as the United States functioned with the protection of three thousand miles of ocean (and the British Navy) it could easily assume that only conditions approximating total war justified such secrecy. Once technology rendered that protection obsolete (and providing the country was not willing to abandon its foreign adventures), the historic assumptions about war, peace, diplomacy and secrecy were inevitably subject to challenge. Clandestine wars were conducted not only because the country required "deniability" vis-à-vis foreign governments but because we continued to insist on our constitutional distinctions and our right to enjoy the moral luxury of denying our own complicity in the dirty business of killing Asians or harassing blacks and radicals. Unless the country and the Congress were willing to assume responsibility for decisions that fell between the traditional democratic absolutes of total war and total peace, and unless they were willing to come to terms with social problems at home on the basis of something other than considerations of law and order (i.e., race and crime), there was no way that the possibility of another Ellsberg prosecution, another National Intelligence Plan and another form of Watergate could be eliminated.

III

Three weeks after the trial ended in Los Angeles, David Nissen left the Justice Department and entered private law practice in Orange County. He felt he had done his best; he was not bitter at anyone, he said, although his contempt for Byrne's rulings was still apparent. He believed that enough evidence had been presented to the grand jury in Boston to sustain another set of indictments. Now all that was over; there would be no prosecution of the *Times* or of anyone else connected with the distribution of the Papers. Ellsberg and Russo had won that for all of them. In the meantime, the Administration's bill making it a felony to disclose any classified document, no matter what its contents or the propriety of the classification, was stalled in Congress.

Daniel Ellsberg went East to testify before a Senate subcommittee on government secrecy, appeared on "Meet the Press" (where he was treated unkindly by representatives of the "honorable" institution), and returned to Malibu to rest on the beach and watch the Senate Watergate hearings on television. There hadn't been many offers from universities; he wanted to write and was thinking about another tour of the lecture circuit, but beyond that his plans were indefinite. In New York there were rumors that he had told friends that he wanted to run for the Senate, where he thought he could become "the Ralph Nader of foreign policy," but there was no rush to his candidacy. Dismissal of the case in Los Angeles had destroyed his chances for martyrdom (which, he said, he never relished) without resolving the First Amendment issues for which he had assertedly been prepared to go to jail. Nor did it immunize him against legally privileged attacks in congressional testimony, or eliminate his usefulness as a pretext for illegal or unconstitutional acts by the government. In Boston someone circulated a fabricated story that he had been blackmailed by a person with whom he had had a homosexual relationship into supplying official secrets to the Russians. In Washington, John Ehrlichman, testifying before the Senate Watergate Committee, retroactively elevated the disclosure of the Pentagon Papers into a full-scale conspiracy to provide classified data to the Russians. ("False, deceptive and slanderous," Ellsberg replied.)

The Administration, through its former members, was making Ellsberg a central figure in what was, in effect, a campaign of *ex post facto* allegation to justify the Plumbers, the political sabotage, and the various elements of the National Intelligence Plan of 1970; he was Nixon's candidate for the Alger Hiss of 1973. Once planted, the rumors and allegations would have an independent life capable of nourishing future reactions against the treacherous sellout of Indochina and the betrayal of fifty-thousand American boys who gave their lives . . .

Tom Hayden, meanwhile, had made arrangements for a group from the defense to visit Hanoi; Weinglass, Donovan and two of the research workers went for ten days and met with assorted officials of the North Vietnamese government. Russo, still disappointed that there was no verdict and frustrated in his efforts to help organize an impeachment campaign, was planning to write a book and went to New York to find a publisher. Katherine Barkley went to British Columbia to "sit on a beach" and subsequently gave up politics in favor of Perfect Knowledge; she became a follower of Guru Maharaj Ji. General Haig succeeded Haldeman at the White House, and Melvin Laird, who acknowledged that he had authorized the secret raids on Cambodia in 1969 and early 1970, succeeded Ehrlichman. Morton Halperin, about whom

Haig had testified for the government, filed suit against Kissinger and others on the wiretapping of his home. And J. Fred Buzhardt, the general counsel for the Defense Department who had been a central figure in the investigation of the leak of the Pentagon Papers and could recall nothing about the exculpatory damage reports or about suppressed evidence in the Ellsberg case, became special counsel to Richard Nixon on Watergate.

On September 4, 1973, a Los Angeles grand jury returned sealed indictments against four of the men involved in the burglary of Fielding's office: Ehrlichman, Krogh, Young and Liddy. Hunt and the Cubans, who had been given immunity for their testimony before the grand jury, were named as co-conspirators but were not indicted. The reporter who first obtained the names in the sealed indictments was William Farr of the *Los Angeles Times,* who had spent seven weeks in prison for his refusal to divulge the source of a story he had written about the Manson trial. The attorney who represented Ehrlichman in Los Angeles was Joseph Ball, who, just two years earlier, had represented Tony Russo in proceedings before another grand jury in the case of the Pentagon Papers.

# Statutes Under Which Daniel Ellsberg and Anthony Russo Were Indicted

## [TITLE 18 OF THE UNITED STATES CODE]

### § 371. Conspiracy to commit offense or to defraud United States

If two or more persons conspire either to commit any offense against the United States, or to defraud the United States, or any agency thereof in any manner or for any purpose, and one or more of such persons do any act to effect the object of the conspiracy, each shall be fined not more than $10,000 or imprisoned not more than five years, or both.

If, however, the offense, the commission of which is the object of the conspiracy, is a misdemeanor only, the punishment for such conspiracy shall not exceed the maximum punishment provided for such misdemeanor.

### § 641. Public money, property or records

Whoever embezzles, steals, purloins, or knowingly converts to his use or the use of another, or without authority, sells, conveys or disposes of any record, voucher, money, or thing of value of the United States or of any department or agency thereof, or any property made or being made under contract for the United States or any department or agency thereof; or

Whoever receives, conceals, or retains the same with intent to convert it to his use or gain, knowing it to have been embezzled, stolen, purloined or converted—

Shall be fined not more than $10,000 or imprisoned not more than ten years, or both; but if the value of such property does not exceed the sum of $100, he shall be fined not more than $1,000 or imprisoned not more than one year, or both.

The word "value" means face, par, or market value, or cost price, either wholesale or retail, whichever is greater.

### § 793. Gathering, transmitting, or losing defense information

(a) Whoever, for the purpose of obtaining information respecting the national defense with intent or reason to believe that the information is to be used to the injury of the United States, or to the advantage of any foreign nation, goes upon, enters, flies over, or otherwise obtains information concerning any vessel, aircraft, work of defense, navy yard, naval station, submarine base, fueling station, fort, battery, torpedo station, dockyard, canal, railroad, arsenal, camp, factory, mine, telegraph, telephone, wireless, or signal station, building, office, research laboratory or station or other place connected with the national defense owned or constructed, or in progress of construction by the United States or under the control of the United States, or of any of its officers, departments, or agencies, or within the exclusive jurisdiction of the United States, or any place in which any vessel, aircraft, arms, munitions, or other materials or instruments for use in time of war are being made, prepared, repaired, stored, or are the subject of research or development, under any contract or agreement with the United States, or any department or agency thereof, or with any person on behalf of the United States, or otherwise on behalf of the United States, or any prohibited place so designated by the President by proclamation in time of war or in case of national emergency in which anything for the use of the Army, Navy, or Air Force is being prepared or constructed or stored, information as to which prohibited place the President has determined would be prejudicial to the national defense; or

(b) Whoever, for the purpose aforesaid, and with like intent or reason to believe, copies, takes, makes, or obtains, or attempts to copy, take, make, or obtain, any sketch, photograph, photographic negative, blueprint, plan, map, model, instrument, appliance, document, writing, or note of anything connected with the national defense; or

(c) Whoever, for the purpose aforesaid, receives or obtains or agrees or attempts to receive or obtain from any person, or from any source whatever, any document, writing, code book, signal book, sketch, photograph, photographic negative, blueprint, plan, map, model, instrument, appliance, or note, of anything connected with the national defense, knowing or having reason to believe, at the time he receives or obtains, or agrees or attempts to receive or obtain it, that it has been or will be obtained, taken, made, or disposed of by any person contrary to the provisions of this chapter; or

(d) Whoever, lawfully having possession of, access to, control over, or being entrusted with any document, writing, code book, signal book, sketch, photograph, photographic negative, blueprint, plan, map, model, instrument, appliance, or note relating to the national defense, or information relating to the national defense which information the possessor has reason to believe could be used to the injury of the United States or to the advantage of any foreign nation, willfully communicates, delivers, transmits or causes to be communicated, delivered, or transmitted or attempts to communicate, deliver, transmit or cause to be communicated, delivered or transmitted the same to any person not entitled to receive it, or willfully retains the same and fails to deliver it on demand to the officer or employee of the United States entitled to receive it; or

(e) Whoever having unauthorized possession of, access to, or control over any document, writing, code book, signal book, sketch, photograph, photographic negative, blueprint, plan, map, model, instrument, appliance, or note relating to the national defense, or information relating to the national defense which information the possessor has reason to believe could be used to the injury of the United States or to the advantage of any foreign nation, willfully communicates, delivers, transmits or causes to be communicated, delivered, or transmitted, or attempts to communicate, deliver, transmit or cause to be communicated, delivered, or transmitted the same to any person not entitled to receive it, or willfully retains the same and fails to deliver it to the officer or employee of the United States entitled to receive it shall be fined not more than $10,000 or imprisoned not more than ten years, or both.

# APPENDIX B

---

# The Indictment
### *(December 29, 1971)*

UNITED STATES DISTRICT COURT
FOR THE CENTRAL DISTRICT OF CALIFORNIA

March 1971    Grand Jury

UNITED STATES OF AMERICA,
Plaintiff,
v.
ANTHONY JOSEPH RUSSO, JR.,
DANIEL ELLSBERG,
Defendants.

NO. 9373 CD
*I N D I C T M E N T*

[18 USC. §371:Conspiracy;

18 U.S.C. §641: Stealing
Government Property; Concealing Stolen Government Property;
Unauthorized Conveying of Government Property; Receiving Stolen
Government Property;

18 U.S.C. §793(c): Receiving National Defense Documents;

18 U.S.C. §793(d)(e): Communicating National Defense Documents;

18 U.S.C. §793(e): Retaining National Defense Documents.]

The Grand Jury charges:
## COUNT ONE
### [18 U.S.C. §371]

Commencing about March 1, 1969, and continuing to about September 30, 1970, defendants ANTHONY JOSEPH RUSSO and DANIEL ELLSBERG, and unindicted co-conspirators Vu Van Thai, Lynda Sinay, and others unknown to the grand jury, agreed, confederated and conspired together:

(1) to defraud the United States and an agency thereof by impairing, obstructing, and defeating its lawful governmental function of controlling the dissemination of classified Government studies, reports, memoranda and communications; and

(2) to commit offenses against the United States as follows:

(a) to embezzle, steal and knowingly convert to their own use and the use of others, and without authority to convey and dispose of classified Government studies, reports, memoranda and communications which were things of value of the United States of a value in excess of $100; and to receive, conceal, and retain said classified Government studies, reports, memoranda and communications with intent to convert them to their own use and gain, knowing them to have been embezzled, stolen, and converted, in violation of Title 18, United States Code, Section 641;

(b) to receive, obtain, and attempt to receive and obtain documents and writings connected with the national defense for the purpose of obtaining information respecting the national defense, and with knowledge and reason to believe that said documents and writings would be disposed of contrary to the provisions of Title 18, United States Code, Sections 793(d) and (e), by their communication, delivery and transmittal to persons not entitled to receive them, in violation of Title 18, United States Code, Section 793(c);

(c) willfully to communicate, deliver, transmit, and attempt to communicate, deliver and transmit documents and writings relating to the national defense, which defendants would have in their lawful and unauthorized possession, to persons not entitled to receive them, in violation of Title 18, United States Code, Section 793(d) and (e);

(d) willfully to retain documents and writings related to the national defense which would be in defendants' unauthorized possession, and to fail to deliver them to the officer or employee of the United States entitled to receive them, in violation of Title 18, United States Code, Section 793(e).

The objects of the conspiracy were as follows: defendants would obtain and cause to be obtained, classified Government documents relating to the national defense, from Rand Corporation, Santa Monica,

California, and Washington, D.C., and from other sources. The documents would be communicated, delivered and transmitted to defendants and others, none of whom would be authorized to receive them. Defendants and their co-conspirators would retain the documents, copy them, and communicate them to persons not entitled to receive them.

To effect the objects of the conspiracy, defendants committed various overt acts in the Central District of California, including the following:

1. On or about March 4, 1969, defendant ELLSBERG brought ten volumes of a 38-volume Department of Defense study entitled "UNITED STATES–VIETNAM RELATIONS 1945–1967" to Los Angeles County, California, from Rand Corporation, Washington, D.C.

2. On or about April 7, 1969, defendant ELLSBERG obtained from Rand Corporation, Santa Monica, California, Part II of a memorandum entitled "NEGOTIATIONS AND VIETNAM: A CASE STUDY OF THE 1954 GENEVA CONFERENCE."

3. On or about August 29, 1969, defendant ELLSBERG brought eight volumes of a 38-volume Department of Defense study entitled "UNITED STATES–VIETNAM RELATIONS 1945–1967" to Los Angeles County, California, from Rand Corporation, Washington, D.C.

4. On or about October 3, 1969, defendant ELLSBERG obtained from Rand Corporation, Santa Monica, California, a document consisting of pages 1, 2, 3, 4, 9, 12, 13 and 14 of a memorandum dated 27 February 1968, entitled "REPORT OF CHAIRMAN, JCS ON SITUATION IN VIETNAM AND MACV FORCE REQUIREMENTS."

5. On or about October 4, 1969, defendants ELLSBERG and RUSSO, and co-conspirator Sinay operated a Xerox copy machine at 8101 Melrose Avenue, Los Angeles, California.

6. On or about October 19, 1969, co-conspirator Vu Van Thai possessed one volume of a 38-volume Department of Defense study entitled "UNITED STATES–VIETNAM RELATIONS 1945–1967," namely volume VI C.4, entitled "SETTLEMENT OF THE CONFLICT, Negotiations, 1967–1968, HISTORY OF CONTACTS."

7. During the period from about March 4, 1969, to about May 20, 1970, defendant RUSSO possessed the following: (1) Nine volumes of a 38-volume Department of Defense study entitled "UNITED STATES–VIETNAM RELATIONS 1945–1967":

| Volume | Title |
|---|---|
| I | VIETNAM AND THE UNITED STATES — 1940–1950. |
| IV.A.2. | AID FOR FRANCE IN INDOCHINA — 1950–1954. |

(2) Pages 1, 2, 3, 4, 9, 12, 13 and 14 of a memorandum dated 27 February 1968, entitled "REPORT OF CHAIRMAN, JCS ON SITU- ATION IN VIETNAM AND MACV FORCE REQUIREMENTS."

8. On or about October 1, 1969, co-conspirator Lynda Sinay pos- sessed one volume of a 38-volume Department of Defense study en- titled "UNITED STATES–VIETNAM RELATIONS 1945–1967," namely volume IV.C.9(b) entitled "EVOLUTION OF THE WAR— US/GVN RELATIONS: 1963–1967 — PART II."

## COUNT TWO
[18 U.S.C. §641]

During the period from about March 4, 1969, to about May 20, 1970, in Los Angeles County, within the Central District of California, defendant DANIEL ELLSBERG did embezzle, steal and knowingly convert to his use and the use of another, the following things of value of the United States and a department and agency thereof:

(1) Nine volumes of a 38-volume Department of Defense study en- titled "UNITED STATES–VIETNAM RELATIONS 1945–1967":

| Volume | Title |
|---|---|
| I | VIETNAM AND THE UNITED STATES — 1940– 1950. |
| IV.A.2. | AID FOR FRANCE IN INDOCHINA — 1950– 1954. |
| IV.B.5. | EVOLUTION OF THE WAR — THE OVER- THROW OF NGO DINH DIEM — MAY–NO- VEMBER, 1963. |

| | |
|---|---|
| IV.C.4. | EVOLUTION OF THE WAR — MARINE COMBAT UNITS GO TO DA NANG — MARCH 1965. |
| IV.C.5. | PHASE I IN THE BUILD-UP OF U. S. FORCES — THE DEBATE — MARCH–JULY 1965. |
| IV.C.8. | RE-EMPHASIS ON PACIFICATION: 1965–1967. |
| IV.C.9(a) | EVOLUTION OF THE WAR — US/GVN RELATIONS: 1963–1967. |
| IV.C.9(b) | EVOLUTION OF THE WAR — US/GVN RELATIONS: 1963–1967 — PART II. |
| VI.C.4. | SETTLEMENT OF THE CONFLICT — NEGOTIATIONS, 1967–1968 — HISTORY OF CONTACTS. |

(2) Pages 1, 2, 3, 4, 9, 12, 13 and 14 of a memorandum dated 27 February 1968, entitled "REPORT OF CHAIRMAN, JCS ON SITUATION IN VIETNAM AND MACV FORCE REQUIREMENTS."
(3) Part II of a memorandum entitled "NEGOTIATIONS AND VIETNAM: A CASE STUDY OF THE 1954 GENEVA CONFERENCE";
which things had a value in excess of $100;
 In violation of Title 18, United States Code, Section 641.

### COUNT THREE
[18 U.S.C. §641]

 During the period from about March 4, 1969, to about May 20, 1970, in Los Angeles County, within the Central District of California, defendant DANIEL ELLSBERG did conceal and retain the following things of value of the United States and a department and agency thereof, with intent to convert them to his own use and gain, knowing them to have been embezzled, stolen and converted:

(1) Nine volumes of a 38-volume Department of Defense study entitled "UNITED STATES–VIETNAM RELATIONS 1945–1967":

| Volume | Title |
|---|---|
| I | VIETNAM AND THE UNITED STATES — 1940–1950. |
| IV.A.2. | AID FOR FRANCE IN INDOCHINA — 1950–1954. |
| IV.B.5. | EVOLUTION OF THE WAR — THE OVERTHROW OF NGO DINH DIEM — MAY–NOVEMBER, 1963. |
| IV.C.4. | EVOLUTION OF THE WAR — MARINE COMBAT UNITS GO TO DA NANG — MARCH 1965. |
| IV.C.5. | PHASE I IN THE BUILD-UP OF U.S. FORCES — THE DEBATE — MARCH–JULY 1965. |

| | |
|---|---|
| IV.C.8. | RE-EMPHASIS ON PACIFICATION: 1965–1967. |
| IV.C.9(a) | EVOLUTION OF THE WAR — US/GVN RELATIONS: 1963–1967. |
| IV.C.9(b) | EVOLUTION OF THE WAR — US/GVN RELATIONS: 1963–1967 — PART II. |
| VI.C.4. | SETTLEMENT OF THE CONFLICT — NEGOTIATIONS, 1967–1968 — HISTORY OF CONTACTS. |

(2) Pages 1, 2, 3, 4, 9, 12, 13 and 14 of a memorandum dated 27 February 1968, entitled "REPORT OF CHAIRMAN, JCS ON SITUATION IN VIETNAM AND MACV FORCE REQUIREMENTS"; (3) Part II of a memorandum entitled "NEGOTIATIONS AND VIETNAM: A CASE STUDY OF THE 1954 GENEVA CONFERENCE";
which things had a value in excess of $100;
In violation of Title 18, United States Code, Section 641.

## COUNT FOUR
[18 U.S.C. §641]

During the period from about March 4, 1969, to about May 20, 1970, in Los Angeles County, within the Central District of California, defendant DANIEL ELLSBERG, without authority, did knowingly convey to Anthony Joseph Russo, the following things of value of the United States and a department and agency thereof:

(1) Nine volumes of a 38-volume Department of Defense study entitled "UNITED STATES–VIETNAM RELATIONS 1945–1967";

| *Volume* | *Title* |
|---|---|
| I | VIETNAM AND THE UNITED STATES — 1940–1950. |
| IV.A.2. | AID FOR FRANCE IN INDOCHINA — 1950–1954. |
| IV.B.5. | EVOLUTION OF THE WAR — THE OVERTHROW OF NGO DINH DIEM — MAY–NOVEMBER, 1963. |
| IV.C.4. | EVOLUTION OF THE WAR — MARINE COMBAT UNITS GO TO DA NANG — MARCH 1965. |
| IV.C.5. | PHASE I IN THE BUILD-UP OF U.S. FORCES — THE DEBATE — MARCH–JULY 1965. |
| IV.C.8. | RE-EMPHASIS ON PACIFICATION: 1965–1967. |
| IV.C.9(a) | EVOLUTION OF THE WAR — US/GVN RELATIONS: 1963–1967. |
| IV.C.9(b) | EVOLUTION OF THE WAR — US/GVN RELATIONS: 1963–1967 — PART II. |

VI.C.4.      SETTLEMENT OF THE CONFLICT — NEGOTI-
ATIONS, 1967–1968 — HISTORY OF CONTACTS.

(2) Pages 1, 2, 3, 4, 9, 12, 13 and 14 of a memorandum dated 27
February 1968, entitled "REPORT OF CHAIRMAN, JCS ON SITU-
ATION IN VIETNAM AND MACV FORCE REQUIREMENTS";
which things had a value in excess of $100;
   In violation of Title 18, United States Code, Section 641.


COUNT FIVE
[18 U.S.C. §641]

During the period from about March 4, 1969, to about December
31, 1969, in Los Angeles County, within the Central District of California, defendant DANIEL ELLSBERG, without authority, did knowingly convey to Lynda Sinay the following thing of value of the United
States and a department and agency thereof: one volume of a 38-
volume Department of Defense study entitled "UNITED STATES–
VIETNAM RELATIONS 1945–1967"; namely, Volume IV.C.9(b),
"EVOLUTION OF THE WAR — US/GVN RELATIONS: 1963–
1967 — PART II"; which thing had a value in excess of $100;
   In violation of Title 18, United States Code, Section 641.


COUNT SIX
[18 U.S.C. §641]

During the period from about August 29, 1969, to about May 20,
1970, in Los Angeles County, within the Central District of California,
defendant DANIEL ELLSBERG, without authority, did knowingly
convey to Vu Van Thai the following thing of value of the United States
and a department and agency thereof: one volume of a 38-volume
Department of Defense study entitled "UNITED STATES–VIET-
NAM RELATIONS 1945–1967," namely, Volume VI.C.4, "SETTLE-
MENT OF THE CONFLICT — NEGOTIATIONS, 1967–1968,
HISTORY OF CONTACTS"; which thing had a value in excess of
$100;
   In violation of Title 18, United States Code, Section 641.


COUNT SEVEN
[18 U.S.C. §641]

During the period from about March 4, 1969, to about May 20,
1970, in Los Angeles County, within the Central District of California,
defendant ANTHONY JOSEPH RUSSO did receive the following
things of value of the United States and a department and agency

thereof, with intent to convert them to his own use and gain, knowing them to have been embezzled, stolen and converted:

(1) Nine volumes of a 38-volume Department of Defense study entitled "UNITED STATES–VIETNAM RELATIONS 1945–1967";

| Volume | Title |
| --- | --- |
| I | VIETNAM AND THE UNITED STATES — 1940–1950. |
| IV.A.2. | AID FOR FRANCE IN INDOCHINA — 1950–1954. |
| IV.B.5. | EVOLUTION OF THE WAR — THE OVERTHROW OF NGO DINH DIEM — MAY–NOVEMBER, 1963. |
| IV.C.4. | EVOLUTION OF THE WAR — MARINE COMBAT UNITS GO TO DA NANG — MARCH 1965. |
| IV.C.5. | PHASE I IN THE BUILD-UP OF U.S. FORCES — THE DEBATE — MARCH–JULY 1965. |
| IV.C.8. | RE-EMPHASIS ON PACIFICATION: 1965–1967. |
| IV.C.9(a) | EVOLUTION OF THE WAR — US/GVN RELATIONS: 1963–1967. |
| IV.C.9(b) | EVOLUTION OF THE WAR — US/GVN RELATIONS: 1963–1967 — PART II. |
| VI.C.4. | SETTLEMENT OF THE CONFLICT — NEGOTIATIONS, 1967–1968 — HISTORY OF CONTACTS. |

(2) Pages 1, 2, 3, 4, 9, 12, 13 and 14 of a memorandum dated 27 February 1968, entitled "REPORT OF CHAIRMAN, JCS ON SITUATION IN VIETNAM AND MACV FORCE REQUIREMENTS"; which things had a value in excess of $100;

In violation of Title 18, United States Code, Section 641.

## COUNT EIGHT
[18 U.S.C. §793(c)]

On or about April 7, 1969, in Los Angeles County, within the Central District of California, defendant DANIEL ELLSBERG, for the purpose of obtaining information respecting the national defense, received and obtained from Rand Corporation, Santa Monica, California, a document connected with the national defense consisting of: Part II of a memorandum entitled "NEGOTIATIONS AND VIETNAM: A CASE STUDY OF THE 1954 GENEVA CONFERENCE," knowing and having reason to believe at the time he received and obtained it, that said document would be disposed of contrary to the provisions of Title 18, United States Code, Section 793(d) and (e);

In violation of Title 18, United States Code, Section 793(c).

## COUNT NINE
### [18 U.S.C. §793(c)]

On or about October 3, 1969, in Los Angeles County, within the Central District of California, defendant DANIEL ELLSBERG, for the purpose of obtaining information respecting the national defense, received and obtained from Rand Corporation, Santa Monica, California, a document connected with the national defense consisting of pages 1, 2, 3, 4, 9, 12, 13 and 14 of a memorandum dated 27 February 1968, entitled "REPORT OF CHAIRMAN, JCS ON SITUATION IN VIETNAM AND MACV FORCE REQUIREMENTS," knowing and having reason to believe at the time he received and obtained it, that said document would be disposed of contrary to the provisions of Title 18, United States Code, Section 793(d) and (e);

In violation of Title 18, United States Code, Section 793(c).

---

## COUNT TEN
### [18 U.S.C. §793(c)]

During the period from about March 4, 1969, to about May 20, 1970, in Los Angeles County, within the Central District of California, defendant ANTHONY JOSEPH RUSSO, for the purpose of obtaining information respecting the national defense, received and obtained from Daniel Ellsberg documents connected with the national defense, consisting of:

(1) Nine volumes of a 38-volume Department of Defense study entitled "UNITED STATES–VIETNAM RELATIONS 1945–1967";

| Volume | Title |
|---|---|
| I | VIETNAM AND THE UNITED STATES — 1940–1950. |
| IV.A.2. | AID FOR FRANCE IN INDOCHINA — 1950–1954. |
| IV.B.5. | EVOLUTION OF THE WAR — THE OVERTHROW OF NGO DINH DIEM — MAY–NOVEMBER, 1963. |
| IV.C.4. | EVOLUTION OF THE WAR — MARINE COMBAT UNITS GO TO DA NANG — MARCH 1965. |
| IV.C.5. | PHASE I IN THE BUILD-UP OF U.S. FORCES — THE DEBATE — MARCH–JULY 1965. |
| IV.C.8. | RE-EMPHASIS ON PACIFICATION: 1965–1967. |
| IV.C.9(a) | EVOLUTION OF THE WAR — US/GVN RELATIONS: 1963–1967. |
| IV.C.9(b) | EVOLUTION OF THE WAR — US/GVN RELATIONS: 1963–1967 — PART II. |

VI.C.4. SETTLEMENT OF THE CONFLICT — NEGOTI-
ATIONS, 1967–1968 — HISTORY OF CONTACTS.

(2) Pages 1, 2, 3, 4, 9, 12, 13 and 14 of a memorandum dated 27 February 1968, entitled "REPORT OF CHAIRMAN, JCS ON SITU-ATION IN VIETNAM AND MACV FORCE REQUIREMENT," knowing and having reason to believe at the time he received and obtained them that said documents would be obtained and disposed of contrary to the provisions of Title 18, United States Code, Section 793 (d) and (e);

In violation of Title 18, United States Code, Section 793(c).

COUNT ELEVEN
[18 U.S.C. §793(d)(e)]

During the period from about March 4, 1969, to about May 20, 1970, in Los Angeles County, within the Central District of California, defendant DANIEL ELLSBERG, having lawful and unauthorized possession of, access to, and control over documents relating to the national defense, consisting of:

(1) Nine volumes of a 38-volume Department of Defense study entitled "UNITED STATES–VIETNAM RELATIONS 1945–1967":

| Volume | Title |
| --- | --- |
| I | VIETNAM AND THE UNITED STATES — 1940–1950. |
| IV.A.2. | AID FOR FRANCE IN INDOCHINA — 1950–1954. |
| IV.B.5. | EVOLUTION OF THE WAR — THE OVERTHROW OF NGO DINH DIEM — MAY–NOVEMBER, 1963. |
| IV.C.4. | EVOLUTION OF THE WAR — MARINE COMBAT UNITS GO TO DA NANG — MARCH 1965. |
| IV.C.5. | PHASE I IN THE BUILD-UP OF U.S. FORCES — THE DEBATE — MARCH–JULY 1965. |
| IV.C.8. | RE-EMPHASIS ON PACIFICATION: 1965–1967. |
| IV.C.9(a) | EVOLUTION OF THE WAR — US/GVN RELATIONS: 1963–1967. |
| IV.C.9(b) | EVOLUTION OF THE WAR — US/GVN RELATIONS: 1963–1967 — PART II. |
| VI.C.4. | SETTLEMENT OF THE CONFLICT — NEGOTIATIONS, 1967–1968 — HISTORY OF CONTACTS. |

(2) Pages 1, 2, 3, 4, 9, 12, 13 and 14 of a memorandum dated 27 February 1968, entitled "REPORT OF CHAIRMAN, JCS ON SITU-ATION IN VIETNAM AND MACV FORCE REQUIREMENTS";

did willfully communicate, deliver and transmit said documents to Anthony Joseph Russo, a person not entitled to receive them;
In violation of Title 18, United States Code, Section 793(d)(e).


## COUNT TWELVE
### [18 U.S.C. §793(d)(e)]

During the period from about March 4, 1969, to about December 31, 1969, in Los Angeles County, within the Central District of California, defendant DANIEL ELLSBERG, having lawful and unauthorized possession of, access to, and control over a document relating to the national defense consisting of one volume of a 38-volume Department of Defense study entitled "UNITED STATES–VIETNAM RELATIONS 1945–1967," namely, Volume IV.C.9(b), "EVOLUTION OF THE WAR — US/GVN RELATIONS: 1963–1967 — PART II," did willfully communicate, deliver and transmit said document to Lynda Sinay, a person not entitled to receive it;
In violation of Title 18, United States Code, Section 793(d)(e).


## COUNT THIRTEEN
### [18 U.S.C. §793(d)(e)]

During the period from about August 29, 1969, to about May 20, 1970, in Los Angeles County, within the Central District of California, defendant DANIEL ELLSBERG, having lawful and unauthorized possession of, access to, and control over a document relating to the national defense consisting of one volume of a 38-volume Department of Defense study entitled "UNITED STATES–VIETNAM RELA- TIONS 1945–1967," namely, Volume VI.C.4, "SETTLEMENT OF THE CONFLICT—NEGOTIATIONS, 1967—1968—HISTORY OF CONTACTS," did willfully communicate, deliver and transmit said document to Vu Van Thai, a person not entitled to receive it;
In violation of Title 18, United States Code, Section 793(d)(e).


## COUNT FOURTEEN
### [18 U.S.C. §793(e)]

During the period from about March 4, 1969, to about May 20, 1970, in Los Angeles County, within the Central District of California, defendant DANIEL ELLSBERG, having unauthorized possession of, access to, and control over documents relating to the national defense consisting of:

(2) Pages 1, 2, 3, 4, 9, 12, 13 and 14 of a memorandum dated 27 February 1968, entitled "REPORT OF CHAIRMAN, JCS ON SITUATION IN VIETNAM AND MACV FORCE REQUIREMENTS";

(3) Part II of a memorandum entitled "NEGOTIATIONS AND VIETNAM: A CASE STUDY OF THE 1954 GENEVA CONFERENCE";

did willfully retain said documents and fail to deliver them to the officer or employee of the United States entitled to receive them;

In violation of Title 18, United States Code, Section 793(e).

## COUNT FIFTEEN
### [18 U.S.C. §793(e)]

During the period from about March 4, 1969, to about May 20, 1970, in Los Angeles County, within the Central District of California, defendant ANTHONY JOSEPH RUSSO, having unauthorized possession of, access to, and control over documents relating to the national defense consisting of:

(1) Nine volumes of a 38-volume Department of Defense study entitled "UNITED STATES–VIETNAM RELATIONS 1945–1967";

| Volume | Title |
| --- | --- |
| I | VIETNAM AND THE UNITED STATES — 1940–1950. |
| IV.A.2. | AID FOR FRANCE IN INDOCHINA — 1950–1954. |
| IV.B.5. | EVOLUTION OF THE WAR — THE OVERTHROW OF NGO DINH DIEM — MAY–NOVEMBER, 1963. |
| IV.C.4. | EVOLUTION OF THE WAR — MARINE COMBAT UNITS GO TO DA NANG — MARCH 1965. |
| IV.C.5. | PHASE I IN THE BUILD-UP OF U.S. FORCES — THE DEBATE — MARCH–JULY 1965. |
| IV.C.8. | RE-EMPHASIS ON PACIFICATION: 1965–1967. |
| IV.C.9(a) | EVOLUTION OF THE WAR — US/GVN RELATIONS: 1963–1967. |
| IV.C.9(b) | EVOLUTION OF THE WAR — US/GVN RELATIONS: 1963–1967 — PART II. |
| VI.C.4. | SETTLEMENT OF THE CONFLICT — NEGOTIATIONS, 1967–1968 — HISTORY OF CONTACTS. |

(2) Pages 1, 2, 3, 4, 9, 12, 13 and 14 of a memorandum dated 27 February 1968, entitled "REPORT OF CHAIRMAN, JCS ON SITUATION IN VIETNAM AND MACV FORCE REQUIREMENTS";

did willfully retain said documents and fail to deliver them to the officer or employee of the United States entitled to receive them;
In violation of Title 18, United States Code, Section 793(e).

A TRUE BILL


Patricia S. Jones

Foreman

DAVID R. NISSEN
Special Assistant U. S. Attorney
Attorney for the Government

# Sources and
# Acknowledgments

THIS book began as a project and became a way of life. The case of Daniel Ellsberg, officially over, may never end, and the story may always be incomplete: every day there are new disclosures, details amplifying details. There are, moreover, the unresolved questions— at this writing—about the fate of Richard Nixon and, more important, the subsidiary questions about the mood and direction of the country in the event or nonevent of impeachment or resignation. The essence of those questions is not who will be in charge on Election Day in 1976, but what the country will think of itself, of its immediate past, and of its imminent future. One generally writes about changes in politics and social outlook with certain assumptions about a moment, a feel about where the country stands and what people are thinking, and with the illusion—the writer's fiction—that, at least for an instant, time can be stopped. In this instance those assumptions are, as they say, untenable. Because no one is in control there are no inside sources, no wise men, who can confidently explain, analyze and predict. There is no order in the present of which one can be reasonably confident. For nearly three months I have been writing, literally, with one eye on the typewriter and the other on the television set.

Certain things have nonetheless been established. If we don't know where we are, we do have an idea of where we've been. The Ellsberg case spans eras, touching almost every major element in the history of the last twenty-five years: the legacies of the Second World War (and much that preceded it), the confident liberalism of the early sixties, the certainties of applied intelligence, Vietnam, Johnson, Nixon, Watergate, a multiple paradigm for almost everything in American politics and political thought. For that reason it was, and is, a highly tempting subject; for that reason also, it will never be a complete story, and one writes, therefore, with a feeling that endless additional questions should be asked, more people interviewed, and more documents read. In the era of Watergate, everyone has an angle, a rumor, something that should be followed and explored. Yet at some point one takes a deep breath, gives a manuscript to an editor, and with the shaky assurance that this is a story about the past—arbitrarily severed from what may happen tomorrow—words are committed to print. Someday it may be possible for authors and publishers to send readers addenda to be inserted in looseleaf books for easy updating. In the meantime, one takes chances. The book stops here.

For two years I have been covering this case. I first met Daniel Ellsberg in the summer of 1971 when I was doing a magazine article about him, and thereafter I saw him in New York, Chicago, Miami, Washington and, over two periods totaling some seven months, almost daily in Los Angeles. I share his feeling, which he expressed in one of our last face-to-face conversations, that I still don't know much about him. (Ellsberg, as I indicated elsewhere in this book, always believed that the press did not talk to him enough, and that he was therefore misunderstood, misquoted and misjudged.) But it was never my intention to write his biography or to break through all the protective shells of privacy that a person constructs around himself. I wanted to understand him only in the context of the case, to view him as protagonist and symbol in a particular age and situation. I interviewed people who knew him in Vietnam and before he went to Vietnam, among them several who knew him as a boy, as a student at Harvard, and, of course, as a military intellectual at the Pentagon and at Rand. I also spoke with scores of people involved in the case, lawyers, witnesses, journalists and government officials. Some of them can't be named, or can't be associated with the information they provided, although the identity of most will be obvious from the text. A great part of the time in Los Angeles we more or less lived together, meeting for meals, discussing the most minute details of the case, and exchanging gossip; the difficulty for a writer, especially in the case like this, is not material, it is distance. The hard work is not getting to people, but getting away from them.

Writers, Joan Didion once said, "are always selling somebody out." And so it is here. One takes advantage of sources, dissecting in print people who have been helpful in interviews and generous in providing material, but that only increases the debt and enlarges the sense of ingratitude. (Perhaps the fair statement should be: "Although X made an ass of himself in court, he was extremely helpful to the writer in explaining the legal background of the Heine case and in analyzing the subtle points of Section 793[e] of the Espionage Act.") Ideally, journalists should have no friends.

The bulk of the material in this book came from the trial itself and the pretrial arguments, from those constant conversations with the participants, from the disclosures related to Watergate, and from a number of confidential sources who provided information with the understanding that they would not be named. Among those who can be named, I'm particularly grateful to Morton Halperin, Charles Nesson, Leonard Boudin, Leonard Weinglass, Mark Rosenbaum, Stanley Sheinbaum, Charles Goodell, Marcia Meyers, Patricia Ellsberg, Harry Ellsberg, Jr., Katherine Barkley, Arthur Berman, Robert Sachs, Norma Whittaker, Marc Stone, Roger Gould, Jay Shulman, Adam Bennion, William Florence, Teri Simon, Carol Sobel, Paul Ryder, David Halberstam, Sanford Ungar, Gene Blake, Martin Arnold, Trudy Rubin, Fred Graham, Tom Oliphant, Anthony Lukas, Studs Terkel, Don Juhlin, Jim Haggard, Bill Carter and Barry Farrell. In the course of the work on this book I also drew on a vast amount of material, published and unpublished, about the case, and particularly Sanford Ungar's *The Papers and the Papers,* the court records of the injunction cases against the *New York Times* and the *Washington Post,* the Gravel–Beacon Press edition of the Pentagon Papers, the Bantam collection of the Papers, Ellsberg's speeches and articles, many of them now available in *Papers on the War,* the record of the Moorehead Committee hearings (*Hearings of the Subcommittee of the Committee on Government Operations of the House*) on Government Information Policies and Practices, the book *Washington Plans an Aggressive War,* by Ralph Stavins, Richard J. Barnet and Marcus Raskin, David Halberstam's *The Best and the Brightest,* and countless magazine pieces about the case. I'm also grateful to the Meiklejohn Civil Liberties Institute in Berkeley, California, which now has, among other things, a complete transcript and all pertinent documents for the Ellsberg trial; Janet Flammang and Susan Cohen for their help in background research; to Peggy Lang for her efficient and incomprehensibly rapid job of producing a clean manuscript from the typographical monstrosity that I gave her; and to Alice Mayhew, a superbly intelligent editor.

# Index